CRIMINAL JUSTICE 101

CRIMINAL JUSTICE 101
A FIRST COURSE

RICHARD C. SPRINTHALL
JOHN J. DEFRANCESCO
ALTHEA LLOYD

Universal-Publishers
Boca Raton

Criminal Justice 101: A First Course

Universal-Publishers
Boca Raton, Florida • USA
2015

ISBN-10: 1-62734-041-6
ISBN-13: 978-1-62734-041-0

www.universal-publishers.com

Cover image © Alancrosthwaite |
Dreamstime.com - American Beginnings Photo

ACKNOWLEDGEMENTS

This book is dedicated to the Sheriff of Hampden County MA., Sheriff Michael J. Ashe. He has been an inspiration to all who know him for his special expertise in the area of prisoner rehabilitation

Putting together a book of this type requires a lot of help. Special thanks must go to the significant others in my academic life. Greg Kimble, then of Brown University; the late Nathan Maccoby, then of Boston University; and the late P.J. Rulon, then of Harvard University. I am also grateful to the literary executor Ronald A. Fisher, F.R.S., and to Dr. Frank Yates, IV.

More recently, I must thank my colleagues at American International College: especially Dr. John DeFrancesco who worked round the clock organizing the material for the publisher, Prof. Dave Kuzmeski and Prof. Jill Paine, Dr. Gregory Schmutte for his valuable contributions to the research chapters, Dr. Gus Pesce for his "spec ed" examples, and Dr. Paul Quinlan for his research help and expertise. I want to thank Marty Lyman, Director of Research at the Hampden County House of Correction, Superintendent Jim Kelleher, and Director Joanne Burke at the Western Mass Corrections and Alcohol Center for their many research examples, especially those involved in rehabilitation. I also wish to extend special thanks to Dr. Marjorie Marcotte at Springfield College for her insightful comments on topic inclusions and exclusions. Also thanks to Dr. Jim Vivian at the University of Hartford, Norm Berkowitz at Boston College, and Dr. Chris Hakala at Western New England University for ideas for statistical analysis on recidivism data.

Karen Dawn McKenna offered invaluable help in proofing my chapters, and to another McKenna, Paul Jr. go my thanks for helping me overcome some of Word's most annoying habits, such as starting each line with a capital letter.

I must thank a number of criminal justice experts for their enormous help with CJ examples, and that includes virtually all the chiefs of police, Bob Siano in Longmeadow, Doug Mellis in East Longmeadow (who is always willing to swap stories over a cup of coffee and a doughnut), and former Springfield's Commissioner Bill Fitchet (without question Springfield's best chief since the halcyon days of Tom Fitzgerald). Tom Fitzgerald, incidentally, is such a statistics fan that he never leaves home without a finely honed number two pencil, in case he has to do an emergency chi square. I also received help from Longmeadow's police captain John Stankewiecz, who provided expertise for the section on questionnaires and polling. Thanks also go to Richard Seligman for the pharmaceutical examples and his insistence on observing the cardiologist's diet- if it tastes good, spit it out. Also thanks go to Bob Watson, in Massachusetts, and Dawn Boyer, in Virginia, for their careful work in spotting typos. And typos can be dangerous. That's why you have to be especially careful reading health studies. You might die of a misprint.

Richard C. Sprinthall
Professor of Psychology, Emeritus
Department of Graduate Psychology
American International College

I would like to thank some special people: First and foremost, Sandra, my wife for her much appreciated patience and support throughout this project, and to my sons Anthony and Joseph for their unyielding exuberance! I would also like to acknowledge my co-author Richard C. Sprinthall, Ph.D. for several decades of mentoring and friendship and arguments about the Yankees and Red Sox; I wish we started our working relationship earlier. Several other professionals have had significant influences, particularly Louis Chandler, Ph.D., Jerome Taylor, Ph.D., and the late Norman Mulgrave, Ph.D. of the University of Pittsburgh who trained me and taught me and …well let's just leave it at that! Also, thanks go to Gwendolyn Zahner, Ph.D., then of Yale University, who invited my collaboration on several research endeavors, Arnold Hyman, Ph.D., then of University of New Haven, who instilled a passion for the science of psychology-particularly B.F. Skinner, Jack Novick, Ph.D., then of Southern Connecticut State University, who offered flexibility and reassurance, Michael Amara, R.N., then of Connecticut Valley Hospital, who encouraged my professional development, Walter Pawelkiewicz, Ph.D., then Director of Research at the CT Department of Children and Youth Services, who provided many professional opportunities for my growth and development, and Karen DeFrancesco, MSW, former spouse and mother of my sons, who sadly passed away during her prime.

Finally, I must acknowledge two individuals who had a profound impact on all aspects of my life: my dad Tony (who left this earth much too early), and my mom Caroline, who still makes the best Italian food on the planet!

John J. DeFrancesco
Professor of Psychology and Criminal Justice
Department of Graduate Psychology
American International College

I would like to acknowledge retired Vermont Superior Court Judge, the Honorable David Suntag, for including me in his vision and implementation in improving outcomes for victims and offenders in domestic violence cases, and my husband, and staunchest supporter, Jurg Jenzer.

Althea Lloyd, Esq.
Integrated Domestic Violence Docket Regional Program Coordinator
Windham Superior Court
Brattleboro, Vermont

TABLE OF CONTENTS

PREFACE

When you picked up this criminal justice textbook you might have noticed that it was a bit smaller and lighter than some of your other introductory texts. We did that on purpose! Whereas other texts may be 15 or 20 chapters long we made ours only 12. We believe that all of our chapters can be comfortably covered in one semester. You will soon also notice that we attempt to present and explain our materials, as much as possible, in an easy to read conversational style. We try to stay away from jargon and other esoteric (understood only by a few) terms and when we can't, we define them for you. Most chapters also contain a "Person of Interest" section and a "Case Study" along with a comprehensive "Summary," a set of "Key Terms," and a "Reference List." An extensive "Glossary" is also provided at the end of the text. One more thing, we attempted to write a real "introductory" book. That is, a book that will expose you to some of the basic and fundamental aspects of criminal justice and not a book that a beginning law school student might use.

Ok, so let us talk about criminal justice. You are likely taking this class because you are a CJ major but some of you might be taking this course because you are thinking of becoming a CJ major, have an interest in CJ, or taking it as an elective, (or maybe your advisor registered you by mistake)!

Well, if you are interested in working in the criminal justice field you should be happy about your future prospects. The field is varied and the types of positions available are many. Publications such as the Occupational Outlook Handbook published by the U.S. Bureau of Labor Statistics indicate that careers in the criminal justice field are projected to grow for the foreseeable future. For example, jobs as police officers, detectives, and correctional officers are estimated to grow 5% until 2022; security positions including gaming surveillance officers will grow 12%; forensic technicians 6%; attorneys 10%; paralegals and legal assistants 17%; criminal justice professors 19%. Further, Federal agencies such as Homeland Security are also looking for law enforcement, security, and prevention professionals. We can keep going but I think you get the drift.

This is certainly an interesting time for those with a criminal justice education. The demands are many and the challenges endless: terrorism, extremism, and cyber-crime; violence in our schools, colleges, and communities; white collar and corporate fraud; the never-ending war on drugs; domestic violence; child abuse, and neglect; immigration concerns; police and law enforcement issues; prison overcrowding; juvenile delinquency and this list goes on.

As you can see, the opportunities in the wide open criminal justice field are many. It can be a tough job but a tremendously rewarding career. As a beginning student, it is our hope that this text will help to pique your interest and ignite your passion.

CHAPTER 1

WHAT IS THIS THING CALLED CRIMINAL JUSTICE?

The Dilemma

What is this thing called criminal justice? Is it, as some have scoffingly suggested, just an oxymoron (contradiction in terms), like "jumbo shrimp," "pretty ugly," "elementary rocket science," or "barely dressed." Let's think about it. Is true criminal justice an impossibility? On one side are those who argue that criminal justice is impossible, that the criminal can never really find justice in our controlled and rigged society. On the other side are those who suggest that justice is not always being fully served, that many judges are too easy, and that many criminals, save for an occasional slap on the wrist, are in effect getting away with it. Society wants a court judge who will make the punishment fit the crime, as was true for the guy who stole a calendar and got one year. Go ahead and groan. These conflicting views are in reality a summary of what the criminal justice dilemma is all about: balancing the safety and security of society against the rights and privileges of the individual.

Criminal Justice Defined

Criminal justice as a discipline can be defined as the government's system of institutions that are primarily directed toward societal protection within the confines of individual rights. The three major components of the system are referred to as the three Cs. 1. Cops (Enforcement), 2. Courts (Adjudication), and 3. Corrections (jails, prisons, probation and parole). As you can see, the criminal justice system is an essential part of any free society. For an organized society to operate at all effectively it must provide the citizenry with safety and security, so that persons can live their lives without being in constant fear. The government is, therefore, charged with ensuring "domestic tranquility." At the same time, the individual must be protected from arbitrary and capricious societal rules and pressures that might deny personal freedom. The citizenry should feel that the system will be fair as well as protective. Thus, the criminal justice system must balance the needs of society vs. the rights of the individual, a delicate balancing act that demands constant scrutiny and supervision. The more secure the society, the less the individual liberty, and the more the individual liberty the less secure is society.

Let's look at two examples that highlight the delicacy of the undertaking,

1. Miranda Rights, and
2. Scientific Jury Selection.

Miranda

The Miranda rights were adopted back in 1966 to prevent law enforcement from over-stepping its role as the protector of society. The Miranda rule was aimed at ensuring that all detained suspects would be told up-front that they don't have to tell the police anything that might be incriminating, and also that they are entitled to legal counsel. Remember, however, that this only applies when the suspect is in custody. If a suspect voluntarily agrees to questioning, and clearly understands that he/she is NOT under arrest, no Miranda warnings have to be given. The Miranda rights were instituted to ensure conformity with the Fifth Amendment to the United States Constitution, which acts as a protection against self-incrimination. It is also based on one provision of the Sixth Amendment of the United States Constitution, which says that all suspects have the right to counsel (lawyer). We have all seen TV shows where one of the officers says to his partner, "Go ahead, and read him his rights." And these rights are as follows: "You have the right to remain silent. Anything you say or do can and will be held against you in the court of law. You have the right to speak to an attorney. If you cannot afford an attorney, one will be appointed for you. Do you understand these rights as they have been read to you?" The officer then says, "Having these rights in mind, do you still want to talk to us?" Once the suspect acknowledges an understanding, he/she is said to be "Mirandized." This whole issue comes from the arrest of Ernesto Arturo Miranda who argued that his rights had been violated while being questioned during his arrest for the kidnapping and rape of a young woman in Phoenix, Arizona. He had admitted to the charges, but based on a Supreme Court decision the confession was later ruled out because he had not been informed of his right to remain silent. Interestingly enough, when Miranda was retried, he was found guilty anyway, even without his previous self-incrimination. This time he got a 20-year sentence that was later reduced to 10 years. Once free he got into a bar fight and was murdered, and irony of all ironies - his assailant invoked his Miranda rights and was never convicted.

The Exceptions

There are two exceptions to the Miranda rule.

1. When a suspect provides information while in a situation that is threatening to the safety of the police officers or the public, as in asking the suspect where his armed accomplice is currently hiding, or where he placed the bomb.

2. When a suspect is accompanied by counsel. Thus, if a suspect is with a lawyer who can give advice during the questioning, then Miranda is waived. As one legal scholar has said "If the attorney is actually present during the interrogation, then this obviates the need for the warning" (LaFave, W.R. et al 2007, p 800)

Confession

If you ever find yourself in the position of being an interrogating officer, once you get a Mirandized confession, that is once you finally hear the words "I did it" then drop the questioning, excuse yourself and leave the room. Whatever you do, don't follow it up with "why did you do it?" All that does is open up the case to all kinds of twists and turns, including an NGRI (not guilty by reason of insanity).

When the Lawyer Intrudes

If you decide on a career in law enforcement you may someday find yourself in the position of investigating a crime and holding a suspect in custody. You may also receive a call from the suspect's lawyer who warns you not to talk to his/her client unless the lawyer is present. However, unless there are local statutes to the contrary, you may continue talking to a Mirandized suspect, with or without the lawyer's presence. "Neither Miranda nor the Sixth Amendment's right to counsel prohibits police interrogation of a willing suspect merely because his attorney has informed police that his/her client is not to be questioned" (Rutledge, 2011).

Casey Anthony

The dilemma posed by Miranda came to the forefront in the sensational 2012 trial of Casey Anthony who was charged with murdering her two-year old daughter, Caylee. Despite the evidence which seemingly supported a conviction, she was acquitted. And even if she had been convicted, the defense could have filed for a mistrial. During the trial, her defense attorney, Jose Baez, questioned detective Yuri Melich as follows:

Baez: Did you read her the Miranda rights?
Melich: No
Baez: Did you tell her she was free to leave?
Melich: No
Baez: Did you tell her she can stop talking at any moment and you'll take her home?
Melich: No

The prosecution then said that the reason she wasn't Mirandized was because when she was picked up and questioned she was not considered to be a true suspect. The defense pointed out that since she was placed in the caged back- seat of a police car and even handcuffed, it was legally a custodial interview (i.e., she was in police custody at the time of the questioning). The public outrage following her acquittal, including death threats, would have been even more vitriolic had there been a conviction and then a Miranda mistrial had been ruled. As it was, authorities were so concerned with her safety that when she was released from confinement several black SUVs with tinted windows were used to take her from the jail to a secret destination and the hordes of reporters and TV trucks could not tell which vehicle contained Ms. Anthony.

Scientific Jury Selection: Forensic Trial and Error?

The famous defense attorney, Clarence Darrow (the model for the role of Billy Flynn in the musical "Chicago") once said "every case is won or lost as soon as the jury is sworn" (1936). Although probably somewhat of an exaggeration, history tells us that Darrow knew how to pick a sympathetic jury. Darrow never used any scientific methods, just his own hunches, intuition and common sense. His oratory was considered to be classic, and in one of his theatrical summations he even moved the judge to tears. He successfully handled many high-profile cases, and he did not hire any expensive jury experts to aid in making his juror decisions. And when his instincts let him down and the wrong juror was selected, it is alleged that he sealed the deal by the use of old-fashioned bribery (Farrell, J. A., 2011). Darrow literally flew by the seat of his pants. That has all largely changed. Today SJS (Scientific Jury Selection) has become a multi-million dollar business that appears to be getting bigger with every passing day. Although there are some exceptions, the vast majority of the SJS consulting firms are operated by psychologists, especially forensic psychologists, who use their knowledge of personality, demographics, group dynamics and even common prejudices to zero in on jurors who would be the most sympathetic to their clients. The issue then becomes whether these scientific intrusions really disturb that important balance between the security of society and the rights of the individual.

Dr. Jo-Ellan Dimitrius

Perhaps the most famous and successful of these jury consultants is Dr. Jo-Ellan Dimitrius. She has been involved in almost 700 trials, and she is so good that she has taken cases that were slam-dunks for the opposition and turned them into upset victories. And she doesn't just work one side of the street. She has provided juries for both the prosecution and the defense (Dimitrius, 1998). Her jury selection techniques occur during what is called "voir dire" a process to be explained a little later in the book. It's during voir dire that she works her magic. Let's look at two of her cases, Rodney King and O.J. Simpson.

Rodney King

In 1991 in Los Angeles California the police spotted a car being driven erratically and attempted to stop the vehicle. The driver, Rodney King, failed to pull over, and a dangerous high-speed chase ensued. When the police finally stopped him, King resisted being restrained, and the police used overwhelming force to subdue him. All of this was caught on videotape, and the world was shown the spectacle of the police beating up on a black motorist. The police officers were tried in court on a brutality charge, but once the jury was scientifically selected by Dr. Dimitrius, the verdict was to acquit the officers. As an aside, before his death (drowning in his own swimming pool at 3 A.M.) King acknowledged that his various civil suits netted him over three million dollars.

O.J. Simpson: Justice by Rhyme?

O.J. Simpson was a retired professional football player who was charged in 1997 with the vicious murder of two people, his wife Nicole, and her friend, Ronald Goldman. The prosecution's evidence seemed to be overwhelming, and it didn't appear that Simpson had any chance of getting off. However, one of the pieces of evidence was a shrunken, blood-soaked glove that had been used in the murders, and the courtroom was treated to the scene of O.J. Simpson struggling mightily to put it on. The defense team, led by Johnny Cochran, gave the jury something to hang on to by repeating the lyric, "If it don't fit, you've got to acquit." Prior to this Dr. Dimitrius had done her work extremely well, and using her big-five selection criteria, race, education, income, age and gender, she was able to select a jury so sympathetic to Simpson that the prosecution's evidence became almost secondary. Simpson was acquitted. Dr. Dimitrius was so acclaimed that it was said that whenever a sympathetic jury was selected it was being "OH-JAYED".

A PERSON OF INTEREST: JO-ELLAN DIMITRIUS

Called the "Seer" by her colleagues and by the American Lawyer magazine, Jo-Ellan Dimitrius has demonstrated an almost uncanny ability to analyze people and predict and anticipate their behaviors. She is what is called a "Scientific Jury Consultant", someone who uses scientific methods to select jurors most sympathetic to their clients, in both criminal as well as civil cases. She has been involved in the selection of over 10,000 jurors, and has analyzed the credibility and psychological profiles of countless witnesses.

She also works with potential witnesses and prepares them for court testimony. She has worked for the defense in many of the highest profile criminal cases, such as those of O.J. Simpson and Casey Anthony. She is an expert in analyzing a prospective juror's personality, attitudes and prejudices, and her analyses form the basis for predicting how a given juror will vote.. Currently she serves as president of the trial-consulting firm, Vinson and Dimitrius. She has appeared on literally dozens of TV shows, such as Oprah, Good Morning America, The Today Show, Larry King Live, Face the Nation, Sixty minutes and Burden of Proof. She is the author of two important books, "Reading People: How to Understand People and Predict Their Behavior" (2008) and "Put Your Best Foot Forward" (2001).

Cognitive Dissonance and the Jury

There is an important concept in psychology that the trial consultants rely on, called cognitive dissonance, and the term is used to understand and explain what happens when an individual gets conflicting thoughts and/or conflicts between thoughts and deeds. Studies show that people strive to achieve a state of equilibrium among their various thoughts, attitudes, beliefs and behaviors. That is, people prefer consistency, or consonance, over inconsistency, or dissonance. Thus, whenever a person has a thought that is not consistent with behavior, or several thoughts and attitudes that conflict with each other, the person is motivated to restore the equilibrium. That is, the person attempts to avoid the internal contradictions by either changing the thought to fit the attitude, or changing the behavior to fit the thought. For example someone who enjoys smoking and who reads that smoking is a health hazard can either conclude that the evidence linking smoking with disease is flimsy, or stop smoking. It has been alleged that one smoker became so nervous after reading the evidence linking smoking with cancer that he gave up reading! This phenomenon of cognitive dissonance is extremely important within the minds of the empanelled jurors. Studies conducted by SJS psychologists support the notion that the thought process of most jurors actually involves the creation of their own stories, sometimes rather fanciful stories, to explain to themselves the reasons underlying the actions of the accused. This does not mean that jurors pay no attention to the details of the case being presented, but it's the interpretations of these details that finally influences their decisions. In fact, studies also show that a large percentage of what the jurors remember had never even been included in the testimony, but created in the juror's own mind in an attempt to reduce the cognitive dissonance by making the events seem more reasonable and consistent with their own personal attitudes and beliefs (Hastie & Pennington, 1983). Also, it is interesting to note that the physical attractiveness of both the defendant and the juror creates an interplay that can affect the decision. In general, it has been found that attractive persons were seen by jurors as more honest and trustworthy, and were therefore more apt to be found not guilty. However, when unattractive jurors are empanelled, they are more apt to side with the unattractive defendant. The scientific jury selector is also very wary of selecting people who are seen to be extremely wealthy or successful, because these are people who may exert too much influence on other jurors. Other variables used for possible juror exclusion are:

1. Anyone who has knowledge of the law or is in any way related to law enforcement.

2. Anyone with strong beliefs, such as total opposition to the death penalty in a murder case.

3. Anyone who is obviously very well educated.

As Schmalleger says "Often the system ends up with a jury that is uneducated, uninformed and inexperienced (Schmalleger, 2011).

Voir Dire

As was mentioned earlier, during jury selection there is a process called "voir dire" (French for "speak the truth"), and this is when the attorneys can challenge a juror on the basis of either (1) "just cause" or, (2) something called "peremptory challenge." This is when Dr. Dimitrius and other trial consultants really go to work and earn their big bucks.

1. Just Cause

A challenge for just cause has to specify the reason for the juror's exclusion. For example the argument could be made that a given juror should be excluded because of seemingly being biased or bigoted or in some way not totally impartial

2. Peremptory Challenge

A peremptory challenge is an automatic dismissal of a juror, and no reason has to be given. It is here that the science of jury selection goes into overdrive, because with these challenges nobody has to know what possible social, psychological, or demographic variables have been used. The attorney may feel that a potential juror's hair style is somehow indicative of an underlying attitude, but the important point is - it doesn't have to be explained. An interesting case involving hair style occurred when one of the prospective jurors in the 2004 Scott Peterson murder case came to court flaunting both her tattoos and her ever-changing hair color. Each day she would show up with hair of varying shades of red. She became known by both prosecution and defense as "Strawberry Shortcake," and although the prosecution at first didn't want her, the jury consultant insisted that she would support a conviction….. and she did! Peterson was convicted.

Death Qualified Jury

Finally, in capital cases the jury can be selected on the basis of being "death-qualified." In the case of Witherspoon v. Illinois, 391 U.S. 501 (1968) it was ruled that in homicide cases the jury should not be composed of persons who are categorically opposed to the death penalty or, on the other hand, totally opposed to considering life imprisonment. Such a procedure is often called "Witherspooning" the jury. Prospective jurors who would not even consider the death penalty can be excluded during voir dire. The trial consultants sometimes have to peel away the veneer of a juror's public posture in order to get at the underlying attitudes and motives. Defense attorneys tend to believe that this process favors the prosecution.

The Dilemma Revisited

So that's the dilemma. As you have now clearly seen, at times the system seems to favor the defendant at the expense of society, and at other times the balance seems to swing toward society at the expense of individual rights and freedoms. Keeping these two powerful and yet opposing forces in careful balance is the real job of the criminal justice system. Someday this may become your job.

Time Out to Think

The United States Constitution has ten amendments, called the Bill of Rights. The Constitution and the Bill of Rights will be covered in some detail in a later chapter on our country's legal system. In this chapter we will look briefly at parts of only three of these Rights, the fourth, fifth and sixth, and then try to use them to determine the possible outcome of some important and fairly recent cases.

The Fourth Amendment

The Fourth Amendment states that law enforcement may NOT conduct a random search and/or seizure. In order to search for or seize possible evidence of any unlawful activity, there must be what is called "probable cause" (reasonable suspicion) as a valid reason for the search procedure. This usually involves obtaining a warrant. Since the terror attack on 9/11, there are emergency exceptions, such as being thoroughly searched before boarding a plane or cruise ship.

The Fifth Amendment

Among other things, the Fifth Amendment guarantees that the individual will be given "due-process protection." That is government actions must be guided by the "Rule of Law" not just by some government official's opinion. This was used to protect the individual from over-zealous prosecution by government officials. The Fifth Amendment states that an individual does not have to
1. Give self-incriminating statements
2. Be tried for the same crime twice
3. Be deprived of life, liberty or property without due process.
4. Be convicted on the basis of unreliable evidence

The Sixth Amendment

In this Amendment the individual is given the right to a public trial by a jury of one's peers and to have the advice of counsel for the defense. The individual also has the right to be told the nature of the accusations and to be able to confront the accuser.

The Case Studies

The following lists six important cases, all six having been ruled on by the United States Supreme Court. Read them carefully and then spend a few minutes thinking about each one and then trying to determine how you would have voted if you were a Supreme Court justice. Also think about whether you believe they lean basically toward individual rights or societal security. If you find later that you guessed wrong on how the Supreme Court voted, don't be dismayed. This exercise is designed to having you think about some important cases and how they relate to the Fourth, Fifth and Sixth amendments to the U.S. Constitution.

1. The Brady Error
John Brady and a friend were both charged with homicide in connection with an armed robbery that went amiss. They were arrested together but later tried separately. Brady pleaded guilty to being an accomplice but argued that he wasn't the one who actually pulled the trigger and therefore should not be sentenced to death. However, the court did not find his argument to be compelling and he was therefore convicted and sentenced to death. When Brady and his attorney later found out that the accomplice had previously admitted to the police that he was the killer, and that this information was withheld from Brady, an appeal was set in motion. The state's (Maryland) court of appeals upheld Brady's conviction but did not affirm the death sentence. The case then went to the U.S. Supreme Court.

2. The Terry Stop
John Terry and two of his friends were seen casing a store prior to what appeared to be an attempted robbery. A Cleveland police detective watched for almost 15 minutes as Terry and his buddies went through their dress rehearsal. The detective then accosted the three suspicious-looking men and found that both Terry and one of his accomplices were carrying concealed weapons. Terry's attorney argued that the fact that guns were being carried should not be used in court because the police had violated Terry's fourth amendment right against unreasonable search and seizure, and that because of this invasion of privacy any evidence confiscated (the hand guns) could not be used by the prosecution. The case was then brought before the U.S. Supreme Court.

3. The Mapp Ruling
On the basis of a police tip, two women living in Cleveland, Dollree Mapp and her daughter, were thought to be harboring a possible terrorist who may have been involved in a series of nearby and recent bombings. The police went to the Mapp home and ordered that they be given entry. Ms. Mapp adamantly refused to open the door and demanded that the police should first show their search warrant. The police did not actually have a warrant, but they broke into the house anyway and showed Mapp what actually later turned out to be a fake warrant. The police did not find their bombing suspect, but they did find a cellar full of illegal pornography of all types and forms. In her defense she said she didn't even know the offensive material was in her house and therefore it must have been left by a previous occupant. Ms. Mapp was taken to court and then convicted of possession of obscenity,

a conviction that she and her attorney quickly appealed. The appeal ultimately found its way to the Supreme Court of the United States.

4. Due Process and Evidence Reliability

A trained Connecticut undercover state policeman, James Glover, was told by an informant that he could buy drugs from a man who lived at a certain apartment. Glover went to the third floor apartment of the address he was given and knocked on the door. A man answered the door, and held out his hand. The light in the hallway was adequate and the man was less than two feet away from trooper Glover. The officer handed him two ten dollar bills, and within minutes the man handed back two bags of a substance later identified by Toxicology as heroin. Trooper Glover then left the building and went to the police headquarters where he described the seller as being "approximately five feet eleven inches tall, dark complexion, black hair, short Afro style, high cheekbones and of heavy build." The description rang a bell with one of the officers who went into the records department and brought out a picture that seemed to fit Glover's description. When Glover saw the picture, he immediately said that it was the man who sold him the drugs. Later, in court, Glover again made a positive identification of the picture, and there was no objection. Glover also made a positive ID of the suspect himself, again with no objection. The suspect was convicted. Later he filed a petition of appeal and although the District Court upheld the decision, the Court of Appeals disagreed and reversed the decision maintaining that the photograph should have been excluded from the trial because it was not reliable evidence.

5. Iris Mena

Because of a drive-by-shooting, the police went to the home of Iris Mena who had rented out a room to a gang member (the apparent target). During the investigation of her home, the police detained Ms. Mena and asked her for her immigration papers. She complied and showed her papers, but later sued the police. Her argument was that the police had no reasonable suspicion of her being an illegal, and that this therefore violated her Fourth Amendments rights.

6. The Code of Federal Regulations (CFR)

Before leaving this section on some of the legalities found in the Bill of Rights, let us also consider the Code of Federal Regulations that specifies the rules and regulations of the country's laws as they are to be **carried out** by the government. The CFR must be constitutionally sound and observe all legal precedents. Whereas the Bill of Rights was intended to protect the individual from the possible abuse of government power, the Federal code spells out the details of how federal law is to be enforced. Because of its importance in shedding light on the current immigration problem, our focus here will be in Title 8, Section 1325, of the regulations which states: "Any citizen of any country other than the United States who enters or attempts to enter the United States at any time or place other than as designated by immigration officers has committed a federal crime, punishable by up to two years in prison".

7. Papers Please

The Governor of Arizona signed into law an immigration bill that, among other things, allowed the police to ask for a person's immigration papers when that person is suspected of being in the country illegally and in violation of the above shown Title 8, Section 1325. Thus, law enforcement officers can demand proof of a person's immigration status when that person is stopped, detained or arrested and there is a reasonable suspicion that the person is in this country without authorization. Opponents of the law contend that this is a blatant case of ethnic profiling and violates basic human rights. The issue was brought to the Supreme Court in Arizona et al v the United States (2012). How would you have voted? Do you think your vote leans toward the rights of the individual or the security of society?

Reasoning Time Out

Let's look at each of the above cases, and see which way you went. Would you have voted in favor of the accused? Also indicate whether your decision emphasizes the rights of the individual or the protection of society.

1. The Brady Error . In this case the Supreme court ruled that by not being informed of his partner's confession, Brady was denied due process. The withheld evidence in this case is called "exculpatory," which is evidence that is favorable to the defendant and that may even exonerate or justify the defendant's actions. Because of this decision, prosecutors are now compelled to seek out any exculpatory evidence and then hand it over to the defense. The prosecutor who fails to follow through on this is said to have committed the "Brady Error". Individual Rights or Protection of Society?

2. The Terry Stop. In case 2 the Supreme Court ruled that the police did have probable cause and were justified in both the detention and search of the men involved. The ruling was that whenever "a police officer observes unusual conduct which leads him reasonably to conclude in the light of his (sic) experience that criminal activity may be afoot, and the person with whom he is dealing may be armed and presently dangerous that he then can be detained and searched". Thus, today when there is reasonable suspicion, a suspect may be both detained and searched, now called a "Terry Stop".
Individual Rights or Protection of Society?

3. The Mapp Ruling . The Supreme court in this case ruled in Mapp's favor, arguing that in this case there was a clear violation of the 4th Amendments' ban on unreasonable search and seizure and also a violation of her 5th Amendment rights against self-incrimination. The court ruled that when the

"Fourth Amendment's ban against unreasonable search and seizure is considered together with the Fifth Amendment's ban against compelled self-incrimination, a constitutional basis emerges which not only justifies, but actually requires the exclusionary rule" (which is the rule that evidence gained illegally must be excluded from use by any law enforcement agencies). This is now part of the law of the land and guarantees that a criminal defendant may have evidence suppressed that was gained by violations of the Fourth and Fifth Amendments, now known as the "Mapp Ruling". Individual Rights or Protection of Society?

4. Evidence Reliability. This case also went to the Supreme Court, (Manson v Brathwaite, 1977), and by an eight to one vote, the original conviction was to stand. The Supreme Court said that since Glover was not a casual observer "but a highly trained police officer who had sufficient opportunity to view the suspect, accurately describe him, positively identify the photograph as that of the suspect, and made the photographic identification only two days after the crime." Individual Rights or Protection of Society?

5. Iris Mena.Although two lower courts ruled in her favor, when the case went to the Supreme Court, the previous rulings were reversed. In Mueller v Mena (2005) the Supreme Court ruled that the reasonable suspicion argument was not relevant in this case because Ms. Mena was already under detention during the time of the questioning. Therefore the conclusion is that authorities may question someone regarding name, age, date of birth and immigration status as long as the person is already under detention for other reasons. Individual Rights or Protection of Society?

6. The Supreme Court in Arizona et al v The United States (2012) ruled that the provision in the Arizona law that allows the police to demand proof of immigration status from a suspect who is reasonably thought to be in violation of the immigration law is constitutional and should be upheld. Individual Rights or Protection of Society?

Although your decisions may even have been preferable, those were the Supreme Court's decisions and they have been solemnly hallowed as the "Law of the Land"

*Some of the cases shown above were summarized in a series of excellent articles by Devallis Rutledge in the "Police Magazine". You are encouraged to read this magazine as often as possible, because it is full of extremely important information for anyone considering a career in criminal justice in general or law enforcement in particular. The column titled "Point of Law" is especially relevant.

A PERSON OF INTEREST: CLARENCE DARROW (1857-1938)

Clarence Darrow may still be America's most famous defense lawyer (the model for the role of Billy Flynn in the musical "Chicago"). His cases and victories are legendary, and he defended rich and poor alike. Perhaps his most famous quote is "every case is won or lost as soon as

the jury is sworn" (1936). And Clarence Darrow knew how to pick a sympathetic jury. He never used any scientific methods, just his own hunches, intuition and common sense, and his oratory is considered to be classic. In one of his theatrical summations it is alleged he even moved the judge to tears. Darrow successfully handled many high-profile cases, and he did not hire any expensive jury experts to aid in making his juror decisions. And when his instincts let him down and the wrong juror was selected, it is alleged that he sealed the deal by the use of old-fashioned bribery (Farrell, J. A., 2011). Darrow literally flew by the seat of his pants.

During his life time he was involved in some of the country's biggest and most notorious cases. He defended the two thrill-killers Leopold and Loeb, (1924), two very rich teen-agers who wanted to kill someone for the sheer joy of reducing their own boredom. He was also the lawyer for the defense in the Scopes trial (1925), also known as the "Monkey Trial", about which the movie "Inherit the Wind" was produced. Although the trial was intended to judge whether John Scopes, a high-school science teacher in Tennessee, had violated the law by exposing his students to Darwin's theory of evolution. In point of fact, it soon became obvious that it was really Darwin who was on trial. The prosecution sought out the oratorical skills of silver-tongued William Jennings Bryan, previously a Democratic candidate for the presidency of the United States. Darrow later became a leader in the ACLU (American Civil Liberties Union), and wrote a number of books on crime and its causes. He argued that there is no clear demarcation between the good and the bad, or right versus wrong, and that the blurry line between them is often arbitrary and shifting.

Criminal Statistics – Keeping Track of Crime – Numbing Numbers

The government provides two major sources for keeping track of criminal activity, crime rates and types of crimes committed in the United States, (1) the Uniform Crime Reports and (2) the National Crime Victimization Survey.

Uniform Crime Reports – UCR and the FBI

The F.B.I. collects information from local, state, and federal law enforcement agencies, and then in Part 1 of these Uniform Crime Reports, the data are organized into categories of what are called "Index Crimes" (the most serious and violent crimes)– (1). Murder,(2). Forcible Rape, (3). Robbery, and (4) Aggravated Assault.   Then in Part 2, the UCR covers what are considered less serious crimes, called property or non-index crimes, such as (1). Larceny-Theft, (2). Motor Vehicle Theft , (3) Embezzlement, (4) Prostitution, (5) Forgery, (6) Counterfeiting, (7) Fraud, (8) Disorderly Conduct, (9), Stolen Property, (10) Vandalism , (11) Weapons Offenses, (12) Burglary. and (13) Vagrancy and/or Loitering. Although the data are reliable, they only cover what law enforcement actually knows – that is, those crimes that have been reported to or detected by the police. The major criticism of the UCR is that there are some crimes that are never reported to the police, and therefore never appear in the UCR.

The FBI also gives us criminal time lines. For example, it was found that among Index crimes:

One murder every 31.5 minutes,

One forcible rape every 5.6 minutes,

One robbery every 1.3 minutes

One aggravated assault every 36.5 seconds

And then among Property crimes:

One burglary every 14.6 seconds

One larceny/theft every 4.7 seconds

One motor vehicle theft every 25.5 seconds

Don't read too much into those time lines. It may look as though crime is being metered out on a regularly timed basis. For example, finding out that murders occur every 31.5 minutes might cause someone to check his watch and decide not to leave home for several minutes in order to avoid that deadly time interval.

National Crime Victimization Survey (NCVS).

These data are collected by surveying representative samples of the population in order to find out information on crimes that have occurred but may never have been reported. The survey focuses on the following crimes: (1) rape, (2) robbery, (3) motor-vehicle theft, (4) larceny, (5) burglary and (6) assault (both simple and aggravated). The results of these surveys indicate that there are crimes that never get reported to law enforcement. The major criticism of the NCVS is that its data are virtually impossible to verify, since at least some of the survey responses may be concocted out of sheer fantasy.

Less Crime

Both of these data sources have consistently shown that crime rates in the United States have fallen sharply over the past 20 years. This is true of both the major crimes, the index crimes, as well as those of a less serious nature. Perhaps the increasing numbers of the population now incarcerated, on probation or parole may be playing a role in the reduced levels of crime. Or, perhaps the increased incarceration rate is due to a higher level of police efficiency. That is, it may be that increased vigilance and more effective police work have led to more arrests and convictions. Finally, it may be that today's judges are handing out longer sentences due to public outcry.

As a student new to the field of criminal justice, keep in mind that these two government sources, U.C.R. and N.C.V.S provide a treasure trove of data that are available to the criminal justice researcher.

The Statistics Vary by State

Incarceration rates do vary by state, with the highest rates occurring in Louisiana, Mississippi and Oklahoma, and the lowest rates in Maine, Minnesota, and New Hampshire. Also it should be noted that 92% of incarcerated felons are male.

White Collar Crime: More Money Stolen with a Pen than a Gun

Before going on to look at some of your career opportunities in law enforcement and/or criminal justice in general, let's take just a few moments to look at what has fast become one of the country's most serious problems – white collar crime. With the current wave of identity thefts and cyber- crimes, the spotlight has definitely turned toward the white collar criminal. Although white collar crimes, such as identity theft and fraud, are not considered to be one of the more serious index crimes, they can and do cost society huge amounts of money. This can be enormous money, such as a corporate accountant "cooking the books" and defrauding stock holders, or perhaps just a few hundred dollars, such as someone cashing your check after forging your name with your social security number. The phrase "the pen is mightier than the sword (or pistol)" was never more true than in the area of white-collar crime. Far more money has been stolen with a ball-point than at the point of a gun. Although the term "white collar crime" has been with us for decades (Sutherland, 1949), its cost to society has risen exponentially over the past dozen years, in part due to the cyber- crimes of the internet. And please never feel sorry for the white-collar thief, because he/she doesn't feel sorry for you. The following case study is a composite character made up of cases covered in "Outsmarting the Scam Artists" (Shadel, 2006)

CASE STUDY- Joey D.

I'm writing this just to pass the time of day, and I have a lot of time to pass and a lot of days to pass it in. I am a college drop-out who majored in accounting and quickly found out that for me things just didn't add up. I worked for H & R Block during tax season, but the rest of the time I just "collected." I am now a victim of California's illegal "three-strikes-and-you're-out" rule. I call it illegal because it is certainly cruel, and for me, highly unusual. I think it must violate some damned amendment. Anyway, I admit that when I needed extra cash I did break the law on occasion, but never anything serious or violent. I guess I did run a few scams. My first few cons were minor league as far as money was concerned, but I did have to do some jail time for each. My third and best con was when I set myself up in the "oil" business, and my sales area was from Los Angeles to San Francisco. I met my suckers by going to local churches, and getting names of parishioners. Then I'd go home and look them up on the net to see who's got anything I might use as an ice-breaking gambit, like "oh I saw on your Facebook page that you like fishing, and I also like fishing." I'd go back to the church and mingle with people at the coffee hour after the service. By the second week I usually had a mark. When I sensed I had a sucker I could hear my inner voice saying "bingo." And when I had that "bingo" moment I would talk to the guy about something fairly personal that I had picked up on the web. Within an hour I usually had a mark. I always picked older men, older because they were more apt to have accumulated some significant cash and men because they were easier to con than women. Women are just too suspicious and paranoid whenever you offer them a real good financial opportunity. Most of the older men I worked with were too greedy and too trusting to be suspicious. I would show the guy some pictures I had of a working oil well that I said was pumping out such great profits that a major corporation (I chose to call it Halliburton) wanted to buy me out. Before I could seal the deal with Halliburton I needed some money to up-date the well structure. I said that for the next few weeks I still had some full corporate units for sale for only $10,000, or quarter units for $2500, and that buyers are guaranteed to quadruple their money in less than a year. Some men would even ask me if I was registered with the Federal Trade Commission, which of course I said I was. I would even give them the FTC's phone number, but rarely did anyone bother to call. They were too anxious to believe me and just couldn't wait to own a unit or two. If a man began to act like he didn't trust me, like saying he had to consult his lawyer , or needed a few nights to sleep on it, I would just drop him, and go on to the next church and the next mark. By the time I was 40, I was a-millionaire, but then one day the roof collapsed on me in the form of a wise-guy F.B.I agent. I got arrested and convicted of violating some damned inter-state commerce laws, and I am now supposed to be sorrowfully paying my debt to society. I have plenty of time now to explore my feelings as I sit here in my H & R Cell Block. Am I really sorry? Yes, sorry that I got caught, but not sorry for those church-going suckers that were too greedy to read the fine print. They got what they deserved.

Note the total lack of remorse. No the crime was not violent, but the emotional level is almost like the person who kills someone and then goes out to a restaurant for a prime-rib dinner (and orders it bloody and rare).

Who Goes to Jail?

The variables which are the best predictors of criminal activity and arrest are 1.gender, 2.number of previous convictions, and 3.age of first arrest.

1. Gender. Currently 92% of those under correctional supervision are male, and gender is the single best predictor of incarceration.

2. Number of Previous Incarcerations. The data indicate that those with the highest number of previous incarcerations are most apt to be re-incarcerated.

3. Age of First Arrest. The younger a person is at the time of first arrest, the more likely it is that the person will be incarcerated.

In a later chapter there will be a discussion of the personality types who have a high probability of being arrested. Many seem to lack a sense of conscience and emotional concern. It can become almost a total inability to feel any remorse, an emotional numbness. At its most extreme level, these people are labeled as psychopaths.

Careers in Criminal Justice – Just Where Do You Fit In?
Now that you have a general idea of what criminal justice is all about, let's take a look at the types of criminal justice careers that are going to be available to you. There are few (if any) other fields of study that offer the wide-ranging diversity and interesting array of job opportunities found in the area of criminal justice. How many variations on the career-theme are there? Let us count the ways. The following will provide a list of thumb-nail sketches for many (but certainly not all) of the types of work you may want to consider. And you thought crime didn't pay! And for you women out there, the vast majority of these jobs are open to females as well as males. Gone are the days when female police officers were known as "meter maids." Today there are women on the criminal justice front lines. In fact, at the time of this writing women outnumber men in criminal- justice doctoral programs throughout the country. However you don't need a doctorate for most of these jobs, but you probably do need at least a two-year college degree. The four-year college degree is definitely preferred, and some careers require academic work beyond the four-year degree (like law school). For most of these jobs there are requirements other than educational, such as age, physical condition, eye sight etc., but our focus, of course, will be on education. If you're able to get a four-year college degree, you'll find it's more than worth the time and effort if you are serious about a career in criminal justice. Although the following is a list of separate and distinct careers, you'll find that many have overlapping responsibilities.

Air Marshal. The Air Marshal is one of the top jobs in the field of criminal justice and involves providing security on commercial air lines as well as securing both the aircraft and the air ports. When traveling on a commercial flight, the Air Marshal usually works undercover and is always armed. Sometimes called a Sky Marshal, the Air Marshal works for the Federal Transportation Security Administration. Requirements include a four-year college degree as well as some law-enforcement experience.

Arson and Fire Investigator. This is a law enforcement job that is concerned with investigating the cause or causes of a fire, and if found to have been set intentionally, to recover evidence for the prosecution of the perpetrator. The fire may have been set in order to file an insurance claim or sometimes to cover up another crime. Arson investigators are often called upon to testify in court. This is a difficult job, because in so many cases the fire itself clears the scene of any evidence. This job requires at least a two-year associates college degree, but recently the four-year bachelor's degree has become increasingly demanded.

ATF Agent. These agents work for the United States Department of Alcohol, Tobacco and Firearms, and are charged with investigating any violations in any of those three areas. It is interesting to note that "fire arms" in this context includes any form of potential explosives. This job requires a four-year bachelor's degree and also involves on-the-job training, especially in surveillance techniques.

Bailiff. A Bailiff is used to ensure security and preserve order in courts of law. The Bailiff may have to search persons entering the courtroom to be sure no weapons are brought in. The Bailiff is usually in charge of escorting the suspects in and out of the court room, and in the case of sequestered juries, escorting the jurors to meals and/or hotel rooms. The Bailiff may also announce both the entrance of the judge as well as the rules of the court. The requirements for Bailiff vary throughout the country and depend on the state or county, with some states requiring formal degree programs and/or law-enforcement experience.

Border Patrol Agent. The United States Border Patrol is in charge of who or who does not enter this country. Border Patrol agents are on the lookout for terrorists or illegal aliens attempting to cross our borders. The job has taken on increased responsibility since the attack on 9/11, and is now the largest federal law-enforcement agency in the United States. The job also involves stopping the smuggling of goods and merchandise (especially drugs and weapons) into the United States. Although the work can be physically demanding, much can now be done with electronic detection devices as well as night-vision scopes. This is a law enforcement job that requires being armed. Most Border Patrol Agents have at least a four-year bachelor's degree and many have Masters degrees.

Bounty Hunter. A Bounty Hunter or **Fugitive Recovery Agent** has the job of locating and bringing back persons who have jumped bail. The Bounty Hunter is usually paid on a commission basis, typically collecting as much as 10% of the bail. The job can be both demanding and dangerous, since the fugitive may be armed, unpredictable and difficult to locate. The Bounty Hunter is usually employed by the bail bond company that had originally put up the money for the fugitive's bail. Most bounty hunters are armed, and there are currently no formal education requirements. Bounty hunting has been popularized in motion pictures (in comedies like "The Bounty Hunter" and seriously, as in Steve McQueen's final film "The Hunter," and on TV shows, such as "Dog the Bounty Hunter."

Corrections Officer. Sometimes called a **Detention Officer** or **Prison Officer**, the Corrections Officer (CO) is charged with maintaining safety, security and discipline within the confined jail or prison population. The job can be stressful due to the inherent potential danger within the confines of any jail/ prison The CO is also usually involved in transporting inmates to their court or medical appearances (a duty often shared with the Bailiff). Some COs may be part of a Swat Team, which then becomes the first responders in case of a jail emergency (riots, escape attempts, or threats to other inmates or prison personnel). Some jobs in this field list either military or law enforcement experience as essential, but may allow a candidate's college credits to act as a substitute. For the federal prison system a four-year bachelor's degree is required.

Crime Laboratory Analyst. This job demands that you become able to analyze evidence from the crime scene, such as bodily fluids that might show traces of toxic agents or drugs. Blood samples can be analyzed for identification, cause of death/injury etc. The crime lab analyst often works closely with the coroner in reviewing autopsies. These are good paying jobs, but require at least a four-year college degree in either chemistry or bio-genetics.

Customs Agent. As a Customs Agent you would be working for ICE, United States Immigration and Customs Enforcement. The job is demanding since you will have to search people, luggage, overseas shipments, and, of course, cars, ships and trucks. Customs Agents have the power of arrest, and are especially on the alert for the illegal shipment of drugs, firearms and laundered money. A four-year college degree is required, with Criminal Justice as the most common major.

DEA (Drug Enforcement Agency) Agent. This is a federal government job under the control of the United States Drug Enforcement Agency. Agents are used to enforce current federal drug laws and are trained in both investigative and legal techniques. To be eligible for this job, the applicant must have a four-year bachelor's degree.

District Attorney. The district attorney is either elected by the people or appointed by a government official, and is the jurisdiction's chief law enforcement agent. The DA handles the court cases and works closely with other law enforcement agencies in gathering evidence for the prosecution. At the federal level, the nation's top law enforcement official is called the Attorney General. In order to qualify as a district attorney, you must first become a lawyer (see lawyer below).

FBI Agent. Working as an agent for the Federal Bureau of Investigation is extremely demanding and requires a thorough knowledge of both law-enforcement procedures as well as expertise in other areas, such as having a background in legal or accounting skills, or having fluency in other languages. This job is basically oriented toward providing national security to the United States citizenry and upholding our federal laws. At least a four-year college bachelor's degree is required, and often there are further educational demands, such as a degree in law and/or accounting.

Fish and Game Warden. These are state jobs and come under the control of the state's Fish and Game Departments. The Fish and Game Warden is assigned to patrolling beaches, rivers, and lakes to ensure that the state's fishing and game laws are not being violated. The warden is usually armed and in uniform. Though a four-year college degree is preferred, with specialties in criminal justice or biology, some states still allow these jobs to be filled by a person with a high-school degree.

Forensic Psychologist. In the vast majority of cases, the forensic psychologist has a doctoral degree in either forensic or clinical psychology. Thus, although fully trained as a psychologist, the forensic psychologist also has to become familiar with criminal law, since a large part of the job is testifying in court as an expert witness, sometimes testifying as to whether a defendant is competent to stand trial, or translating technical psychological terms into language the court can understand. The forensic psychologist may also be employed by a corrections facility in order to aid in the inmates' rehabilitation efforts. Finally, a large part of the job is testing defendants and inmates for psychological issues and problems.

Fraud Investigator. Fraud is both a crime and a violation of civil law. It is defined as willful deception used for personal gain, usually monetary gain. The fraud investigator can be involved in civil as well as criminal investigations, and may be called upon to serve subpoenas, investigate insurance and mortgage claims and gather criminal evidence. The fraud investigator is often required to give court testimony and often works closely with the forensic accountants. A four year bachelor's degree is required.

Homeland Security. This is an area with increasing numbers of jobs. Its mission is to make a "concerted national effort to prevent terrorist attack within the United States, reduce America's vulnerability to terrorism and minimize damage if attacks do occur." The numbers of departments within its umbrella are far ranging and include: U.S National Guard, U.S. Coast guard, U.S. Customs, Border Patrol, Immigration Service and FEMA (the Federal Emergency Management Agency).

IRS (Internal Revenue Service) Special Agent. The IRS Special Agent works in the investigative branch of the IRS and is involved in probing tax violations, money laundering, and other financial irregularities and crimes. The Agent could be assigned to several arms of the IRS, including the Organized Crime Unit, the Telemarketing Fraud Unit or the Computer Fraud Unit. Many of the agents are themselves, or work closely with, the Forensic Accountant. The job demands at least a four-year bachelor's degree, and an accounting degree is a definite plus.

Judge. The position of judge is determined either by popular vote (an election) or by a government appointment. The judge is the presiding officer in the court room, and sometimes renders the verdict, either as part of a panel of judges or by him/herself. When juries are involved the judge keeps the court's rules and the court's decorum. Usually wearing a black robe and wielding the gavel, the judge determines what can or cannot be legitimately offered by either the prosecution or defense. In most court rooms the judge is addressed as "your honor." Judges are required to first become lawyers, (hold a JD degree).

Lawyer. In general terms the job of a lawyer (attorney) is in the application of the law, and this involves many different areas within the legal system. The following are examples of some of the jobs available: court-room prosecution and/or defense, drafting wills, conveying legal documents such as deeds, drafting contracts, preparing wills, and of course, giving advice. Preparation to become a lawyer takes at least seven years, four years of undergraduate education and three years of law school. The law school degree is called a Juris Doctor (JD), and once that is achieved, the student must then pass the bar exam for his or her particular state.

NSA (National Security Agency) Police. The National Security Agency Police wear uniforms and as is the case for other police jobs, the NSA police must carry agency issued firearms. Members of this group are charged with protecting any and all NSA functions including counter terrorism and worldwide counter intelligence. Head quartered at Fort Meade in Maryland, NSA is considered to be one of most respected agencies in the Federal government. This job requires at least a two-year degree in Criminal Justice or previous military service in security work.

Park Ranger. Park Rangers work for the United States Park Service and provide security for visitors, wild life, and the eco systems in American parks. Most Park Rangers must wear uniforms and have at least an Associate Degree, preferably in criminal justice or forestry. The Park Ranger is especially alert to the possibility of fires. Some of the most famous cases solved by Park Rangers concerned successful searches for lost hikers.

Penologist. A penologist is responsible for setting jail or prison policies, for securing the jail or prison and preventing any disruptions. The penologist sets up programs for rehabilitation of the inmate population. Such programs as substance abuse counseling or anger management come under the purview of the penologist. Penologists typically work closely with the corrections officers and other jail/prison personnel. A bachelor's degree from a four –year program is required in most states and counties. As a penologist you could work for the Federal Government or for the State and/or County governments.

Police Officer or Detective. Police Officers and Detectives are usually employed by the city or town and are trained to protect and serve. These jobs can be both dangerous and stressful, especially in large cities. The job involves protecting lives and property and standing ready to apprehend law breakers, either through arrest, citations or warnings. The job also demands a large amount of paper work in the form of report writing and record keeping. The difference between the police officer and the detective is basically that the police officer is the first responder to the violation, whereas the detective comes in later and continues the investigation with detailed analyses. Also, whereas the police officer is in uniform, the detective is almost always in plain clothes. Detectives are virtually always selected from persons who have already served as police officers, and it is becoming the norm that both police officers and detectives obtain four-year college degrees, with criminal justice as the preferred degree.

Private Security Agent. These jobs are offered by private-sector industries, and involve protecting company personnel and/or company property. The Private Security Agent often employs video technology as well as conducting personal visual patrols. The primary method used is often labeled as the DDOR, Detect, Deter, Observe and Report. A two or four-year college degree, usually with a Criminal Justice major, is adequate, although special training following the degree may be required.

Probation-Parole Officer. The probation officer is in charge of anyone who has been granted probation while the parole officer is responsible for monitoring and supervising parolees. The probation or parole officer's job could be at the Federal level or the city, county, or state level. Careful records must be kept and violations of the terms of probation or parole can result in re-confinement. Most probation/parole officers hold a four-year bachelor's degree.

Secret Service Agent. Now under the control of the Department of Homeland Security (previously under the Treasury Department), the secret service agent must protect the President of the United States and first family, including past presidents and their families. They control who comes and goes at the White House, and are involved in security wherever the president or former presidents may go. Other duties include investigating counterfeit money or bonds, or any discrepancies in the country's monetary system. A four-year bachelor's degree is required.

Sheriff. The duties of the sheriff vary from state to state and even county to county within a given state, but they all have one thing in common – a Sheriff is a preserver of the peace. The word Sheriff comes from the old English term "shire reeve," defined as a royal official charged with keeping the peace. Also, although the office of Sheriff is typically a county position, in some local areas, especially rural areas, the Sheriff's office is the major police department. In other areas the sheriff may serve the duties of a bailiff and also be in charge of the county jail. The sheriff may also serve warrants and eviction notices to foreclosed mortgage holders. You must hold at least an Associates' Degree, but a four-year bachelor's degree is preferred.

United States Park Police. As with the Park Ranger, the Park Police work under the aegis of the National Park Service (a bureau of the department of the Interior). This is a uniformed police force that is charged with protection of the national parks and the country's most famous monuments. Park Police are required to carry fire arms. The job requirements include at least an Associate's college degree.

Summary
Criminal justice is the government's system of institutionalized laws and rules for both the protection of society and the preservation of individual rights. The dilemma facing the criminal justice system is in the difficulties encountered in trying to balance both sides of this sometimes tenuous equation, that is, balancing both sides without leaning too far in one direction. Some have argued that the government goes too far in favor of individual rights at the expense of society's security. The Miranda rights, for example, have often been portrayed as favoring the suspect, rather than the safety of society. The Miranda rights demand that law enforcement officers carefully inform suspects that they don't have to talk, and that if they do talk whatever they say can be used against them in a court of law. Critics of Miranda allege that this makes it too easy for the suspect and is therefore a danger to society. Before Miranda, on- sight confessions were often extremely helpful to law enforcement's attempt at conviction, (a conviction that kept the suspect off the streets and away from society). Another example of the challenge to fair and equitable justice is the practice of scientific jury selection, SJS. The use of scientific techniques for selecting a jury has become wide-spread, and involves evaluating a prospective juror on the basis of at least five major variables: (1) race, (2) education, (3) income, (4) age, and (5) gender. Even the

juror's looks, attractive or unattractive, may impact that juror's decision, especially when combined with the attractiveness of the defendant. The juries that result from these careful selections have been shown to favor the defendant in some cases, or, on the other hand, sometimes favor the prosecution. The goal of the selection is to empanel a jury that is already one-sidedly sympathetic. As was also pointed out, jurors are not always basing their decisions on the presented facts. Because of a phenomenon called "cognitive dissonance" jurors may create their own images and scenarios that seem more logical and consistent than are those contained in the actual details of the case. The process of jury selection and questioning is called "voir dire" and it is used by both the prosecution and the defense. Each side is given a number of challenges, and the prospective juror can be dismissed either by "just cause" (where the reason for the dismissal is publicly announced ... as in the case of the wife of an investigating police officer), or via the "peremptory" challenge (where the reason can be withheld).

The combined techniques for meting out justice must be continually examined in order to maintain that careful balance between one side of the equation (the safety of society – typically the prosecution)) and the opposing side (individual rights – typically the defense). And this balancing act between society's safety and individual freedom can be seen in many non-courtroom situations that you may encounter throughout your life. For example, should the safety of the air-traveling public demand that invasive scans and body pat-downs be performed on every prospective passenger? The coverage in this section includes six very important Supreme Court decisions, which were presented to allow you to think about that critically thin line that divides individual rights and the safety of society. The white collar criminal, non-violent criminal, has come under increased scrutiny with the rise of computer-driven cybercrimes and identity theft. These felons often show a complete lack of any remorse. The chapter concludes with a large and varied list of potential careers available to you as a student of criminal justice. Perhaps no other field of study offers as many different and interesting jobs as can be found in the area of criminal justice. Spend some time thinking about each one and see which way your interests lead you.

Key Terms

Brady Error
Code of Federal Regulations (CFR)
Cognitive Dissonance
Criminal Justice
Death Qualified Jury
Mapp Ruling
Miranda Rights

Peremptory Challenge
Terry Stop
Sequestered Jury
Scientific Jury Selection (SJS)

References

Darby, B.W. & Jeffers, D.J. (2000). The effects of defendant and juror attractiveness on simulated courtroom trial decisions. *Society for Personality Research, 16,* 67-84

Dimitrius, J. (1998). *Reading people.* New York: Random House.

Farrell, J.A., (2011). *Clarence Darrow: Attorney for the damned.* New York, Doubleday.

Hastie, R. , Penrod, S.D. & Pennington, N (1983). *Inside the jury.* Cambridge, MA: Harvard Univ. Press.

La Fave, W.R., Israel, J.H. & King, N.J. (2007). *Criminal procedures, 3rd Ed.* St.Paul, MN: West Publishers

Rutledge, D. (2011). Don't talk to my client. *Police Magazine,* February, 64-65, p 65.

Rutledge, D. (2011). Point of law. *Police Magazine,* December, 56-58

Schmalleger, F.(2011). *Criminal justice today.* Upper Saddle River, NJ: Prentice-Hall

Shadel, D. (2006) . *Outsmarting the scam artists.* New York: Wiley.

Sutherland, E.H. (1949). *White collar crime.* New York: Dryden Press.

CHAPTER 2

A SEARCH FOR THE ROOTS OF CRIME

Psychology, Sociology, Biology, and Economics
In this chapter we will launch an investigation into the various theoretical positions regarding the roots of crime. There will be, as you will soon see, conflicting theories, but by the time you get to the end of the chapter, a unifying theme begins to emerge. And let's be clear. There is nothing inherently wrong with theory building, but theorizing and construct building should ultimately rest on the bed-rock of observational research, rather than mere armchair speculation. As Sheriff Michael J. Ashe said "As a criminal justice practitioner for nearly 30 years, I have come to believe that just as criminal justice theory without practice can become esoteric, criminal justice practice without theory can become wanting in perspective and vision" (Ashe, 2004)

The criminal justice literature abounds in theories of why people turn to crime, and why some persons are more susceptible than others to the lure of criminal activity. Even the Bible mentions the fact that certain types of individuals seem to be prone to crime, and the early Greek theorist, Hippocrates (circa 400 B.C) identified a number of physical characteristics associated with specific behavioral traits such as anger and excitability. Incidentally, this is the same Hippocrates to whom every physician still swears an oath. Hippocrates looked at what he called the four humors (bodily fluids), black bile, yellow bile, blood, and phlegm. Persons were categorized on the basis of which of their four humors was in ascendance. If it were black bile, you were brooding, despondent, irritable and suffer from insomnia, and if it were yellow bile you were quick tempered, easily angered and irascible. If your main humor was blood, you were a happy optimist, amorous and courageous, but if it were phlegm you were slow to react, calm, unemotional and phlegmatic. It seems that the early Greeks loved dividing things up into four categories. For example they saw the world as being composed of four elements, earth, air, fire and water. And many centuries later, the English dramatist, William Shakespeare, expressed a similar view when he described one of the Julius Caesar assassins as having a "lean and hungry look...and such men are dangerous."

As you will soon see, some of the theoretical positions to be presented here are not scientifically substantiated, but it is important for you to at least know what they are, because they keep returning, dressed differently perhaps, but still conveying the same messages. This is not meant to be just a museum tour, showing off dust-covered relics, but instead it is designed to provide a background for understanding the many and varied theories of crime we have today. A little history of what theories have preceded the current views should make you better able to sift the wheat from the chaff in your own reading of the literature. Actually, some of these positions you will read about again later in the research chapter.

The Backgrounds

We will use broad brush strokes in laying out these positions and categorize them four ways:
1. Theories based on heredity (the bad gene theories)
2. Theories based on environment (the behaviorists and social-learning theorists)
3. Theories based on the interaction of heredity, environment and time.
4. A brief look at the economy

1. The Hereditarians Speak: Bad Seed or Bad Science?

Phrenology

Probably the first organized attempt to determine the genetic origin of crime comes from the work of Gall and Spurzheim (early 1800s). They called their discipline "Phrenology" and defined it as the study of personality characteristics associated with and determined by the shape of the head. Gall and Spurzheim (early 1800s) literally felt a person's head, and characterized that person's personality according to the location of certain bumps, nodes, and skull depressions. It was a lock-step system, a bump here and you were a thief, a node there and you were a musician, a dent over there and you were an athlete. Amazingly, phrenology was still part of both the literature of criminology and the actual process of classifying felons well into the 20th century. You may still hear it being seriously discussed on some late-night, conspiracy-theory radio talk shows.

Cesare Lombroso (Late 1800s) – The Body of a Criminal

Cesare Lombroso believed that some people were born to be criminals, and that they come into the world with inherited tendencies of aggression and "savagery." He stated that there were certain inherited physical characteristics that associate with mental traits which could then be used to profile the born criminal. The physical traits included a long, sloping forehead, long and ape-like arms, ears with no lobes, and asymmetry of the head. For mental traits, the born criminal was said to have had a low threshold for pain but a greater sensitivity to sights and sounds. Psychologically he/she had no sense of remorse, or what Lombroso called "moral sense." The criminal was also described as being vain, impulsive, vindictive and cruel. In setting forth these traits, Lombroso is portraying very closely the behavior of what we now call the psychopath. Finally, if Lombroso is right, you should beware of persons with excessive tattoos or the inability to wear ear rings.

The Jukes: Margaret the Mother of Criminals

In 1877 Richard Dugdale (described as a "gentleman-sociologist" and a member of the Executive Committee of the New York Prison Association) published a book called "The Jukes: A Study in Crime, Pauperism, Disease and Heredity." In it he described a family, descended from an early Dutch settler that he called the Jukes (a pseudonym), a family that was definitely over represented in the criminal records of the time. The family owed much of its genetic endowment, said Dugdale, to a woman who he affectionately called "Margaret the Mother of Criminals." Over the years the family produced hundreds of prostitutes, brothel keepers, welfare recipients, convicted criminals and mentally ill people of all types. Although Dugdale believed that much of this dysfunction could be attributed to heredity, he did acknowledge that environment might still play a role and may even impact heredity. He said "environment tends to produce habits which may become hereditary" (Dugdale, 1877, p66). In short, although he definitely saw the roots of crime in one's genetic endowment, he did give some credit to the influence of environmental stressors, especially the lack of financial resources. And as shown above, he actually believed that a poor environment could change one's genetic nature.

Henry Goddard and the Kallikaks – Early 20th Century Inheritance Gone Wild

In 1912 Henry E. Goddard published an account of the damaging effects of an inferior genetic endowment on generation after generation of a family named Kallikak. According to Goddard, who gleaned this material from books, newspapers, personal interviews and other records, Martin Kallikak (a pseudonym chosen by Goddard to protect the family) was an American Revolutionary War soldier who was responsible for developing two completely different family strains. The "good Kallikaks" (and Goddard traced this strain through 496 descendants) resulted from Kallikak's marriage to a "worthy Quakeress." She bore him seven upright, worthy children and from these seven children came hundreds of the highest types of human beings, doctors, lawyers, businessmen and even college presidents. Only two of the nearly 500 good Kallikaks were of below average intelligence. However, Martin Kallikak also had an amorous adventure with a "feeble-minded tavern girl." The result of this affair was an illegitimate son, later known to his friends and neighbors as "Old Horror." Fortunately for Goddard's story, Old Horror was not seen as horrible by everyone, because even he went on to father ten children of his own.

Goddard identified 480 of these descendants, the so-called "bad" Kallikaks, and found nothing but the lowest forms of humanity, from horse thieves and prostitutes to alcoholics and murderers. In this account Goddard wasted no time on details, such as the dramatic environmental differences between the good and bad Kallikaks or his serious misunderstanding of genetics. Unlike Dugdales's account of the Jukes family, Goddard paid no heed to any environmental inputs. Goddard's evidence, which was still taken seriously by some psychologists as late as the 1940s, is considered to be highly fanciful by today's genetic standards. Even if psychological traits were as directly and simply related to genotype as eye color, there would still have to be far more upstanding members of the bad Kallikaks and vice versa. After all, Martin Kallikak was himself half responsible for "Old Horror." But this was Goddard's point of view, and a cherished belief clouded his scientific vision.

Davenport and Turn-of-the-Century Genetics

Charles Davenport, one of America's leading geneticists at the time (1911), even went so far as to say that a large number of human traits had straight Mendelian explanations, laziness and aggressiveness being inherited through dominant genes and ambition and motivation through recessive genes. Davenport viewed personality traits as being as directly inherited as eye color. He also identified a number of diseases as being totally inherited, such as psoriasis, cirrhosis and goiter. Davenport's books, articles and lectures were used as primary sources in most medical schools at that time.

William Sheldon – Somatotypes – Mid 20th Century

Another theorist who looked for the physical correlates of inherited mental traits was William Sheldon who coined the term "somatotypes" as a way of describing various body types and their concomitant personalities. (Sheldon,1954). The three somatotypes were called (1) Endomorphy, (2) Mesomorphy and (3) Ectomorphy

1. Endomorph - This is the overweight individual, with small bones.

2. Mesomorph - This is the stocky, well-muscled person, usually with a medium to large bone structure.

3. Ectomorph - The thin, underweight individual, also with small bones.

Sheldon believed that all persons carried the above three types in differing degrees. He graded these each on a seven point scale, with the three extremes being a 7-1-1 for endomorphy, 1-7-1 for mesomorphy and 1-1-7 for ectomorphy. However, he found very few extreme body types, with most persons having somatotypes that fell in between, such as a mesomorph being perhaps a 2-6-4. Sheldon insisted that each body type was correlated with a certain personality type. For example, the endomorph was characterized as having a Visceratonic personality: out-going, jolly, a lover of comfort and luxury, and somewhat extraverted. The mesomorph had a Somatationic personality, courageous, active, aggressive and willing to take risks. Finally the ectomorph had a Cerebratonic personality, withdrawn, introverted, artistic and sensitive. Sheldon believed that the mesomorph was the most prone to criminality, the endomorph to mental problems, and the ectomorph to suicide. In later writings he made distinctions among types of criminals and their relationship to somatotyping. For example, whereas the mesomorph might be the bank robber or hit man, the ectomorph might be the quiet book keeper kiting checks, and the endomorph an out-going salesman on a scamming mission.

Genetics and the Super Male

As you probably remember from some past biology course, the human genome is composed of pairs of tiny rod-like structures called chromosomes. One of these pairs determines sex, XX for the female, and XY for the male. Patricia Jacobs discovered a chromosomal anomaly based on the fact that some men appeared to carry an extra Y chromosome and were labeled as being XYY, or as she called them "super males" (Jacobs & Hassold, 1986). These men were found to be aggressive, prone to acne, above average in height, and not blessed with an overabundance of IQ points. Jacobs found them to be overrepresented in the prison population, especially for property crimes and crimes of violence. Even the mass murderer, Richard Speck , was alleged to be an XYY, and therefore his lawyer argued for a reduced sentence.

Beware Wide faces – Such Men Are Dangerous

Today's researchers seem to be casting Lombroso in a more favorable light than was true just a few years ago. In fact in one recent study scientists found that unethical behavioral traits were linked with the width of a man's face, (Haselhuhn, & Wong, 2011). Unless there are some hidden environmental forces that can be shown to shape the structural contours of the face, this is probably best interpreted as being due to the forces of heredity. Using a measure called the WHR (Facial Width to Height Ratio), researchers found that men (but not women) with wide faces were three times more likely to lie, cheat, and deceive than were men with narrower faces. As an aside, if you've ever seen the extremely wide face of the murderous gangster Al Capone you might tend to agree. The authors even speculate on whether wide-faced men have actually evolved to be less ethical. One of the authors said the study reminded him of the horror novel, "The Bad Seed" in which a murderous genetic trait was passed on from generation to generation, suggesting that some men are born to be bad. However it must be kept clearly in mind that even if all criminals have wide faces (which is certainly a stretch), it does not logically follow that all wide faces have to belong to criminals. Think of it this way. Suppose we could assume that all dogs bark. That doesn't mean that everything that barks has to be a dog. For example, the barking might come from a trained seal or even some child in the school-yard doing his best cocker spaniel imitation

Instinct Theories

Before leaving the hereditarian position, there will be a quick side-trip into the world of instincts. The two most famous instinct theorists are Charles Darwin and Sigmund Freud. In his book, "The Origin of Species," Darwin created a theory of evolution that used the concept of instincts as one of his major building blocks (Darwin, 1859). He defined instincts as inherited and unlearned patterns of behavior that are triggered by specific stimuli. Instinctive behavior is therefore genetically based and not based on past experience. Although Darwin was careful not to extrapolate beyond his own naturalistic observations, his concept of the instinct was picked up by numerous other theorists and generalized to almost all animal and human behavior. As an example, it was alleged that people fight because of their aggressive instinct. And if asked how they know people have an aggressive instinct, the answer was "because they fight." In logic this is called the "nominal fallacy" because the behavior itself is used as its own explanation. Why do people get together in groups? Because they have a gregarious instinct. Why do people commit crimes? Because they have a criminal instinct. Why do people twiddle their thumbs? Because they have a thumb-twiddling instinct. This kind of reasoning confuses explanation with description and is not likely to lead to scientific advancement. The other major instinct theorist was Freud who insisted that humans had a built-in aggressive instinct that was as basic to human behavior as sex. The urge to violence is a result of pressure from what Freud called our innate and irrational id, a part of the human personality that contains a seething cauldron of pleasure and aggressive drives that demands immediate satisfaction. (According to Freud, the other two parts of the personality were the ego, that aspect of one's consciousness that is in contact with reality, and the super-ego, which is the stern voice of conscience.)

The problem with pure instinct theories, such as those shown above, is that by trying to explain everything, they may really not explain anything at all. If law enforcement were to be told that people rob taxi drivers because they have a taxi-robbing instinct, that explanation plus a couple of dollars might buy a cup of coffee.

2. The Environmentalists Speak

John B. Watson – Give me the baby

The strict environmentalists allied themselves with the great English philosopher, John Locke (1691), who said that the mind was a blank slate (tabula rasa) upon which experience writes. To the environmentalists, the baby is really nothing more than a lump of protoplasmic clay that can be molded and fashioned into any desired shape by that master craftsman, the environment. The most eloquent spokesman for this position is without a doubt John B. Watson. It was Watson's belief that people are made, not born, and that the baby can be molded into any adult form, trapeze artist, musician, hold-up man or master criminal - through the judicious use of conditioning techniques. Watson began writing about the same time as Pavlov's (1913) conditioning study of dogs was beginning to be recognized in the United States. Watson reasoned that if a dog could be conditioned to salivate at the sound of a bell, then so too could a baby. In a now classic study, Watson tested this assumption by conditioning a nine month old baby, named Albert, to fear a whole variety of objects (stimuli). By the time the study was concluded, poor little Albert was intensely afraid of white rats, rabbits, dogs, fur coats, a Santa Claus mask, cotton, wool and anything else that remotely resembled animal fur, and this was all done by presenting Albert with a white rat, (what else would an American psychologist have hanging around the lab?) and then banging loudly on a steel bar a few inches behind Albert's head. Albert soon associated the rat with the terrific din and thus learned to fear the rat and other similar stimuli. In order to "cure" Albert of this conditioned phobia, Watson proposed, but never carried out, presenting the baby with the fear provoking object and then following it with stimulation of the erogenous zones (tactual). "We should first try the lips, then the nipples and as a final resort the sex organs." Watson believed that he had come upon ultimate truth, and that no matter what the genetic background, environmental stimulation in the form of conditioning could produce any behavioral trait.

A few years later Watson thundered his now famous words, "Give me the baby and I'll make it climb and use its hands in the construction of buildings of stone or wood...I can make it a thief, a gunman, or a dope fiend. The possibilities of shaping it in any direction are almost endless. Even gross anatomical differences limit us far less than you think. Make him (sic) a deaf mute and I will build you a Helen Keller. Men are built, not born". After reading about how Albert had been scared half to death by the sound of a steel bar being pounded behind his head and being dropped, and how it was proposed to cure him by manipulating his genitals, the mothers of America did not line up to give Watson their babies.

B.F. Skinner and Conditioned Behavior

B. F. Skinner picked up where Watson left off, and by mid-century he was America's most influential behaviorist. Instead of inferring any inner causes for behavior, Skinner believed in simply analyzing the behavior itself. In his 1938 book, "The Behavior of Organisms" Skinner outlined a system of response analysis that was far more thorough and detailed than anything seen before. While behaviorists, such as J.B. Watson were concerned with response analysis up through the mid-1930s, Skinner's arrival changed this preoccupation to a near obsession. To Skinner every little squiggle on the cumulative recorder (a device for measuring learning) is seen as fraught with profound significance. Skinner is not concerned with what might be going on inside the person, such as one's motivational or emotional state, or even one's neurology. Skinner's psychology is called an "empty organism" psychology, a psychology of environmental conditions (stimuli) associating with and affecting the organism's response repertoire. As was the case with Watson, Skinner's psychology is totally environmental. The Skinnerian theme song is that since the consequences of a response influence further actions, and since those consequences occur in the outer environment, it is the environment and only the environment that can cause changes in behavior.

Skinner tells us that if an aggressive response is followed by any type of reinforcement (which is Skinner's general term for reward), it becomes conditioned, and its response rate increases. Like any other possible response in the organism's repertoire, when the aggressive response produces rewarding consequence the behavior becomes fixed and is then maintained and repeated with increasing strength and frequency. Skinner also insisted that aggression breeds aggression, and that aggressive responses at one level may be met with aggressive responses at more intense levels. In one study, by using food as a reward, a pigeon was trained to attack another pigeon (Reynolds, 1983). A high and consistent level of aggression was observed and maintained. However Skinner also believed that a society could be engineered by scientific application of his theory in which most of the ills of mankind could be eliminated. As with Watson, Skinner was convinced that the criminal is made, not born. To Skinner a society could be controlled and engineered in which criminal behavior would be eliminated! During this process the criminal would participate in what Skinner described as a reciprocal arrangement. Said Skinner, "The relationship between the controller and the controlled is reciprocal." The scientist in the laboratory, studying the pigeon's behavior, designs contingencies and observes their effects. The behavior of the pigeon determines the design of the testing apparatus and the procedures in which it is used (Skinner, 1971, p169). Thus, just as the scientist in the laboratory is under the control of the pigeon, so too will the controller of society (presumably Skinner) be influenced by its members. Despite Skinner's view on the apparent equality between the controller and controlled, some of you may feel that you'd rather be wearing the lab coat than being cast in the role of the pigeon.

Social learning Theory and Modeling
Another important psychologist, Albert Bandura, has long been arguing that a significant part of what a person learns occurs through imitation or what he likes to call "modeling." Bandura has concentrated his studies on learning that takes place in the context of the social situation. During social interactions an individual learns to modify his/her behavior as a result of how others in the group are responding. Thus behaviors can be learned by imitating the behavior of other persons, or models, and this learning takes place even though these imitative responses may not be directly reinforced. For example, a young child may stand up when the Star Spangled Banner is played because his parents are standing. The child's response in this instance was

not necessarily followed by a reinforcing stimulus, such as a candy bar, or any other primary reinforcer. In the previous example, the child's ability to stand up was already part of his behavioral repertoire, but Bandura goes on to say that even new responses can be learned through modeling. The child can learn to ski or play tennis simply by imitation. The list of new responses that can be learned through modeling are probably endless, and although the examples shown above involve positive forms of learning, modeling also has a darker side. Modeling has also been shown to create undesirable and anti-social responses. A child may learn to be overly aggressive, deceitful, and dishonest through the modeling mechanism.

Learned Aggression

In a now classic study, Bandura subjected a group of young children (ages 3 to 6) to the improbable spectacle of watching adult models punch, kick, and yell at a large inflated "Bobo" doll. When later given the chance to play with Bobo, these children displayed twice as many aggressive responses as a control group of children who had not witnessed this adult performance. And the form of the imitation was startlingly direct, with the children even yelling the same phrases as the adults had used, such as "kick him" or "sock him in the nose". One might assume that had the adults danced with Bobo, rather than socking him, the children would have also behaved in this more gentle fashion.

The Role of Reinforcement - It's So Rewarding

As shown above, although learning through modeling does not always require direct and immediate reinforcement, Bandura has also suggested that reinforcement may still also be strongly involved. First, many of the models in the child's life (i.e., parents and teachers) are also in charge of a great deal of the possible reinforcers. Parents not only provide the modeling stimulus, but they may also reinforce the child when the behavior is imitated. Second, a child is more apt to imitate adults when the adults themselves are being reinforced for those same responses. In other words, the child who sees an adult getting praise for a certain action is more likely to respond the same way than is a child who only views the action but not the subsequent reinforcement. Thus, reinforcement and modeling together can create very potent conditions for behavioral change. Many of our most persistent habits, traits and attitudes can result from this combination of powerful forces.

Bystander Effect: The Fear and Apathy of Crowds

The bystander effect is a concept used by psychologists to explain why people who are part of a large crowd of bystanders are less apt to help out in an emergency situation than if the crowd were smaller. Some of this may be explained on the basis of modeling, but not all. This is often called the "Genovese" syndrome and is based on a famous case where a girl (Kitty

Genovese) was stabbed to death in front of what was alleged to have been a large crowd of apathetic bystanders. There is some suspicion that the Genovese story may have been overstated by the news media, but in any event it led to a series of studies that did lend support to the theory that when a large group of witnesses are involved, individual responsibility is reduced due to what has been called the "diffusion of responsibility" or the fact that each witness assumes that someone else will probably jump in and be the savior (Darley & Latane, 1968). Although that is one possible reason for the apathy, there are probably many more, some very personal, including
the fear of bodily harm, or even the fear of legal consequences. However, when there are only one or two witnesses, the urge to help becomes far more compelling.

CASE STUDY-Two Witnesses
An elderly woman (age 75) drove to her doctor's office one morning, arriving at 11:30 AM. She parked her car in the medical building's parking lot, but as she was getting out a 34 year-old man assaulted her, grabbed her purse and then ran off. Two nearby men, one a postman, saw what happened and made chase. When they caught the assailant he tried to attack them with a box cutter, but after a lengthy scuffle they were finally able to subdue him. When the police arrived, they charged the assailant with assault to rob while armed, and assault on a person over the age of 65. The arresting officers commended the two good Samaritans and told them they had actually caught a dangerous felon that the police had been looking for.

Frustration Aggression
Led by Miller and Dollard, a group of Yale psychologists in the late 1930s introduced the now famous, "Frustration Aggression Hypothesis" (Dollard et al, 1939). Aggression was explained as being the result of having one's goals blocked. Said Miller, "The occurrence of aggression always presupposes frustration" (Miller, 1941, p339). In many instances The Miller-Dollard hypothesis is obviously valid. We have all seen people become angry, sometimes to the point of irrationality, over having a goal blocked, such as a person already late for an important appointment becoming furious when the car won't start, even getting out and kicking the car, or a teen-age boy gets in a fight on the way home from school after having been "cut" from the varsity football team. The frustration-aggression hypothesis, however, does have some serious short-comings as an explanatory model. Some people react to frustration, not with overt aggression, but merely by sitting quietly and seething inwardly. Another person may respond to frustration by regressing, that is, acting in a less mature fashion. Also there are countless examples of aggressive behaviors that were not triggered by any frustration. Being annoyed or attacked by another person often results in aggression aimed at the source of the annoyance. For example, a student was playing poker in the dorm

when, without provocation, another student moved quietly behind him and then playfully poured soda on his head. Five seconds and two punches later, the "playful pourer" was on his back nursing a bruised eye and jaw.

The Revision: Frustration-Aggression Today

The original frustration-aggression hypothesis has been revised a couple of times by Leonard Berkowitz. First, any unpleasant stimulus, not just frustration can produce a general response repertoire consisting of a wide range of negative-emotion responses (sometimes called "negative affect") not just aggression (Berkowitz, 1989). The negative-emotion responses can include anger, aggression, anxiety, and/or annoyance. Second, Berkowitz makes an extremely important distinction between two types of aggression, reactive and instrumental (Berkowitz, 1993). Reactive aggression is an impulsive, strike-back response usually triggered by some perceived threat. Reactive aggression has no other agenda, just fighting back. Instrumental aggression, however, is far more calculating and less impulsive because it is based on an attempt to achieve a goal. Beating someone up to grab a purse or billfold is definitely instrumental aggression, and can be found as part of the behavioral repertoire of many antisocial personality types.

The Interaction Theories: Heredity, Environment and Time

Since the eras of extreme environmentalism and naïve hereditarianism, there has been a literal sea- change in our understanding of the internal factors of organisms up and down the phylogenetic ladder. Today's psychology is no longer an empty organism psychology. Great attention is now being paid to the organism's internal factors (neuroanatomy, physiology and bio-chemistry) and barely a week goes by without some important new physiological discoveries hitting the front pages. And the focus has also now turned to the timing of the interaction between heredity and environment, and the concurrent changes within the organism. Because of this change in focus, psychology and personality theories have indeed taken on a new-look.

Learning and Early Experience

Much of this new-look traces back to an Austrian psychologist and ethologist by the name of Konrad Lorenz. The term "ethology" refers to the study of organisms in their natural habitat, not just in the sterile confines of the laboratory. Lorenz cast the old nature-nurture debate in a new light by adding an important third dimension – time. He found that certain organisms will become imprinted on the first moving stimulus object in their visual field, and they will then follow this object, usually of course their mother, with marching-band precision (Lorenz, 1937). This is how the young organisms, especially birds, know which species they belong to, and it also accounts for their flocking behavior. The timing for this type of learning turned out to be critical. Lorenz found that this form of learning, which he called "imprinting" could occur in ducks only up to 32 hours after hatching (although the optimal time period was between 13 and 16 hours of age). Thus, certain behavioral changes depended, not just on external stimuli, but even more importantly on when those stimuli (the environment) interacted with the organism's internal timing mechanisms (heredity). Lorenz also learned that if he presented himself to these ducklings during that critical time period, they would flock after him with the same devotion usually reserved for their natural mother. Nature, therefore, is not just a blank slate, but is set to unwind at certain critical time- points in the organism's life. At the human level these are usually called "sensitive" periods, and they account for the fact that many environmental factors have their most profound impact during a child's first few years. Psychologists have found that stimulus variety early in life, as long as it's not overly stressful, can have a positive impact on a person's later level of intelligence. Benjamin S. Bloom in a now classic book has analyzed, sorted and sifted through virtually all the studies on intellectual growth and found that with increasing age there is a decreasing positive effect from a positive environment (Bloom, 1964). Three-year old children profit far more from enriching experiences than do ten or twelve year-old children. Bloom argues that a beneficial early experience is absolutely essential for healthy cognitive growth. He has found that two-thirds of one's ultimate intellectual abilities are formed by the time a child is six years old, the age, incidentally, when most children are just entering first grade. That is, by the time formal schooling begins, the child's potential for further intellectual development is already beginning to top out. Bloom insists that early intervention is required, especially among the disadvantaged groups. Experience has its most profound effect very early in life, during the period of most rapid growth.

Bonding, Attachment and Early Experience

Healthy personality development depends on the ability of the infant to form secure attachments with significant adults in the environment – often called "bonding." Attachment theory was first presented by the English psychologist John Bowlby, and it suggests that the developing infant must bond with at least one primary caregiver in order for healthy personality and emotional development to occur (Bowlby, 1973). This again points to the importance of early experience on one's emotional health. Thus, the bonding should occur very early in life, during the baby's critical and sensitive developmental periods. Just as early experience is such a powerful factor in one's cognitive development, it is also just as important in one's emotional development. Bowlby maintains that attachment, especially to the mother, should be fully formed by age three. And further, he sees a direct relationship between the lack of a firm attachment and later involvement in delinquency and crime. He says that crime, like some infant diseases such as rheumatic fever, may have its origin in childhood and it continues to attack in later life through the process of constant recurrence. Thus, there is increasing evidence for an emotional critical period that occurs within the first three years of life. The research of Jay Belsky points to the crucial importance of maternal affection and its concomitant bonding as the basis for the child's later development of a conscience and moral empathy (Belsky, 1988). This view has also been espoused by Robert Hare (creator of the Hare Psychopathy test) , who says that the psychopath is lacking in an early attachment to an adult care giver. However, psychopathy expert James Blair (Blair et al.,2010) wonders if the attachment failure is one of the causes of psychopathy, or whether the latent seeds of psychopathy prevent the child from securing normal bonding. It may be that the mother is incapable of allowing the bonding to occur. She may herself be a single mother and emotionally unattached. She may have substance- abuse or emotional problems that prevent her from bonding with her child, or even being capable of giving her child any consistent supervision or emotional support. Or she herself may be the object of spousal abuse, both physical and psychological. Thus, since the process is indeed an interaction, it is therefore difficult to establish whether bonding limitations are primarily due to problems with the care-giver, the environment, the baby's own physiology, or all three acting in concert.

Childhood Stress
Environmental stressors early in life have far more impact on the developing child than had they occurred at a later age. It has even been shown that early stress can cause changes in the architecture and circuitry of the brain and nervous system, as well as its hormonal activity (Charney, 2003). Some of these changes lurk behind later aggressiveness and a heightened probability of offending. The young child who feels constant threat, either from negative family stimuli, or sometimes from total family neglect, may become far more anxious and/or aggressive than children from more secure environments. "The neurochemical response to threat can be profoundly affected by prior threat experience, particularly if this occurs early in life" (Blair et al p 102). It has also been found that the physical abuse of children causes higher rates of later vandalism, theft and drug use (Gelles, 1992). Even verbal aggression has been linked to increases in the probability of delinquency and excessive aggression (Vissing et al, 1991). In short, violence seems to beget violence. Children who have been abused or have witnessed violence in the family are more likely to themselves later commit crimes of violence. In fact, one researcher found that sexually and physically abused boys are later found to have committed the most violent felonies (Widom, 1999).

Age Related
That the roots of crime are formed early and are age-related is summed up in the words of the researcher Patrick Fagan: "Inconsistent parenting, family turmoil, and multiple other stressors (such as economic hardship and psychiatric illness) that flow from these problems compound the rejection of these

children by their parents, many of whom became criminals during their own childhoods. With all these factors working against the child's normal development, by age five the future criminal already will already tend to be aggressive, hostile, and hyperactive. Four-fifths of children who later become criminals will be antisocial by 11 years of age, and fully two-thirds of antisocial five-year olds will be delinquent by age 15" (Fagan, P.F., 1995, p. 8). There will be more emphasis on the importance of early experience and its relationship to personality formation and criminal activity in a later chapter.

The Economy as a Possible Root Cause

Although it may seem as though unemployment is a major cause of crime, the evidence for that relationship is far from conclusive. It may be a reasonable assumption that the unemployed are more apt to steal and rob, but on the other hand it may also make the unemployed more home-bound and more apt to keep their homes and cars protected. During the 1920s ("the roaring 20s") there was a booming economic prosperity, but alas also a high crime rate. And during the great depression of the 1930s there was a staggering unemployment rate that topped 30%, and yet there was very little crime. During the 1940s unemployment and crime were simultaneously at low levels, but in each decade, other variables must be examined. The 1920s was an era of prohibition (making alcohol illegal) that produced an underground of bootleggers and violent gang fights for turf and distribution rights. During the 1940s (World War 2) there was both low unemployment and also low crime rates. Young men (the prime group for committing crimes) who might otherwise be unemployed and possibly committing felonies were drafted into the armed forces and sent overseas to fight the Germans and Japanese. Finally, over the past dozen years, some crime stats have been in decline, even though today's economy is not optimal. David Kennedy, director of the Center for Crime Prevention and Control at the John Jay College has warned us that although crime going up in a recession is one of those things everyone thinks is true, it is in fact not always true (Kennedy 2008). And Mark Kleiman, professor of Public Policy at UCLA's School of Public Affairs has pointed out that there seems to be no correlation between crime rates and economic indicators, such as unemployment (Kleiman, 2009).

Broken Windows

Associated with the economic theories of crime is what has become known as the "Broken Windows" theory, a theory that suggests that crime is spawned by a decaying neighborhood, especially a decaying urban neighborhood (Kelling & Coles, 1996). If windows are left broken, if garbage and trash are left in the streets, if graffiti is left out in the open, then the conditions become ripe for crime. Even though these may all seem like minor violations, if left unattended, they create the impression that nobody cares and therefore anything goes. Such a neighborhood will descend into disruptive chaos and is alleged to be hard to reclaim. Police are urged to get out of their patrol cars, meet with members of the community and enforce the seemingly trivial violations. In fact the broken window theory was one of the major factors in the creation of the community policing effort. Evidence in favor of the theory came in the form of an expectation of afflicted neighborhoods. The problem with this explanation is that crime rates went down everywhere, even in neighborhoods not so closely monitored. Also, the theory would seem to predict that those in the blighted areas would commit fewer crimes if they moved or were moved to more stable neighborhoods. Research, however, found that those tenants who did move continued committing crimes at the same rate (Harcourt & Ludwig, 2006). Community policing has become very popular in recent years and its proponents have heaped it with high praise. It is said to break down the barriers between police and the community, to engage people and groups who don't usually get consulted and change both police and community attitudes toward each other. A federal program called COPS (Community Oriented Policing Services) has provided huge amounts of money (in the billions) to move this initiative forward. Critics have said that community policing puts too much on the backs of police personnel, that they can't balance the job of being both social workers as well as arresting officers. After all, law enforcement must be judgmental. Even though there is testimonial evidence for the effectiveness of community policing, such as preached by then Mayor Rudolph Giuliani and other politicians, the empirical evidence is not so convincing. When the quantitative evidence is placed under the high-powered lens of statistical scrutiny, no significant differences in crime rates have been found between those areas where community policing efforts were in effect versus those areas covered by conventional policing methods (Mulhausen, 2011). It seems that what ought to be isn't always what is.

Is There a Racial Factor?
Although there may be a statistical correlation between race and felony arrests, it must be stressed that correlation does not necessarily imply causation. This will be fully explored in a later chapter devoted to research methods. Suffice it to say here, that although there is a statistical correlation between shoe size and reading ability among elementary school children, it doesn't mean wearing a large shoe increases a child's reading ability. A third variable, age, might better explain this correlation, because older children do have larger shoes and on average they are more experienced and better readers. Also although there is a correlation between the use of umbrellas and the occurrence of rain, it is obvious that umbrellas don't cause the rain. While it is true that some minorities are disproportionately represented in the criminal justice system and as welfare recipients, this relationship is not based on cause-and-effect factors. Using United States census data, a Brookings Institute study found that if a person does three things: (1) graduates from high

school, (2) waits until marriage to have children, and (3) gets up and goes to work, the probability of being poor drops to .02, and this is true regardless of race (Haskins & Sawhill, 2009). In fact, when race is factored out, it becomes clear that it's the lack of family structure that remains as the underlying predictor of poverty and crime, and this is true whether it be minority families or white families. The predictors of white criminality are in fact the very same as the predictors of minority criminality….children being raised in broken, dysfunctional families.

Summary

We have now been witness to a long line-up of suspects in our search for the roots of crime. The theories were sorted according to whether they were based on heredity, environment or an interaction of heredity, environment and time. Although hereditarian views could be found in some of the early Greek philosophies, the Bible and many theories right up to the present day, our focus was on the post 1800 theorists. Theories that assumed criminality as based on heredity included Gall and Spurzheim, Cesare Lombroso, Richard Dugdale, Henry Goddard, Charles Davenport, and William Sheldon. Gall and Spurzheim created a theory called "phrenology" and they argued that personality traits, including a criminal nature, could be detected by examining the various bumps, dents and furrows in the human skull. The Italian sociologist, Cesare Lombroso, primarily used facial characteristics, such as a long sloping (ape-like) forehead, as the major clues for identifying those whom he believed were born to be criminals. Then Richard Dugdale treated us to the spectacle of Margaret, the "mother of criminals," whose innate criminality was passed on to generation after generation of a family called the Jukes. Although Dugdale did give a nodding mention to the influence of environment, he viewed the root cause to be genetic. Next, came Henry Goddard and a family dubbed as the "Kallikaks." This family had two separate roots, the good Kallikaks, resulting from Martin Kallikak's marriage to a woman referred to as a "Worthy Quakeress," and the bad Kallikaks, spawned by Martin Kallikak's dalliance with a half-witted bar maid. Goddard found that all of the best human qualities were transmitted to the good Kallikaks and the worst to the bad Kallikaks. The two families were portrayed as good or bad, with no shades of gray in between.

Then, in the early 1900s came Charles Davenport, who was an extremely famous and honored geneticist of his time. Davenport produced a theory of human traits as being totally inherited in straight Mendelian fashion, citing dominant and recessive genes as being as directly tied to such human characteristics as laziness and aggressiveness. These traits were shown as being as directly controlled by heredity as eye color. Then, much later (in the 1950s), William Sheldon created a theory that attempted to explain personality factors as being linked with bodily characteristics. The three body types, called "somatotypes" by Sheldon, were the endomorph, overweight and tending to obesity, the mesomorph, solid and muscular, and the ectomorph. long and thin. Each of these body types had a distinct personality cluster, the endomorph being out-going, jolly and a lover of ease and comfort, the mesomorph being courageous and aggressive, and the ectomorph being withdrawn, introverted and artistic. He also listed various types of felonies as being linked to these somatotypes. For example the mesomorph would be more apt to be a bank robber or hit man, the ectomorph a quiet book-keeper committing fraud, and the endomorph might be the extraverted salesman setting up personally-enriching scams.

Then, in the mid-1980s geneticist Patricia Jacobs found that certain men, called "super males," were found to be carrying an extra Y chromosome and were also over represented in the prison system.

Running alongside the extreme hereditarian views of human nature were the instinct theorists. Although some of these theories kept instincts somewhat in perspective, such as the theories of Darwin and Freud, others extrapolated beyond the bounds of rudimentary logic. To explain every conceivable human behavior as based on a specific instinct is to explain all by explaining nothing. For many it was an issue of simply relabeling (called the "nominal fallacy") such as saying that fighting is caused by an aggressive instinct. And asked how they know there is an aggressive instinct, the answer comes back, "because they fight, don't they?"

Next came the theories based on extreme environmentalism, typically products of psychology's learning theorists, such as John B. Watson and B.F. Skinner. Watson used Pavlovian conditioning techniques to shape behavior, and claimed that he could condition any baby to become any type of adult from a thief to a dope fiend. As he said so often, "men are built, not born." Skinner picked up the environmental message and although changing the conditioning techniques (from Pavlovian to what Skinner labeled as "operant"), came up with very similar conclusions. Behavior is a result of reinforcement contingencies, and this includes any type of behavior, including aggression. Skinner even offered suggestions for eliminating all criminal behavior (and also "all the ills of mankind") by using his principles of operant conditioning. The social learning theorists, although not as extremely environmental as Watson and Skinner, explained that behavioral changes came about on the basis of imitation or modeling. That is, behaviors are learned on the basis of imitation, imitating the behavior of other persons, or models. This form of learning may take place even in the absence of reinforcement. To these social-learning theorists, such as Albert Bandura, the environmental influences come from the actions of others in the group. The influence of the group is also shown in what is called the "bystander effect," or that a person who is part of a crowd is less apt to help another person in distress than if that person were alone. In a large crowd of bystanders the individual tends to be more apathetic than if alone. This was explained on the basis of the crowd as offering a diffusion of responsibility.

That aggression is a learned phenomenon was proposed by Albert Bandura, and was based on an experiment he did with children who had witnessed an adult kick and punch a doll (the now-famous "Bobo doll"). And what did the children do when they later played with the doll? They kicked and punched it, even in the absence of reinforcement. The key to understanding aggression, according to Bandura, was found in the study of what he called "modeling."

Next came Miller and Dollard's frustration-aggression theory, or that frustration in the form of goal blockage, is the direct cause of aggression. Over the years this hypothesis has been modified, and frustration has been found to cause not just aggression but many other behaviors, including a wide range of negative emotional responses. Also they proposed two forms of aggression, reactive aggression, such as a person striking back when threatened, or instrumental aggression, which is aimed at obtaining a goal, such as a thug beating up someone to get his wallet.

Finally, the interaction theories were presented, theories based on heredity interacting with environment, interacting with time. Because of the profound effect on behavior of early experience, the time variable assumes great importance. Konrad Lorenz demonstrated that imprinting could occur with young ducklings only during their first few hours of life. During this critical time period they would follow the first moving stimulus in their visual field (of course this was usually the mother). However Lorenz could present himself to the ducklings, and they would march faithfully behind him wherever he went, which must have made a dent in his social life. The importance of early experience in human development came from several sources, including Benjamin Bloom and John Bowlby. Although Bloom concentrated more on cognitive development, much of his work can be easily generalized to emotional development. Bloom stressed the critical importance of early experience in the process of intellectual growth, and that with increasing age there is a decreasing positive effect from a positive environment. In fact, Bloom concluded that two-thirds of the growth occurs before the age of six. Bowlby, also using an early-experience perspective, suggested that for healthy emotional development, the infant should form secure attachments (bonding) with at least one significant adult, usually the mother. This attachment should be fully formed by the age of three. The bonding process links directly to the later development of conscience and social empathy, as well as concomitant delinquency and crime. Feelings of stress and isolation have far more impact on the emotional growth of a child than were the stress to occur later in life. Stress in the early years may even cause physiological changes in the brain and hormonal activity.

The physical and psychological abuse of the child has been shown to predict later vandalism, theft, and substance abuse. Timing is crucial and the roots of crime are definitely age related. Some data suggest that by the age of five the overly aggressive child may already be on the road to criminality.

The possibility of economic conditions laying the groundwork for crime was also examined. Although it seems on the surface to make intuitive sense that being out of work is an important motivator for criminal activity, the other side is that being out of work is more apt to keep people at home and better guardians of their property. It has also been shown that the facts simply don't seem to support the theory that crime goes up during an economic recession. Some data shows no correlation between economic indicators, such as unemployment and crime. Deteriorating neighborhoods have also been nominated as fertile areas for crime. Often called the "broken windows theory," it suggests that if garbage and trash are left out in the open and minor infractions are left unpunished, crime will thrive. This has led to the philosophy of community policing, where the police are asked to go into the community on foot, and then communicate with and befriend residents. Although politicians hailed it as almost a panacea in the war against crime, the results are decidedly mixed. In fact some studies have found no difference in crime rates between areas involved in community policing and those areas subjected to conventional methods. Finally, the possibility of a racial factor in crime was dismissed when it was pointed out that the predictors of minority criminality are precisely the same as those that predict white criminality – children being raised in dysfunctional homes and families.

Key Terms

Attachment and Bonding
Community Policing
Conditioned Behavior
Critical Period Hypothesis
Dugdale, Richard
Economics and Crime
Freud, Sigmund
Frustration Aggression Hypothesis
Goddard, Henry
Heredity, Environment, Time
Instinct Theories – Darwin
Instrumental Aggression
Learned Aggression
Lombroso, Cesare
Phrenology
Reactive Aggression
Sheldon, William
Social Learning Theory
The Bystander Effect
The Super Male-XXY

References

Ashe, M.J. (2004). Progressive criminal justice with sensible public safety. Speech delivered on Sept. 20, 2004 to the_Criminal Justice Public Policy Coalition

Belsky, J. (1988). Development and risk factors of juvenile antisocial behavior and delinquency. *Early Childhood Research Quarterly, 3*, 235-272.

Berkowitz, L. (1989). The frustration-aggression hypothesis: An examination and reformulation. *Psychological Bulletin, 100*, 59-73

Berkowitz, L. (1993). *Aggression: Its causes, consequences and control.* Philadelphia PA: Temple Univ. Press.

Bloom, B.S. (1964). *Stability and change in human characteristics.* New York: Wiley.

Darley, J.M. & Latane, B. (1968) Bystander intervention in emergencies: Diffusion of responsibility. *Journal of Personality and Social Psychology ,89*, 277-383.

Darwin, C. (1859). *The origin of species by means of natural selection.* London: John Murray Publishers.

Davenport, C.B. (1911). *Heredity in relation to eugenics.* NY: Henry Holt.

Dollard, J. M., Doob, L. W., Miller, N.E., Maurer, G.H. & Sears, R.R. (1939). *Frustration and aggression.* New Haven, CT: Yale University Press.

Dugdale, R.L. (1877). *The Jukes: A study in Crime, Pauperism, Disease and Heredity.* New York: Putnam.

Fagan, P.F. (1995). The real root cause of violent crime: the breakdown of marriage, family, and community. *The Backgrounder, 1026*, 1-31.

Freud, S. (1923). *The ego and the id.* New York: W.W. Norton and Company.

Gelles, R.J. (1992). Poverty and violence toward children. *American Behavioral Scientist, 35*, 258-274.

Goddard, H.E. (1912). *The Kallikak family.* New York NY: Macmillan

Harcourt, B.E. & Ludwig, J.(2006) Broken windows: New evidence from New York city and a five-city social experiment. *University of Chicago Law Review, 73*, 743-84.

Haselhuhn, M. & Wong, E. (2011). Bad to the bone: Facial structure predicts unethical behavior. *Proceedings of the Royal Society, 21*, 38-47.

Haskins, R. & Sawhill, I.V. (2009). *Creating an opportunity society* .Washington, DC: Brookings Inst. Press .

Jacobs, P.A. & Hassold, T. (1986). Chromosomal abnormalities: Origin and etiology. In Vogel, F.& Sperling, K, Editors. *Proceedings of the 7th International Congress of Human Genetics.* Berlin: Springer Verlag

Kennedy, D.M. (2008). *Deterrence and crime prevention.* New York: Routledge

Kleiman, M.A.R, (2009). *When brute force fails: How to have less crime and less punishment.* Princeton, NJ: Princeton Univ. Press.

Lorenz, K. (1937). The companion in the bird's world. *Auk, 54*, 245-273.

Miller, N. E. (1941). The frustration aggression hypothesis. *Psychological Review, 40*, 337-342.

Reynolds, G.S., Catania, A.C. & Skinner, B.F. (1963). Conditioned and un-conditioned aggression in pigeons. *Journal of the Experimental Analysis of Behavior, 6,* 73-75.

Sheldon, W.H. (1954). *Atlas of men: A guide for somatotyping the adult male.* New York, NY: Gramercy Publishers.

Skinner, B.F. (1971). *Beyond freedom and dignity.* New York: Knopf.

Vissing, Y.M., Strauss, M., Gelles, R.J. & Harrop, J.W. (1991). Verbal aggression by parents and psychosocial problems of children. *Child Abuse and Neglect, 15,* 223-238

Watson, J.B. (1913) Psychology as the behaviorist views it. *Psychological Review, 20,* 158-177.

Watson, J.B., & Raynor, R. (1921). Conditioned emotional reactions. *Journal of Experimental Psychology, 3,* 8.

Watson, J. B. (1927) A behaviorist looks at instincts. *Harpers Magazine,155* (July)

Widom, C. S.(1999).Child abuse, neglect and violent criminal behavior. *Criminology, 27,* 251-271.

CHAPTER 3

PERSONALITY, CRIME, AND VIOLENCE: FROM BULLIES TO SERIAL KILLERS

Theorists today are studying an individual's personality as a factor in crime. Are some personalities more prone to crime than others? If so, are these personality differences due mostly to internal factors, such as the brain's hard wiring or perhaps a hormonal imbalance? Or are they due to a person's experiences, to his/her socialization? If environment is involved, which environmental experiences or stressors are the most powerful? We will first look at the personality types and disorders that have been most closely linked with crime.

Personality Disorders and Aggression

The personality disorders to be discussed here all contain an aggressive component and all have been in some way associated with crime. These include: Bullying, ODD (Oppositional Defiant Disorder), CD (Conduct Disorder), ASPD (Anti-Social Personality Disorder) and Psychopathy. Some of these personality disorders have now been found to be somewhat related to problems in the neuroanatomy of the nervous system as well as the body's hormonal system, especially as they concern generating feelings of anxiety, empathy and aggression.

Aggression: Two Types

In the following discussion it is important to remember the distinction that was made in Chapter 1 between two major types of aggression, reactive aggression and instrumental aggression. Reactive aggression is an anger reaction triggered by some frustrating or threatening event, whereas instrumental aggression is used to achieve a specific goal (Berkowitz, 1993). Instrumental aggression is primarily aimed at a victim's possessions or to create a feeling of power over the victim, rather than the infliction of pain on the victim per se. Whereas reactive aggression may be a venting release, an emotional cleansing, instrumental aggression is more calculating and goal directed . If you are assaulted because you have stopped someone from gaining some desired goal, or because you have backed someone into a corner, the aggression is probably reactive. If you are assaulted because someone is trying to steal your purse, the aggression is instrumental.

Bullying

Bullying is the repeated physical or psychological mistreatment by someone (usually a peer) who is typically physically or psychologically stronger than the victim. These are acts of instrumental aggression that are committed over a period of time to enforce one person's power over another person. The victim is called the target, and for bullying to occur the target must be part of the cycle by producing an inadequate response to the bully. Ironically, it's the victim who becomes the enabler. That is, the bully and the target form an implicit contract. In the words of an old song, "It takes two to tango." Like the wolf looking for vulnerable prey, the bully tends to select a target who is already fragile and easily intimidated. Dan Olweus cites evidence showing that the victims of bullying are more likely to attempt suicide than are children in general, and far more likely than are the bullies themselves (Solberg & Olweus, 2009). This has had serious consequences especially in the teen-age population where some victims may have been pushed into stress-related illnesses and possibly even suicide. Studies show that boys bully more than girls, but that both bullies and victims have poor problem-solving skills within social situations, and that bullies tend to do worse than the victims in academic areas. Bullying can be emotional, verbal, physical, or cyber or any combination of the four (Kim & Leventhal, Koh, Boyce,2009)

Oppositional Defiant Disorder

This is defined by the American Psychiatric Association (2013) as an ongoing pattern of hostile and/defiant behavior toward adults and authority figures (which goes beyond the bounds of normal childhood disobedience). The criteria for ODD include excessive and persistent anger, frequent temper tantrums and a blatant disregard for authority. To be diagnosed with ODD the child (typically before age ten) must persist in these behaviors for at least six months and be the source of considerable distress to the family and/ or interfere with academic or social functioning. Many ODD children continue in these behaviors for several years and approximately 50 % will later develop a Conduct Disorder.

Conduct Disorder

Persons with a conduct disorder (APA, 2000/2013) present a pattern of behavior resulting in the repeated violation of the rights of others and/or social norms. Individuals with this diagnosis may inflict injury on other people, but are also themselves at a greater risk of depression, substance abuse, and death by homicide or suicide. Approximately 6% of children and adolescents between the ages of 10 and 17 have been diagnosed as CD. Some theorists find CD to be linked to a more serious condition called psychopathy, since both involve a distinct lack of empathy and any real concern for how others may feel. It is suggested that empathy can inhibit feelings of aggression, and the lack of empathy prevents normal emotional feelings toward others in distress.

When a conduct disorder is limited only to the adolescent years, the years of hormonal turmoil, it is labeled as an "adolescent-onset" conduct disorder. The Bureau of Justice has shown the relationship between age and arrests. For example there are less than 1% of arrests below age 10, and the peak occurs between the ages of 17 and 22, (over 40%). By age 67 the trend levels off at an extremely low level (less than 1%).

ASPD: Anti-Social Personality Disorder
ASPD is a pervasive pattern of disregard for, and violation of, the rights of others that may begin in either childhood or early adolescence and continues into adulthood. This diagnosis can be considered if a person meets the following criteria set forth in the American Psychiatric Association's Diagnostic and Statistical Manual of Mental Disorders (2000, 2013)
Behavioral Symptoms
1. Failure to conform to societal norms with respect to lawful behavior by repeatedly doing things that are reasons for arrest.
2. Deceitfulness, as shown by repeated lying, use of aliases, and conning others for personal profit or pleasure.
3. Impulsivity and/or failure to plan ahead.
4. Irritability and aggressiveness as indicated by repeated physical fights or assaults
5. Reckless disregard for safety of self or of others
6. Consistent irresponsibility as shown by repeated failure to sustain consistent work habits or honor financial obligations.
7. Lack of remorse and being indifferent to having hurt, mistreated or stolen from someone else.
The following criteria are also considered:
1. The individual must be at least 18 years old
2. There is evidence of conduct disorder with onset before age 15
3. The antisocial behavior does not only occur during the course of schizophrenia or a bi-polar manic episode

As you can see, ASPD covers a wide range of behaviors, and although it only accounts for a small fraction of the general population, it is overrepresented in the prison population. Estimates indicate that ASPD occurs in about 3% of males and only 1% in females. However, estimates are that roughly 70% of the prison population meets the above criteria for ASPD

The Psychopath
Psychopathy is basically an emotional disorder that is characterized by an incredibly low level of empathy and a callous disregard for the feelings of others. This dysfunctional emotional-processing system creates a lack of empathy and inhibits any of the usual aggression-controlling mechanisms. The psychopath is a glib (often charming) fast talker who can do or say virtually anything with no feelings of remorse. Accompanying this is the psycho-

path's lowered levels of fear and anxiety, often resulting in a willingness to engage in many reckless and daring activities. The generally lowered emotional arousal levels keep the psychopath constantly seeking new avenues of excitement. In short, psychopathy is characterized by severe emotional detachment.

Only Two Percent

Although it is found in only 2% of the general population, psychopaths account for over 25% of the inmate population (Blair et al 2010). A large part of the inmate population presents with both psychopathy and ASPD. Evidence shows that compared to other inmates, the psychopath is three times more likely to recidivate and four times more likely to recidivate following a violent crime (Blair et al 2010). They are a definite danger to society in innumerable ways. For example, psychopaths account for over 50% of felons who kill police officers, and the average psychopath will be convicted of four violent crimes by the age of forty. However, convicted psychopaths often present themselves so schemingly well that they get parole or even early release.

The Psychopath Defined

Psychopathy can be defined on the basis of a series of behavioral and emotional traits which include:

1. Lack of concern for the feelings of others
2. Egocentric and self-aggrandizing
3. Lack of both empathy and feelings of guilt or remorse.
4. Manipulative and ready, willing and able to lie, cheat and steal.
5. Outwardly charming and glib, but emotionally superficial.
6. At least average IQ
7. And usually associated with a biological predisposition.

Because of the psychopath's lack of personal insight, it has been assumed that attempting to do research based on a psychopath's self-report would be an exercise in futility. However studies are now reporting that the psychopath's self-evaluation can be fairly accurate (Jones & Miller, 2012). In short, they know who they are. Although the American Psychiatric Association's Diagnostic and Statistical Manual (DSM) has attempted to lump psychopathy into the broader category of ASPD, Hare disagrees and has provided strong evidence showing that psychopathy is an independent and separate condition, and in fact is a condition with a tighter constellation of traits than is true for ASPD (Hare et al, 2000). You may have noticed that the DSM list of criteria overlap several of the above-mentioned personality types. Although it's true that not all psychopaths wind up in prison, over half have arrest records. They can be found in many areas of life including politicians, business executives and, of course, a number of notorious figures (i.e., Adolph Hitler). The condition is made worse when combined with alcohol and/or drugs. Not all psychopaths are necessarily overtly aggressive, some running vicious financial scams that cost society enormous amounts of money. There are many warning signs of impending psychopathy as children move into adolescence. They tend to be cruel to animals, bully other children, lie, cheat and often set fires. As adolescents many quickly fall into the category of juvenile delinquency and are usually extremely promiscuous. Unfortunately, at the present time many professional clinicians consider psychopathy as untreatable and not responsive to treatment, which creates a tragic dilemma for society. Robert Hare has a reliable test for diagnosing the psychopath, called the Hare PCL –R, which is a 20- item symptom-rating scale. This test, although primarily used for diagnosing the level of a person's psychopathic tendencies, has been increasingly used in courts of law and in prisons to alert authorities as to the risks involved if the person were to be set free.

The Sociopath
Although there are some who use psychopathy and sociopathy interchangeably, researchers such as Hare draw a clear distinction and insist that sociopathy is primarily a function of social influences (Hare 1999). The term sociopathy is preferred by sociologists, and is based on the belief that the origin of the condition is based on negative social factors, especially poverty, parental neglect and a failure to introject societal norms. Therefore although psychopathy and sociopathy describe very similar (often the same) behaviors, the major difference is oftentimes based on whether the term is used by psychologists or sociologists (Lykken, 1999).

The Psychopath, Emotions, and the Brain
As you read this section, just relax. You don't need to go to medical school to understand the basics of the science behind the study of the physiology of crime. Since psychopathy is an emotional disorder, just spend a few minutes thinking about what is called the brain's limbic system. Are you still awake? The limbic system is a grouping of brain structures that are primarily involved in the control of emotions, and the two parts of the limbic system that are of special interest in the study of personality disorders are the amygdala and the hypothalamus, both of which are found on both sides of the brain. Next time you're having a dorm discussion, throw in the phrase "limbic system" and watch the room clear.

The Amygdala
The amygdala is a small, only about an inch long, almond-shaped brain structure located on both temporal lobes and is primarily involved in the fear emotion and the memory of those situations producing fear, anxiety and general excitement. Incidentally your temporal lobes are situated just behind your ears (and you wondered what was between your ears).

The Hypothalamus, The Amygdala and the Four Fs

The hypothalamus, however, is located down at the base of the brain and controls both the autonomic nervous system and the endocrine systems. It is the seat of what are called the emotional four F's: fighting, feeding, feeling and let's just call it – frolicking.

Neuroanatomists have found that psychopaths have distinctive anomalies in both the amygdala and the hypothalamus (Blair, 2008). Because psychopathy is primarily an emotional disorder it is little wonder that distortions have been found in the areas of the brain that are the most heavily involved in emotion (Koehler, 2006).

The Amygdala and You

Without question, there are going to be times when you will have to confront your own amygdala, and this is especially true if you are involved in law enforcement. The problem is that the amygdala reacts instantly to any potential threat (the mother bear syndrome) and yet the prefrontal cortex (where you think and process information) reacts more slowly. Have you ever had to do any public speaking? If so, you might recall that perhaps you began to sweat, breathe more rapidly, with legs shaking and heart pounding. You were afraid you might say something stupid or look foolish (Meyers & Nix, 2011). Daniel Goleman calls this "the amygdala hijack" (Goleman, 1996). What happened was that the amygdala, which is part of the old reptilian brain (the part of the brain you share with alligators) instantly takes over and sends SOS messages to the adrenal glands, assuring you of becoming totally adrenalized and ready for action. The blood comes out of your prefrontal cortex, which short-circuits the thinking brain and then in turn floods and activates your muscles. You are ready for fight or flight. And if this is a confrontation you are reacting to, then you must remember that the suspect is probably more crazily aroused than you are. The following suggestions have been offered for retraining yourself by using an emotional learning program that may change your mind set (these suggestions are based on slowing down the process in order to give the thinking brain enough time to react with some degree of reason and rationality):

1. Take a deep breath and stay as calm as you can by thinking of something that might be humorous enough to take the edge off the situation.
2. Use the old six-second rule, which prescribes that you count to six before taking any action. This gives enough time for the 'thinking" part of the brain, the prefrontal, neo cortex, to kick in. However, if the suspect is armed, find cover before you start the six count. As a law enforcement officer nobody expects you to start a fight, but you are expected to deal with it.
3. Make a clear determination of what it is that is causing the threat. This again gives some more time for the neo-cortex to provide you with some intel.

4. If it's a situation, like public speaking that brings on the attack, the best approach is to stand your ground by repeatedly putting yourself in the uncomfortable situation. This process is called desensitization.

5. When the situation is resolved, think about it in as much detail as possible. The amygdala operates on past experience, and if you spend some review time clarifying the experience, you'll be less prone to the next amygdala hijack.

MRI Evidence

MRI stands for Magnetic Resonance Imaging, and it is used to create an image or picture of the body's internal structures. It is especially useful for brain imaging because it provides a high-contrast image between the various soft tissues in the brain. Prof. Kent Kiehl has conducted a long series of MRI studies that have consistently shown differences in brain activity between the brains of "normals" and those of diagnosed psychopaths. In some of these studies, the person undergoing the MRI, is shown a series of pictures, some very gruesome, and then asked to rate the scene as to whether it portrays a moral violation. The psychopath may even be able to describe a scene, for example a picture of a man pointing a gun at a child, as morally reprehensible, but the brain scan tells a different story. When a normal person sees this picture, the brain's emotional area (limbic system) lights up, but with a psychopath the emotional circuit just does not engage (Kiehl et al 2006).

Serotonin

The neurotransmitter serotonin has been studied in the context of psychopathy. Serotonin is a hormone that acts to suppress aggression and increase feelings of well-being. In fact it is often called the "happiness hormone" and is related to something called tryptophan. Tryptophan is a protein-based constituent found in many foods, especially in turkey. Do you remember that turkey dinner you had last Thanksgiving and how it was then hard to stay awake long enough to watch the football game on TV?

With tryptophan and serotonin coursing through the body, a person would rather nap than fight. Studies have shown that any increase in the level of serotonin in the brain tends to decrease both instrumental and reactive aggression (Swann, 2003). As would be predicted, the psychopath has been found to have significantly lowered levels of serotonin.

Testosterone

Testosterone is a steroid hormone and is found in both the brain and testes of men (ovaries in women). Men of course have more testosterone than do women (about ten times more), and there are several lines of evidence linking it to aggression. Correlational studies show that testosterone levels peak at just about the same age as do crimes of violence (mid-to-late teens). Experimental evidence shows that large doses of testosterone can increase aggression in some men, but not all, and men who use anabolic steroids are significantly more likely to be involved in violent crime. Among the prison population testosterone levels are highest among those males who were convicted of violent crimes. Even among imprisoned women, testosterone levels were found to be related to aggressive behavior and crimes of violence (Dabbs & Hargrove, 1997).

Minor Physical Anomalies (MPA)

There is evidence that minor physical anomalies, usually caused either at birth or during the first trimester of pregnancy, may be associated with both psychoses and antisocial behavior (Raine, 2002). These include such things as a furrowed tongue, high palate, crossed eyes, low-seated ears, or adherent ear lobes. Adherent ear lobes are those that adhere (are attached very closely) to the head, making the wearing of ear rings somewhat difficult. The ear lobes appear to be almost glued to the head. Are we hearing echoes of Cesare Lombroso? All these anomalies were stressed by Sheila Cantor as factors predicting the onset of schizophrenia in children (Cantor, 1988).

The Psychopath and the Influence of Environment

Psychology's most basic axiom is that behavior is a result of the interaction of heredity, environment, and time . And these interactions begin immediately, at the very moment of conception. To be sure, the uterine environment is relatively stable, but not totally or always so. Toxic agents in the mother's uterus, sometimes produced by drugs and alcohol, can modify, damage or even halt fetal development. The physical abuse of the expectant mother can also cause unalterable fetal problems that may become life-long. The evidence presented above points to at least some level of biological substrate for the psychopathic personality. But what about the environment ? Since not everyone with these specific brain anomalies and antisocial tendencies becomes psychopathic, what are the most influential environmental risks, and when do they occur? That is, what types of environmental events are most likely to interact with these latent tendencies and then evolve into criminal behavior?

Economic and Social Problems

Although there is no clear relationship between overall crime rates and national unemployment rates, living conditions in blighted areas can serve as precursors to crime.

Because socio economic status can have an effect on a person's living situation, it is little wonder that the interaction of low economic status and underlying personality factors can have a profound influence on behavior. A low socio-economic status can severely reduce the number and variability of available behavioral choices (especially legal choices). The combination of poverty and the effects of a blighted neighborhood can increase the appeal of the quick score promised by a life of crime. This limitation of life's choices therefore may increase levels of instrumental aggression, the violence that is activated in the pursuit of tangible goals and rewards. This of course is goal-directed aggression. However the insecurity of a threatening neighborhood can also cause reactive aggression that is aggression used only as an act of protection. Because SES (socioeconomic status) so often acts as a proxy for race, some people have inappropriately assigned race as a causal factor in evaluating the incidence of crime.

Problems Within the Family Unit

Without question family variables can influence the developing personality in both healthy and unhealthy directions. As we saw in Chapter 2, a dysfunctional family can act to bring out anti-social tendencies within children. To begin with, some parents are very poor role models. For example, parents who abuse drugs and alcohol, or who are themselves antisocial, may set the child on an antisocial life course. Because some parents can be such poor role models, the developing child may look to others in the neighborhood for support, and these others may project very destructive and illegal alternatives. The parent who fails in the role of being a parent, who provides little supervision and inconsistent discipline, can set the stage for the child's unhealthy personality development. Some forms of antisocial behavior are more the result of environmental influences than is the case with psychopathy, especially adolescent- onset antisocial behavior (Blair et al, 2010). For example, shoplifting, and fare dodging, may offer a stronger social-environmental explanation than would, say, robbery. Thus, since the environment can breathe active life into latent biological tendencies, biology is not destiny. As Blair et al say "While we would argue that there is a biological basis to the antisocial behavior of the 5 percent of criminals who commit the disproportionate percentage of crime (mostly individuals with psychopathy), we would not argue that there is a biological basis to the antisocial behavior of most criminals" (Blair et al, 2010 p154).

Serial Killers

Some psychopaths move on to seek even higher levels of the worst forms of excitement by committing multiple homicides. Known as serial-killers, they are the persons who have killed at least three people in separate events over the course of a few months. Currently the country's foremost expert on serial killers, Dr. Jack Levin, has said that although serial killers do share many common characteristics, there is not just one criterion that fits each and every case (Levin, 2008). Most serial killers, however, are what Levin and the F.B.I call "collectors of injustice." That is, individuals who think the world is out to get them, and so to remain as safe as possible they become motivated by a compelling drive to experience the rush of power and control that can accompany murder. The need to control becomes so great that these killers become desperately compelled to enjoy the heady excitement of determining who will live and who will die. As Levin says, "They like playing God." These are not the so-called "hit men" who kill for money or fulfill some gang leader's orders. These are killers who kill for the sheer joy of the killing itself, an act which supplies them with their feelings of power, control, superiority and attention. In fact sometimes the need for superiority and its accompanying fame, leads to their undoing. The now-famous BTK Killer (Blind, Torture, and Kill) began feeling ignored by the press, and so he sent letters to the police and media to try and get back in the public spotlight. The letters were soon traced back to him, and he was caught. Levin says "If he hadn't wanted so much to be a celebrity, he might still be on the loose." Levin also reports that Charles Manson told him personally that he, Manson, was the most famous person in history. The Unabomber ,Ted Kaczynski, became so envious of Timothy McVeigh's headline-grabbing killing of 168 men, women, and children, that he started writing to the media and even phoning the police. This turned out not to be the Unabomber's best idea, because again authorities were able to trace everything back directly to him.

There are, as said above, some differences among these killers, the most notable being whether it's based on a spur-of-the-moment frenzied impulse or on a cold and calculated, meticulously planned operation Thus there are said to be two types of serial killers disorganized and organized. The disorganized assailant, usually an impulse killer, is actually easier to track down, since more clues are left behind. The organized killer, who meticulously plans the details, is less likely to leave clues and in fact often gets better at hiding clues with each successive murder.

CASE STUDY: Brian Dugan – "Please, I don't want to die"

Brian Dugan, a New Hampshire native, was charged in a series of vicious, murderous sexual assaults on females, some as young as 7 years of age. He was born in Nashua, N.H, and at the time of his birth he had an older sister and would later have three younger brothers. His birth was not without incident. He started emerging before the doctor arrived, and so in an attempt to delay the delivery process a nurse pushed his head back in and strapped his mother's legs tightly together. As a child all the way up to his teen-age years he suffered headaches and was on a regimen of pain medication. His family believed the headaches were due to what they thought was his birth trauma. He was also a bed wetter, all the way up to his teen-age years. His mother, Jenny, was the disciplinarian in the family, and to punish his bed-wetting, she made him sleep in soiled bedding which made that part of the house reek with urine. When he was six years old the family moved to Illinois, and when he was eight years old, as an omen of what was to come, he burned down the family garage. As he grew older he was charged with a series of arsons.

When he was 13 he decided to pour gasoline on a cat, light it up and watch it burn. He then laughed and told his brother that it gave him a great feeling.

When his mother caught him lighting matches in the house, she forced him to keep holding the match down to where it burned him. She also beat him with a whip and made him drink extremely hot liquids. He was sexually active at 13, not only molesting his brother, but also having a sexual affair with an older woman. In a case of "it takes one to know one," Dugan alleges that in 1972 he was picked up by the clown-killer, John Wayne Gacy. He said that Gacy took him to a place out in a lightly-wooded area, and forced him to wear a bikini while performing sexual acts on Gacy. Actually, unless this was just another one of his lies, Dugan was lucky to have lived through that ordeal, because Gacy (who worked as a clown at children's parties) murdered a grand total of 33, mostly boys but even some men. Later that year Dugan was arrested for burglary, and this was soon followed by convictions for a variety of crimes, more burglaries, arson and assault and battery. In 1974 he was charged with, but not convicted of, abducting a 10 year old girl. Despite all this, his mother said that he had a fairly normal childhood, and that he liked to read and play various sports, his favorite being baseball. His father was a neer-do-well, traveling salesman, who drank heavily and died in 1975 – The cause? Cirrhosis of the liver. Dugan's high school years were not happy, and he quit school at age 16, (although he later obtained a GED while in prison). In 1975 he threatened to kill his older sister. He also broke the headlights on her car and threatened to "chop up" her son, his own nephew. As a result she turned against him and later after one of his killings she told police she thought he did it, and that if it were proven true she hoped he would get the death penalty. Dugan, of course, denied threatening her. Then from 1979 to 1982 he served time at the Menard Correctional Center, where he alleges that he himself was sexually abused.

In February 1983 he broke into the home of Jeanine Nicarico, a 10-year-old girl who was at home that day because of an illness. He kidnapped her, sexually assaulted her and then bludgeoned her to death. Her body was found a few days later. In July of 1984 he saw 27 year-old Donna Schnorr in her car as she stopped for a red light. He then followed her and when he saw the opportunity he ran her off the road, and viciously assaulted and raped her. He then finished by drowning her in a quarry. On May 6, 1985, he stopped his car to help a 21-year-old woman who was sitting at the side of the road trying to start her car. He pulled her into the car, held a knife to her throat, and tied and gagged her. He drove to a secluded spot, and then raped her in the back seat of the car. She somehow got away and lived to tell the story. A couple of weeks later he spotted a 19-year-old woman walking alone on the side of the road. He grabbed her and tried to drag her into his car, but she wriggled free and escaped. Not to be denied, the very next day, he forced a 16 year-old girl into his car, threatened her with a tire iron and raped her. She was also able to get away. The next girl, however, wasn't so lucky. Just a few days later, he spotted seven-year-old Melissa Ackerman and her friend, Opal Horton, riding bikes near Melisa's home. Dugan grabbed both of them, but while pinning Melissa down, her friend was able to get away. He then raped and murdered little Melissa.

This is the story of Brian Dugan, a psychopathic serial killer. At his trial he begged that he not be executed – "Please I don't want to die" he repeated, and even that was said without much affect. He also said he was sorry, but as District Attorney Matthew Ryan said many years ago – "They're all sorry when they get caught." Dugan's trial is especially important because it points out the societal dilemma of whether a person who may not be in full control of his actions should be held responsible. During the trial the results of the Hare psychopathy test were used, showing that Dugan scored at the 99th percentile, and when asked why he went on the killing sprees he replied "it might have been for sex, but I don't understand why. I wish I knew why I did things, but I don't." Again, be reminded that you are reading the words of a psychopath, and so these words may be being used for purposes of manipulation. During the trial the defense argued that persons should not be sentenced for a condition that they were born with, because it's not their fault. Dr. Steven Erickson, a forensic psychiatrist, then testified that Dugan should be sentenced, that a person should not be given a free pass for killing someone, even if there is an abnormality. He countered that some depressed patients have been shown to have brain abnormalities. Should they be entitled to kill? The court ruled that nobody should be set free on a murder conviction, regardless of any possible anomaly. Dugan was sentenced to life in prison without parole. Claiming such inanities as "the devil made me do it" does not guarantee freedom from confinement.

Women and Violence

Although women are less prone to violence than are men (accounting for only about 14% of crimes of violence), they are currently on the upsurge. During the past 40 years the number of incarcerated Americans has gone from 1.125 million to 2.25 million for a 100% increase. However, during that same time frame the number of incarcerated women has gone from 12,000 to 90,000 for an increase of 650%. Also, since women are more likely to be in contact with children, they are more likely to commit crimes of child abuse (Pearson, 1997). There have also been cases of female serial killers, although they don't seem to have the same motives for sex and power as are exhibited by men (Pearson, 1997). Also, whereas male killers tend to shoot, stab, batter or strangle their victims, women are more likely to use poisons and suffocation. As with males, female serial killers are clearly psychopathic.

Schizophrenia and NGRI (Not Guilty by Reason of Insanity)

Finally, we must also look at another serious mental condition called schizophrenia, and especially paranoid schizophrenia. Schizophrenia is a condition usually first diagnosed in the late teen-age years, and is characterized by major thought disorders, including hallucinations (seeing and hearing things that aren't there) and delusions (usually of either grandeur, or as in the case of paranoia, persecutorial). Because someone suffering from paranoid schizophrenics often believes someone or something is out to get them, they may become violent as a means of personal protection. Many of these people are homeless and often end up as a patient in a hospital or as a perpetrator in a jail. Sometimes the courts may allow a person with schizophrenia who has committed a crime to enter a NGRI plea (not guilty by reason of insanity). The insanity defense demands that the defendant undergo a psychological/psychiatric examination, and if then found not guilty in court because of the mental impairment, the individual can be remanded to a hospital or other such facility rather than to prison. Despite media attention, the NGRI defense is rarely used and when used is rarely effective.

Schizophrenia and Violence
It has been found that rates of violence among men are significantly higher for men diagnosed with schizophrenia than for the male population at large, but for women the difference is even greater. Although in total numbers, men commit far more violent acts than do women, women diagnosed with schizophrenia are twice as likely to engage in violence than are women in the general population (Hodgins, 2008). Because schizophrenia is so often accompanied by violence, you are probably going to encounter an individual with this disorder if you enter the field of law enforcement.

Schizophrenia – The Causes and Cures
Although scientists seem to agree that schizophrenia has a genetic basis, there are some environmental factors that may come into play. On the genetic side are studies showing that there is a high concordance rate between identical twins (who share the same genetic endowment), but the agreement is not 100%. And as we have already discussed in Chapter 1, environment in this context is far more than just the neighborhood or room that one lives in. It is everything that is not genetic and thus includes an enormous number of variables, from the past (the chemical and nutritional uterine environment) to the present (social stressors, substance abuse), and every experience in between. Fortunately there are now a variety of medications that may lessen the severity of the symptoms, but so far there is no absolute cure. Finally, individuals with schizophrenia, especially those living in the community, are not always faithful about taking their "meds," and for these tragic cases the symptoms often get worse. For you psychology students, schizophrenia is classified in the DSM-5.

Irresistible Urge

One variation on the NGRI "don't-know-right-from-wrong "theme is when an insane action is alleged to be based on an uncontrollable impulse. This again is a rarely used legal defense, but when it is used it can be a headline grabber. Back in 1994, in a trial that received world-wide attention, a young married woman, Lorena Bobbitt, admitted that she cut off her husband's penis with a carving knife. The defense used the irresistible-urge argument, and, believe it or not, she was acquitted.

Mass Shootings

Although mass shootings are certainly headline grabbers and appear to be happening regularly, they are relatively rare. Unfortunately these horrific mass murders are not at all easy to prevent, especially since the mentally disturbed are free to walk the streets. In the name of freedom and individual rights, it has become extremely difficult to force a person into involuntary commitment to a psychiatric facility for treatment. Too many mentally disturbed individuals are living on the street, homeless and unable or unwilling to take their medications. And for them, the law seems to be irrelevant, since although the law may act to deter the rational it seems to have no effect on those who are irrational. In fact studies show that those states whose civil commitment laws are the strongest, have significantly fewer homicides. (Segal, 2011).

An Obligation

Knowledge of the various personality types shown above is essential to any of you who hope to profit from the literature in the field of criminal justice. Although this chapter has only skimmed the surface of the subject, a thorough reading and analysis of the material it contains should pay rich dividends in your future career. The student who is serious about becoming a professional is urged to follow this up with at least a one-semester course in the psychology of personality and abnormal psychology.

Summary

Personality types and disorders have been studied as factors associated with crime, especially disorders with an over-load of aggression. The two components of general aggression are (1) reactive aggression (brought on by frustration or threat) and (2) instrumental aggression (used to achieve a specific goal). Bullying is the continued physical or even psychological mistreatment by someone who is stronger than the chosen victim. The victim, who tacitly agrees not to break the relationship, is seen as actually being a part of the bullying cycle. ODD or Oppositional Defiant Disorder is a disorder of childhood and adolescence and is characterized by excessive anger and defiance toward an adult or authority figure. CD or Conduct Disorder is more severe than ODD, and involves overt aggression, violation of the rights of others and a failure to understand the consequences. Some forms of CD are limited only to the adolescent period and do not continue into adulthood. ASPD or Anti-Social Personality Disorder is a constellation of personality traits that often develops into some form of criminal behavior. The person who presents with ASPD lacks responsibility for actions, is deceitful, impulsive, aggressive and indifferent to the suffering of others. Currently about 7 out of 10 prison inmates meet the criteria for ASPD. Even more serious is Psychopathy, an emotional disorder characterized by low levels of empathy, high levels of aggression, being manipulative and often charmingly glib. Of all the personality disturbances shown above, the evidence for some sort of biological basis has been most clearly shown with psychopathy. The areas of the brain which most closely associate with psychopathy are the amygdala and hippocampus, both part of what is called the limbic system - the brain's emotional-controlling circuit. Environmental influences impact all the above mentioned disorders. These environmental issues include a low socio-economic status, family problems, and lack of a clear bonding with a parent or any other primary-care giver during the infant attachment stage.

The serial killer, typically a psychopath, is defined as anyone who kills at least three people in separate events covering a period of at least a month. Some of these killers are organized and plan their activities with great care. Others are disorganized, spur-of–the-moment, thrill killers, who also may be more apt to leave incriminating evidence as to their identities. Sometimes the need for fame and attention is so strong that they inadvertently provide clues that can bring authorities directly to their doors. As an example of a serial killer, the case of Brian Dugan was presented. This case illustrates the dilemma caused by recent discoveries of possible organic causes of the behavior, with society's need for the security of having these people confined and unable to repeat. Another personality condition that may put a person on the wrong side of the law is a mental disease called schizophrenia. Individuals with this disorder, especially paranoid schizophrenia, may be delusional as well as exhibiting hallucinatory behavior. The schizophrenic, both male and female, show higher rates of violence than occurs in the general population, and this is especially true for women.

Key Terms

Amygdala
Antisocial Personality Disorder
Attachment
Bullying
Conduct Disorder
Hippocampus
Limbic System

MRI
NGRI
Oppositional Defiant Disorder
Psychopathy
Schizophrenia
Serotonin
SES
Testosterone

References

American Psychiatric Association (2013). *Diagnostic and Statistical Manual of Mental Disorders-5*. Author.

American Psychiatric Association (2000). *Diagnostic and Statistical Manual of Mental Disorders-IV*. Author.

Blair, R.J. (2008). The amygdala and ventromedial prefrontal cortex: Functional contributions to psychopathy. *The Royal Society, 1503*, 2557-2565.

Blair, J., Mitchell, D. & Blair, K. (2010). *The psychopath: Emotions and the brain*. Malden MA: Blackwell Publishers

Bowlby, J. (1973). *Separation, anger and anxiety*. London: Hogarth

Cantor, S. (1988). *Childhood schizophrenia*. NY: Guilford.

Dabbs, J.M. & Hargrove, M.F. (1997). Age, testosterone and behavior among female prison inmates. *Psychosomatic Medicine, 59*, 477-480.

Goleman, D. (1996). *Emotional intelligence: Why it can matter more than IQ*. New York: Bantam Books

Hare, R.D. ,Clark, D., Grann, M. & Thornton, D. (2000). Psychopathy and the predictive validity of the P.C.L. –R. *Behavioral Sciences and the Law, 18*, 623-645.

Hare, R.D. (1999). *Without conscience*. NY: Guilford

Hodgins, S. (2008). Violent behavior among people with schizophrenia. *Royal Society 8, 363*, 2505-2518.

Jones, S. & Miller, J.D. (2012). Psychopathic traits and externalizing behavior: A comparison of self- and informant reports in the statistical prediction of externalizing behaviors. *Psychological Assessment, 24*, 255-260.

Kim,Y, Levanthal,B., Koh,Y & Boyce,W. (2009). Bullying increased suicide risk.. *Archives of Suicide Research,13*, (1), 15-30.

Koehler, K.A. (2006). A cognitive neuroscience perspective on psychopathy. *Psychiatric Research, 142*, 107-128

Kiehle, K.A., Bates, A.T., Laurens, K.R., Hare, R.D. & Liddle, P.F. (2006). Brain potential implicate temporal lobe abnormalities in criminal psychopaths. *Journal of Abnormal Psychology, 115*, 443-453

Kosson, D.S., Smith, S.S. & Newman, J.P. (1990). Evaluating the construct validity ofthe psychopathy construct in blacks. *Journal of Abnormal Psychology, 99*, 250-259.

Levin, J. (2008). *Serial killers: Up close and personal.* Amherst, N.Y: Prometheus Books

Lykken, D.T. (1995). *The anti-social personalities.* Hillsdale NJ: Erlbaum

Meyers, P. & Nix, S. (2011). *As we speak: How to make your point and have it stick.* New York, Simon and Shuster.

Pearson, P., (1997). *When she was bad: Violent women and the myth of innocence.* Toronto: Random House.

Raine, A. (2003). The role of prefrontal deficits, low autonomic arousal and early health factors in the development of anti-social aggression in children. *Journal of Child Psychology and Psychiatry, 43,* 417-434.

Ronson, J. (2011). *The psychopath test.* New York, NY: Riverhead Books.

Segal, S.P. (2011). Civil commitment law, mental health services and US homicide rates. *Social Psychiatry and Psychiatric Epidemiology, 10,* 45-57.

Solberg,M. & Olweus,D. (2003). Prevalence estimation of school bullying with the Olweus Bully/Victim Questionnaire, *Aggressive Behavior,29,* 239-268.

Swann, A.C. (2007). Neuroreceptor mechanisms of aggression and its treatment. *Journal* of Clinical Psychology, 64, 26-35.

CHAPTER 4

LAW ENFORCEMENT: TO PROTECT AND SERVE

The Three Cs

As a student of Criminal Justice you may have heard about Cops, Courts, and Corrections or the three Cs. Keep them in that order. For example, if you were suspected of committing a felony you would first meet the Cops, and if you were then arrested and charged your next contact would be the Courts. Finally, if convicted and sentenced you would then have to confront Corrections, either Institutional or Community. This chapter is focused on that first C, Cops. The Cops in this context stand for and symbolize law enforcement in general, and as you saw in Chapter 1, Law Enforcement is a huge enterprise and includes a long list of potential careers.

Town or City Police

However, when you think of law enforcement, the image of your own town or city police force probably is the first thing that comes to mind. And well it should. Throughout the United States, our local and state police departments combine to be the largest crime-fighting group in the country. There are currently well over a million persons working on a full-time basis in local and state police agencies. Perhaps not as glamorous as the Sky Marshall, the Elite Hostage Negotiator or the FBI's Swat (Special Weapons and Tactics) Team, it's the local police who do most of the country's enforcement work. And when there's trouble in your neighborhood, don't call the CIA! And if you, as you should, dial 911 it won't be the Sky Marshall who answers. No, it's your own town or city police officer who answers the call and becomes the first responder.

Law Enforcement

Since this chapter is about law enforcement, let's take a moment to look at what is being enforced - the law, and in this case criminal law as opposed to civil law. In the next chapter we will be taking a much closer examination of our legal system, but we do have to take a brief look at the law in this chapter. After all, it would be most difficult to discuss law enforcement without some knowledge of what it is that's being enforced. The legal system in the U.S. can be categorized in two ways: Federal Law vs. State Law and Criminal Law vs. Civil Law.

Federal Law vs. State Law

Federal laws refer to laws that apply to the entire country, and they are said to reflect the "will of the people." Federal laws are, of course, enforced by the federal government, via such agencies as the FBI. The U.S. Constitution also allows states to have their own laws under the provisions of the 10th Amendment, which says that "the powers not delegated to the United States by the Constitution, nor prohibited by it are reserved to the states respectively." Obviously state laws are enforced by the state, via such agencies as the State Police.

Criminal Law vs. Civil Law

Criminal law refers to those governmental rules, which if broken, can result in confinement for a period of more than one year for a felony, or less than a year for a misdemeanor. In short, breaking a criminal law can get you locked up. Criminal law involves issues between the government and the individual. A person accused of violating a criminal law, however, is afforded special protection under what the U.S. Constitution calls "due process" – an extremely important concept in any free and democratic society. Due process means that the accused has the (1) the right to an attorney, (2) the right to a speedy trial by a jury of one's peers, and (3) the right to remain silent. Criminal law in the United States is rooted in what is called English common law. English common law was patched together over many centuries by combining judicial rulings and opinions from local levels and applying them to the entire country of England. It is called common law because it became the common and unified legal code that applied to everyone throughout the country. Civil Law refers to issues between private parties, or sometimes even corporations. Civil disputes arise as a result of private issues between individuals over such things as divorce, wills, estates, contracts, finances and libel/slander. For example if you were to be injured in an auto accident, you could sue the other driver for the cost of your treatment as well as your pain and suffering. Your case would be brought to a civil court for the decision. Unlike criminal law, civil law is rooted in the rules of ancient Rome, as opposed to English common law.

The Importance of Law

To some, the law is thought of as nothing more than a nuisance. "Laws are made to be broken," some may sneer. To others, however, the law is equivalent to the ultimate truth. These people, especially after a close Supreme Court decision, talk of the "law of the land" in hushed and reverent tones, betraying a kind of holier-than-thou attitude regarding lapses in human behavior. The law, however, is critical to maintaining an orderly and safe society. Laws are proposed by the people's representatives in Congress. Congress offers what is first called a bill, which is then debated and if passed by both houses of congress then goes to the executive branch (President or Governor) for a signature. If signed, the bill becomes a new law added to our legal system. Any new law must first and foremost be consistent with the United States Constitution. If the law is challenged, the judicial branch (the Supreme Court) decides its legality. There are also Ordinances which are typically local laws created by the cities and towns to enforce rules that may not apply to the entire state or country. But upholding and enforcing the laws and statutes isn't the only job for the police and other law enforcement agencies. The police are also charged with maintaining order, providing service, and preventing crime.

Enforcing Law

The police are empowered, first and foremost, to enforce the law. Any time a violation of the law is detected, the police officer can utilize his/her power of arrest. That is the violator can be detained, and does not have the option of resisting the officer's order to arrest. This is a responsibility that often carries over to off-duty time, meaning the police officer's job can sometimes be a twenty-four- seven profession.

Maintaining Order

The police are not only focused on law enforcement. They are also called on to handle situations that threaten public order, but may not always be criminal. For example, a loud party may get out of control, and the police might be called, not to make arrests, but simply to break up the party and quietly send everyone home. Although the threat of arrest my get the party goer's attention, it's the maintenance of peace and tranquility that was the police officer's first challenge. There are also domestic disputes that can get loud and unruly, and the police might be called to intervene before any real crime has been committed. Situations involving domestic disputes can be threatening events for the responding officer. Crowd control is certainly aimed at maintaining order, and the police may be called to break up a crowd before any riot occurs – even after such seemingly innocuous events as a high-school football game.

A PERSON OF INTEREST: ELIOT NESS (THE UNTOUCHA-BLE) 1903-1957

Considered to be one of the all-time great crime fighters, Eliot Ness and his tiny group of eleven men (called by the media "The Untouchables") did an outstanding job of cleaning up the racketeers in both Chicago and later in Cleveland. The group became known as the untouchables because Ness and his carefully-selected men could not be bought out or bribed, even though the crime-boss, Al Capone, and others made repeated attempts. Ness and his elite group also survived several Capone-ordered assassination attempts. He began his law-enforcement career working for the U.S. Treasury Department during the prohibition years and was charged with trying to control illegal alcohol production and distribution. Through the use of extensive wire taps, Ness was able to close down dozens of illegal stills and breweries and convict many of the associated mobsters (Heimel, 1997). Ness often used a specially built armored car with an attached battering ram to knock down the steel-reinforced doors of the stills and breweries. Although it was the I.R.S. (Internal Revenue Service) that finally got the long-sought conviction of Capone, Ness and his group did collect much of the criminal evidence needed to put him in prison. Capone died while in prison from the ravages of syphilis. When prohibition was repealed in 1933, the boot-legging business was finally broken up, and the entire enterprise opened up to legitimate companies. Alcohol was no longer the exclusive life-blood of the racketeers. Ness then went on to Cleveland as the Public Safety Director, and rooted out a network of Cleveland corruption, including a link between organized crime and the Cleveland police department. Ness was long interested in joining the F.B.I., but was turned down, perhaps because, as some have suggested, J. Edgar Hoover didn't want to share media headlines with him. He later ran unsuccessfully for the office of mayor of Cleveland. His career took an unfortunate downward path following an early morning Cleveland auto accident, from which Ness fled the scene. Eliot Ness became world famous because of the television series "The Untouchables" starring Robert Stack (1959) and the hit movie of the same name starring Kevin Costner (1987).

Providing Service

The police are also called upon to provide a wide variety of public services, including giving driving directions, helping stranded motorists, opening cars for motorists who locked their keys inside, and even assisting women undergoing the birthing process. The police may also be used to escort funeral processions, or simply stand by at the dedication of new buildings. Police are often used in other routine ways, such as alerting drivers to road work on the highway ahead, but they may also be used in life-or-death situations, such as trying to reason with a suicidal jumper who may be perched high on a bridge. Police departments receive far more calls for service than for violations of the law. A listing of the various services police provide to the public is almost endless.

Crime Prevention

Sir Robert Peel, chief of London's first organized police force (circa 1820s) always maintained that crime prevention was the number one responsibility of the police. Peel insisted that the measure of any police department's effectiveness was the absence of crime, rather than the various efforts used to solve a crime. There are numerous ways that the police can deter crime, but perhaps the most obvious and perhaps most effective is to increase the number of patrols working at the street level. During the last several years there has been a fairly dramatic increase in the number of state and local police agency employees, and it may be working. During that same time period crime rates have gone down. This of course cannot be a direct cause-and-effect conclusion, since there have also been changes in other criminal justice areas, such as longer prison sentences. The U.S. Defense Department likes to talk about the success of our troops in the Iraq war as a result of what was called "the surge" – a huge increase in the number of U.S. troops on the ground. This would almost certainly work in the case of local law enforcement. Cops on every corner of every neighborhood would go a long way toward preventing crime, but can society afford it? Currently there are discussions regarding the placement of armed police officers in every U.S. school in order to prevent such horrendous incidents as the massacre of school children in Newtown Connecticut. The decision will almost certainly be partly based on economics.

A Look to the Past: Our English Heritage – From London to Boston

It has been alleged that history professors tell us that if we don't learn from history we are doomed to hearing it repeated. Although our historical focus in this brief section will be on the 1800s and on the organized police departments of London and Boston, this doesn't mean that previously there were no attempts to preserve law and order. Some cities and towns had what were called "Night Watchmen" or "Day-Night Police." These were really tough guys who often worked alone and carried a pole with a hook on one end and a solid bat on the other. They could hook a fleeing suspect with one end and send him into oblivion with the other end. They also carried what was a called a rattle, a noise-maker that could be used in an emergency (like today's siren) to call for a back- up. It was not a high-tech world back then.

London

Our starting point in this little historical foray will be London, England. Try to remember the name Robert Peel, because he's the man who organized that first modern police department, which he set up in London in 1826. From that day on the English police became known as "Bobbies" (for Robert," Bobby" Peel), and even today the British police academy is called the "Peel Centre" in his honor. Peel demanded that the police department be highly disciplined with an organizational structure based on the military tradition. Under Peel the police in London became paid employees, not volunteers. His emphasis was always on crime prevention, and he demanded that the police be directly responsible to him alone (as a quasi- General). Ironically, he became the target of a deranged shooter, who mistakenly shot and killed one of his aids, thinking it was Peel himself. The shooter, Daniel McNaughton, pleaded not guilty by reason of insanity, and was acquitted on the grounds of not knowing right from wrong. This became known as the McNaughton Rule, which until 1972 was the standard defense for insanity, even in this country. Peel is probably best known today for the formulation of his "Nine Principles of Police Behavior," principles that still have a very modern ring to them, especially his foreshadowing of today's community police philosophy (Gaunt, 2010). If you ever get a job in law enforcement, you are encouraged to copy and frame these nine rules and display them prominently on your desk.

Peel's Nine Principles of Police Behavior
1. The basic mission of the police is to prevent crime and social disorder.
2. The ability of the police to perform their duties depends on public acceptance.
3. The police must try to obtain the willing cooperation of the public in order to maintain the respect of the public.
4. The degree of cooperation that can be obtained with the public diminishes to the extent that the police find it necessary to use physical force.
5. The police will seek public favor not by catering to public whims but by constantly demonstrating absolutely impartial observance of the law.
6. The police will use physical force only to the extent necessary to secure the law or to restore order (when persuasion and warning are not enough).
7. The police should strive to maintain a relationship with the public that gives reality to the historic tradition that the police are the public, and the public are the police
8. The police should strive to assure that their actions stay limited to their function of law enforcement and never appear to usurp the powers of the judiciary.
9. The final test of a police department's efficiency is the absence of crime and disorder, rather than the identification of any police action needed to deal with it.

Although he emphasized police-public cooperation, Peel was not always enamored of the whims of the public's attitudes. At one point he said, with a hint of exasperation, that public opinion was a compound of folly, weakness, prejudice, right feeling, wrong feeling, obstinacy and the most recent newspaper articles. Peel went on later to become England's top government official – the Prime Minister.

Boston Massachusetts
One of the first police departments in the United States (some say "the first") was established in Boston, Massachusetts. Boston continued in the tradition of Sir Robert Peel and organized its police force according to Peel's rules and military protocol. Although not formally founded until 1854, the department had actually been operational ever since 1838 when the Massachusetts General Court passed a bill authorizing Boston to appoint police officers on a

paid basis. Boston's first Irish born police officer was Bernard "Barney" McGinniskin, appointed in 1868, and who now lies buried in St. Augustine Cemetery in South Boston (an area of Boston affectionately known as "Southie"). In 1871 the Boston police department appointed Horatio J. Homer as its first African-American, and in 1921, Irene McAuliffe was sworn in as the department's first female officer. Another historical fact of interest was the Boston police strike of 1919, which was called because the city would not allow for the formation of a police union. The issue went all the way up to then-governor of Massachusetts, Calvin Coolidge who ruled that the police did not have the right to strike because it threatened the safety and security of society.

The Wickersham Commission
In the early 1930s, President Herbert Hoover formed a group, called the Wickersham Commission, to look into major problems that were occurring in the criminal justice system, especially enforcement and corrections. Although they found problems in many areas of criminal justice, some of the most blatant issues were uncovered within the country's local police departments. They found that the police in some areas were using far too much force, in some cases virtual torture, in their efforts to enforce the law. The Commission finally concluded that the methods being used, brutal though they were, were not having enough effect on crime rates, and they charged the police departments of too often being inefficient, lazy and even corrupt. Corruption was especially evident in cases where police officers took bribes in lieu of arrests, or took weekly money from brothels and drug dealers. One corrupt New York officer was found to have accumulated several million dollars during his 35 year career. These findings actually did have an effect and did lead to cleaning up many departments.

The Blue Wall of Silence – Cops Don't Tell on Cops
One of the difficulties encountered when trying to clean up police corruption is a police social code, called the blue wall of silence, or the doctrine of not incriminating a fellow officer. Part of this doctrine is rooted in the fact that police officers have a "cops-don't-tell-on cops" sub culture, as well as the strong feeling that officers have to trust each other in all situations. When an officer tells his partner that he "has his back" it means he would literally lay down his life to protect his fellow officer. The blue wall is obviously difficult to break down, and yet both police corruption and the blue wall are not as pervasive today as they were 20 or 30 years ago. Back in the 1960s a New York police officer named Frank Serpico uncovered and brought public some police actions that were definitely tainted with corruption. Serpico then endured harassment from officers in his own department, and eventually was "accidentally" shot in the face while busting up a drug ring. He recovered from the shooting and retired from the department. At the time of this writ-

ing he is still alive and is a tireless supporter and advocate of police accountability.

Police corruption and the department's blue wall still exists in places, but the evidence seems to indicate that things are changing. Some say that these changes may be due to the increased hiring of women and minorities, and some may also be due to the work of the department's bureau of internal affairs, a bureau charged with investigating even the slightest hint of police misconduct. There are now also civilian review boards which are local committees composed of community leaders who volunteer their time to investigate any accusations of police misdoings.

Quis Custodiet Ipsos Custudes? - Who Is Watching the Watchmen?

That the job of the Bureau of Internal Affairs is not new, is clearly shown in the Latin quote shown above. Actually the Latin quote is a translation of a section on political corruption taken from Plato's "Republic" which was written back in circa 380 BC. In the Republic, Plato suggested that the guardians of public trust must learn to guard themselves against themselves – hence a prophecy of today's departments of internal affairs. T'was ever thus.

Sworn

In order to have the right to detain a suspect, the officer (state or federal such as the police officer, sheriff, sheriff's deputy or government agent) must be "sworn," which means affirming the following: "I do solemnly swear that I will support the Constitution of the United States and the Constitution of this state and that I will faithfully discharge the duties of the office according to the best of my ability."

Although the department may have jobs that do not require being sworn, writing parking tickets or answering the phone, for example, only the sworn officer can make an arrest. One irony is that of all those being sworn to uphold the constitution, only about 20% acknowledge having ever read it.

Police and the Use of Force

Any sworn officer of the law is empowered with the right to use force. There are times, obviously, when the use of force is needed. If an unruly, combative suspect suddenly strikes a menacing pose and then, after a long line of profanities, becomes physically threatening, then the officer may have no choice but to use force. How much force is allowed? Only enough to calm the situation and gain control of the suspect. By far the better method of control is, as one veteran officer has said, to use "sweet talk." Quietly tell the suspect that you're an understanding officer, and that he's a good guy, and that if he just quiets down a little and becomes cooperative, things will go a lot easier for him. Some officers find this technique difficult, because it requires total personal control, and in an adrenaline-filled moment, perhaps with invective filling the air, that level of self-control may be difficult to maintain. However, as every police officer knows, the job of police is not about being strong enough to use force, but about being strong enough not to.

Brutality

There have been times when over- zealous police officers have exceeded their limited authority to use force. On occasion police have used tactics that have been described as nothing short of brutality. There are several examples as of late that are still being litigated but two previous examples that grabbed headlines throughout the country were the 1991 case of Rodney King (discussed previously), and the 1997 case of Abner Louima.

Rodney King

As you may remember from Chapter 1, Rodney King was an African-American living in California. He had ignored a police request to stop his car, and then after a high-speed chase was pulled out of his car and beaten by the pursuing officers with fists and night sticks. A by-stander recorded the scene on video tape. The officers were then tried in court where the defense hired a high-priced jury consultant, Dr. Jo-Ellan Dimitrius. Using scientific jury-selection techniques, a panel was installed who heard the case and then brought in a verdict of innocent. A public outcry greeted the verdict causing rioting throughout the country. Rodney King eventually received a court settlement of over three million dollars, but he later died of drowning in his own swimming pool at three in the morning.

Abner Louima

Louima was a Haitian immigrant who was involved in a brawl outside a Brooklyn New York Night club. The police had an especially difficult time controlling Louima, but when he was finally quieted and cuffed, he was brought to the station. It was in the police station's own rest-room that the major violations took place. Two white officers beat Louima to near unconsciousness, and then forced the handle of a toilet plunger up his anus and then into his mouth - which broke off several teeth. Louima later required surgery to both his rectum and gall bladder. He also needed extensive dental work. Only one officer was actually convicted of the assault, and he is now serving out a 30-year prison sentence. Louima brought legal action against the city of New York, and was awarded a total of 8.75 million dollars.

Deadly Force

Only as an absolute last resort may deadly force be used. Although deadly force can be applied in a variety of ways, by far the most common method is through the use of fire arms. Anytime a police officer is involved in a fatal shooting a thorough investigation always follows. The following three important milestones set the guidelines for the use of deadly force.

Tennessee v Garner - 1985

First, in 1985 in the case of Tennessee v Garner, the U.S. Supreme Court ruled that deadly force may never be used to prevent a suspect's escape. Said the court, "The use of deadly force to prevent the escape of felon suspects, whatever the circumstances is constitutionally unreasonable."

Graham v Connor - 1989

Then in 1989, in the case of Graham v Connor, the court added that deadly force may only be used when it is evaluated on the basis of reasonableness and not 20/20 hindsight. "Reasonableness must embody allowances for the fact that police officers are often forced to make split- second judgments in circumstances that are tense, uncertain, and rapidly evolving".

A Federal Order - 1995

Finally, in 1995, federal agents were told that deadly force could only be used when they felt that their lives, or the lives of others, were in imminent danger.

COP - Community Oriented Policing and Neighborhood Watches.

The Public Safety Partnership and Community Policing Act of 1994 stressed the philosophy of police-public interactions as being an integral part of crime reduction and community security. The Act also provided funding for (1) increasing the number of officers who will work interactively in the community, (2) providing more police training to increase the social skills needed for community involvements, (3) adding to the development of more new and innovative techniques for working interactively in the community and (4) educating police officers to the fact that the real job of policing is to prevent crime rather than merely reacting to crime. This new policing philosophy has since become increasingly popular throughout the country, especially in large metropolitan areas. The police are being urged to get out of their squad cars and patrol their assigned areas on foot. That is, the police should walk among the people. The theory is that by getting more involved with the people and the culture of the communities they supervise, the police become more effective in preventing and controlling crime. It does demand that the police develop more positive attitudes toward the members of the community, and that, in turn, community members begin viewing the police in a more positive way. The process is therefore reciprocal. The members of the community must be equally involved with the police and be ready to work closely with the police in a joint effort to deter and solve crime. The community must be persuaded that this is a cooperative effort to increase their own safety and preserve order in their own neighborhoods. The goal of this effort is to create a police-public partnership aimed at reducing crime and establishing neighborhood security. One veteran police officer has listed steps that can be taken to help strengthen the police-community bond

1. Talk to the people and ask how they are doing.

2. Become a guest speaker at local organizations.
3. Become a member of at least one local organization.
4. Join a service organization such as the "Habitat for Humanity"
5. Donate time and/or money to local charities (Murgado, 2013).

Community policing is said to break down the barriers between police and the community, to engage people and groups who don't usually get consulted and change both police and community attitudes toward each other. There is also a federal program called COPS (Community Oriented Policing Services) that has provided huge amounts of money (in the billions) to move this initiative forward. As community-police experts Skolnick and Bayley have said, "Policing should be grounded on the notion that together the police and the public can be a more effective and a more humane co-producer of safety and public order than can the police alone" (Skolnick & Bayley, 1988). Before leaving this section, spend a few minutes reviewing Sir Robert Peels' NINE principles of police behavior. As you can see, Peel could be viewed as the father of community policing.

Neighborhood Watch: The Eyes of the Law - not the Muscle
As a community-policing side effect, there is now a movement called the "Neighborhood Watch," a national program that solicits volunteers to patrol their own neighborhoods and report any suspicious activity. Members are instructed not to confront a possible suspect nor attempt any heroic citizens' arrests. The volunteer's job is to call the police, not apprehend the suspects or take the law into their own hands. Neighborhood watch programs distribute many signs and window decals warning possible intruders that the "watch" program is in effect.

The Critics Speak
Although community policing has become very popular in recent years and its proponents have heaped it with high praise, there are still those who are unconvinced. For example critics have said that community policing puts too much on the backs of police personnel, that the police can't balance the job of being both social workers as well as arresting officers. After all, law enforcement must be judgmental. Even though there is testimonial evidence for the effectiveness of community policing, the empirical evidence is not so convincing. When the quantitative evidence is placed under the high-powered lens of statistical scrutiny, no significant difference in crime rates has been found between those areas where community policing efforts were in effect versus those areas covered by conventional policing methods (Mulhausen, 2011). It seems that what ought to be isn't always what is.

DARE – Drug Abuse Resistance Education in the Schools
DARE came into being in 1983 with great fanfare and the fond hope of eliminating or at least reducing drug abuse and its associated criminal compo-

nents. Police officers were selected and sent to 40-hour training sessions to prepare themselves to lead these drug awareness groups in school systems all over the country. The children who participated had to swear an oath not to take drugs, join gangs, or ever be violent. In 2004, however, the U.S. Department of Education began demanding proof that the program worked before there could be any further funding. But, alas, there were absolutely no studies that could prove that DARE had any impact on drug use, and in fact there were some that showed a boomerang effect which in fact increased drug use (Lilienfeld, 2007). The program began quietly making changes that are said to increase effectiveness but to date have not yet been fully evaluated.

Researching Crime: Kansas City and Flint Michigan

In one famous criminal justice experiment, areas of a city (Kansas City) were matched for ethnicity, income, calls for service and crime rates, and then designated as to various levels of police presence (Kelling, 1974). Based on the area assigned, the police were asked to be proactive, reactive, or used in a control situation (where the area was treated as business as usual). The area's police treatment was, of course, seen as the causal variable, and the resulting crime rate was to be the effect. In the proactive area, there was a marked increase in police presence, with more patrol cars (and more visibility of the patrol cars). In the reactive area, the police only entered in response to citizen calls for help, and in the control area the typical level of patrol activity was maintained. It was bold and, at the time, a very innovative study. However the results, unfortunately, showed no difference in crime rates as a result of the differential treatments. There were also no differences in arrests, citizen fears, traffic accidents or the time it took police to answer calls. In short, the variations in police response did not influence any of the hoped-for effects.

In Flint, Michigan, an early attempt was put forward to implement and study the effects of community policing (Trojanowicz, 1982). Officers were ordered to get out of their cars and join neighborhood foot patrols. Although this program produced significant positive differences in police attitudes toward community members and vice versa, the drop in crime was minimal - less than the tax payers had expected. It may be that Flint Michigan is not the best model for show-casing community policing, since for three years in a row, 2011, 2012, and 2013, Flint led the nation (for cities of 100,000 or more) in rates of violent crime. There are even some skeptics who say that police officers, no matter how many deployed, cannot reduce crime rates, because the problem can only be solved by a change in societal attitudes and a thorough sociological understanding of the roots of crime.

Profiling Drivers

One researcher compared the number of drivers' citations issued by the police to the number of persons in the driving population for various demographic characteristics, such as gender (Farrell et al, 2004). It was found that males, especially young males, were being stopped, cited, and searched at a rate that was disproportionate to their total numbers. One interpretation of these data was that the police were "profiling" male drivers or ambushing young males in general rather than focusing on any individualized suspicion of the driver's behavior. Another interpretation might be that driving behavior itself may differ across age and gender groups. Driving patterns may not be the same for a young 21-year-old male and his 60 year-old grandmother. Other studies have shown that young males are overrepresented when it comes to risk-taking behavior in general. One government study of over 40,000 persons found that males between the ages of 18 and 25 are three times as likely as women not to wear seat belts. The study also found less seat-belt use among lower income groups, especially among those with low levels of education and fewer employment opportunities (Chu, 2005). The police also use many exterior cues before ordering a stop, such as broken tail lights and missing registration tags. Perhaps young males are also less careful about vehicle repairs than are members of other demographic groups.

Routine Traffic Stops?

Newspaper accounts of police activity often refer to something they call routine traffic stops. These are street and highway vehicle stops that are considered safe and virtually automatic. However, law enforcement disagrees vehemently and maintains that there is no such thing as a routine traffic stop. Whenever a car is pulled over it creates the potential for an explosive situation. Veteran police officers talk of vehicle stops (along with checking an unlocked building or home), as one of the most unnerving of all their activities (Murgado, 2012). The officer is stepping into the unknown and never knows if there might be weapons and contraband in the car, and whether the occupants may decide to resist, sometimes deciding to shoot it out rather than go submissively. When pulling over a driver, officers are urged to always remember to use the radio first and report the TLC – tags, location, and car color (also the number of occupants if they can be observed). Unless it's called in first, problems could occur during the stop, and the officer's location might remain unknown. To underline the danger, LEOKA (Law Enforcement Officers Killed or Assaulted) reports that in a recent nine-year period, traffic stops led to 95 officers being killed and almost 5000 being assaulted.

In the Line of Duty

Although this may leave you more shaken than stirred, you must realize that the James-Bond, high-speed car chases and running gun battles are not the norm, and in fact are really relatively rare. And yet the life of a police officer is certainly filled with the potential for danger. As one expert in law enforcement phrased it "a police officer's work is filled with long hours of sheer boredom, punctuated by moments of sheer terror" (Lab et al, 2008). Officers often complain about the boredom of writing and filing voluminous police reports. But every investigation and every arrest has to be followed by the filing of a written report.

Nevertheless, when the terror comes, it is real. As illustrative of this point, the National Law Enforcement Memorial in Washington DC now contains the names of over 14,000 officers who were killed in the line of duty. Of those who were killed, almost 50% were killed by gun fire with another 30% killed by vehicle accidents, and 10% by vehicles deliberately aimed at them. The FBI's yearly report of Law Enforcement Officers Killed or Assaulted (the same LEOKA mentioned above) is another sad reminder of the dangers lying in wait for police professionals. In 2011 of those officers killed by firearms, 43% were shot in the head. There is currently a serious move afoot suggesting that police officers be required to wear ballistic helmets. LEOKA also tells us whether the officers were wearing body armor or while driving if seat belts were in place. Although some police fatalities may be unavoidable, every effort should be made to keep these numbers as low as possible (Griffith, 2012). An interesting aside shows that whereas armed citizens shoot the wrong person less than 3% of the time, police officers do so 11% of the time (Poe,2001). Some have interpreted this to mean that police officers are more careless and less vigilant than are armed citizens. Critics of this interpretation are quick to point out that civilians can pick and choose whether to get involved in the situation in the first place. They can avoid situations that are confusing and extremely threatening. Police, however, must take action every time and thus are put in situations where guilt or innocence are not always clear cut, and in which the chance for mistakes is far higher

The Police Personality

Is there an overall police personality, and if so, do these personality characteristics occur as a result of police training and environmental stressors, or are they already a part of the young recruit before becoming an officer? If the latter is true, perhaps it's this very factor that caused the person to seek out police work at the outset. Let's spend a few moments looking at what personality is and whether it is at all malleable.

First, personality is best defined as a person's unique constellation of patterns of thinking feeling and behaving, and it affects virtually every aspect of one's life. Second, though researchers tell us there is an innate genetic pattern for the origin of personality, it actually develops through environmental experience, especially social interactions. Studies conducted over the past several years have found that police officers have above average levels of the following traits: suspiciousness, conservatism, cynicism, assertiveness, action-orientation and pragmatism (Shannon, 2010). The fact that a police officer is unusually suspicious is almost surely an occupational asset (Twersky-

Glassner, 2005) but this trait in some other jobs might even be detrimental. Although a trait such as cynicism may exist even in the police recruit, it almost certainly develops and grows as the officer has increased experience with criminals. Police officers have also been found to view emotional expression in another person as a deficit and weakness, whereas the same trait would be an asset in some other jobs, such as a psychologist. There are also some data that suggest that the police officer is also a high-risk taker, a trait which again certainly fits the demands of the job (Cullen, et al 1987). Others have pointed out that the police personality contains a large degree of both authoritarianism and a need for dominance. Authoritarianism, however, has been shown to lessen as the police officer gains more on-the-job experience, (Laguna, et al, 2012). Day after day of seeing and arresting criminals (some, over and over) probably does not generate the traits associated with happy optimism. Despite the dangers and burdens of the job, however, perhaps the police have stronger, more healthy, personalities for dealing with such stressors than might be found among those in the general public (Terry, 1991). It's not everyone who can handle this stress level.

Stress Indicators
Studies aimed at determining stress levels among police officers versus the general public typically utilize three assessment measures: suicide, divorce rates, and alcoholism.

Suicide
Available data on suicide rates are decidedly mixed. Because life-insurance companies do not honor insurance policies when death is determined to be by suicide, there may be some deaths that are misreported. However, there seems to be a consensus that police officers have higher suicide rates, 17 per 100,000, than is true in the general population, 11.5 per 100,000. But when statistical controls are used for equating the groups on the basis of age, gender and race, the difference becomes significantly lower (Sheehan & Warren, (2002).

Divorce
Though many have assumed that because of the stresses of the job, divorce rates and domestic abuse might be higher among officers of the law, the data seem to dispute that theory (McCoy & Aamodt, 2010). Using data from the U.S. Census, researchers compared the divorce rate for law enforcement professionals with those for other occupations. After controlling for age, ethnicity and numerous other job-related variables, it was found that the divorce rate for police officers was in fact lower than that of the population at large. This was also found for levels of domestic abuse, with law enforcement proving to have lower levels than was the case for persons in other jobs.

Alcoholism

The rates for DUI or DWI (driving under the influence or driving while intoxicated) seem to be lower for police officers than for the public at large. One must be reminded, however, that it's fellow officers who are stopping the drivers and issuing the citations. That is, the off-duty driver and the on-duty officer are both members of the same team and also the referees. In an earlier section of the chapter, the "Blue Wall of Silence" was used to illustrate an example of the police sub-culture that virtually demands that cops don't tell on cops. Because of this possibility, these driving-alcohol data may not be fully trusted. However, the rates of treatment for alcohol addiction do seem to be higher for police officers than for the general population.

Arms and the Man and/or Woman

Whereas the traditional police weapon has been the 9mm or .38 caliber revolver (the Police Special) , there has been a recent move to increase police fire power by issuing 45 caliber semi-automatic pistols. In some gun battles the police can be simply overwhelmed by superior fire power. In one famous example, Los Angeles police officers were faced with a pair of bank robbers wearing body armor and carrying AK 47 assault rifles - with armor-piercing ammunition and 100 clip magazines. The outgunned police officers were finally successful, but only after they called up the SWAT team's armored personnel carrier. The entire fire fight took over 20 minutes and was broadcast live on TV.

The police also do have a number of non-lethal techniques for preventing a suspect from escaping. For example, police may use such items as the stun gun (especially the Taser), tranquilizing darts, incapacitating gas, or even the old reliable tactical baton (night stick). These can be extremely effective in subduing a disruptive or fleeing suspect. For example the Taser can incapacitate a suspect from a distance of several feet by causing the suspect to experience strong, involuntary muscle contractions. The Taser can be set in either the "Drive Stun" mode (which can inflict serious pain) or the Non-Pain mode.

The Sting

The sting is a police operation aimed at catching the suspect by setting up a deceptive ploy to lure the supposed perpetrator into action. The police officer, in plain clothes, might pretend to be someone who himself is involved in criminal activities and is therefore seeking some kind of partnership with the suspect. Sting operations are allowed in the United States, but they must avoid any semblance of entrapment. That is, the techniques must be clearly aimed at catching the thief, not provoking the thief into creating a crime.

The John Detail

One form of the sting is to use young, female undercover officers posing as prostitutes in order to identify and arrest pleasure-seeking men (known as "johns"). These are men who are cruising around trying to look for and pay for sexual favors. Or, it could go the other way around, where a young male officer is used to pose as a john in order to discover the location of a certain "house of ill-fame" – often known as a "brothel."

The following case study was written especially for this volume by Thomas F. Fitzgerald, Professor of Criminal Justice at American International College, in Springfield MA.

Case Study of a Sting

Wilma M. was a middle-aged police sergeant who had come up through the ranks, but had at times complained about her rate of promotion, claiming she had been discriminated against because of her gender. One early evening she volunteered to be part of a sting operation aimed at arresting "johns" (men prospecting for prostitutes). She dressed herself in as provocative a manner as was possible for a woman of her age and weight. Two male officers dutifully, but doubtfully, drove her to a prearranged location on a city street corner. They parked the patrol car out of sight, and spent the next two hours watching and waiting. But during that time, nobody approached her, nor did any car even slow down. When the officers drove over to pick her up and bring her back to the station, she protested vigorously saying they hadn't given her enough time. The male officers stifled their laughter and brought her back. The news of her failure had somehow preceded her, and there was a group of officers waiting for her in the hallway, and feigning a happy welcome home.

Types and Levels of Police Departments

Metropolitan, City, and Town

These departments are at the town or city level, and range in size from a small town's one-officer agency to the almost fifty thousand members of New York City's police department. Most metropolitan and town departments act cooperatively with other agencies and share jurisdiction. These cooperating departments are sometimes called task forces, and they help to centralize the overall command and prevent the outrage of a fleeing suspect thumbing his nose at his pursuers as he crosses the city or state line. The metropolitan police take their name from the city or town they serve, such as the (BPD) Boston Police Department, or the smaller (LPD) Longmeadow Police Department (both serving areas of Massachusetts).

Large city police departments usually organize around a chain of command that starts from the Chief at the top. The Chief (sometimes in larger departments called the "Commissioner") plans and organizes the administrative direction for all police services, including security and overall law enforcement. The Chief also provides cooperative services with other city departments, and is involved in the preparation of the budget. Next comes the

Deputy Chiefs, as many as a dozen. These are the Chief's stalwart backups. The Chief depends on the Deputies for quick answers and detailed strategies. By covering his back and carrying out some of his many duties, the deputies allow the chief time to think out solutions and assign responsibilities. Just under the Deputies are the Captains. The Captains work as subordinates to the Chief and Deputies, and have as their primary responsibility, management duties, rather than direct responses to calls for service (although that's also possible during emergency situations). Directly under the Captain is the Lieutenant, who works in a mid-management position and supervises patrol and investigative services. The Lieutenant is in charge of the training of both sworn and unsworn staff members. The Sergeant is next in line, and supervises and evaluates the work of both Corporals and Police Officers. This job also entails preparing cases for court (and may involve personally testifying). The Sergeant still has the responsibility of responding to service calls. Just below the Sergeant is the Corporal, whose job entails a wide variety of police duties, such as crime prevention, enforcing laws and ordinances, court appearances, and investigating crime. The Corporal may assume the Sergeant's supervisory responsibility if the Sergeant is not available. Finally there is the Police Officer, who is usually the face of the police department to the public. The Officer performs a long list of non-supervisory jobs, such as street and patrol duties, and preparation of court cases. The Officer provides assistance and information to the public, and is usually a first responder when needed. Examinations (some are Civil Service) must be taken at each level and, of course, must be passed. Obviously, the organization of a police department is quite different in small towns, where in some cases there is only one sworn officer (who must wear many hats). However, there are very few local police departments who don't require a four-year college degree, so if you're serious about choosing this career – stay in school.

As a point of interest in this high-tech age, most metropolitan police departments are now using data-driven response systems, where statistical data are analyzed, trends spotted, and appropriate police responses put into action. One of the first to use this method was the New York City Police Department's program called CompStat, the acronym standing for Comparative Statistics (Henry, 2002). The program was designed to utilize a data bank from which statistical deductions could be made regarding police reactions, targeting both the city area and the resources necessary for intervention. In order to spot any changes in criminal activity, new, up-dated information is constantly fed into the program In effect, it profiles the city and calculates the probabilities of various response options and their chances of success.

But all is not serene out there in number land. Although CompStat can be an effective tool in managing response options, the numbers it spews out are being used for far more than that. In fact, in some departments the numbers have become, not just guides, but the rules themselves in virtually every aspect of enforcement, To begin with, the budget negotiations with the mayor or town council can be determined by what are now called "performance-based standards" and these are based on everything from numbers of arrests to the numbers of still-unresolved cases. Even though the phrase "performance-based- standards" is used as a proxy for quotas, it has been alleged that patrol officers have actually been given citation quotas. As one critic puts it, "Modern police budgeting and management have become an exercise in statistical analysis, manipulation of data, CompStat presentations and control. It is not about public safety or what the men and women of the agency actually put on the line for their society. It's about the numbers they produce" (Libicer, 2013, p16).

Private Police and Campus Police

There is also a private category of police, that is, police departments and agencies that work directly for businesses, corporations, railroads and the like rather than for any form of government. Private police are paid by the employer, not the tax payer. An example of private police that you probably see every day is your own campus police. In some states campus police can be armed, as in Virginia, and be sworn with full powers of arrest, as in Rhode Island.

Detective

Detectives are criminal investigators, usually in plain clothes, who collect evidence and prepare court cases. Most detectives have already attained the rank of Sergeant, and have also attended a law enforcement academy. When first on the job, the fledgling detective goes through a probationary period and works under the guidance of a field training officer (a training period that can last up to two years). Although not a first responder to the crime, the detective goes through the crime scene thoroughly and collects and preserves evidence, interviews and interrogates suspects and witnesses, writes a detailed report, and provides testimony in court.

Any evidence collected at the crime scene must be handled with great care, and each transfer of the evidence from, say, one officer to another (and eventually on to the Evidence Clerk for storage) must be fully documented, including the time and date for when it was passed along. The integrity of the evidence must be scrupulously guarded in order to avoid any charge of tampering. Evidence integrity is important in both criminal and civil cases.

County Police

County law enforcement can be maintained by either the County Police, or far more often, by the Sheriff's Deputies. The Sheriff's Department is typically the basic arm of law enforcement at the county level. The Sheriff acts as the chief of police in the county, and the deputies act as the officers. Unlike the chiefs of police, however, the sheriff is usually elected by the people of the county. The sheriff's department has certain specific tasks, as well as those that are shared with the local police departments. The specific tasks include the following: being in charge of the county jail, bringing prisoners from the jail to and from court appearances, serving court writs, serving eviction notices to behind-payments home owners, and finally as patrol officers (often working in concert with police officers). Sheriff's deputies are sworn officers of the law, and of course have arrest powers throughout the county.

State Police

The largest law enforcement agency at the state level is the State Police Department, which is organized into smaller geographic units called "Troops," hence the name "Troopers." The majority of state-police work consists of keeping our roads safe by patrolling the highways, especially inter-state highways and connections. When a state police officer detects a violation, a citation may be issued that can result in fines and even the loss of license. The state police do far more than just patrolling highways. They are also called upon to handle a wide variety of situations, including locating missing persons, finding escaped felons and, on occasion, engaging in fire fights when the situation demands it.

A Bit of Whimsy: Could It Happen?

A young man, late for work, and driving on an Interstate highway with its speed limit of 65 MPH, suddenly heard a siren and saw the accompanying flashing blue lights. He quickly pulled over, and when the state-police officer stood beside him, pad and pen in hand, he politely asked the officer what the problem was. The trooper replied tersely "speeding." The young man said that he was only going 70, and that usually the police allow for that slight margin of error. The trooper replied that he clocked him at 82, and that was beyond any margin he ever allowed. Finally, the young man pleaded that there were other cars going at that same rate, and he had even seen a car pass him "like I was standing still." "Why didn't you pull them over"? Handing the young man a ticket, the trooper asked, "Did you ever go fishing?" The young man acknowledged that he had on occasion gone out on a fishing trip. The trooper, now smiling broadly, asked, "Did you catch all the fish in the sea?" "No" admitted the young man. The trooper replied simply "case closed."

Federal Law Enforcement

Federal law enforcement crosses state lines and is supposed to be involved in only those laws that are listed in the (CFR), United States Code of Federal Regulations. The CFR includes about 200 federal crimes. Two examples of these are kidnapping and bank robbery. Most federal law enforcement is organized under the auspices of the Department of Justice (DOJ), and includes the F.B.I. (Federal Bureau of Investigation), the DEA (Drug Enforcement Administration) ,the A.T.F. (Bureau of Alcohol, Tobacco Firearms and Explosives), the U.S. Marshall's Service, and the BOP (Bureau of Prisons). Also, at the federal level is the Department of Homeland Security (DHS), originally organized in response to the terrorist attack of 9/11. Homeland Security includes – Immigration and Customs Enforcement (ICE), the U.S. Customs and Border Protection (CPB), the United States Secret Service ,and the Transportation Security Service. (which includes the famous Sky Marshalls). The FBI is currently spending much of its resources in an attempt to solve the severe problems inherent in high-tech, cyber-crimes.

Today's high-tech age has brought on new problems, and even some old problems dressed in new disguises. Foreign nationals, as well as some mis-guided U.S. citizens, have recently been engaging in world-wide cyber- at-tacks, using computer programmers and hackers to pry information out of the U.S. military, the U.S. state department, as well as corporate computers – even you or your local bank could be targeted.

Over the last ten years, the FBI has assembled a team of hundreds of computer professionals whose expertise in information technology is of the highest order. The FBI now leads a federal group called the National Cyber Investigative Joint Task Force (NCIJTF), an organization designed to investigate and curtail cyber threats from nation-states, terrorist organizations, and both foreign and domestic criminal enterprises. The task force has the job of identifying, mitigating and disrupting cyber threats.

A PERSON OF INTEREST: J. EDGAR HOOVER (1895-1972)

J. Edgar Hoover was the FBI's (Federal Bureau of Investigation) first and most famous director. He gained wide-spread media attention during the 1930s when his agents were able to capture (and sometimes kill in shoot-outs) such notorious gangsters as John Dillinger, Bonnie and Clyde, Pretty Boy Floyd, and Baby Face Nelson. Hoover became the symbol for crime-fighting, and his power grew exponentially. He often by-passed his nominal boss, the Attorney General, and went straight to the president for help and advice. Although he remained a bachelor, he also drew attention for his flamboyant life style, such as dating Hollywood's most glamorous actresses (despite rumors of bi-sexual orientation). Hoover saw Communism as a danger to the country, and he aggressively went after all those he considered to be active subversives, and sometimes even their sympathizers. Other groups that he targeted were The Klu Klux Klan, the Black Panthers and the Socialist Workers Party. Over the years Hoover also did secret investigations of various political figures, and it has been alleged that he used that information to increase his own political power. During the 1960s Attorney General Robert Kennedy ordered Hoover to tap Martin Luther King's phone in order to get any personal information that might be incriminating and possibly useful to the Kennedys as a political power advantage. He worked closely with local police departments throughout the country and provided them with the latest scientific methods for fighting crime. He set up the country's largest fingerprint and DNA data bases. Although critics accused him of being a secret cross dresser and perhaps homosexual, these issues were never verified.

The FBI also engages in behavioral profiling. Behavioral profiling has become a very important analytic tool, a tool that has saved many lives. The FBI's Behavioral and Analysis Department in Stafford, Virginia (near Quantico) is divided into three units; internal terrorist threats, crimes against adults, and crimes against children. Since human beings, good and bad, are largely creatures of habit, behavioral analysts look for certain, often unique, patterns of behavior. Criminals are usually betrayed by their characteristic actions, not their words. FBI profilers analyze enormous data files and attempt to match certain aspects of the crime with their statistical computer data. By correlating evidence at the crime scene with information in the data bank, profilers can sometimes narrow the search, and in some cases narrow it to the point of such uncanny accuracy as to seem almost clairvoyant (Kessler, 2008).

Going Forward

The U.S. Bureau of Labor Statistics states that there are currently well over a million persons working in law enforcement at the city-town, state, and federal levels. They also estimate that from now until 2020, there will be an increase in the number of law- enforcement personnel employed in this country. This rather optimistic forecast is based largely on both economics and society's demands for increased security. This is especially true at the local level. Whereas state and federal jobs may face increased competition, continued demand for public safety will generate new opportunities at the local level. These forecasts, of course, are not set in stone, and could be revised based on a number of factors, such as

1. A strengthening economy could lead to increases in government revenue – which could dramatically increase job opportunities in law enforcement.

2. Significant changes in the crime rate could change the job picture. If the crime rate were to increase, it could put increasing pressures on the government to provide society with more security. However, if crime rates went

down, it might possibly lead to a smaller increase in the numbers of law-enforcement.

3. Changes in the law could change the crime rate by redefining areas of legality. If there were legislative changes that alter the definition of various violations, such as legalizing certain drugs such as marijuana there could be less crime to enforce. This would, in effect, mean that legislation itself could therefore reduce some crimes rates, in this case drug crimes. On the positive side, this could free up law enforcement to spend more time on other more serious felonies, such as crimes of violence.

Summary

This chapter puts the spotlight on law enforcement and opens with a discussion of the three Cs, Cops, Courts and Corrections, which is the order in which a felon would be greeted by the criminal justice system. This chapter is about that first C - Cops.

Although it's only one of the levels of law enforcement, the majority of police work is actually conducted at the local (metropolitan, town and/or city) level. The police are charged, first and foremost, with enforcing the law. The legal system was examined on the basis of two dichotomies: state versus federal and criminal versus civil. The U.S. Constitution allows the states to have their own laws that may differ from federal law. However, the states may not have any laws that violate the U. S Constitution. Federal law governs the entire country, and at the federal level the laws to be enforced are those contained in the C.F.R. or Code of Federal Regulations. When violations of criminal law occur the offender may face detention (a person can get locked up for violating criminal law). Civil law contains those provisions that allow a person to sue another person or group of persons for damages brought about by the wrongful acts of another. The usual penalty is monetary. The next section outlines the duties of the police officer such as maintaining order, law enforcement, controlling a crowd and providing services. Finally the police are always asked to be involved in crime prevention.

A brief history of police organizations includes the Nine Principles of Police Behavior written almost two hundred years ago by London's first chief, Sir Robert Peel. This is the same Robert after whom the English police (Bobbies) are named. The London police force under Peel's guidance is said to be the first department to have a modern organization according to standards that still apply today. The first U.S. police department is said to have originated in Boston, Massachusetts. It was in Boston (in 1919) where the police attempted to go out on strike for higher wages and better working conditions, but the governor (Calvin Coolidge) ruled that the strike was illegal because of its threat to public safety. During the 1930s the Wickersham Commission was formed. This was an investigative body that looked into all areas of the criminal justice system, especially corrections and cops. The police were subjected to a scathing denouncement based on the Commission's uncovering of blatant corruption and the use of torturous grilling tactics. The report did lead to a number of prosecutions and indictments - and produced many changes for the better. Of the many people involved in the overall business of law enforcement, only those who are sworn are allowed to have powers of arrest. These officers swear to uphold the constitutions of the state and nation. Police officers are allowed to use some level of force when attempting to control a suspect. Veteran police, however, say a better method is to "sweet talk" the suspect, in which case nobody gets hurt. There have been several examples of the police using too much force, perhaps even brutality. The cases of both Rodney King and Abner Louima were used as illustrations. The use of deadly force as a last resort has been defined and limited by both the Supreme Court and a federal order. In separate cases, the Court said that deadly force may never be used to prevent a suspect's escape and that its use must be evaluated in the light of the changing circumstances, not 20/20 hindsight. Finally a federal order stated that deadly force can only be used when the lives of the officers or others are in imminent danger. One fairly recent (over the past several decades) trend in policing is something called COPS, for Community Oriented Police Systems. Officers are urged to get out of their patrol cars, and walk through neighborhoods and interact with the citizens. The concept is based on the theory that the police and community working interactively are better able to solve and prevent crime than either could alone. Critics counter that the police are not trained to be social workers and should spend their time on enforcement not as therapists. Studies have not shown any reduction in crime as a result of the community policing initiative. A byproduct of community policing is something called the Neighborhood Watch, where the community attempts to police itself by having citizen-volunteers patrol their own streets. They are only supposed to alert police to any problems, not attempt any sort of citizen confrontation or arrest. In 1983 the police became involved as teacher-counselors in a program called DARE (Drug Abuse Resistance Education) that was alleged to reduce drug use among school children. Unfortunately there were no studies that could provide evidence supporting this claim. Two quantitative studies, Kansas City and Flint Michigan, were cited showing the difficulty of establishing techniques that can be proven as crime reducers. The Flint Michigan study showed a slight decrease in crime as a result of community policing. The Kansas City study used an assortment of differing police methods (such as cruiser visibility), but showed no resulting crime reduction. Veteran police officers warn young officers that there is no such thing as a routine traffic stop, since each one has the potential for trouble. The hazards of police duty were illustrated by data supplied by the National Law Enforcement Memorial in Washington DC, which contains the names of over 14,000 officers who were killed in the line of duty. Also the FBI's yearly report of Law Enforcement Officers Killed or Assaulted (LEOKA) shows that 43% of those killed by gun fire were shot in the head – a fact that has led to urging officers to wear protective helmets. Whether there is a police personality that attracts people to the job or traits that are acquired on the job was examined, but no solid conclusions were offered. The following traits: suspiciousness, conservatism, cynicism, assertiveness, action-orientation, pragmatism and authoritarianism were found among many officers. Some of these traits are obviously a benefit for someone involved in police work. Certainly suspiciousness is almost surely an asset in this profession. Because law enforcement has to contend with so many on-the-job stress situations, studies examined three possible stress indicators: suicide, divorce and alcoholism. The only significant difference was found for alcohol-treatment rates, somewhat higher for police officers. Some fire fights have found the police facing superior fire power and have led to departments now issuing 45 caliber semi-automatic pistols (and even assault rifles). Before becoming a law-enforcement agent, the individual is trained at a police Academy where educational and physical requirements are stressed. There are also private police organizations, where an agent works, not for the government, but for a private company or corporation. Your own Campus Police are an example of private policing. The types and levels of government police include: 1. Metropolitan - City and Town, (which along with the state police are the largest law enforcers in terms of numbers). These departments have recently turned to data-driven response analysis, or the use of computer-generated statistics to predict the most advantageous responses. 2. County – usually covered by the Sheriff's Department and its cohort of Deputies. 3. State – most commonly the state police (troopers). 4. Federal – encompassing a large number of agencies and departments. At the federal level, two aspects of the FBI's crime-fighting efforts were examined: The Cyber Crime unit, using information technologies to fight the new battle against computer hacking by criminals and terrorists and the FBI's profiling team who have had extraordinary success in narrowing the crime search to (sometimes) a single individual .

As we look forward, the Bureau of Justice estimates are for an increase in law-enforcement jobs from now to 2020. Although the rate of increase in jobs may be lower at the state and federal level, there are projected to be many opportunities at the town-city level. There are, however, several variables that could change these estimates, such as a growing economy, a change in crime rates, or a legislative change that would redefine what is considered to be legal, such as a change in drug laws.

Key Terms

Blue Wall of Silence
Department
Civil Law
Community Policing

References

Aamodt, M.G. & Stalnaker, N.A. (2002). Police officer suicide: frequency and officer profiles. In Sheehan, D, & Warren, J. (Eds) *Suicide and Law Enforcement.* Washington DC: U.S. Government Printing Office.

Cullen, P.T., Link, B. G., Travis L.F. & Lemming, T. (1987). Paradox in policing: Perceptions of danger. *Journal of Police Science and Administration, 11,* 457-462

Graham v Conner, 490 U.S. 396-397 (1989)

Griffith,D. (2012). Beyond the numbers. *Police Magazine,* December.

Henry, V.E. (2002). *The compstat paradigm: management accountability in policing, business and the public sector.* Flushing, NY: Looseleaf Pub.

Kelling, G.L., Pate,T., Dieckman, D. & Brown, C.E. (1974). *The Kansas city patrol experiment.* Washington DC: The Police Foundation

Laguna, L. Kinn, A., Ward, K. & Rupslankyte, R. (2012). An examination of authoritarianism traits among police officers: The role of experience. *Journal of Police and Criminal Psychology, 25,* 99-104.

Libicer, S.R. (2013). Bring back qualitative policing. *National Academy Associates,* May/June, 3, 14-19.

Lilienfeld, S.O. (2007). Psychological treatment that causes harm . *Perspective on Psychology Science, 2,* 53-70.

McCoy, S.P. & Aamodt,M.G., 2010. A comparison of law enforcement divorce rates with those of other occupations. *Journal of Police & Criminal Psychology*. *25*, 1-16

Murgado, A. (2012). Traffic stops. *Police Magazine*, November.

Murgado, A. (2013), Community involvement. *Police Magazine*, June

Plato, (circa 380BC). *The Republic*

Skolnick, J. H. & Bailey, D.H. (1988). *Community policing issues and practices around the world.* Washington, DC: National Institute of Justice

Tennessee v Garner, 471 U.S. (1985)

Terry, W.C. (1991) Police stress: The empirical evidence. *Journal of Police and Science and Administration, 9*, 61-75.

Trojanowicz, R.C. (1982). *An evaluation of the neighborhood foot patrol in Flint Michigan.* East Lansing, Michigan: The National Neighborhood Foot Patrol Center, Michigan State University.

Twersky-Glassner, A. (2005). Police personality: What is it and why are they like that? *Journal of Police and Criminal Psychology, 20*, 342-355

CHAPTER 5

THE COURT SYSTEM

Order in the Court

This is the second C in that "CCC" series, Cops, Courts, and Corrections. You probably didn't sign up for this course in order to be put through the rigors of law school. However, it is critical that if you really want to venture into some area within the criminal justice system, you really have to become familiar with some of the basics of our court systems. You may even have to go court yourself someday for some reason, and the list of reasons is almost endless: you might be a victim, or you might have assaulted someone (obviously in your case the other person deserved it), or you might be a witness, or you may even be sued. The odds are that you will at some level become a participant in the legal system, and if you go into some form of law enforcement the probability of involvement becomes a certainty. So turn off the TV and the cell phone because the judge has just called for "Order in the Court".

Order in the Court: An Introduction

TV shows such as "Law and Order" or "CSI" might give you the impression that law enforcement solves crimes within an hour, or at the most a week, that court systems move quickly, all cases go to trial, and that the courtroom proceedings are compelling and riveting. You know who the "bad guys" are and they are quickly punished. Go to your local courthouse and observe criminal proceedings. You might be shocked at how long each case takes as it winds its way through the system. Actually you might be even more shocked to discover how few cases actually go to trial and how busy the courts and attorneys are. Did you know that before a case even gets to court the ground work necessary by law enforcement can be painstaking and tedious involving untold hours, months and even years?

The Background

To better understand how the court process works let's start with some background. As said earlier, the American system of jurisprudence has its roots in what is called the British "common law," which is derived from the British practice of organizing and combining the various local legal customs and traditions (many unwritten at the time) in order to provide a common basis for the entire nation. The origin of this process dates back to the Norman invasion of England (circa 1066) when William the Conqueror wanted to gain some fair and consistent legal control.

However it is the US Constitution which sets American law apart from the rest of the world. The Constitution defines the judiciary as one of the three branches of government: the executive branch (the President), the legislative branch (Congress) and the judicial branch (Courts). The American legal system provides a vehicle for its citizens to bring complaints against each other, corporations or the government to the courts for adjudication (final decision), and for the government to protect its citizens by bringing lawsuits on the public's behalf (remember the BP oil spill ?). Lady Justice symbolizes the expectation that justice and truth will prevail, and that the courts will render impartial and fair decisions. Lady Justice is always shown as blindfolded, indicating that only the facts specific to the case before the court are relevant, and personal bias does not impact upon judgment. She holds the scales of justice upon which evidence is weighed and balanced, and the rights of all parties are taken into consideration. In a perfect world "truth" is discovered, and the outcome of any particular case would be the same regardless of where the case was heard. However, humans are unpredictable and divergent. Perception, prejudice, and the subjectivity with which each person views the world come into play in each and every case. Judges, jurors, witnesses, attorneys, plaintiffs and defendants are impacted by their upbringing and life experiences, which greatly influence how cases are presented and decisions are rendered. The same case heard by different juries and judges may have dramatically different outcomes.

Fundamental Civil Rights

Ours is an adversarial system in which two opposing parties (prosecution and defense) present their positions in front of a neutral party, the judge and/or jury. This system places great value on due process, assuring that innocent persons are not charged and punished without proper evidence and a right to cross examine that evidence and present a defense. "Innocent until proven guilty" is one of the basic tenets of our criminal justice system. Our Constitution's Bill of Rights' fifth and sixth amendments afford defendants (persons accused of crimes in which a case is filed with a court) procedural rights including the right against self-incrimination, the right to cross examine witnesses, the right to have a jury of one's peers, the right to a speedy trial, and the right to have an attorney.

Exhausting Remedies

The usual course of a case is for it to be tried at the trial court level, and, if further relief is sought, to be reviewed by an appeals court. The law, and rules and regulations, define specific pathways that must be followed in order to appeal a case. This requirement is provided in order to "exhaust remedies." For example, a defendant cannot file for an appeal at the US Supreme

Court until all of the underlying federal or state courts having jurisdiction in that particular case have been utilized or "exhausted." The term "jurisdiction" refers to the authority the courts have to hear various types of cases, rather than to any geographical area or region. The proper processes and procedures are set forth in federal and state laws and statutes (the federal law is also known as the federal code). The state and federal laws have corresponding rules of criminal procedure.

Federal Courts

The Federal Courts include (1) the United States Supreme Court, (2) the United States Courts of Appeal and (3) the United States District Courts. The US Constitution in Article 3, Section 1 gives federal courts jurisdiction over implementing the laws of the United States. State courts have jurisdiction over state laws. However, when a case involves commission of a crime spanning two states, or involves interstate commerce, authorities must decide whether to prosecute in federal or state court, because both courts might have jurisdiction. If a defendant is acquitted (found not guilty) by one court s/he cannot be tried again in another court for the same crime. This is known as "res judicata" - a final judgment by a court of competent jurisdiction is conclusive.

In a child pornography case, the defendant, Eric Achenbach, a popular Vermont high school teacher, was first charged by the state with possession of child pornography. Photo albums with pictures of children being sexually molested were found by some hunters in a tree house in the woods on Mr. Achenbach's property. He was first charged by Vermont state authorities with possession of child pornography, however, when it was discovered that the defendant used his computer to receive these photos the United States District Attorney's office took over the case charging him in federal court because the receipt of pornography via the internet is a form of interstate commerce. The state dropped its case and on December 28, 2011, in United States District Court in Rutland, Vermont, Mr. Achenbach entered a guilty plea to one count of receiving child pornography, in violation of 18 U.S.C. 2252(a)(2), and one count of possession of child pornography, in violation of 18 U.S.C. 2252(a)(4)(B). He was sentenced to serve 79-months of imprisonment, a lifetime term of supervised release, and was ordered to pay restitution to the victims of his offensive conduct in the amount of $33,126.83 (press release, from the Office of the United States Attorney for the District of Vermont, January 11, 2012.)

The United States Federal Court System

The US federal court system has 94 District Courts (each state has from one to four such courts with the District of Columbia having just one), 12 U.S. Courts of Appeal which are regionally based (and also known as circuit courts), and the court of last resort, which is the U.S. Supreme Court.

The District Courts

The District Courts are the trial courts and have one sitting judge. The Judge, or Judge and jury, hears the facts of the case. The facts are introduced into evidence through the testimony of witnesses who are subject to both direct and cross examination. The difference between direct and cross examination is that during examination a witness, who is under oath, is asked questions first by the prosecutor (direct examination) and then the defense counsel may question the same witness (cross examination). Also, when the defense is finished with a direct examination of a witness, the prosecutor may counter with a cross examination. Physical evidence may be presented and include documents, photographs, audio or video tapes, or other evidence such as a weapon or drugs seized by police. Oral and written arguments (called briefs and memoranda of law) by counsel (attorneys) for the prosecution and defense then summarize these facts, analyze the prevailing law and search past records to find out how other courts have decided similar cases (case law) in an effort to persuade the judge and jury to find in their side's favor.

The U.S. Courts of Appeal

The U.S. Courts of Appeal have jurisdiction to review federal and state appellate court cases on substantive and procedural issues involving the rights guaranteed by the US Constitution. Appellate courts do not re-try the case; rather they consider legal arguments regarding an error of law made at the trial level (for example, arguing that evidence admitted was actually inadmissible). They may also review the imposition of a sentence or other action which exceeded the authority of the lower court, or a trial court misinterpreting the case law. Due to the high volume of cases filed for appeal, many are decided without oral argument and are based only on written submissions by the parties. These submissions may include the briefs and transcripts and other records from the lower court. Appellate review is not guaranteed and a court may choose which cases it hears on appeal. Typically, a defendant has one guaranteed right of appeal and thereafter it is within the discretion of the court whether to accept the case for further review.

The United States Supreme Court

The US Supreme Court is the highest appellate court of the land. It is known as the "court of last resort" hearing appeals from both state and federal courts. The nine Supreme Court justices are appointed for life terms and may choose which cases to hear. Thousands of requests for review and appeal are filed each year and only a handful are chosen for review, usually those cases accepted involve important constitutional rights impacting the rights and liberties of citizens. Cases accepted by the Supreme Court may include factually similar matters in which lower courts have rendered different decisions, or have interpreted the law or constitution differently. Supreme

Court decisions have far-reaching consequence because the lower courts must follow the rulings of the Supreme Court. This is known as setting case precedence. Attorneys and judges at the trial level cite Supreme Court decisions in crafting arguments, briefs and opinions. Attorneys will use case precedent to argue that a decision by a higher level court is either the same as, or different from, the facts of the case they are presenting to a court. Interpretation of case law is crucial in all court cases and judges must decide how case precedence impacts each and every case they hear. Judges certainly do not want their decisions to be overturned on appeal.

State Courts
At the state level, the court systems include (1) the State Supreme Court, (2) the State Courts of Appeal, (3) Superior Court and (4) Trial Courts (District, Family, Probate Municipal, Drug, Juvenile and other specialty courts).

Trial Courts
Each of the 50 states has trial and appellate level courts similar to the federal system, including a top-tiered court in every state (usually known as that state's Supreme Court). Each state decides how many courts to have, what to name them, and how to allocate cases. For example, in Massachusetts its Probate Court hears divorce, wills and estates among other matters, and there is a separate Juvenile Court system. In Vermont it's the state court's Family Division that hears divorces and juvenile cases, whereas the Probate Division has jurisdiction over wills and estates. You will hear states' trial courts called by various names- District Courts, Criminal Courts, Municipal Courts, and Felony Courts.

Specialty Courts
Many states use specialized courts that hear only very specific types of cases. For example, Juvenile courts hear cases relating to children charged with crimes and CHINS petitions (Child In Need of Services). The CHINS petition is filed by the state when attempting to separate children from their parents due to abuse or neglect. Hearings in juvenile matters are confidential and are called closed hearings, because the records of these proceedings are not public records and only the parties directly involved with the case are privy to the court's information. Similarly, a state agency charged with child protection has strong laws which seal records from public scrutiny. Children being charged with juvenile delinquencies, are given conditions of release and probation just like adults receive. There are, however, major differences between the juvenile and adult criminal court systems. The juvenile court system attempts to rehabilitate young offenders, rather than simply hand out punishments as so often happens in adult courts. For many years the juvenile system used a philosophy called "parens patriae," or the theory that the state may take the role of the parent. Even the word "delinquency" is substituted

for the word "crime" in the juvenile system. Also, whereas records of conviction for adults are open to the public, records of juvenile delinquencies are confidential and maintained as sealed records. The child's probation officer is usually a child-protective-services case worker and there are periodic court review hearings to check on how the youthful offender is doing.

Drug courts handle cases related to substance abuse, and in some jurisdictions these courts also handle the affiliated domestic abuse cases since there is strong correlation between domestic violence and substance abuse (see Drugs and Crime Chapter). A drug court attempts to closely monitor the defendant and requires frequent court appearances to report on treatment progress. There are strict terms for compliance and prompt intervention if a defendant is not following the court's orders. These courts have proven to be more effective in reducing recidivism than the non-specialized court's handling of similar charges. According to the National Justice Reference Service's report from the Bureau of Justice Assistance, National Institute of Justice, and Office of Juvenile Justice and Delinquency Prevention, 2013, drug courts generally reduce recidivism resulting in lower costs per offender, when compared to traditional criminal court outcomes.

Another study of four adult Drug Courts in Suffolk County, MA found that Drug Court participants were 13% less likely to be re-arrested, 34% less likely to be re-convicted and 24% less likely to be re-incarcerated than probationers who had been carefully matched to the Drug Court participants (Rhodes et al, 2006).

Integrated Domestic Violence Courts
These courts bring related criminal and civil cases and parties involved in domestic violence before one judge. Because the same incident of domestic violence is typically heard and ruled upon by civil and criminal judges in separate proceedings there are often inconsistent and conflicting orders. Integrating these dockets results in court orders being consistent. By addressing both victim and offender needs through referral to appropriate programming, such as batterer's intervention, and services such as mental health and substance abuse screening, parties work collaboratively instead of in the traditional litigation model. A study of an Integrated Domestic Violence docket in Bennington, Vermont from 2007 – 2010 found "a 38 percent reduction in recidivism for new violent crimes and a 42 percent reduction in recidivism for new crimes of domestic violence for those convicted and supervised in the IDVD program, as opposed to those similar offenders in the traditional criminal justice process statewide over a three-year period" (Suntag, 2011).

Traffic courts
As you might suspect, these courts handle speeding tickets and license suspension and other traffic related matters which do not involve juries, or any

possible imprisonment or probation. Therefore, DUI, (Driving Under the Influence), is not typically handled by a traffic court since its jurisdiction is limited to imposing fines, suspending licenses, and other civil remedies. Someone charged with DUI can face imprisonment and is entitled to a jury trial. These cases are heard by the criminal courts.

There are other kinds of specialty courts. It is best to familiarize yourself with your state's court system and learn the names of the courts in which you might someday be working.

Appellate Courts & State Supreme Courts

As in the federal system, trial courts are the triers of fact, and appellate courts focus on questions of legal error or abuse of discretion by the lower court. Just as in the federal system an appeal will be afforded the opportunity for oral argument, or will simply be decided on the written record and attorney's briefs. This is at the discretion of the appellate court. States can have several tiers of appellate courts. Some states divide appellate courts into criminal and civil appeals, while other states have appellate courts which hear all appeals from the trial level. In 39 of the 50 states there are intermediary appellate courts, and in some states there are no intermediate appellate courts. When there is no intermediate appellate court the state's Supreme Court hears all appeals directly from the trial courts.

Attorneys in the Criminal Justice System

1. Federal Court Attorneys
   a. Prosecutors – U.S. Attorneys
   b. Defense Attorneys or Federal Public Defenders
2. State Court Attorneys
   a. Prosecutors – District Attorneys
   b. Defense Attorneys or State Public Defenders
3. Private Attorneys in all courts
4. Appellate Attorneys in Federal and State courts

In both the federal and state court systems there are government employed attorneys who represent the government. These are the prosecutors, usually called some variation of "district attorney" or "chief prosecutor." Defendants are often represented by public defenders, who are also employed by the government. While these attorneys are all government employees, they represent differing interests of the government versus the defendant. Cases are entitled *State v. John Doe*, where the prosecutor represents the state and the public defender represents John Doe.

A PERSON OF INTEREST: MARCIA CLARK

Marcia Clark was born in California but then attended public schools in Staten Island, New York. In college she became a political science major at UCLA, and later received her law degree at the Southwestern

University's School of Law in Los Angeles, California. After working as a defense attorney for a Los Angeles law firm, she decided that she really disliked her role of trying to free violent suspects . After successfully defending a man who had been charged with the sexual assault and fatal stabbing of a woman he had picked up on the street, Clark knew that a career change was necessary. And change she did when she took the job of assistant district attorney, a move that allowed her to prosecute rather than defend. She had basically a law-and-order personality, and she had felt a strong sense of sympathy for the victims in those cases in which she had previously defended the alleged perpetrators. However in her new role as a prosecutor, she had a job that was more closely allied with her feelings, and it brought her great success and acclaim. At one point in her career she a string of nineteen homicide convictions. Then, with the O.J. Simpson trial, Clark stepped out onto the world's stage and did battle with an incredibly strong defense team that included Johnny Cochran (of "if-it-don't fit fame"), F. Lee Bailey, and Barry Scheck. In her role as the lead prosecutor in this case, Marcia Clark became at that time the most famous lawyer in the United States. In 1995 Esquire Magazine named her their "Person of the Year" and in 1997 she wrote a very successful book about the trial, titled "Without A Doubt." In 2011 she turned her hand to fiction and coauthored a gripping crime novel, "Guilt by Association."

Who Represents Whom?

Prosecutors represent the state-government's interest in protecting its citizens. Therefore, the victim of a crime is not the client of the prosecutor, but instead is a witness who can provide the court with evidence of the crime. This is quite different from the defense attorney who represents the defendant directly and must proceed with the defense based on the client's wishes, even if the defense attorney disagrees with those decisions. A defense attorney might recommend a plea agreement, but it is the defendant's decision whether to accept or reject that deal. Because a prosecutor is not actually representing the victim of the crime, s/he has no duty of representation for the individual victim and can make deals without the victim's consent. In reality prosecutors do try to work with the victims and attempt to reach agreement on how the case will proceed. However, the prosecutor is not bound by what the victim wants. For example, in a domestic abuse crime, if the victim decides not to prosecute the defendant, the district attorney might still have enough evidence to go ahead anyway and, ironically, might even call the victim of the crime a "hostile witness." Conversely, the victim might want to go forward in a case in which the prosecutor might feel there is insufficient evidence to warrant filing a case.

Prosecutors

In federal courts U.S. Attorneys are the chief federal law enforcement officers in their districts, responsible for federal criminal prosecutions and civil cases involving the United States Government. The Executive Office for U.S. Attorneys provides support and oversight for the 94 offices across the country. The US Attorneys are part of the United States Department of Justice (DOJ).

The United States Attorney General is the head of the DOJ and is the nation's chief law enforcement officer. The attorney general is considered to be the chief lawyer of the U.S. government and is concerned with the legal affairs of the U.S government. The Attorney General serves as a member of the president's cabinet, and is only one two cabinet department heads who is not given the title of "secretary" (the other being the postmaster general). The Attorney General is nominated by the president of the United States and takes office after confirmation by the United States Senate. He or she serves at the pleasure of the president and can be removed by the president at any time. The Attorney General is also subject to impeachment by the House of Representatives. The Senate may hold the Attorney General for trial for "treason, bribery, and other high crimes and misdemeanors." The office of Attorney General was established by Congress by the Judiciary Act of 1789.

District Attorney

The state is represented in its trial courts by district attorneys. Many district attorneys are elected in state-wide elections, often at the county level. You might be familiar with seeing a billboard or ballot for your local district attorney. District attorneys work closely with the police and other law enforcement personnel in deciding what evidence is necessary to move forward for prosecution through the court system.

States also have their own office of the attorney general which is the lead agency for the state in all of its legal affairs. Unlike the President choosing his/her US Attorney General, many states vote for their attorney generals, but, the state attorney general reports to the governor.

Defense Counsel

Because the Constitution dictates that defendants have a right to an attorney if being charged with a crime, defendants have the option of hiring private attorneys to represent them, or, if indigent, they may qualify for a low cost or free-of-charge counsel to be appointed. The Office of the Federal Public Defender has locations in each of the federal districts, and in each state there are comparable public defender agencies to represent financially needy defendants. The Court will determine the financial need of each person who applies for a public defender.

If the public defender has been found to have a conflict of interest, another lawyer, called a "conflict counsel" will be appointed by the court. Conflict counsel are private attorneys hired by the state to represent indigent defendants when the public defender has a conflict. A conflict might arise if a public defender represented someone in a criminal matter and the defendant who now needs an attorney was the victim in the prior case. The public defender's office could not represent the new defendant without being in conflict with the prior representation. Another example is when several defendants are charged in the commission of a crime, the public defender cannot represent all of the defendants since the interests of each defendant may not be the same and may be in conflict with another defendant's interest. When an attorney takes the job of being a conflict counsel the contract usually specifies a year of work at a flat rate and the condition that all the cases which the court assigns must be taken. The case load is often overwhelming.

Hiring a private attorney can be very expensive, since the attorney's hourly rate can be hundreds of dollars per hour and mounting a criminal defense is time consuming. The attorney will ask for a retainer fee, which is the amount of money paid up-front even before the attorney begins work on the case. When the retainer funds are running low the attorney requires the client to replenish the account before continuing work. However, the attorney cannot simply stop work on the case even though no additional funds are being paid by the client. The court must give its permission for an attorney to withdraw. If the court denies a motion to withdraw, the attorney might eventually be working for free. This may happen when the case is close to the trial date. In this situation the judge must balance the interests of the defendant for a speedy trial with the interests of the attorney in getting paid (another example of a criminal justice dilemma).

Some private attorneys accept cases without pay, called pro bono. Many large law firms have specialized attorneys who will do *pro bono* work especially on death penalty cases. The Court might request that a firm, or specific attorney, accept such work, and the court keeps lists of attorneys who are willing to be appointed *pro bono*.

Courts also have limited funds to hire private attorneys, called ad hoc counsel. This would be necessary if there are several defendants and the public defender and the conflict counsel are already representing defendants in the case. When the court appoints an *ad hoc counsel* there is a dollar and time limit included in the court's order of appointment. The rates paid for ad hoc counsel are considerably lower than private-attorney rates, and the number of hours permitted are often not enough to take the case to its conclusion. However, when accepting such a case the attorneys are on notice that only a specified fee and number of hours is permitted and that they may be working pro bono if the time necessary to defend the case exceeds the court ordered amounts. Courts, like the rest of the economy, are hurting financially and budgets are being cut. Such cost-cutting measures as closing some courts one day per month and reducing the size of court staffs have become commonplace. Needless to say, the funds for hiring private counsel are very limited despite the need.

Appellate Attorneys

Typically the trial attorneys who work for the government, public defenders or prosecutors do not handle cases on appeal. Rather the government agency has attorneys who specialize in appellate law. These specialized attorneys will review the record, write the briefs and make oral arguments at the appellate levels in both state and federal courts. In cases where a private attorney already represents the defendant, this private attorney will often handle the appeal also.

Court Administration

Courts are run by Clerks, administrators who oversee the processing of cases and who work closely with judges and staff to ensure timely and smooth handling of all cases. Clerks of court hold positions of management and they are accountable to the court administrator's office, or sometimes to similar agencies higher up the management chain. The clerks are in charge of hiring and training the staff, coordinating with the judges about docket management at the day-to-day level, and the handling of emergency filings.

Docket clerks are staff who do everything from entering all of the necessary information into computers- from names, dates of birth, social security numbers to chronological events that occur in each case. They handle motions and other filed paperwork for the judge's review, prepare the daily list of cases to be heard, get the files to the judge, answer constantly ringing phones from the public asking myriad questions, and assist the public at the clerk's office window. Court staff usually have a wealth of knowledge and are trained to be polite and efficient, but they cannot give legal advice. Docket clerks are invaluable employees without whom the wheels of justice might grind to a halt. You probably know a company or school that relies on its support staff to keep the wheels turning - it is no different in a court of law.

Naturally the vast majority of courts have extensive security systems in place. Screening at the front entrance includes metal detectors and x-ray scanning of all bags and/or the use of wand detectors. The front-end security will take items deemed as potential weapons, such as glass or metal water bottles and small pen knives.

A Bailiff or armed court officer inside the courtroom assures the safety of the judge, litigants, jury, attorneys and others in the courtroom. Bailiffs may be dressed in police/sheriff uniforms and equipped with a gun, baton, handcuffs, and a communication device. Everyone knows who they are and why they are there. Bailiffs will announce the judge's entrance into the courtroom and ask everyone to please stand. They administer the oath to witnesses, ferry paperwork and evidence from the counsel table to the judge, escort a defendant to and from the courtroom if the defendant is coming from a holding cell or lock-up, and assure an orderly and respectful process in the courtroom.

Court officers make sure cell phones are off, and that no one is chewing gum, talking or otherwise distracting from the proceedings. Court officers can and will arrest people in the audience for failure to follow instructions.

The Judge presides over everything in the courtroom. Judges are sometimes elected officials, but are often appointed by the governor of the state, or, in the federal system, appointed by the President with confirmation by the Senate. In a few states, lower level judges are called magistrates or justices of the peace. Their jurisdiction is limited and defined by the state. Judges wear black robes and sit in the front of the court on a raised podium (called the bench). Just in front of the bench is the court reporter who records all of the courtroom proceedings both on audio tapes as well as on the computer. The reporter will also log all evidence introduced in a case and keep a list of all the exhibits that have been entered. An exhibit is an object or document shown in court as evidence, such as a blood-soaked glove in a murder case. The bailiff has a desk just off to one side of the bench. Attorneys and their clients are seated at counsel tables. Jurors are seated in what is called the jury box, which is off to one side of the bench. Witnesses who are called to testify take the stand which is located to the side of the judge's bench. Behind the counsel tables are seats for the audience, usually made up of family and friends of the defense or victim, as well as anyone else who might want to observe. After all, criminal proceedings are open to the public. Finally, attorneys and defendants who are waiting for their case to be heard, and journalists can be found seated in this area.

Going To Trial
You may now be thinking that you definitely know a lot about the theory and terminology of the court process, but you may now be wondering how it all actually works. How does a criminal case go from an arrest to court?

Probable Cause/Indictment/Preliminary Hearing/Arraignment
In order to better understand the process, let's take a look at the following case study.

CASE STUDY: The Case of Tim V. – the "Morning Person"
Tim dropped out of high school as soon as he turned 18, not because he couldn't do the work (with a tested IQ of 115) but that he wouldn't. Tim was an only child, and his parents were especially upset that he didn't graduate and ordered him to either go back to school or get a job. Over the next two years he had several jobs, but was either fired or left them on his own, usually for reporting to work late, or not reporting at all. He insisted that he was just

not a morning person and had to stay in bed each morning until noon. He rejected the notion that he was lazy down to the core, and actually that was only part of his problem. The problem was also what he did the night before. Tim discovered hard liquor (rum) when he was only 15, and from then on his level of consumption went continually up, always drinking at night. Of course, he had to spend the next morning sleeping it off. His two passions were rum and sports on TV. When Tim was 21, both of his parents died in an auto crash, and Tim inherited the mortgage-free family home which he immediately sold for almost $200,000. With that load of cash, Tim went on a spending spree, replete with a fancy apartment, fast cars, fast women and expensive trips. He later became very involved with a waitress named Andrea, and he gave her both his attention and some expensive gifts. But the money soon ran out, and Tim had to move in with Andrea, in a rundown apartment for which she was only paying $500 per month. By now, however, Tim was so broke he couldn't even help her out with that level of rent. She demanded that he get a job. But instead he went on a mini crime spree and committed almost a dozen B&Es (Breaking and Entering), both at night and during the day. He never got much from them, some jewelry, cameras, watches and a couple of laptops, all of which he took to the local pawn shop. The most he ever received was about $200. In two of those capers he was caught and charged, but never got more than a slap on the wrist - community service and probation. One night Andrea came home with the story of a man who frequented the restaurant where she worked who had been showering her with attention and showing her a large wad of cash. He also told her that he didn't trust banks. Tim suddenly became excitedly interested. The next night Tim went to the restaurant, waited for the man to show up, watched him eat and then followed him home. For a week Tim followed him everywhere, knew all his habits and especially the times when he was not in his apartment. Tim cased the apartment, and a few days later, he went there alone, climbed an outside fire escape and expertly cut out a window pane and made his entry. He first looked through some bureau drawers, and then under the mattress and blurted out "bingo." To his surprise and glee, he found what turned out to be a little over $10,000. That night he and Andrea celebrated at an expensive restaurant that Tim had formerly frequented. What could be easier and better paying than the few minutes it had taken him to find and steal that money? Crime was good, and this time it paid well. Tim thought he had found the perfect job. However, two of the city's police detectives, Fuentes and Udall, (known affectionately in the department as F&U) were also doing their job and after questioning Andrea's boss at the restaurant and learning of the attention Andrea had been given by the victim, they decided to go to her apartment and ask her a few questions. It was late when they arrived, and Andrea was already home from work. Tim was still drinking and watching TV. One of the detectives, Fuentes, recognized Tim from a previous encounter. On a hunch he asked Tim for a drink, and when he got the bottle he picked it up with gloved hands and announced loudly that he now had Tim's fingerprints (and DNA if he needed it). Tim was drunkenly enraged, and asked why his prints were taken. One of the detectives replied bluntly that they wanted to know if they matched prints taken at the victim's apartment. The next day his prints were sent to the crime lab and a perfect match was uncovered. The detectives went to a judge they knew, told their story and provided enough evidence (the prints) to secure a warrant to search Andrea's apartment (and for Tim's arrest). When they got back to Andréa's apartment the detectives found none of the cash, but they did find Tim and they dutifully read him his rights (Mirandized him). Tim got up off his chair and started lurching toward the door. Fuentes said flatly "if you try to run you'll only go to jail tired." Tim was then cuffed and started complaining about how tight the cuffs were, but was told that they were new and that they would stretch after he wore them awhile. They took him to police headquarters, where Tim said he didn't want or need a lawyer because he was innocent and would prove it himself. He was booked by the desk sergeant and placed in a police department lock-up, where both Fuentes and Udall took turns questioning him. After eight straight hours they promised Tim a drink if he confessed. He then wrote and signed a full confession and was, amid uproarious laughter, given a drink - of water. Two days later Tim was brought before a lower-court judge for his initial appearance. Because it was assumed that Tim still had most of the money and was therefore a threat to skip town (or even perhaps skip the country), bail was denied and he was placed in preventive detention. The next step was a preliminary hearing where a judge did determine that there was enough evidence (the prints and confession) for probable cause. He would be charged with both the B&E and grand larceny. Tim remained in custody and was next scheduled for arraignment before still another judge. At this point, Tim asked for and was given a public defender who told him to give back the money and cop a plea. He said that if found guilty Tim could get up to two years in state prison, but if he returned the money they could plea bargain down to 90 days in an Alcohol Corrections Center (where he could also get treatment). Tim would not disclose where the money was, and decided to plead guilty. The judge summarily sentenced him to serve one year in a minimum security facility, where he was rousted out of bed each morning at 6 AM. Tim was quickly transformed into becoming a "morning person."

How It Worked

As you've seen, the prosecutor works with law enforcement to decide when a case should be filed, and in this case the police obtained evidence implicating Tim in the crimes of grand larceny and breaking and entering. Prosecutors must decide if the evidence brought by law enforcement is strong enough to warrant filing a criminal case, as they must be sure that the evidence they have can withstand the scrutiny of the criminal trial system. Even though

Tim was arrested and detained, he will not be the named defendant until the case is filed with and accepted by the court.

In some states and in the federal system a grand jury is convened to determine if there is enough evidence against the defendant to proceed with a case. A grand jury consists of between 12 to 23 persons who conduct private proceedings to evaluate the evidence. Witnesses can be subpoenaed and the power of the grand jury is very broad. Only the prosecutor, not the defendant, nor his/her attorney, is present during grand jury proceedings. If the grand jury issues an indictment (charge) the case continues and is then filed with the court.

When a case (also called a complaint) is filed, the court determines if probable cause exists. Is there enough evidence on the face of the information provided, (the affidavits are sworn written statements) to make it probable that a crime was committed? Some court systems use a preliminary hearing to make the determination of probable cause, and unlike the grand jury proceedings, the accused and his/her attorney are present and can dispute the charges.

Once the court determines that probable cause does exist the case is opened, a docket number is assigned and the charges are listed. Tim's case might be docketed as State v. Tim V., Windham Criminal Division, Docket No. 1234-12-12 Wmcr. If the judge determines there is insufficient evidence for probable cause, the case is not opened and is returned to the prosecutor who then must decide whether to instruct the police to gather more information to meet the probable cause standard, or not to prosecute the case.

Tim appeared for the first time in court for his arraignment. The charges against him were read aloud in open court by the judge and he could enter a plea- guilty, not guilty, or nolo contendere (no contest). A plea of nolo contendere (no contest) is basically the same as a guilty plea and the defendant is usually convicted and sentenced. It is at these first court appearances that defendants request the services of a public defender if they cannot afford an attorney. The prosecutors are also present at the arraignments and often will be discussing with defense counsel possible plea agreements (or sometimes called plea bargains) so as to avoid the cost and time of going to trial. These negotiations at the time of arraignment do not usually result in plea agreements, but cases usually reach a plea at a later date once the prosecutors and defense attorneys have conducted discovery. Discovery is the process of finding out all the facts and information before going to trial, or sometimes on the first day of the trial. All the evidence must be presented during discovery. The defense, especially, should not have to deal with any last-minute surprises.

Most courts set aside a specific day or days for arraignments when public defenders and prosecutors are present in the courtroom. The court determines if the accused lacks sufficient funds to afford counsel on their own and, if so, assigns a public defender to represent him/her. Public defenders must accept all the cases the court assigns them and are typically overburdened with too many cases per attorney. Similarly, the prosecuting attorney/ district attorney/ state's attorney, must accept all the cases which are deemed worthy of prosecution, and they too are overworked. Once a plea is entered by the defense, the court will discuss conditions of release for the defendant.

In our case study Tim was told by his public defender to "cop a plea," but instead of meeting the prosecutor's terms necessary for him to have received a lesser sentence, such as alcohol treatment, he pled guilty to B & E and grand larceny. He refused to disclose where the money was or to return it. The judge sentenced Tim to one year in prison because clearly he had not learned from experience - his prior convictions, his community service and his probation.

Tim's prior convictions included community service and probation as a means of addressing his then-still-youthful and relatively harmless offenses of theft under $200. The court has the discretion to apply sentences to such offenses. In the best of all worlds these sentences rehabilitate the offender. Probation conditions would include meeting regularly with the probation officer, finding gainful employment, and other terms that the probation officer deems necessary. If it were known at the time of his earlier offenses (that Tim had a history of alcohol abuse issues), probation would have included alcohol treatment.

Tim's willingness to plead guilty at arraignment and be sentenced immediately is not the norm. How might things have gone differently for Tim if he had entered a plea of not guilty?

Conditions of Release: Bail, Detention, Release on own Recognizance
Had Tim pleaded not guilty, the judge would make decisions regarding his release or detention pending trial. Bail and other conditions would be set if the court agreed to release him prior to the trial. Bail is money paid to the court to ensure the defendant's appearance at trial. The 8th amendment to the Constitution states that excessive bail shall not be required. If the defendant skips the trial, the defendant can be arrested and the bail money is forfeited. If a defendant cannot afford bail he/she may be housed at the corrections center until the funds can be obtained or, until trial if they cannot pay. If bail is paid it will be refunded to the defendant at the conclusion of the case whether the person was convicted or not, as the money was required to ensure attendance at court.

Other conditions of release might include reporting daily to the police, staying at a certain residence, not contacting or harassing named victims, electronic bracelets and other terms specific to the crime being charged. Sometimes, defendants are released on their own recognizance if the crime committed was non-violent and they can show no flight risk (e.g., live and work in the community). If a defendant violates any conditions of release prior to trial they will be brought back before the court to determine appropriate measures, which might include preventive detention. Always remember that a person charged with a crime is innocent until proven guilty, however, the judge must weigh and balance the nature of the crime with the rights of the defendant and the right of public safety. Finding that balance goes right to the heart of the entire criminal justice system. Preventive detention at a corrections facility pending trial might be ordered when the charges are of serious crimes, violent or otherwise, and when the offender has a history of arrests, convictions or violations of probation/conditions. The court may feel that allowing release will put the offender's family, employer or community in general at too much risk.

Pre-Trial

Before a trial occurs, both the prosecutor and defense camps are working to prepare for trial. Discovery is conducted, witnesses are interviewed, the crime scene may be examined, and experts are enlisted to review evidence and give opinions. The scope of discovery is broad and governed by special sets of rules. Witnesses are deposed, asked a series of questions under oath at the attorneys' offices where both sides are present. There are also requests to produce documents and other evidence from both sides, and written interrogatories (questions to be answered in writing and under oath) are sent to and from each side. All of these discovery tools have to conform to the rules of procedure. Be aware that the prosecution has both an ethical and a legal obligation to give the defense all exculpatory evidence (evidence which might justify or excuse the defendant's actions), regardless of whether the defense asks for it or not. This is an important aspect of due process. If it is later discovered that the prosecution failed to produce exculpatory evidence an appeal might result in overturning a guilty verdict and the prosecutor may face disciplinary action for a breach of ethical responsibility.

Since the defendant has a right against self-incrimination (5th amendment) they cannot be deposed or otherwise questioned by the prosecution, and may choose not to testify at the trial. Any information given to the defense counsel by the defendant is confidential and privileged. The defense attorney has an ethical obligation not to reveal anything the client says. However, if a client were to disclose a dangerous and immediate threat, the defense attorney would have a duty to report it to the police. As you can see, the ethical obligations of the defense attorney can be confounding and there are no easy answers.

Throughout this pre-trial process, the prosecutor and defense counsel discuss settling the case to determine if a plea is possible. Plea bargaining can entail an agreement to plead guilty to a lesser charge in exchange for a sentence which both sides can agree on, or, dismissal of one charge and agreement on another charge and sentence. The variations are endless and these negotiations can occur right up to, and even sometimes during, the trial. Though often viewed by the public as favoring the criminal, plea bargains are probably necessary in order to reduce the volume of court cases. One researcher estimated that 90% of the potential court cases are settled by plea bargaining (Carp & Stidham, 1990).

Juries

A defendant has a constitutional right to have a jury of one's peers as provided by the 6th amendment. A defendant can opt to have a judge hear the evidence and waive the right to a jury trial. A jury trial might be waived when the defense believes that the judge will respond more favorably to the evidence than a jury would. That might depend on the particular sitting judge and the type of case being tried. For example a judge who was a public defender prior to being seated on the bench might be seen as more impartial in a case of a sex offense against a child if the defense worries that a jury might be inflamed about the nature of the offense. In this situation, the defense may feel that a jury might be more likely to find the defendant guilty.

There are typically 12 jurors seated (6 in some jurisdictions) to hear a case. Jury summonses are sent out to many community members who must appear for a jury draw on dates specified in the summons notice. A Summons goes out to many more than 12, because it is expected that some folks will be excluded from the jury pool. The courts are sympathetic to conflicts that jurors might have with these summons dates, conflicts such as an already-scheduled vacation or caretaking responsibilities. The court does its best to work with the schedules of the summoned jurors and excuses them if possible. Work conflicts will generally not be sufficient to excuse a juror. Some courts have one or two alternate jurors who hear all the evidence in case one of the jurors becomes ill and needs to be replaced. These alternate jurors do not sit in on jury deliberations.

How does the court determine if jurors are right for the job?

Voir Dire

Jurors are supposed to be impartial and unbiased in each case. A process called voir dire is used to question potential jurors to determine who should, or should not, be seated on the jury. The jurors assemble in the courtroom and the judge and/or attorneys will pose various questions for each juror to answer. The defendant is also present in the courtroom during this questioning. Questions such as "do you know the defendant or anyone related to her/him?" "were you ever a victim of a crime?" "do you think you would be able to render an impartial verdict based on the evidence produced at trial?" "have you read or heard anything about this charge, or defendant?" "do you have any family members or close friends who are in law enforcement?" The answers to these questions will cause some jurors to be dismissed. Someone who was the victim of an assault might not be able to be impartial in a case involving charges of violence. These types of dismissals are for cause, and there is no limit on how many jurors can be dismissed. Both sides are also permitted a limited number of preemptory challenges. The attorneys can simply say that they wish to exercise such a challenge to juror "X" without stating a reason. Usually there are 3 preemptory challenges for each side.

Presenting the Case

The state and defense attorneys make opening arguments to the judge and jury. These speeches are not "facts" but are a summation of the case that the attorney will present to the court through witnesses and physical evidence. Of course the attorneys do their best to convince the court that the evidence they will introduce will undoubtedly show guilt/innocence. Attorneys can vary widely in their presentation skills.

Burden of Proof

The state presents its case first and has the burden of proof. Evidence must show that the defendant committed the crime beyond a reasonable doubt. It is very important to remember that the defense does not have to prove that the defendant did not commit the crime. Meeting this high standard depends on the evidence and how it is presented to the court and jury. If the defense can raise a doubt about whether the defendant committed the crime then the judge or jury will have to decide if that doubt is reasonable. Because a defendant has a right not to testify, the jury or judge may not infer guilt from the lack of a defendant's testimony.

Specific procedures and rules must be followed by the attorneys in presenting their cases, including how they question witnesses and how they introduce the physical evidence into the record. Witnesses are called, including experts, and they are asked questions on both direct and cross examination. The attorney who has called the witness asks direct questions, the opposing attorney asks questions on cross examination. Lawyers are adept at phrasing a question in such a way as to elicit the answer they wish to have. If an eyewitness is asked by the defense attorney to describe in general "what happened," that witness may say something the defendant's attorney does not want the court to hear. Instead, the questions are usually posed so that they require only a "yes" or "no" answer. If a witness tries to elaborate and explain the answer, the attorney will ask the judge to stop the testimony. Good attorneys only ask questions to which they already know the answers. However, there can be surprising testimony that no one anticipated which might change the outcome of the trial.

Physical evidence, documents, weapons, fibers, and other objects may be introduced into the record. Once the state rests (is finished introducing evidence) the defense has its turn.

When the defense puts forth its case the same rules apply for witnesses and for other evidence being introduced into the record. Sometimes the defense will not have any witnesses, but will poke holes in the prosecution's case through cross examination sufficient to cast "reasonable doubt." The defendant often will not testify. In some courts the jury is asked if they have questions of witnesses which are then written down and handed to the judge. The judge will decide if these questions should be asked of the witness.

Closing Arguments

When the case is fully presented both attorneys make closing arguments to the jury. Again these arguments are a summation of the evidence produced and tailored to convince the jury of the guilt or innocence of the defendant. The question of what could cast a reasonable doubt is specific to the facts and evidence of each case. However, since there are many appellate courts that have given opinions about this standard, the attorneys may refer to these decisions and draw parallels to the case they are arguing.

The Rules of Evidence

How evidence comes into the court and whether it is accepted by the court as being admissible is a constant challenge to the judge who must rule on admissibility in accordance with the "Rules of Evidence." Attorneys must be aware of the latest case law concerning these evidentiary rulings and be prepared to argue why the court should allow or exclude certain evidence. The attorneys may make objections, and the judge will decide if the objection should be sustained (allowed) or overruled (not allowed). These rules govern, among other things, exactly what witnesses may or may not disclose during testimony. For example, hearsay (testifying about what someone else said when the witness did not actually hear it or see it) is not allowed except in limited circumstances. An example of an exception to the hearsay rule is the "excited utterance.

The Case of the Excited Utterance

Eddie, Sam, and Joe were hanging out. Sam and Joe were arguing when Eddie left the room. When Eddie returned a few minutes later Sam was very upset and exclaimed, "Joe attacked me!" Eddie did not see Joe attack Sam and cannot testify about the attack, because Sam's statement to Eddie is simply hearsay. However, the prosecutor might be able to have Eddie testify to Sam's statement as an exception to the hearsay rule based on it being an excited utterance. The exited utterance is a statement made while the person is in a stressed or excited state, and is deemed to be more trustworthy than some contrived statement given in a more cool and calculating way.

Physical and Documentary Evidence

Physical and documentary evidence must be admitted through the testimony of someone who can prove the trustworthiness of the evidence. Medical records, for example, can only be admitted if the custodian of those records testifies to their authenticity and that the records sought were maintained in the normal course of business.

Expert Opinions

Expert opinions may be given based on the person's expertise, but attorneys must first establish that expertise with a series of questions about the expert's education, background, training, and experience. A medical examiner will be permitted to testify as to the cause of death while a police officer could not. The officer could describe what was observed at the crime scene, and what actions they took, but only a doctor or toxicologist could establish the cause of death. If the witness is providing scientific evidence, it must conform to either Frye, Daubert or both. The Frye Rule, (which dates back to 1923) demands that the evidence being presented must be proven to have general acceptance in the scientific community. The Daubert rule (initiated in 1993) states that the scientific evidence must not only have consensus in the scientific community, but also that it be both reliable and valid. It is up to the presiding judge to determine if the evidence has a true scientific basis. Both Frye and Daubert standards can be applied in state court rooms, but Daubert supersedes Frye in a federal court. More on this important topic will be covered in a later chapter.

The Judge, Prosecutor, and Defense Counsel

The judge controls the courtroom and oversees all the proceedings. The judge rules on evidentiary objections, may have side bar meetings (both attorneys go to the front of the courtroom for a brief, off the record and private conversation with the judge about procedural matters), gives the jury instructions, and rules on motions that may be introduced during the trial. There are some motions that require the jury to be excused briefly, since these motions may affect what evidence the jury should or should not hear. The judge even decides when to have a recess (a break in the action, often a welcome break). The attorneys cannot simply take as much time as they would like with their opening and closing arguments or when questioning witnesses. The judge will discuss all these factors with the attorneys and then decide how much time each will be afforded. The judge's job is not an easy one. It is a formidable task to orchestrate all these proceedings. Most prosecutors and defense attorneys have worked together on many cases, often with the same judges. This collegiality can sometimes seem like the attorneys are all in it together, and that they are not zealously prosecuting or defending the clients.

A PERSON OF INTEREST: F. LEE BAILEY

F. Lee Bailey, a defense lawyer, went from the very peak of the legal marquee down to the valley of being disbarred in both Florida and Massachusetts. He certainly had his moments in the spotlight, but then later had it all come crashing down with his conviction for financial misdoings with money he took from one of his clients. Often a guest personality on top-rated TV programs, he showed both the charisma and charm needed to enchant a jury with his flair and rhetoric. The first case to bring Bailey media attention was that of Dr. Sam Sheppard, a physician who was convicted of killing his wife. Sheppard then hired Bailey to present the appeal, and Bailey took it right to the Supreme Court where he argued successfully on behalf of Sheppard's innocence. Bailey then got a verdict reversal of not guilty. This case caused so much media and public interest that both a TV series and motion picture were based on its essentials (The Fugitive, 1968 and The Fugitive, 2008). He also defended Albert DeSalvo, AKA the Boston Strangler, who was charged with a series of sexual assaults (called the Green Man assaults), as well as strangling 13 women, ranging in age from 19 to 85. Although he was convicted of the sexual assaults, he was NOT convicted of the stranglings. DeSalvo was later stabbed to death while serving time in prison. Bailey also wrote about this case in his book "The Defense Never Rests." DeSalvo was the central character in two motion pictures, "The Boston Strangler,"1968 and "Copy Cat," 1985 and was also quoted directly in "Midnight Rambler" by the Rolling Stones. On his own TV show, Bailey perpetuated the "Paul is dead" rumor (the story that Paul McCartney of the Beatles died in an automobile crash in 1966 and was secretly replaced by a look-alike). He even went so far as to cross examine an alleged witness. Bailey later defended newspaper heiress Patty Hearst, who had been kidnapped by a group calling themselves the "Symbionese Liberation Army" and then went along with the group by aiding and abetting their bank robberies. This was one of the few times that Bailey didn't meet the challenge. Patty Hearst was convicted, and later in her autobiography she claimed that Bailey's closing argument was both disjointed and the product of too much alcohol-self-medication. Bailey got back on the winning side when he worked for O.J Simpson's defense team (what prominent lawyer didn't?). His cross examination of Mark Fuhrman (the lead Los Angeles Police detective in the case) was said to be brilliant and is still used as a model in many law schools today.

A Respected Position

The judge is accorded the respect due her/him by the members of the bar (attorneys). They refer to the judge as "your honor," and prior to speaking will stand up and ask "if it please the court..." Attorneys are never allowed to approach the bench without first asking for the judge's permission. As we have seen, court officers handle the evidence being given to the judge for consideration by taking it from the attorney up to the bench. Counsel are under ethical obligation to be courteous and polite to each other and to the witnesses. Attorneys can even have ethics violations lodged against them with the state's licensing board due to bad behavior in the courtroom, such as an angry outburst. A judge can also hold an attorney (or witness) in contempt of court for failing to behave appropriately (a finding by a judge when some-one does not follow the court's order. It is a serious breach and can result in a fine or jail). Unlike many TV portrayals, most court proceedings do not often have people behaving badly. The attorneys and judges are all called officers of the court, that is symbols of the entire judicial process, not indi-viduals who may be liked or disliked. The judge will never refer to him or herself in the first person, but will always say "the Court" when answering a question you or I would respond to with "I..." For example, a judge might say, "The Court understands the defense objection to the admission of this witnesses' testimony and overrides the objection."

The Rule of Law

We are a country which prides itself in our rule of law. As a society we do not countenance vigilante justice. The individual likes, dislikes, or quirks of a particular judge or opposing counsel are all irrelevant. Everyone deserves a fair trial conducted in a respectful manner and the application of the law without bias. Most judges address the defendants as "sir" or "madam," or Mr. /Ms. Appropriate attire is part of courtroom etiquette and defendants who never owned a suit in their lives appear in court in a suit with fresh hair-cuts.

Jury Deliberations

Once both the state and defense rest, the jury will meet privately, outside the hearing of the judge, attorneys, and defendant, to conduct deliberations. All the evidence is discussed and sifted through. They may request that the judge answers questions which may be written down and given to the court officer in charge of the jury. They may request to hear portions of the taped testimony or see certain pieces of physical evidence. The jury is given a set of oral or written jury instructions by the judge before they retire from the courtroom. These instructions include a statement of the law which governs the case (e.g., the elements of breaking and entering or grand larceny and so on) and may also be relevant to the specific case. Attorneys can submit in-structions and the judge will decide which ones to include. Appeals are often lodged on a claim of error in jury instructions.

Sequestered

Juries do not have a time limit for deliberations. In some cases they meet over a period of days. If the case is extremely serious, or sensational, a jury may be sequestered – kept away from the outside world with no access to newspapers, TVs, or computers for the duration of the trial.

The Jurors Return

Once the jury has reached its decision, the jurors return to the courtroom. All parties are present and the judge asks the foreperson to reply to each charge as it is read out loud by the court by indicating guilty or not guilty. In all but a few states the jury must have unanimous agreement on the verdict. A few states require 11 – 1 or 10 – 2 verdicts. In states with only 6 jurors the decision must be unanimous. The jury must meet the particular state's requirements to reach its majority decision to convict or acquit.

There can be a hung jury if a majority decision cannot be reached. This is also known as a jury deadlock. Usually the judge will instruct the jurors to return to deliberations and keep trying to reach a verdict. However, if despite best efforts a verdict cannot be reached, a mistrial will be declared by the judge. The prosecution can request a new trial and the process begins all over from square one! The prosecutor must decide if another trial is worth it, based on the nature of the crime, the time and cost of another trial, and the likelihood of conviction.

What Happens After the Trial?

If a defendant is found not guilty, they are free to go. The prosecution cannot file the same charges against the defendant as this would be put the defendant in double jeopardy which is prohibited by the US Constitution. The Fifth Amendment prohibits a person from being charged "...for the same offense to be twice put in jeopardy of life or limb..."

If the defendant is found guilty, the court will decide if the person can remain free until sentencing or needs to be detained at a corrections facility prior to sentencing.

Appeal

Defendants have an automatic right to appeal a first conviction. Further appeals are at the discretion of the appellate level court, including the US Supreme Court. In most cases the prosecution does not have this right, or, if there is a prosecutorial appeal avenue, it is limited to claims of the constitutionality of the law. If an appeal is taken on the conviction the questions which the appellate court is faced with can include errors of law or procedure at the trial court level, ineffective assistance of counsel, erroneous or biased jury instructions, just to name a few. If the appellate court finds that there are sufficient grounds for appeal it may reverse the ruling and order a new trial. If the lower court's decision is upheld, the case is over and further appeals are discretionary in either higher state or federal courts.

Back to the case of Tim V, he might have appealed on grounds of ineffective assistance of counsel -Tim's public defender did not raise questions of possible legal error, such as: (1) obtaining the glass was an unreasonable search since there was no search warrant at that point, and (2) Tim's confession was coerced since he was promised a drink and the confession came after lengthy questioning without food or water. The promise of a drink was misleading as Tim believed he would receive an alcoholic beverage. Instead of pursuing these possible errors, his attorney encouraged Tim to "cop a plea" at the time of the arraignment. Denial of bail and continued detention at the probable cause stage was improper given the circumstances of the case, especially since there was no violent crime; and failure to have Tim sign the Miranda warnings ("you are under arrest, you have the right to any attorney, everything you say, can be used against you at a trial...") was an error. Whether Tim would prevail on one or more of these points would be up to the appellate court. The court would examine the pertinent laws of the jurisdiction as well as the case law and precedence as argued by the attorneys.

Sentencing

There is a separate sentencing hearing, usually within a month of the conviction. The probation office will prepare a pre- sentencing report for submission to the court which reviews the defendant's personal life and criminal records, interviews the victims and looks at other information relevant to sentencing such as what treatment programs are available within the community. The Court will hear from the prosecution, defense counsel, and often the defendant him/herself. Victims, and/or their families sometimes testify about the impact of the crime. Sometimes the defendants are not present in court but prepare written statements which are then read aloud. This may be the time when a defendant apologizes for the crime, or shows some kind of remorse in hopes that the judge will be lenient and hand down a less severe sentence.

Judicial discretion comes into play in sentencing. The judge has latitude and, depending on the crime, has statutory sentencing guidelines for maximum and minimum terms. There are some crimes for which a sentence is mandated by law and the judge or jury cannot override the mandate.

In a few states the jury may recommend a sentence to the judge that may or may not be followed. In Virginia, Texas, Oklahoma, Arkansas and Missouri the jury does in fact issue the sentence.

A guilty defendant can be sentenced to pay a fine (for minor crimes and misdemeanors), or to pay the victim (restitution), or to serve jail time, and in limited cases and states, the death penalty can be imposed. It's also possible that the defendant gets none of the above and is instead given probation. You may find this ironic, but there are many defendants who do not want probation, and instead prefer doing jail time and then being free of having to report to anyone. It is not unusual for the court to sentence a defendant to jail time, but then to defer the sentence as long as probation terms are complied with. If the defendant successfully completes the sentence on probation, the case will be closed, usually upon the completion of a successful report submitted to the court by the probation officer.

Probation

Probation is the most common form of sentence in the United States. Terms and conditions are determined by the court and the defendant's probation officer. These conditions are based on the type of crime and the available resources to meet the defendant's supervisory and treatment needs. For example, those found guilty of assault that also have substance-abuse issues might have to meet with their probation office daily. They may also have to submit to random drug testing, and then document their attempts to find work. They may also have to serve on a community work crew, attend therapy or other treatment programs, and have no contact with the victim. These terms might change over time if the defendant can comply with the more rigorous terms, and may gradually be allowed to have contact with the victim and/or the defendant's family – the latter is often the 'carrot' to promote compliance. If the defendant is sent to jail, in most cases the court will set a minimum and maximum length of prison time. Specific incarceration sentences are handed down less often. Once the minimum time, or specific time, is served the defendant is eligible for parole. A parole board will decide whether the prisoner is ready to be released and supervised by a parole officer. The parole board looks at many key factors, such as the conduct of the prisoner while incarcerated, statements from the victims, where the prisoner will live, if a job is available and so on. If released on parole, specific parole terms and conditions will be set and supervision by a parole officer will be enforced. Of all the jobs in the criminal justice system, being on a parole board may be one of the most stressful and unappreciated. Two of the most difficult questions the criminal justice system has to answer are:

1. Should there be a parole system?
2. If so, what should the parole criteria be?

If there is to be a parole system, parole board members will continue to be faced with a thankless and incredibly difficult task. The data indicate that although the vast majority of cases are ruled wisely, when mistakes are made they are followed by screaming headlines, as in the case several years ago of Willie Horton (that may have caused one presidential candidate to lose the election). The latest data for Hampden county Massachusetts show that of the 417 inmates who filed for parole, only 221 were granted. It is also interesting to note that there is a significant difference in the rates of recidivism between those paroled, 28.5%, and those who served their full sentence, 42% (both figures incidentally are below the national averages).

As shown above, not every inmate chooses to opt for parole, which typically results in the most troubled inmates serving out their full sentences. This is because there are some inmates who would rather do the time than have to face the reality of having to report to and be supervised by a parole officer.

If probation or parole is violated the court has a hearing on the violation and decides what should happen next. The defendant can present evidence at this hearing, but the standard for finding that the violation occurred is not beyond a reasonable doubt. Usually the court only has to find that it is likely to have occurred. If a violation is found, a defendant may be sent back to serve the remainder of the sentence in jail. However, due to the overcrowding of prisons and the questions many raise concerning whether serving prison time actually increases the risk of recidivism (reoffending), intermediate sanctions are considered by the court. These could include more intensive supervision, house arrest, work camps, boot camps, and drug/alcohol/domestic violence intensive treatment programs.

The Three Strikes Laws

Due to growing public perception that our society is not tough enough on offenders, over 30 states and the federal system have enacted sentencing based on the "three strikes and you're out" laws. These laws were passed in the late 1990's and typically call for mandatory prison terms, often long prison terms, for a person convicted of a third violent crime or felony. There is a strong public debate about the pros and cons of these laws. Those who favor them see retribution for the crimes committed as being necessary to protect the public, and those who decry them argue that we are warehousing young offenders for the remainder of their lives at great cost to the society. It is argued that as some of these offenders age, they may change their ways as part of a normal maturation process. Without question, young men make up the bulk of the prison population and young African American and Latino men are disproportionately jailed. The costs of incarceration are growing. Given the fact that the US prison population has quadrupled since the 1980's these debates are likely to continue.

Summary

The United States Constitution is the basis for the American legal system. It affords all citizens with civil rights such as the right to a speedy trial by a jury of one's peers, the right against self-incrimination, the right to cross examine witnesses, and the right to an attorney. It also dictates the basic court structure with the U.S. Supreme Court being the court of last resort.

Federal Courts include the U.S. Supreme Court, 12 U.S. Courts of Appeal, and 94 U.S. District Courts. The makeup of state courts is decided by each state and include a state Supreme Court, appellate, and trial level courts, as well as specialty courts. Prosecutors are attorneys who represent the government to protect its citizens; the head of all the federal government prosecutors is the Attorney General of the United States. Defense attorneys include public defenders, who are also government employees, as well as private attorneys who may be hired by a defendant or appointed by the court. When a case is appealed the case is usually handled by separate attorneys who specialize in appellate law. Courts are run by staff that process all the cases, assure the security of the building and courtroom, and record all of the courtroom proceedings. The most important player is the Judge. A case will land in court when a defendant is charged with a criminal act, and that charge can originate from a judge finding that probable cause exists to open the case, or a preliminary hearing is held by the court to assess the evidence to decide if probable cause exists, or a grand jury hands down an indictment. A named defendant appears in court for the arraignment at which time a plea is entered as guilty, not guilty, or nolo contendere. The attorneys may discuss resolving the case through a plea agreement at this, and later stages. The judge will decide if, prior to the trial, a defendant may be released on his/her own recognizance with or without conditions of release. Bail may be required and, if so, it will be determined how much money must be pledged, or perhaps the defendant will be held in preventive detention at a correctional facility pending trial. Pretrial preparations include discovery of information from each side, witness lists, depositions and interrogatories, and other tools designed to give each side as much information as possible prior to the trial. Prosecutors have an ethical obligation to provide exculpatory evidence to the defense. Negotiations to see if a plea bargain is possible can be ongoing during the pretrial process. Defendants have a right to have a jury trial, or can waive that right and have only a judge hear the case and render a decision. If there is a jury trial the jurors are chosen from a pool of local people who are asked a series of questions to decide who should be chosen for the trial. This is called voir dire. Jurors will be dismissed if there is evidence of bias, if they know any of the parties in the case, or there are other reasons they cannot be impartial. Each side also has a few preemptory challenges to dismiss jurors. At trial, the prosecution has the burden of proving beyond a reasonable doubt that the crime was committed. The defendant is presumed to be innocent until proven guilty. The defendant has the right against self-incrimination, and the jury should not infer from the defendant's lack of testimony any evidence of guilt. Attorneys will give opening and closing arguments to weave together all the evidence in an effort to convince the judge and jury of their view of the case. The judge presides over the courtroom and decides all questions of law and admissibility of evidence before and during a trial. The judge also gives jury instructions, and answers their questions during the trial and jury deliberations. The judge has the power to hold persons in contempt if they fail to follow court rules, and must always assure that justice is done in a fair and impartial manner. A verdict can be returned for guilty on one or more counts of the crimes charged, or, there can be a hung jury if the appropriate number of jurors fails to reach a unanimous(or 11-1 or 10-2 as dictated by the state) decision.

If there is a hung jury, the prosecutor must decide if another trial will be sought and must then start from the beginning. Upon a finding of not guilty the defendant is free to go. Because of the double jeopardy clause found in the Fifth Amendment, the prosecution cannot ever bring the same charges against the defendant again. If there is a finding of guilty there will be a sentencing hearing at a later time. At the sentencing hearing the judge will consider the following options: (1) Restitution, (2) Probation, (3) Prison time, or even (4) the Death penalty. The so-called "three strikes and you are out" rules are mandatory sentencing laws the majority of states enacted in the late 1990's for offenders who have committed three violent or felony crimes. In these cases the judge has no discretion and must apply the sentence as dictated by the law.

Once a defendant has met the conditions of the sentence he/she will be released without further conditions. However some sentences require a life time of supervision or other long-term parole conditions. If the death penalty is exacted the person will be imprisoned until the sentence is carried out or overturned by a higher court. Appeals are usually filed by the defense after a conviction. The prosecution has very limited options for appeal. While a defendant has an automatic right to appeal in the first instance, further appeals are at the discretion of the appellate courts.

Key Terms

Adjudication
Appeal
Arraignment
Attorney General
Bail
Bailiff
Beyond a Reasonable Doubt
Burden of Proof
Closing Argument
Contempt
Cross Examination
Defense Attorney
Deposition
Direct Examination
Discovery
Evidence
Exculpatory Evidence
Expert Opinion
Federal Court
Hearsay Evidence
Hung Jury
Indictment
Interrogatories
Judge
Jury

Mistrial
Nolo Contendre
Opening Argument
Parole
Plaintiff
Plea
Peremptory Challenge
Preliminary Hearing
Probable Cause
Probation
Pro Bono
Prosecutor
Recidivism
Rest
Restitution
Rules of Evidence
Self-Incrimination
Sentencing
Sequestration
Specialty Courts
State Courts
Three Strikes Law
Voir Dire

References

Carp, R. & Stidham, R. (1990). *Judicial process in America*. Washington, DC: Congressional Quarterly Press.

Gifis, S. H. (2008). *Barron's Dictionary of Legal Terms*. New York: Barron's Educational Series, Inc.

Rhodes, W., Kling, R., & Shively, M. (2006). *Suffolk County Court Evaluation*. Cambridge, MA: Abt Associates.

Sax, R. (2009). *The Complete Idiot's Guide to The Criminal Justice System*. New York : Penguin.

Siegel, L. J. (2010). *Introduction to Criminal Justice*. Belmont, CA: Wadsworth Cengage.

Suntag, D. (2013). *Procedural Fairness Swift and Certain Sanctions: Integrating the Domestic Violence Docket. Trends in State Courts, 25th Anniversary Edition*. Williamsburg, VA: National Center for State Courts.

CHAPTER 6

INSTITUTIONAL CORRECTIONS: LIFE ON THE INSIDE

Corrections is the third C in the CCC trio (Cops, Courts, and Corrections) and of the three, corrections involves the fewest participants. As you probably know, there are far more infractions than arrests, far more arrests than convictions, and far more convictions than incarcerations. This chapter will delve into that fraction of violators who do have to be confined. And even that fraction is not a tiny number. Currently there are over 2 million Americans now incarcerated and another 5 million on probation or parole, which is almost double what it was in 1989. That's a lot of super-bowl crowds. However, on the other side of the coin the total number of reported crimes in the United States has declined over that same time period by over 42%. And don't spend time bemoaning the fact that those who are locked up are leading the good life. You know the drill, "Oh they get dental and medical care, three meals a day and yes even color TV." You've heard the public complaints, "It costs more to put someone in prison than it does to send them to Harvard." And "that's a lot of tax-payer money for giving these bums a place to live along with three squares a day." Don't buy into it. You would not want to spend one over-night in prison, TV or no TV. Think about it! Don't for a minute assume you can leave your cell and just go across the street and a grab a quick cup of coffee. Forget it. You'd be locked up, perhaps even threatened with assault or rape by another inmate. You would be under the total control of the system. You will have to do as you're told when you are told. Most prisons have reasonable rules strictly enforced, but they are strictly enforced. This chapter is about institutional corrections, and the focus will be on those lock-up institutions where persons are totally detained.

Changes in Prison Philosophy

Over the years, the United States has gone through several changes in philosophy regarding how institutional corrections are to be viewed, managed and understood. American prisons have gone back and forth through several variations of the same two basic themes – harsh and punishing versus rehabilitative and reforming. We will see these two themes playing out in varying degrees throughout our brief look at the history of corrections. Before surveying American corrections, we will take a very quick peek at a long-ago British prison off the coast of Australia known as Norfolk Island. This prison was doubly famous. First, it's where the sailors from Captain Bligh's ship,

"The Bounty" were imprisoned for their crime of mutiny, and second because of the extremely cruel level of punishment that was used routinely. In
one case, an incorrigible prisoner named Charles Anderson was given over a
thousand lashes and then chained to a rock that overlooked one end of the
harbor. Each day one of the guards pushed something generously defined as
food up to him at the end of a long pole. The cruel plight of Charles Anderson actually became a point of human interest for scenic boat tours of Sydney
harbor, and the tourists would gape up at him and even try to throw food up
to him. When Alexander Maconochie (born in Scotland) was sent by the
British government to take charge of the prison in 1840, he immediately got
Anderson down off the rock, gave him some nourishing food and had his
wounds cleaned up and medicated. It is alleged that through a system where
inmates could earn points for good behavior (an early form of what is now
called behavior modification) Maconochie's treatment of the prisoners led to
the rehabilitation and release back to England for the majority of those long-
suffering inmates.

Another early prison reformer was John Howard who was the High
Sheriff of England's Bedfordshire County. He made many attempts (some
successful) to correct what he labeled as the "evils of our prisons." Ironically
he died of Typhus, a disease he contracted while visiting one of Europe's
prisons.

In the Beginning: The Punishment Philosophy at New-Gate

The first state prison in this country, 1773, was set up in an abandoned copper mine in East Granby, Connecticut. Known as the New-Gate prison,
(named after the notorious New-Gate prison in London), it was located 70
feet below ground. Like its counterpart in England, the conditions in this
prison were, to put it kindly, very rudimentary and the supervision was rigorous and often severe. Not surprisingly, the New-Gate prison recorded America's first prison riot, and several of the inmates were shot to death by the
guards. There was no thought of rehabilitation in this prison, as the punishment philosophy reigned supreme. The prisoners were rarely (if ever) allowed
to see the light of day, and the mine was cold, damp, and forbidding. In
short, conditions at New-Gate were harsh and by all accounts inhumane.
Remember, this was before the United States with its Bill of Rights even
came into being. The punishment in this prison could easily be considered
"cruel and unusual" (now forbidden by our Eighth Amendment). The New-
Gate prison operated continuously for the next 50 years, only to be turned
back into a copper mine when new veins of ore were found (by the prisoners). To this day, some of New-Gate's neighbors in East Granby consider
the prison to be haunted, claiming to hear moaning and screaming wafting up
the mine shaft from far below on quiet nights. The prison is now a museum
and is operated by the state of Connecticut. If you ever have the urge to

break into a prison, the New-Gate museum awaits, and you will find your guided tour to be very interesting as well as educational.

The Walnut Street Jail

By 1790 (post 1776) in Pennsylvania, what has been called the first true corrections center in the United States was established on Philadelphia's Walnut St. This facility was designed to house all convicted felons other than those sentenced to death (Allen & Simonsen, 2006). The corrections philosophy that dominated the Walnut St. Jail was one of silent repentance.

Our Penitentiaries

From the early 1800s up until the Civil War, two competing corrections styles were most common in the United States, the Pennsylvania system and the Auburn (sometimes called the New York) system. The Pennsylvania system grew out of the Walnut St. Jail and was totally focused on repentance (hence the term penitentiary). To repent meant keeping your mouth shut and silently thinking of your many sins. Not only was strict silence enforced, but the prisoners were not allowed to leave their cells. They ate, slept and worked within the confines of a small cell, and they had zero contacts with the outside world. Things were somewhat better in the Auburn system, even though it also demanded total silence. But the big difference was that in the Auburn facility prisoners were allowed out of their cells during the day to see, work, and eat with other prisoners. Thus, the Auburn inmates were actually allowed to see other human beings, rather than living in the solitary confinement demanded in the Pennsylvania system. Finally, prisoners were allowed to work in groups, and work they did. One irony is that Auburn prisoners were used to construct the famous prison in Ossining, New York, that you probably know as "Sing Sing."

Change Is In the Air: The ACA and Rehabilitation

In 1870 a dramatic change took place in the philosophy of corrections. A commission was formed, now known as the American Correctional Association, to oversee America's jails and prisons. The first president of this association was a future president of the United States, Rutherford B. Hayes. This group leaned toward a rehabilitation philosophy that fit more closely with the rules of the Eighth Amendment's insistence that there be no cruel and unusual punishment. Four major points were stressed by this commission:
1. Silence was abolished
2. Vocational and educational training were introduced
3. Rewards, rather than punishment alone, were introduced in hopes of changing inmate thinking and behavior
4. Good behavior could lead to early release

The model institution for showcasing these new rules was the Elmira Reformatory in New York, but even there the way the rules were enforced didn't always conform to the rehabilitation philosophy as outlined by the American Correctional Association. As an aside, the American Correctional Association is still alive and well today, and is in charge of evaluating and accrediting all the various jails and prisons throughout the U.S.

The Wickersham Commission

As we saw in a previous Chapter, President Herbert Hoover formed a commission to look into problems that were becoming apparent in both corrections and law enforcement in general. Known as the Wickersham Commission, the group looked into virtually all aspects of the criminal justice system and even delved into what they saw as the root causes of crime. The findings were a shocking delineation of excesses in the entire criminal justice system, including virtual torture, both mental and physical. It also concluded that the zealous methods being used by many prisons were not having any effect on crime rates or recidivism. Although the general public tended to blame crime on the immigrant population, the Commission (though taking a decided sociological view of the causes of crime), made clear that the problems stemmed, not from the immigrants, but from an inefficient police-corrections system that was lazy and sometimes even corrupt. The report aroused the public as well as the elected government officials, and corrections philosophy took another look at the rehabilitative approach.

Nothing Works?

In the early 1970s Robert Martinson and others published a summary of the results of over two hundred journal articles on the issue of whether prison rehabilitation programs have a direct impact on recidivism (Lipton, Wilks & Martinson, 1972). The critical conclusion was that "nothing works." The news that rehabilitation did not affect recidivism came as a severe blow to the corrections officials who stood by the rehab philosophy. However, Martinson may not have been the most objective critic of the corrections industry, and his analysis did contain several flaws. One critic said "Martinson drew his conclusions selectively from broader studies, only citing evidence that was unduly pessimistic" (Lipton, 1998). In short, Martinson may have cherry-picked the studies and used only those studies that agreed with his mind-set. And, in fact, in 1979 he did a complete about-face and said "some treatment programs do have an appreciable effect on recidivism." And also "Some positive results are found again and again for treatment programs as diverse as individual psychotherapy, group counseling, intensive supervision, and what we have called individual help (aid, advice, counseling)" (Martinson, 1979). But the apology came too late. The public fell in love with the "nothing works" mantra and demanded a "get tough" policy, rather than coddling prisoners with what the public now saw as worthless and costly rehabilitation programs. (As an aside, Martinson started having severe bouts of depression, and in 1980 he committed suicide by jumping from a high-rise window while his son looked on).

By 1982, even the Attorney General at the time, Edwin Meese, talked of the "discredited theory of rehabilitation." The rehabilitation model was being replaced by the retribution approach. However, in 1987, with little fanfare, a publication appeared that presented convincing evidence in support of the rehabilitation model (Gendreau & Ross, 1987). Using metaanalytic and statistical techniques not available to Martinson, they said that the "nothing works" theory is not grounded in scientific truth, and they went on to cite study after study showing successful inmate rehabilitation. In some cases the success rate was substantial, as much as 80%, and they found these positive results in a considerable number of well-controlled studies. The most positive results stemmed from a form of therapy called C.B.T. or Cognitive-Behavioral Therapy (Ross, 2013). The world, however, has not greeted these new findings with enthusiasm. The "nothing works" slogan has persisted, especially because it was endorsed by both liberal and conservative politicians. The liberals thought that rehabilitation meant forced treatment and longer sentences to complete these treatments, and the conservatives urged that if rehabilitation doesn't work then let's increase both the length of prison terms and the use of capital punishment (Sarre, 1999).

Retribution

The net effect of the Martinson study was to reissue a call for stronger punishment, such as the "get-tough" measures and the "three-strikes-and-you're-out" rule (which means that a third felony conviction could result in a life sentence). The retribution philosophy has led to a dramatic increase in the U.S. prison population, which now leads the world in the total numbers of persons incarcerated.

Types of Institutional Corrections Today

Before getting into levels of prison security, let's take a look at the various lock-ups. These include police holding cells, jails and prison-correctional facilities.

Holding Cells

Most police departments throughout the country have their own holding cells (sometimes referred to as "drunk tanks") for those whom the police have just picked up for everything from loitering to murder. For very small police departments these holding cells might be shared among several closely situated police departments. The holding cell is supervised by detention officers, both male and female, and their job begins the moment a hand-cuffed suspect is brought before the booking sergeant. And if you ever find yourself in this situation, the booking officer will do the questioning, and you will do the answering. This will not be just an exchange of pleasantries. The discussion will be direct, one-sided and often containing veiled threats. A female officer takes charge of female suspects as well as some juveniles. The detention officer must search and observe the suspect, looking for subtle mannerisms or anything that may appear to be unusual, especially anything that might be used as a possible weapon. The suspect cannot be placed in the cell until the initial search is over. Any personal property is inventoried, recorded and placed under lock and key until the suspect is released for arraignment. Many suspects enter the booking process afraid, injured, medicated, suicidal, homeless, drunk, and even with open wounds. After an initial clean up, the detention officer may escort the suspect to the photo lab for pictures and fingerprints.

Jails (Detention Centers)
Until suspects have been tried in a court of law, they are usually held in a jail where their range of personal freedom is severely limited. Historically, that's what the jail was for – short-term confinement for those awaiting trial. Today, however, along with these pre-trial offenders there are also inmates who have been given short-term sentences, usually less than a year. Currently there are over half a million Americans doing jail time, ten times as many men as women. And they're not all adults, since there are well over 50,000 jail inmates who are younger than age 18. In most states, jails are operated at the county level, usually under the supervision of the Sheriff's department. The levels of security in a jail can vary widely. For example the same jail may hold a dangerous murder suspect, or perhaps a gentle vagrant. Until sentencing, they all may occupy different levels of the same jail. In most cases, the pre-sentenced inmates wear yellow or orange jump suits, versus green for those already sentenced. Although the majority of this country's jails are relatively small, holding fewer than 100 people, there are now many new larger jails, and these are where the majority of the jail-inmate population is now being housed.

Orientation and Classification
During orientation, the rigorous process of classification begins. Here again, the delicate balance between security and inmate needs is carefully analyzed. As with the holding cells, those inmates first entering the jail, usually in leg irons and handcuffs, may be highly agitated, heavily self-medicated and often very aggressive. It is a trying time for both inmates and staff. During these first few days of confinement, however, the inmates are put through an orientation process that usually also includes classification. The classification is based on a number of important factors, such as medical and mental health records, educational level, job skills, marital status, and, of course, criminal record and type(s) of offenses. The process is twofold: custody level and treatment programs.

Custody Levels

The assigned custody level is based on the safety risk presented by each inmate. Inmates who present the highest risk are assigned to the highest level (maximum) security, and within this group some may even have additional control restrictions. These added restrictions are designed for the protection of the staff and other inmates. This classification, however, is not set in stone. Inmates may earn their way out of some restrictions by good behavior.

Treatment Programs

Classification also includes the assignment of rehabilitative programs that are focused on self-improvement and eventually preparing the inmate for reentry. Each inmate is given an individual profile that includes the inmate's strengths and weaknesses, and perceived potential for change.

The New-Generation Jail

Today there is a movement toward what are called NGJs, New- Generation Jails. These are architecturally different, because they are being built using the pod system which is a system where the jail is composed of several independent and smaller units called "pods." The pods may hold only about 40 or 50 inmates tops. Thus these new jails are being built to include a grouping of smaller jails (the pods) within the same walls. The inmates remain in their pod, together, work together and enjoy relaxed times together. The pod is really just one small section of the jail. Although the jail may have many pods, each pod is virtually a self-contained unit within the larger jail. The pod may be made up of up to 30 cells, and each pod is supervised by its own staff of corrections officers (CO) who only work that particular pod. In this way, the staff gets to know the inmates at a personal level, and the inmates know the staff. And because of the pod's smaller size, COs and other staff members get to know the inmates on a first-hand basis. The NGJ concept also addresses the issue of both inmate and staff security. There can still be disturbances, even riots, but with the pod system they are on a much smaller and less dangerous scale. This new system came into being because those larger jails were very impersonal, and it seemed as though the inmates were simply being warehoused, with little or no attention to any rehabilitation efforts. In those days it seemed as though jails were just a "lock'em-up-and – throw- away the-key business" and not a rehabilitation business. The emphasis now, however, is on rehabilitation and preparation for re-entry.

Prisons (Including Penitentiaries and Corrections Centers)

The prisons in this country are run by either the state or the federal government, and it's actually the state prisons where the majority of inmates are housed. In most cases, anyone convicted of a felony and sentenced to more than one year will be sent to a prison. A person who is convicted of a federal crime, such as racketeering (RICO) or bank robbery will be sent to a federal prison. RICO, or the Racketeer Influenced and Corrupt Organization Act is a federal law that was passed in 1970 and demands heavy penalties on violators, almost all of whom are members of organized crime. This legislation has been very helpful to law enforcement in prosecuting suspects who are involved in threatening retaliation against witnesses and so-called whistle-blowers. RICO convictions result in sentencing to Federal Prisons.

There are only about 100 federal prisons in the United States, far fewer than the 1800 state prisons. Less than 10% of federal prisoners were convicted of a violent crime, whereas the state prisons house almost 55% of persons convicted of crimes of violence (the rest are doing time in jails). Conditions have long been considered much better in a federal vs. state prison. Persons who have been in both have alleged that compared to a state prison, the federal prison is almost like being in a hotel – even calling it "Club Fed." Certainly the federal prison is not as dangerous in terms of prisoner-on- prisoner assaults as is the state prison, but to compare it to a Hilton is a stretch. Federal prisons are operated by the US Bureau of Prisons (BOP), a highly structured and efficient government program. There are, however, differences among the various federal prisons which have been thoroughly illustrated by Alan Ellis in his book "The Federal Prison Guidebook" (Ellis, 2005). Minimum security federal prisons are usually called "camps" and Ellis maintains that the prison a convict is sent to is almost as important as the length of the sentence. There are some camps where the felon is more apt to do "easy time" than is the case with other camps with the same security designation. There are even privately-run national firms, such as National Prison and Sentencing Consultants, that not only use sentencing reduction strategies but also techniques for aiding their clients in finding the least aversive federal or state prison in which to serve out the sentence. State prisons, of course, are run by the state in which the inmate has been convicted.

Levels of Prison Security
Security levels in U.S. prisons are rated by the BOP (Bureau of Prisons) on a five-point scale, with 5 being the most secure and 1 the least secure. As mentioned above each inmate is given an assigned security level during classification, with the most violent offenders going to the level 5 facilities. Corrections officers are trained to use different tactics depending on the security level of the facility.

The Super-Max
There is also one level of prison security that rises above all the others in terms of tightness of control. Such a facility is called a "Super-Max" prison, with perhaps the most famous being in Florence, Colorado. Called the "ADX" this prison is said to be the most secure in the entire prison system. There are only about 500 inmates at the ADX, but they consist of the most

dangerous males in all of confinement. Each prisoner resides in an individual cell, and is only allowed out of the cell for one hour per day, usually into an exercise area that is double-fenced and electrified. Inmate actions within the exercise yard are tightly monitored and controlled. There are no communal showers, toilets or sinks, and there are no lockers for storing personal possessions. You may have seen this super-max prison on various TV shows, and quickly decided that this is not the place where you would like to spend your "golden" years.

Minimum Security

At the other end of the scale are the minimum security facilities and they are used to house the non-violent offenders, such as the "white collar" criminal. Many inmates in these facilities are not put in actual cells, but instead may live in what are called dormitories, and the showers, toilets and sinks are often communal. Inmates in these facilities are often allowed to work outside the prison walls, many doing such things as highway clean-up jobs or landscaping work in public areas. These minimum-security facilities also allow certain inmates to attend twelve-step meetings, such as Alcoholics Anonymous and Narcotics Anonymous that are located outside the prison walls. In between the maximum and minimum security facilities stand the medium security facilities. Here, supervision is far more relaxed than in the super-max, and inmate movement within the prison is allowed and sometimes encouraged. The most popular activities are physical conditioning, watching TV, and reading.

Prison Industries

Both for reasons of vocational training and what is seen by some as economic necessity, convicts have long worked in factories, road gangs, coal mines ....the list is almost endless, often working directly for the state but also even for private industries. Inmates have made a variety of items inside the prison, such as furniture and clothing that can then be sold on the outside. In one prison, inmates made prison jump-suits and other uniforms that were sold to prisons throughout the country. Convicts have also been leased by the state to private companies with the money usually returning directly into the state treasuries. Most of the convict-leasing programs occurred during the 1920s and 1930s, but when trade-unions became more powerful, legislation was introduced both at the state and federal level that severely curtailed the use of inmate labor in the private sector. However by 1975 prison workers were again allowed to create products inside the prison to be distributed and sold by private companies, such as J.C. Penney, Victoria's Secret, Jostens and many others (Sexton, 1995). Some prisoner-made-clothing is sold directly from the facility to the general public. A prison in eastern Oregon manufactures a line of clothing called "Prison Blues" – with the slogan "Made on the Inside to be Worn on the Outside." Finally, imagine a scene in a New Hampshire state prison where inmates are busily making automobile license plates - with the state's motto emblazoned on each "Live free or Die."

The Eighth Amendment

Whereas a suspect (and counsel) usually focuses on the Bill of Rights' Fourth, Fifth and Sixth Amendments (the amendments designed to protect the suspect), once convicted the Eighth Amendment becomes the inmate's best friend. The Eighth Amendment states that the government cannot use "cruel and unusual punishment," and this phrase has been used to open up a multitude of legal actions, including some frivolous suits. Among Eighth-Amendment prisoner complaints are the following:

1. Complained of feces on the cell's wall (but he put it there).
2. A fan made the cell too cold (but it was during the summer, and he later complained of not having air conditioning.)
3. A night light outside the cell caused insomnia (but also complained that the light was not bright enough to read by).
4. The cell was dirty (but then complained of an allergic reaction to the liquid used to clean it).
5. One of the nurses had a bad attitude.
6. The food was bad, but even worse was the drinking water that he said had been poisoned by the staff.
7. Scheduled his dental and medical appointments during the part of the day when he wanted to work out at the gym. And there was not enough exercise equipment.
8. The totality of the prison experience was cruel (but could not give one example).
9. Complained that his prison jump suit did not fit properly and was also degrading. (he weighed over 330 pounds).
10. Did not enjoy the food but ate it anyway, and alleged that he was forced to take his "meds."
11. And finally the "Irony Prize" goes to the 500 pound condemned killer who says that his execution would be cruel and unusual because it would be painful for him to have to suffer while the executioner struggles to find his fat-covered veins for the injection.

Suspect vs Convict

It's important to keep in mind that the Bill of Rights and due process still applies to a suspect, but once the judge and/or jury render a guilty verdict, the person is a convict and is no longer afforded all protections provided by the Constitution. For example it would certainly be the height of folly to expect a Corrections Officer to get a judge's warrant to search a prison cell in case there is a suspicion that the inmate may have hidden weapons, drugs, or other contraband inside his cell.

Capital Punishment

We are now entering one of the most controversial issues in all of criminal justice. This topic is so fraught with religious, moral, and philosophic overtones that it can lead to incredibly emotional debates. Because of this we will keep this section short on rhetoric and try to just stick to the facts - to what is actually known. We will first define the term and then focus on four major concerns: deterrence, constitutional legality, the rights of prisoners, and the formation of the jury.

Definition

The word "capital" in this context derives from the Latin word "capitalis" which translates as "of the head" and is meant to be defined as "beheading." The use of capital punishment has a long history and dates back at least to ancient biblical times. The bible's Old Testament and Hammurabi's Code argues in favor of the death penalty as a form of revenge when it speaks of "an eye for an eye and a tooth for a tooth." If someone is murdered, the retaliation is therefore to murder the murderer. Although capital punishment in the United States is almost entirely for homicide, there are still other crimes on the books that may qualify, such as espionage, using weapons of mass destruction resulting in death, terrorism and in a few states, aggravated rape (especially of a child).

Deterrence

One of the key issues in this debate is whether capital punishment can really act as a deterrent to those who may be considering this form of violence. It is certainly obvious that it is a significant deterrent to those being executed. He/she can kill no more. But does it have an effect on others? Here our vision gets cloudy. Supporters on both sides have provided what seems like hard evidence in favor of either one position or the other.

Statistics are paraded before us, and what is actually known is that the final answer still eludes us. One anecdotal and specious argument against the deterrent effect of capital punishment is that it simply does not deter crimes of any type. The argument states that many years ago in England when convicted pickpockets were publically hanged, other pickpockets would work the crowd and pick the pockets of those who were there to witness the hanging. Can you spot the flaw in this logic? The fallacy is that there is no comparison group (or, as it will be called later in the book, control group). To draw the comparison, we would have to look at the number of pockets being picked at other less grisly events, like horse racing or a carnival. If the frequency of pocket picking was lower at the public hangings, then perhaps capital punishment did have a deterrent effect, but without the comparison group we'll never know. One of the first major studies using quantitative evidence was provided by Professor Isaac Ehrlich (Ehrlich, 1975), Ehrlich's evidence was seen by many as proof that not only did capital punishment save lives and deter homicide, but it even lowered the rates of other, less serious felonies. Then later, Radelet and Akers(1996) surveyed both a group of experts in the field of criminal justice as well as the general public, and their results showed an overwhelming consensus among the experts against the effectiveness of capital punishment as a deterrent, although there was support for capital punishment among members of the general public. So therefore what is really known regarding capital punishment and deterrence? What we know is that the jury is still out on this crucial question.

Constitutional Legality

The United States has gone back and forth regarding the constitutionality and use of capital punishment. For example the Supreme Court in Furman v. Georgia (1975) seemed to be putting an end to capital punishment when it ruled that this form of punishment was indeed cruel and unusual and violated the provisions of the Eighth Amendment. And over the years it may indeed have been cruel and unusual. It was used in a variety of forms, such as firing squads, burning at the stake, bludgeoning, hanging, the electric chair and the gas chamber. But then in Gregg v. Georgia (1976), the death penalty was restored by the Supreme Court, and it has remained legal ever since. However, states currently use lethal injection as virtually the only form of execution (in order to uphold the Eighth Amendment's prohibition of cruel and unusual punishment). There are some states that have legislatively abolished capital punishment altogether, and all the states have abolished capital punishment for anyone under the age 18.

The Jury

The Supreme Court in 1968 ruled that the jury in a capital case must become "death qualified." This means that the juror must neither be totally opposed to the death penalty, nor believe that the death penalty can be the only verdict in a case of homicide (Witherspoon v. Illinois, 1968). Therefore the jurors must be open-minded, and be willing to see both sides of this important issue. It is also interesting to note that when a jury has been "death qualified" it is often called having been "Witherspooned."

The Supreme Court and Prisoner's Rights

In 1964 the Supreme Court ruled (Cooper v Tate) that prisoners had the rights granted to every U.S. citizen by the Constitution's Bill of Rights. This meant that the court system was now open to prisoners and could be used to hear their grievances. It was also used to prevent any treatment programs from being forced on the inmates. Then, in a series of court decisions, one as recent as 2010 (Brown v Plata), it was ruled that the government had to provide all inmates with free medical care. When combined with the 1964 prisoner-rights decision inmate rights rose to new heights, and the Court's health rulings have had some interesting consequences (perhaps some unintended).

For example, an inmate named Michelle K. (previously known as Robert K.) sued the Department of Corrections for refusing to allow a free surgical sex-change operation. He/she was serving a life-time sentence for the violent, slashing-murder of his/her wife in 1990. Calling it a medically valid gender identity disorder, a Massachusetts judge in 2012 ruled in favor of the inmate, saying that this was the "only adequate treatment" for this particular inmate and withholding it would violate his/her constitutional rights, citing especially his/her Eighth Amendment rights forbidding cruel and unusual treatment. Although a group called the "Gay and Lesbian Advocates and Defenders" were clearly pleased by the decision, a spokesman representing the American Society of Plastic Surgeons said that along with the surgery there will be hormone injections, medical and psychotherapies, electrolysis and other procedure, all of which would cost the state as much as $80,000.

Jail House Lawyers
Many inmates complain that although the court system is open to them they simply can't afford the cost of legal representation for each grievance. Prisons are therefore charged with providing legal reference material to those inmates who feel they want to represent themselves in court (or represent friends and cell mates). Some prisons have complete law libraries modeled on those found in top-level Law Schools.

Freedom of Religion
The Supreme Court has said that inmates do have their First Amendment rights, including freedom of religion, and that the prison must provide inmates with an opportunity to practice their religion of choice (Cutter v Wilkinson, 2005). The Court also stated that prisoners may have fewer overall rights than free citizens (because the withholding of some rights may be viewed as a legitimate punishment). This has made the freedom of religion issue a sometimes thorny problem. The issue is complicated by the fact that some of the alleged religions are not always easy to define, and/or have religious practices that are difficult if not impossible for prisons to allow and still maintain security. Also there are some religions whose dietary requirements are virtually impossible for a prison to satisfy. While many non-traditional religions have been incorporated into prison practice, there are some, such as the Church of the New Song, Satanism, Witchcraft, the Aryan Nations and the Five-Percenters who have not been fully accepted by the government or by prison officials. It may be of interest to know that the prison population has a far higher percentage of some of these non-traditional belief systems than exists in the free population at large.

Special Needs Inmates
Many inmates enter confinement with special needs, such as: health problems, substance abuse, mental illness, and old age.

Health Problems

The Supreme Court has ruled that inmates must receive free medical and dental services as needed. (The only other persons to have such free services are those serving in the military). The number one health problem among persons entering jail is being HIV positive or having AIDS. AIDS is primarily transmitted through the sharing of dirty needles and/or sexual contact. Both of these activities are prohibited in our jails and prisons, and yet they secretly continue and some inmates contract the disease while under detention. Other sexually-transmitted-diseases (STDs) are syphilis, gonorrhea, chlamydia and herpes. The percentage of persons with STDs is higher among the inmate population, both men and women, than in the general population at large. It is also higher in jails than in prisons because while in jail awaiting sentencing inmates may have only just started to begin treatment. Almost a quarter of STD cases, including HIV, now occur among women. This is partly due to the fact that conviction for prostitution is one of the leading reasons for women being in the prison system (along with property crimes, sometimes called "poverty crimes," and drug crimes). Drug crimes are often linked to prostitution because some women use that line of work to pay for their drug and alcohol habits. AIDS is now both the number- one health problem (and the leading cause of death) among inmates. As the prison population ages, however, other health problems are beginning to close the gap, such as heart problems, cancer, liver disease and hepatitis.

Substance Abuse

The large majority of prison inmates are afflicted with substance abuse problems, problems that often sent them to jail in the first place - such as selling drugs and/or stealing in order to get the money to buy the drugs. In fact the National Center on Addiction and Substance Abuse found that although the majority of inmates meet the criteria for substance abuse and addiction, only 11% receive treatment. They also reported that drugs and alcohol are often implicated in violent crimes, property crimes, and weapons or public-order crimes. The report also stated that if inmates could be treated and sent back to the community drug and alcohol free, each such inmate would save society over $90,000 per year. This is obviously an extremely difficult goal to reach, but it does point to the extraordinary need for our jails and prisons to provide such treatment. Of course no substance treatment program can be 100% effective, but for every success story society would be that much safer and more secure. Within any prison drugs are sometimes smuggled in, usually by friends or family during visitation hours. An effective prevention measure is to implement a non-contact visiting policy, with visits only taking place with a glass partition between visitor and inmate. To measure its effectiveness, random drug testing of large samples allows for an accurate estimate of the overall drug use in the total prison population.

The Mentally Ill and the Other Asylums

Because of the large number of mentally ill inmates, prisons today are often called "the other asylums." For what was then seen as upholding the rights of the individual, the government back in the 1960s began closing state-run mental hospitals, and some of the consequences, though unintended, are still with us. Called "deinstitutionalization" inmates were released with little or no supervision, and too many ex-patients found themselves in medical hospitals as victims of assault or in prisons as perpetrators of assault or some other crime. Two recent studies show that persons with mental disorders are more apt to be violent (Coid, 2013), and also more likely to be victims of violence, including murder (Crump, 2013). The mentally ill have been found to be up to 23 times more likely to be victims of rape, robbery, and assault than is the case for the general population (Teplin, et al, 2005) . It has been estimated that about 12% of all prison inmates have severe mental health issues, including paranoid schizophrenia, and that the current system has failed them. But the current system wasn't designed to treat mental illness. The burden on the corrections system has become enormous, both financially and administratively. Corrections officers find mentally ill offenders difficult to control, and assaults on officers have risen with this influx of mentally ill inmates. Nor are things getting any easier for the officers. In March of 2012, a District Court Judge in Massachusetts ruled that mentally ill patients may no longer be segregated because segregation violates their constitutional rights (Hanlon, 2012). It was pointed out that during a certain 28-month time period, 11 segregated mentally-ill patients committed suicide. Unfortunately we don't have a good comparison group, such as how many non-segregated mentally-disturbed inmates also committed suicide, or how many non-institutionalized, mentally-ill persons killed themselves. It has also been suggested that juveniles being detained also have high rates of psychiatric disorders, such as substance abuse and "disruptive behavioral disorders" (Teplin, 2002).

An Aging Prison Population

Just as the population of older Americans at large is growing, so too is the aging population in jails and prisons. Also, the fact that persons are now serving longer sentences due to such get-tough policies as the "three strikes" rule, has increased longevity within the corrections system. Some have called the aging problem the result of a "perfect storm" of events in the criminal justice system – such as harsher sentencing, limiting the power of judges, and the curtailment of parole within the federal system. This has become a challenging issue for corrections authorities, and has led to the creation of special geriatric units within the prisons, which of course increases the costs of corrections. The average health cost per inmate in the United States has increased by 31 percent since 1995, and these costs are destined to rise dramatically over the next few years. A report released by the ACLU found that by the year 2030, if the current trend continues, there will be almost half a million federal and state prisoners who are 55 and older (ACLU Report, 2012). This would constitute over one-third of all inmates.

Compassionate Release

Some inmates, especially among the sick and elderly, have been granted what is called "compassionate release." This is only granted when inmates are judged to be terminally ill and deemed to pose no threat to society (or themselves), and who have family members or close friends who are willing to care for them. Terminally ill inmates who are not given compassionate release are often cared for in prison hospice units. The prison hospice units are led by an Interdisciplinary Team of doctors, nurses, social workers, counselors, and clergy. Although there are security issues involved when inmates are used in these team roles, prisons are continuing to utilize prison volunteers.

CASE STUDY- The Case of Donald R.

Donald R. had led what seemed to be the "good" life. He had served his community in several important areas, especially as a long-time member of the School Board and as a major contributor to many of the city's charities. He had his own insurance agency, which was successful enough to afford him with many of life's pleasures. He lived in an expensive home in an exclusive part of the city, and he always drove top-of-the-line luxury cars. He and his wife had also enjoyed extensive travel. He was a faithful member of his church and spent much of his time on various church committees. He had raised a family of five, and his oldest son was heavily involved in politics and was currently considering, with his father's encouragement, a run for mayor. Although he himself had gone to a local community college, he sent all five of his children to prestigious colleges and universities. Up to a year ago he had never had any problems with the law, not even a single moving violation. Nor had he had any problems with alcohol. But then, in his twilight years, things changed. During the past year he had two reported DUIs, but in fact had been stopped several other times by police-officer friends who gave him a wink and a nudge and even helped him get safely home. But then, at the age of eighty two, it happened! While backing out of his driveway and while heavily intoxicated he hit and killed a young girl riding by his house on her bicycle. He was, of course, charged with vehicular homicide and despite pleas for leniency was convicted and sent to prison for five years with no parole for at least one year. His drinking problem had started only a year and a half ago, just after his wife of fifty years had passed away. Here he was in prison, frail and stooped over, surrounded by young toughs who threatened him almost daily. His health deteriorated significantly during his first few months in prison, and although he was, as is every inmate, entitled to medical care, the care he received may not have been adequate for his age and condition. To add to his problems, he slowly drifted into dementia, and after less than a year in prison he died. His felony, though unintended was of course horrendous, and nobody could say that prison conditions alone killed him. But a long sentence for someone that age might be seen as a "death sentence."

Inside Education

As part of their rehabilitation programs, America's prisons have been providing inside-the-walls education both vocational as well as academic. Vocational training has been focused especially on landscaping, plumbing, hair-cutting, electricity, carpentry, clothing design, cooking, and computer technology. These courses prepare the inmate directly for employment on the outside. Academic education runs the gamut from elementary levels through college. Though there are courses in basic literacy at the elementary level, perhaps the most popular prison education programs are those that lead to the G.E.D. , which stands for General Education Development. The G.E.D. is also commonly called the Graduate Equivalency Degree, and is the official high school diploma equivalent. This program offers the inmate a chance to create a life-changing situation when it comes time for release. It even allows the inmate-student an opportunity to apply for a college degree. There are colleges that offer within-the-prison courses taught by the college's own faculty. One of the most successful and respected of these is the Bard College Initiative that offers a liberal arts degree in five different New York state prisons and enrolls about fifty students in each prison. Inside education has proven to be one of the best dollar-for-outcome services ever authorized by prison officials. Although you probably have heard skeptics talk about prison education programs only producing smarter criminals, the data belie that negative assertion. Carefully designed studies have shown the importance of education on the prison's bottom line – recidivism (Harer, 1994). Another study found that one million dollars spent on correctional education prevents about 600 crimes, whereas incarceration alone prevents less than half that number (Erisman & Contardo, 2010).

Institutionalization and Reentry

There are two more problems, both very serious, that the corrections establishments are trying to solve, and these are institutionalization and reentry. Some inmates become "institutionalized," that is they become so accustomed to life inside the walls that they adjust almost completely to the prison environment and don't want to leave it. Prison seems safe and secure when compared to the surprises and inconsistencies of the outside world. Life inside the prison is predictable and therefore seems less threatening than the life they left behind. Insecurity mounts as the day of release approaches. In the movie "The Shawshank Redemption" (1994), Red Redding (played by Morgan Freeman) says:

"The walls are funny. First you hate 'em, then you get used to them. Enough time passes, you get so you depend on them," and later, "No way I'm going to make it outside. All I think about is ways to break my parole, so maybe they'd send me back. I want to be back there where things make sense, where I won't be afraid all the time."

This is a dramatic example of the phenomenon of institutionalization, a serious condition that affects many in the system. And this is just one problem of the many which beset the inmates who have paid their debt to society and are ready for release. Along with the many insecurities attached to this process is the job problem. Finding a job for the poor and uneducated, which defines a large part of the prison population, is never easy, but when combined with a prison record it can become even more challenging. There are almost certainly family issues that may have to be resolved. Are the family members still intact as a unit, and if so how accepting and understanding will they be? What about friends? Will they be supportive, or will they be destructive and perhaps encourage more criminal behavior? Sometimes it's better not to go back to the same old friends and same old neighborhood.

Post-Prison Adjustment
Without question the prison system should provide assistance to the about-to-be-released inmate, sometimes called a "decompression program" (Haney, 2001). In one case, David Randa, who had been convicted in 1990 for killing a Rabbi, had his sentence overturned after spending 23 years in prison. On his second day of freedom he suffered a massive heart attack. Perhaps decompression could have helped this man. And for those who do obtain assistance, it should include therapeutic sessions to acclimate the inmate to the changes that have taken place in the world outside the prison walls, and also to changes that may have taken place within the inmate as a result of the prison experience. There should be some personal counseling, family counseling, and vocational counseling and, of course, special help in finding a job. These programs should start well before the release date and should stress the importance of the community-based services that will be available on the outside.

Reentry Programs – A Model Facility
A model detention facility, where intensive reentry treatment is provided, is located in Springfield Massachusetts. Although called the Western Massachusetts Correctional and Alcohol Center (WMCAC), a large number of drug offenders, men and women, are also housed in this facility. The inmates at WMCAC are all serving their last three months of confinement, and each inmate is involved in both individual and group counseling. The emphasis is on rehabilitation and reentry into society, and because of the importance of reintegration the inmates dress in civilian clothes (the men must even wear a jacket and tie to evening meals). The person responsible for this facility,

Sheriff Ashe, has said, "the program is demanding and is based on the disease concept that combines confinement with substance abuse treatment as a means for residents to develop enough self- discipline to live a drug and alcohol-free life style" (Ashe, M.J., 2012). The effort made at this facility has resulted in a recidivism rate that is significantly below the state's and country's average, which of course is of great benefit to society. Recidivism may not be the only measure of corrections success, but when it remains low year after year, it certainly bodes well as a step in the right direction. More on reentry will be covered in the Chapter on Community Corrections.

The Ashe Principles of Best Practices in Institutional Corrections

As we saw in the Chapter on Law Enforcement, Sir Robert Peel laid down the principles of police behavior, and these will now be followed by the principles of institutional corrections as formulated by Michael J. Ashe Jr, who is the high Sheriff of Hampden County in Massachusetts (Ashe, 2013). His success in corrections has been well documented throughout the country. The American Correctional Association has awarded his facility top scores, 100 percent, in seven out of eight categories, and a 98.6 in the eighth. The best principles are:

1. Within any correctional facility or operation, there must be an atmosphere and an ethos of respect for the full humanity and potential of any human being within that institution and an effort must be made to maximize that potential. This is the first and overriding principle from which all the other principles emanate, and without which no real corrections are possible.

2. Corrections facilities should seek to positively impact those in custody, and not just be mere holding agents or human warehouses.

3. Those in custody should put in busy, full and productive days, and should be challenged to pick up the tools and directions in order to build a law-abiding life.

4. Those in custody should begin participating in positive and productive activities as soon as possible in their incarceration.

5. All efforts should be made to break down the traditional barriers between correctional security and correctional human services.

6. Productive and positive activities for those in custody should be understood to be investments in the future of the community

7. Correctional institutions should be communities of lawfulness. There should be "zero tolerance," overt or tacit, for any violence within the institution. Those in custody who assault others while in custody should be prosecuted as if such action took place in the free society. Staff should be diligently trained and monitored in the appropriate "use of force" that is necessary, but non-excessive, in order to maintain safety, security, order and lawfulness.

8. The operational philosophy of positively impacting those in custody and respecting their full humanity must predominate at all levels of security.

9. Offenders should be directed toward understanding the full impact of their actions on their victims and on their community and should make restorative and reparative acts toward their victims and the community at large.

10. Offenders should be classified at the lowest level of security that remains consistent with public safety and is merited by their own behavior.

11. There should be a continuum of gradual, supervised and supported programs of re-entry for all offenders.

12. Community partnerships should be cultivated and developed for offender reentry success. This partnership should include the criminal justice and law enforcement communities as part of a public safety team.

13. The staff should be held accountable and be positive and productive

14. All staff should be inspired, encouraged and supervised in order to strive for excellence in the work to be done.

15. A spirit of innovation should permeate the operation. This innovation should be data-informed, evidence based and include both process and outcome measures.

16. In-service training should be ongoing and mandatory for all employees

17. There should be medical programs that link with public-health agencies and public-health doctors from the home neighborhoods and communities of those in custody and which takes a pro-active approach to finding and treating illness and disease in the custodial population.

18. Modern technological advances should be integrated into a correctional operation for optimal efficiency and effectiveness.

19. Any correctional facility no matter what its locale should seek to be involved in, and to involve, the local community, to welcome within its fences the positive elements of the community and to be a positive participant and neighbor in the community life. This reaching out should be both toward the community that hosts the facility and to the communities from which those in custody come.

20. Balance is the key. A correctional operation should reach for the stars but be rooted in the firm ground of common sense.

The Future of Institutional Corrections
There are three strong head-winds that may have an impact on the future of institutional corrections: Over Crowding, Prison Abolitionism, For-Profit Prisons.

Overcrowding
The incredible increase in the country's jail and prison population has put severe constraints on the government-run (tax-supported) institutional corrections system. The numbers are stark but generally indicate that as the numbers of persons in corrections increases, crime rates decrease somewhat. The total crime rate has indeed decreased whereas the incarceration rate has increased but whether there is a direct cause-and-effect relationship can't be

determined by these data alone. It does, however, give us dramatic evidence of the burden being placed on the corrections system today (FBI, 2012).

Abolitionism

There is a growing movement demanding the total abolition of all prisons and the prison system itself. The abolitionist's arguments focus on three major points: 1. The system doesn't work, is ineffective in deterring crime and results in high rates of recidivism, 2. It actually acts as a breeding ground for new and more sophisticated criminals, 3. It is biased against the poor and the minorities. This third argument is usually accompanied by statistics showing minorities and the unemployed-poor to be overrepresented in today's prisons (criticalresistance.org, 2015).

For-Profit Prisons

Because of prison over-crowding, many new prisons have been built and operated by private "for-profit" corporations, such as the Corrections Corporation of America. Private corrections facilities now house almost 10% of the nation's inmates, and the percentage is increasing at a rapid rate. In 2012 Corrections Corporation of America offered to buy and maintain a large number of state prisons (including maximum security prisons), in exchange for the promise of at least a 90% occupancy rate and a twenty year management contract. So far these private facilities are saving money for the tax payers, but the question remains as to the quality of the staffs and the services they supply. Are they as professionally trained as those who work in state and federal prisons? Are we jeopardizing the security of society for the financial savings the private prisons offer? The American Correctional Association has accredited the vast majority (over 90%) of these privately-run prisons, and the few still on probation are also said soon to be accredited. Finally, most of these private prisons are adhering to the rehabilitation philosophy and are offering inmates vocational training, education, addiction treatments and recreational opportunities (CCA, 2013).

Summary

The prison philosophy in the United States has gone through several important changes over the years, but has almost always stressed either punishment or rehabilitation. These two themes have permeated U.S. prison policy since its very first days. And those early days can be illustrated in America's first prison, the New Gate Prison in Connecticut. Built in a copper mine, 70 feet below ground, conditions at New Gate were harsh and probably both cruel and unusual. However, when New Gate opened, 1773, the United States was not yet formed, and therefore there was no U.S. Constitution with its Bill of Rights. The next landmark in the history of American prisons was the Walnut St. Jail in Philadelphia (1790). This jail became the model for a philosophy of incarceration called the "Pennsylvania System," which was characterized by two major elements, penitence (hence the term penitentiary) and silence. And the silence was complete – no talking, ever- just a silent reflection on one's sins. Nor was there anyone around to talk to, since all the inmates had to remain inside their cells as though in solitary confinement. The competing philosophy at the time was called the "Auburn System," and although this was seen as enlightened in its day, it would be considered barbaric by today's standards. In the Auburn system, inmates, although remaining silent, could leave their cells on occasion and at least see other human beings (guards and other inmates). They could also work, and one enormous irony is that the inmates were used to build other prisons, including New York's famous Sing Sing. Thoughts of rehabilitation were clearly beginning to surface, and were brought to the forefront in 1870 by a new organization called the ACA – American Corrections Association (still in operation today and evaluates and accredits all U.S. jails and prisons). ACA's actions resulted in: (1) prisoner silence being abolished, 2) vocational and educational training being introduced, (3) rewards, not just punishment, could be used to change behavior, and (4) good behavior could result in early release. This was a giant step forward, but even more so was the Wickersham Commission, organized in the early 1930s, that gave new impetus to the rehabilitation philosophy. The Wickersham Commission did a thorough investigation of law enforcement and corrections, and uncovered major violations, including corrupt police practices and a prison system that allowed for, sometimes even encouraged, virtual torture. The Wickersham report aroused public and governmental concerns and caused another shift toward the rehabilitation model. During the early 1970s, Robert Martinson published a study which concluded that prison rehabilitation efforts are a waste of time. His statement that "nothing works" became a rallying cry for the critics who stridently urged a retribution and "get-tough" policy on all inmates. It soon became obvious, however, that Martinson's analysis was seriously flawed, and could not be used to prove his "nothing –works" theory. Also new and rigorously- designed studies began appearing that provided convincing evidence that the rehabilitation model did indeed work, and that Martinson was wrong. Just before his suicide, Martinson recanted his position and actually apologized. The types of institutional corrections today consist of police department holding cells, jails (usually for those awaiting trial), and prisons for those who have been convicted. An inmate entering prison is given an orientation and classification regarding prison programs and levels of security. Prisons are run by either the state or the federal government. The majority of inmates are in state prisons. There are only 100 federal prisons, as opposed to over 1800 state prisons. Inmates seem to think that prison conditions are better (more lenient) in federal prisons. The levels of security range from minimum, through maximum ,and all the way to the "Super Max." Most prisons today do adhere to the rehabilitation model and do provide counseling, vocational training, and education to the inmates. In fact some vocational efforts have resulted in prison industries that now manufacture many items for sale to the general public. Although the effectiveness of capital punishment as a deterrent has yet to be fully established, the U.S. Supreme Court has ruled that it is a legal form of punishment. There is, of course, great controversy around this issue – many questions and few answers. Jurors in capital cases must be "death-qualified," meaning they must prove to be open minded on the issue before they can serve on the panel. There are some states that have abolished capital punishment completely, and in no state can a person under the age 18 be executed. In 1964, the Supreme Court ruled that prisoners now have some of the same citizen rights as granted by the U.S. Constitution's Bill of Rights. This means that prisoners could now use the court system to address their grievances. The prison also had to supply legal reference material (in effect law libraries), and this has resulted in many inmates becoming so knowledgeable that the term "Jail-House Lawyers" has been applied. One of the recent challenges for the jails and prisons is the right to freedom-of-religion. There are so many religions, some appearing to be made up on the spot, that catering to all their various non-traditional diets and practices becomes virtually impossible. The Court also ruled that the government had to provide inmates with free medical and dental care (just like members of the armed forces). Health problems, especially HIV and AIDS, are prevalent in both male and female populations. AIDS, of course, is one of the number one health problems and the leading cause of death among inmates. Health problems also include mental illness, and Corrections is now charged with the treatment of the mentally ill making it difficult for Corrections Officers to be both jailers as well as mental health workers. The increase in the number of older persons in the prison population has also added to the costs of confinement. Some elderly and sick inmates, judged to be terminally ill, have been given what is called "compassionate release." Jails and prisons have also provided educational opportunities for inmates (although they cannot be forced to become involved). The reentry problem and post-prison adjustment is a difficult issue for Institutions to handle, and yet it is important to do as much as possible for the inmate who is now ready to reenter society. The prisoner who has "done the time" and is ready to leave often finds that the new-found freedom comes with many new and difficult challenges, including those of jobs, family and friends. The more the institution can aid in this process, the higher is the percentage of success (non-recidivism) for the now-free inmate.

Ashe's principles of good practices lists a series of solutions to many of the problems faced by today's corrections facilities. Among the future issues and challenges for the Corrections Systems are overcrowding, the movement to abolish the prison system, and the advent of private (for-profit) prisons, such as those run by the Corrections Corporation of America. It has been found that private prisons are more cost effective, but the quality of the staff and the services they supply may not always be up to the standards of today's state and federal prison professionals.

Key Terms

American Correctional Association
Auburn System
Capital Punishment
Compassionate Release
Custody Levels
Death Qualified (Jury)
Education Within the Walls
Eighth Amendment
Elmira Reformatory
For-Profit Prisons
Freedom of Religion
Health Problems and Special Needs
Holding Cells
Jails
Martinson, Robert
Mentally Ill Prisoners
Minimum
Maximum
New Gate Prison
Overcrowding
Pennsylvania System
Prison Industry
Prison Security
Prisoner Rights
Punishment Model
Rehabilitation Model
Retribution
Silence and Repentance
The Aging Population
Walnut Street Jail
Wickersham Commission

References

Allen, P.E. & Simonsen, C.E. (2006). *Corrections in America.* Upper Saddle River, NJ: Prentice Hall

American Civil Liberties Report (2012). *At America's expense: the mass incarceration of the elderly.* June

Behind Bars (2010) . *Substance Abuse and America's Prison Population.* National Center on Addiction and Substance Abuse. New York: Columbia University Press

Coid, J.W., Ullrichs, S., Constantinos, K., Keers, R., Barker, D. Cowden, F. & Stamps, R. (2013). The relationship between delusions and violence. *Journal of the American Medical Association*, 1-7.

Correctional Association of America (2013). *Standards and Accreditation.* Nashville, TN Author.

Critical Resistance (2015). *What is abolition?* Retrieved from critical resistance.org.

Crump, C., Sundquist, K., Winkleby, S.W., Sundquist, J. (2013) Mental disorders and vulnerability to homicidal death, *The BMJ*, 346-357

Ehrlich,I. (1975). The deterrent effect of capital punishment: A question of life and death. *American Economic Review*, *65*, 397-417.

Erisman, W. & Contardo, J.B. (2010). Learning to reduce recidivism. *Journal of Correctional Education*, Dec, 316-334

Ellis, A. & Henderson, M. (2005). *The federal prison guide book.* San Rafael CA, The Law Offices of Alan Ellis.

Federal Bureau of Investigation (FBI). 2012. *Crime in the US.* Retrieved from www.fbi.gov.

Gendreau, P. & Ross, R.R., (1987). Revivication of rehabilitation: Evidence from the 1980s. *Criminal Justice Quarterly*, *4*, 575-608.

Gregg v. Georgia,428 U.S. 153 (1976)

Haney, C. (2002). The psychological impact of incarceration: Implications for post- prison adjustment. *U.S. Dept. of Health and Human Services Conference*, Jan. 2002.

Hanlon, P. (2012). Policy changes affect isolation for prisoners with mental illness. *New England Psychologist*, *6*, July, 2012

Harer, M. (1994). *Recidivism among Federal prisoners*. Washington DC: Federal Bureau of Prisons.

Lipton, D, Wilks, J & Martinson, R. (1972). *The effectiveness of correctional treatment: A survey of treatment valuation studies.* Praeger Press, NY: New York

Martinson, R, (1979). New findings, new views: A note of caution regarding sentencing reform. *Hofstra Law Review*, 7, 243-258.

Radelet, M. & Akers, R. (1996). Deterrence and the death penalty. *Journal of Criminal Law and Criminology*, *87*, 111-165

Sarre, R. (1999). Beyond what works: a 25 year jubilee retrospective of Robert Martinson. *Paper presented at the History of Crime, Policing and Punishment Conference*, Dec 10, Charles Sturt Univ., Australia

Sexton, G. (1995). *Working in American prisons: A joint venture with the private sector.* Washington DC: National Institute of Justice.

Teplin, L.A., Welty, L.J., Abram, K.M., Duncan, M.K. & Washburn, J.J. (2012). Prevalence and persistence of psychiatric disorders in youth after detention. *Archives of General Psychiatry*, *69*, 1031-1043.

Teplin, LA., McLelland, G.M., Abram, K.M. & Weiner, D.A. (2005) . Mentally ill become victims of violent crime. *Archives of General Psychiatry*, 62, 911-921.

CHAPTER 7

COMMUNITY CORRECTIONS

Introduction

In numerous sections of this book we have addressed the issue of the over-burdened and overcrowded prison system. Indeed, the Government Accounting Office (2012) released a report entitled 'Growing Inmate Crowding Negatively Affects Inmates, Staff, and Infrastructure' that outlined the stressful and sometimes dangerous conditions of our nation's prisons. This report found that these overcrowded facilities foster frustration and promote violence against other inmates and staffs. Further, this overcrowding was found to substantially reduce the amount of support and rehabilitative services that can be provided to inmates which oftentimes results in many inmates being released without the appropriate life, occupational, and social skills needed to re-enter society. One approach to relieving prison overcrowding is to provide alternatives to incarceration (FAMM, 2009). That is, to closely supervise and provide services to offenders outside of the prison system. This alternative is often referred to as community corrections.

Benefits of Community Corrections

Not every offender is eligible or appropriate for community corrections, particularly repeat violent offenders, but this type of programming can help to alleviate prison overcrowding and also provide valuable services to offenders who do not need to be incarcerated. Community corrections is also more cost effective than incarceration. It is estimated that State and Federal governments would realize savings of about 3 billion dollars per year if the prison population was reduced 10 percent through the use of community based correctional services (Justice Policy Institute, 2009). In addition to cost effectiveness, community corrections also offers the following benefits (Justice Policy Institute, 2009; Center for Effective Public Policy, 2013):

1. Overcrowding. Reduction in prison overcrowding leaving room and services for the more serious offenders.
2. Treatment. Increased accessibility to rehabilitative programs and treatment interventions not typically available in prisons. This is particularly important given the increase in the number of inmates requiring mental health services.
3. Family. The offender is often able to live with and/or maintain close contact with family and other community institutions such as church, civic organizations, and the work place thereby allowing the offender to reintegrate

into society much more effectively than the offender who spends his sentence incarcerated.

4. Society. The offender in the community will continue to be a contributing member of society. For example, the individual will continue to help support a family and pay their income taxes.

5. Associations. The offender is not associating with other offenders and is less likely to acquire other criminal skills and the 'techniques of the trade' needed to engage in additional criminal activities.

6. Independence. The offender will be able to acquire more readily and practice the appropriate life skills, education, and other adaptive behaviors that will make them more independent and will also assist in reducing recidivism rates.

Despite these benefits, many individuals believe that community corrections are not punitive enough. They believe that offenders should be removed from society and not be allowed to avoid prison time. But correctional programs that are located in the community are not meant to pamper, indulge, or pander to the offender. Rather, these alternatives to incarceration programs are actual sentences imposed by the courts and these programs mandate that the offender engage in specific programming. This programming is accompanied by the provision of stringent supervision and monitoring requirements, typically by an officer of the court such as a Probation Officer. If these requirements are not met the offender can be incarcerated.

Community corrections is seen as an acceptable alternative to incarceration for many offenders. The number of convicted offenders who participate in community corrections programming far outnumbers the number of offenders who are incarcerated. At the end of 2011 approximately 1 of every 50 adults was involved in some type of community correctional program such as probation while 1 of every 107 adults was incarcerated (Bureau of Justice Statistics, 2012).

Types of Community Corrections Programs

There are several types of community based correctional programs that we will be addressing including the various types of probation services and several programs commonly referred to as intermediate sanction programs. Parole is considered a community corrections program for reporting purposes by the Bureau of Justice Statistics and will be briefly addressed, however, parole services in a strict sense is not a community corrections program.

Probation

Probation is the most utilized type of community and correctional program (see Table 1.1). The State of Massachusetts was at the forefront in community corrections development. John Augustus, a Boston shoemaker and temperance advocate, was concerned about those individuals who violated temperance laws and in 1841 he petitioned the Boston Police Court to release an individual who was charged with a temperance law violation. He posted bail and the individual was released into his care and supervision for a three week period. At the end of this period the individual returned to court and the Judge was convinced that the individual was reformed. The Judge found that he did not need to be incarcerated and ordered that he only needed to pay a small fine. Subsequently, Augustus was able to secure the release of thousands of carefully selected adults and juveniles whom he thought could be rehabilitated and as such is considered the 'Father of Probation.' His work, however, was voluntary but it did set the stage for the Massachusetts legislature to establish, in 1880, the first statewide probation system and hire the first probation officers. By 1920, 21 additional states had established probation systems. In 1925 President Calvin Coolidge signed the National Probation Act and currently all states and the federal government have official probation departments (APPA, 2010)

Table 1.1 Status of Correctional Population 2012

Population Types	Population Numbers	Percent of Total
Probation	3,910,600	56.7
Parole	853,200	12.4
Prison	1,574,700	22.8
Local Jail	731,200	10.6
Total*	6,899,000	100

*Estimates may not equal total because of rounding. Total excludes those with multiple statuses. Source: Adapted and retrieved from Correctional Populations in the U.S. 2013, Bureau of Justice Statistics, United States Department of Justice, Washington, D.C. 201.

The term probation comes from the Latin 'probatio' meaning a period of proof or testing. Probation is a sentence imposed by a state or federal court of law that allows for the conditional release of a convicted offender into the community under the supervision of a probation officer. It is conditional because, in order for the offender to remain in the community, the offender must prove that they can meet the requirements (conditions) set forth by the courts. Some of these conditions can be attending counseling sessions or AA meetings, paying restitution, maintaining gainful employment, random drug testing, weekly meeting with the Probation Officer, engaging in community service, and, of course, not committing another crime (Petersilia, 1998; Bureau of Justice Statistics, 2014). There are several types of probation but before we address them let us review the role and responsibilities of the Probation Officer.

The Probation Officer

There are State and Federal Probation Officers but all are officers of the court who are primarily responsible for monitoring and supervising the behavior of offenders who have been placed in the community. Their responsibilities, however, reach far beyond monitoring and supervision and also include presentence investigation and development of the pre-sentencing report (PSR).

The purpose of the PSR, sometimes referred to as the pre-sentencing investigation (PSI), is to provide to the court a comprehensive evaluation of a defendant to assist the court in reaching a fair and just sentence. These reports address numerous components of an offender's life including offense history, family and social functioning, employment history, alcohol and drug abuse history, and educational attainment. These reports may also include information from previously conducted psychological evaluations and other mental health contacts and, in some instances, may advise on sentencing recommendations. The value of the PSR has been debated for decades but it is required in the majority of states (NYC Board of Corrections, 1973; APPA, 2010). So, in order to effectively fulfill their job responsibilities as investigators and supervisors Probation Officers need to be trained and educated not only in the internal workings of the court but also in areas such as criminology, psychology, and casework (see Figure 1.1).

Figure 1.1 Massachusetts Probation Officer Job Description
POSITION SUMMARY:
The probation officer, under the direct supervision of the chief probation officer, first assistant chief probation officer, or assistant chief probation officer, investigates thoroughly offender personal history, background and environment; reports findings to the court and is prepared to make appropriate recommendations on dispositions; periodically interviews probationers to determine the effectiveness of probation supervision and areas in which casework counseling are needed; refers probationers to social resources in the community for assistance in rehabilitation; enforces court orders; recommends revoking of probation and/or modification of court orders when necessary.

Adapted and retrieved from www.mass.gov/courts/probation/po/html January 12, 2013.

Certainly, the duties of the Probation Officer are varied and complex and require a great deal of preparation, education, and according to Federal Probation Officer Patrick Norton, M.S. of the District of CT, a great deal of "on the job training." Having defined probation and the roles and responsibilities of the Probation Officer, we now focus our attention on the various types of Probation.

A PERSON OF INTEREST: JOHN AUGUSTUS (1785-1859)

John Augustus is considered to be the "Father of Probation", since he personally and privately initiated the program in Boston, MA back in 1841. Although he was mainly employed as a maker of shoes and boots, he spent his spare time and money helping first-time offenders avoid the rigors, and what he thought were the damaging effects, of prison life. In fact, Augustus coined the term probation, which he took from the Latin "probation," translated as " proof." He was a member of the "Total Abstinence Society," a group dedicated to the elimination of all alcoholic beverages. He became especially interested in the plight of poor alcoholics who were being sent off to prison because of mandatory sentencing. He was convinced that given the right setting and a nurturing environment, these petty offenders could be rehabilitated and even remain alcohol free. He was able to convince Boston authorities to allow convicted offenders to be placed in his care on the condition that their fines would be paid and that they would reappear in court every three weeks. Augustus would pay the fines himself, find jobs for the offenders, and make them sign a pledge never to drink again. When Augustus brought them back to court , the offenders appeared to be "changed men," industrious and completely sober. Because of his success, the court allowed Augustus to take many others, which he did on a carefully selected basis. He seemed to have a gift for picking out those best able to profit from his efforts. In 1843 he decided to add children to his list of those in need of help. He started with three children, two boys and a girl, all of whom had been convicted of stealing. He paid their fines and brought them back to the court once a month to show their progress. Because of his success with the first three, many more juveniles were placed under his supervision over the years. By the time of his death, Augustus had personally supervised over 2000 men, women and children, out of which there were only four who were considered failures. A few years after his death (and because of his work), the Commonwealth of Massachusetts ordered the mayor of Boston to hire a professional probation officer, and by 1880 courts throughout the state had followed Boston's lead and had their own probation programs.

Probation Types

A review of the literature will find numerous and sometimes confusing names for a variety of probation types (Probation Officer, 2013, APPA, 2010). Generally, probation can be seen as formal or informal. Informal probation, sometimes referred to as unsupervised probation, usually happens when an individual has committed a relatively minor offense. The offender will typically need to agree to not engage in further illegal activities, perhaps pay a fine and abide by other conditions set forth by the court, and occasionally meet with a probation officer. More formal types of probation involve more stringent monitoring and supervision and will almost certainly require strictly regulated conditions. These formal types of probation can include:

1. Suspended-sentence probation. The court imposes a sentence but then suspends the sentence on the condition that the offender will successfully meet all conditions of his probation.

2. Standard/Straight probation. The court sentences the offender to probation with specific conditions and supervision requirements.

3. Shock probation. The court sentences the offender to prison but after a short period of incarceration the offender is returned to court and placed on probation. Apparently, this serves to 'shock' the offender into realizing the magnitude of their actions and thereby into adhering to the conditions of their probation (the offender is unaware of this arrangement).

4. Split-sentence probation. The judge actually 'splits' the sentence between prison time and probation. The offender is sentenced to a specific prison sentence before being placed on probation.

5. Intensive supervision probation. This type of probation requires consistent monitoring and supervision by the probation officer, perhaps on a daily basis. Probation officers who supervise probationers on intensive supervision probation (ISP) generally have smaller caseloads.

Probation Violations

Probationers are required to adhere to all of the conditions of probation set forth by the court. There are General Conditions that can apply to most such as meeting with a probation officer at a certain time and place, not engaging in illegal activities, abstaining from substance possession and use, notifying authorities about any change of address, maintaining employment, and not leaving the jurisdiction without their Probation Officer's permission. Other Special Conditions can be much more stringent and are typically ordered to address the specific circumstances of an offender. These conditions can include, but are not limited to, substance abuse testing and treatment, mental health interventions, paying restitution or fines, community service, or not possessing, owning, or purchasing a firearm or other type of weapon. If these conditions are not met by the probationer then the probation officer must decide if the person's probation should be revoked. That is, should probation be repealed and more stringent conditions, including the possibility of incarceration, be imposed. The Probation Officer has some latitude in this situation. Generally, minor infractions such as a missed appointment with the probation officer or being late for an appointment, might only result in a warning. Repeatedly missing appointments or violating a special condition such as purchasing a firearm, however, would most likely result in a recommendation for revocation. A recommendation for revocation involves informal and formal inquiries and hearings. These inquiries and hearings could lead to a modification or strengthening of probation conditions or to incarceration (Legal Information Institute, 2013). So, probation is a popular and regularly utilized type of community corrections program. One can hypothesize that, given the overcrowded prison system, it is a necessary program and one that is vital to the operations of the court and correctional system, the safety of the community, and the rehabilitation of the offender. There are situations, however, when probation is not warranted or appropriate and incarceration in a crowded prison system is not advisable. Many see probation as being too lenient but also realize that prison time may also not be the solution. This has led many to advocate for a system of intermediate sanctions.

Intermediate Sanctions

Intermediate sanctions are considered alternative sentences imposed by a court. These sanctions typically fall between court ordered probation and incarceration. Intermediate sanctions are seen as being more individualized and tailored to the offense and to the personality of the offender and tend to be viewed by many as being more punitive (and thus justified) than probation. Probation, as previously mentioned, is sometimes considered by many to be too lenient. Intermediate sanctions are usually imposed using strict standards that outline specifics that can be utilized to guide sentencing. Some jurisdictions, however, have adjusted their guidelines and now employ 'zones of discretion' whereby the courts have some latitude in imposing these sanctions (Tonry, 1997). There are many types of intermediate sanctions such as restitution, fines, home confinement, electronic monitoring, halfway houses, intensive supervision, drug courts, mental health courts, boot camps, and community reporting centers. Many of these sanctions can be combined and many are imposed as conditions of probation. Adherence to these intermediate standards is oftentimes supervised by a probation officer or other law enforcement personnel and violation of the sanctions can result in more stringent sanctions or incarceration.

Home Confinement/Electronic Monitoring

Home confinement, sometimes referred to as 'house arrest,' is a sanction where the convicted offender is mandated to remain in their homes rather than be sentenced to prison. There are often preauthorized exceptions to this confinement such as the offender being able to go to work, medical or mental health appointments, attend church, or other preapproved activities. The General Conditions of probation might also be enforced as would several Special Conditions. The use of Home Confinement as an alternative sanction has become much more popular since the advent of Electronic Monitoring Systems. These systems allow officers of the court to monitor an offender electronically. There are basically two types of electronic monitoring. The first requires the offender to wear an electronic bracelet connected to a home monitoring device that is placed in their residence. The second requires the offender to wear a bracelet and carry a GPS like monitoring device on his person. Both systems provide the probation officer with information regarding the offender's location. Further, both systems can be activated as Active or Passive Monitoring (Norma-Eady, 2007). Active monitoring provides the probation officer with current real time information about the location of the offender. Passive monitoring provides information about the location of the offender at a later time, typically the next day. The cost of electronic monitoring is sometimes paid by the offender but exceptions are often made for financial hardship. Violation of the conditions of house arrest and/or electronic monitoring can result in more stringent sanctions or incarceration.

Halfway Houses

Halfway houses, referred to as 'residential reentry centers' by the Bureau of Prisons, are community correctional homes/residences that serve as an alternative to incarceration in a prison or jail. These facilities are sometimes used to house offenders after they are released from being incarcerated as a way of gradually acclimating the offender to life outside of prison. Nevertheless, these halfway houses are increasingly being utilized as an alternative to incarceration. Halfway houses are typically located in residential homes or apartment buildings and staffed with professional and para-professional employees who provide supervision, support, and guidance to the offender. Generally, there is specific programming, rules, and regulations, and strict conditions that offenders must follow. Many of these homes serve offenders who have been placed on probation and many are offense specific. For example, offenders who reside in a particular halfway house might all have drug convictions and be in need of substance abuse treatment. Residents are normally restricted to the facility but under certain conditions, such as work, the resident may be allowed to leave for a specific period of time. Further, staff members often assist residents with employment, medical, and mental health appointments, educational endeavors, and other activities designed to aid the offender in transitioning back into society. Some of these services, such as psychotherapy, may be provided on-site if a licensed mental health practitioner is on staff. Otherwise, referrals are made to community facilities to provide these services. Placement in a halfway house might also afford the offender the opportunity to maintain or reestablish relationships with family members and significant others (Bureau of Prisons, 2013; Klein-Saffron, 1995). Halfway house programs certainly decrease prison overcrowding and can effectively assist residents in obtaining the necessary resources to transition back into society. Also, offenders who successfully complete their halfway house sentence and participate in programming are less likely to reengage in serious criminal activity (James, 2011; Seiter & Seiter, 2003; Klein-Saffron, 1995). As with other alternative sanctions, violations of the conditions of sentencing and rules of the halfway house can result in additional sanctions or incarceration.

Fines

Fines are widely used as sanctions in the criminal justice system. Fines can be imposed for relatively minor offenses such as possession, in some states, of small amounts of cannabis, or motor vehicle infractions but are also imposed for more serious offenses such as simple battery or providing alcohol to a minor. Fines can also be levied in conjunction with or as a condition of probation or fines can be combined with other types of sanctions (Hillsman & Greene, 1991). Fines are generally generated through the use of guidelines. There are two types of fines used by the courts, Tariff Fines and Day Fines. Tariff Fines are fixed fines that are applied to every offender who commits a particular type of crime. For example, a $100.00 fine for travelling twenty miles over the posted speed limit. This fine is applied regardless of the person's financial circumstances or ability to pay. Day Fines are not fixed fines. These fines are based on the offense that has been committed but also takes into consideration the financial circumstances of the offender and their ability to pay. Tariff fines can be problematic for the poor who might have difficulty paying and subsequently end up being incarcerated while, conversely, tariff fines can be meaningless and of little consequence for the wealthy who can afford to pay. Day fines do appear to be advantageous when compared to tariff fines in that day fines can be considered a sanction that is fair and just.

Restitution

Restitution, like fines, can also be considered a financial sanction. Restitution is payment made by an offender to their victim. The victim has experienced some type of loss or harm that was found by the courts to be caused by the offender. In most situations this loss can usually be quantified. Courts are authorized to mandate that offenders pay restitution to their victims. Restitution can cover the cost /expense of any loss incurred by the victim. It does not cover damages for pain or suffering experienced by the victim. According to the National Center for Victims of Crime (2012) these expenses can include:
Medical costs
Therapy and counseling expenses
Prescription charges
Lost wages
Lost or damaged property
Insurance deductibles
Expenses related to participating in the criminal justice process such as travel expenses and child care.
Crime scene clean up
Any other expense related to the crime

Similar to fines, restitution is also influenced by the offenders' ability to pay. There are, however, alternatives to financial restitution such as community service and direct service to the victim (OJJDP, 2013). A judge can sentence an offender to community service to repay society for the crime that was committed. For example, an offender who was convicted of vandalizing a school might be required to repair the damage or perform another type of community service such as picking up litter or landscaping the grounds of the school. Direct service to the victim is an option but is not used as often. Nevertheless, there are supervised programs where the offender and victim meet to attempt to repair the emotional harm that has been done to the victim and to develop an agreement to make the victim whole. This might involve performing some task for the victim. For example, an offender who vandalized someone's home might repair the damage. As can be seen in Table 1.2 the most common type of restitution for both juveniles and adults is community service followed closely by monetary restitution. Direct service to the victim is by far the least popular type likely due to the fact that most victims would rather not have contact with their offender.

Table 1.2 Restitution by Group and Type

	Type of Restitution (Percent)		
Group	Monetary	Community Service	Direct Service to Victim
Juveniles	91.2	94.0	39.9
Adults	81.8	98.2	33.6
Juveniles and adults	82.2	91.4	34.2

Source: Adapted and retrieved from National Directory of Restitution and Community Service Programs. Office of Juvenile Justice and Delinquency Prevention. Washington, D.C. 2013.

Mental Health Courts and Drug Courts

Drug courts were previously discussed in the Drugs and Crime Chapter. Mental Health courts are somewhat similar in that these courts also attempt to divert the offender from incarceration. Currently, prisons are seriously overcrowded with offenders with mental disorders. Reportedly, more than half of all prison inmates were found to have mental health problems (James & Glaze, 2006).The purpose of Mental Health Courts is to divert offenders with mental disorders from ever having to be incarcerated and instead place them in strictly supervised mental health treatment programs located in the community. These courts attempt to not only reduce the number of mentally ill offenders in prison but also attempt to provide these individuals with much needed treatment that is likely not available in prison. Typically, the person's offense is somewhat related to not having received mental health interventions in the past. Offenders are carefully screened by mental health

professionals before they are placed in a program. Once in a program offenders are monitored for compliance with the treatment program and treatment progress is tracked carefully. Noncompliance can result in additional
sanctions or incarceration. Outcome studies have indicated that Mental
Health Courts can be cost effective, that participants were less likely to recidivate than nonparticipants, and that participants reported improved interpersonal functioning (Justice Center, 2008; Urban Justice Center, 2013).

Other Types of Intermediate Sanctions
There are various other types of intermediate sanctions that are utilized by
the courts. As with other intermediate sanctions, the following can also be
used in conjunction with probation or other sanctions or can be implemented
singularly.

Boot Camps. Boot camps are militaristic like placements that involve fairly
intensive physical regimens and strict discipline. Often, these camps are actually staffed with former military personnel and offenders are usually required to dress in uniforms and look and act like soldiers. That is, to salute,
stand at attention, and address their superiors as soldiers would. Offenders
who complete the program successfully are typically able to apply for early
release from their sentences. The goals of Boot Camps are to provide an
alternative to incarceration, to build self- discipline, self- esteem and the ability to work in groups. Outcome studies provide mixed results with some
indicating adequate short term but limited long term benefits (NCJRS, 2003).

Day Reporting Centers. Day reporting centers are a relatively new type of
alternative to incarceration that originated first in Great Britain in the early
1970s followed by the opening of the first center in the United States in Massachusetts in 1986. Offenders are allowed to live at home but must report to
the center daily for supervision. Further, during the time that they are at the
center offenders must take part in activities such as counseling, education,
and groups and may be required to undergo substance abuse screening and
treatment. These centers are cost effective, alleviate prison overcrowding,
and allows the offender to remain with their significant others (Contino,
2011).

Forfeiture. The forfeiture or seizure of assets by the government occurs
when it is determined that assets were somehow connected to criminal activity. For example, the luxury items purchased by drug dealers or the businesses of criminals involved in money laundering can be seized. The government
only needs to show probable cause. The Department of Justice Asset Forfeiture Program is noteworthy: "The primary mission of the Department of
Justice Asset Forfeiture Program is to employ asset forfeiture powers in a
manner that enhances public safety and security. This is accomplished by

removing the proceeds of crime and other assets relied upon by criminals and their associates to perpetuate their criminal activity against our society. Asset forfeiture has the power to disrupt or dismantle criminal organizations that would continue to function if we only convicted and incarcerated specific individuals"(DOJ, 2013). In this context, forfeiture can be considered an alternative sanction at the community level in that it attempts to discourage crime by taking away the incentive.

Parole. Whether parole can actually be considered a community corrections program is debatable. Community corrections focuses on alternative sanctions that strive to keep the offender out of prison. Probation, for example, is an actual sentence imposed by a court that keeps the offender in the community and out of prison. Parole, on the other hand, is not a sentence and is granted after the offender has served a set amount of time incarcerated. Decisions on parole are typically made by a parole board using release guidelines. An offender who is granted parole is released from prison into the community under the supervision of a parole officer who is responsible for monitoring the conditions of parolee. There are some similarities between probation and parole. Both help to relieve prison overcrowding, both can require the offender to take part in community interventions such as counseling, and both require supervision. Nevertheless, the parolee has served a prison term and the probationer has not which might make the transition to the community a bit more arduous for the parolee.

A PERSON OF INTEREST: ALEXANDER MACONOCIE (1787-1860)

Alexander Maconochie, dubbed the "Father of Parole", was born in Scotland in 1787, joined the Royal Navy in 1803 and saw action in two wars, including the War of 1812 against the United States. In 1840 he was appointed by the British government to take charge of a penal colony at Norfolk Island off the coast of Australia. Norfolk Island was famous for two things: (1) it's where the mutineers from Captain Bligh's ship "the Bounty" had been incarcerated, and (2) It was known for its incredibly cruel conditions. In fact, when Maconochie arrived at the island there was one convict, Charles Anderson, who had been given 1200 lashes and then chained to a rock overlooking the harbor. He was fed by having food pushed up to him on a pole. It is said that he became famous as one of the stops on scenic boat tours where tourists would throw food up to him. Maconochie was appalled at the conditions and the treatment meted out to these men. One of his first acts was to get Anderson down off the rock and clean up his condition and wounds. He put Anderson in charge of taking care of some gardens on the island. He soon introduced a totally new system that is very similar to what psychologists' today call "behavior modification."

The inmates could earn points, or what became known as "marks" for good behavior. Maconochie called it a system of "moral reform." He also tried to eliminate the cruelties that went on, and he encouraged the convicts to be more responsible and more honest. The reforms he introduced did not go smoothly at first as many of the guards and island personnel resisted any changes in their routines. However, change did take place. During his four-year service on the island over a thousand convicts were discharged, and he proudly pointed to their low recidivism. This program is seen now as the first attempt to institute a parole system.

CASE STUDY: Sean S.

Sean is a 44 year old male residing in a small New England town. He lives with his wife of 18 years and their 2 children. Both Sean and his wife are college graduates. Sean graduated with a B.A. in Sociology but never pursued a career in that area. Rather, he began working construction jobs and learned enough carpentry over the years to become an expert framer and finisher. He and his wife, a school nurse, earned enough money to afford a fairly comfortable middle class life style complete with home ownership, cars, vacations, and other amenities. Sean and his wife were involved in several community activities such as little league, Kiwanis and the garden club. In 2008, however, the construction business took a dramatic turn for the worse because of the recession. Sean was making less money and the future was not looking positive but he was keeping his head above water, at least for a time. Then the jobs stopped coming and he found himself only working 2-3 days per week. Even though his wife was working the bills were now beginning to accumulate. Sean tried to find additional work but to no avail.

After several months of searching he became a bit desperate. He had never been unable to find work. One day while at a job site he took a box of nails. The next week he took several power tools. He believed that he could sell some of these items online. The site foreman, however, began to receive complaints that items were missing and installed a security camera at the work site. Sean was then caught on video stealing several sheets of plywood and drywall. The police were called and obtained a warrant to search Sean's home. They found all of the stolen goods in his garage. Sean was arrested and charged with Larceny. In court he told his story. Important was the fact that he had no previous criminal record and was a model citizen in the community. The judge sentenced him to 2 years of supervised probation and he was required to make restitution to the construction company. In addition to his legal difficulties Sean no longer had any type of job and has been unable to find work of any kind. Sean is another statistic of the recession but his foray into criminal activity has severely impacted his ability to find work and his overall life situation. For Sean and his family the future, because of his criminal behavior, will be certainly be challenging.

The Future for Community Corrections

Community corrections has always been controversial. Many believe that community correctional programs are lenient and soft on the offender and allow the offender to 'skip out on a prison term.' Further, many question the efficacy of these programs because there is a paucity of robust outcome studies that address their effectiveness. These programs do, however, reduce prison overcrowding, provide the offender with services that are not typically available in prison, and appear to be a cost effective alternative to prison. Community corrections will be part of the criminal justice system for many years and it is necessary to provide the resources and research that will ensure that they are a positive alternative for many.

Summary

The benefits of community corrections are many and include reducing prison overcrowding, providing treatment and therapy not available in prisons, maintaining connections with society and family, and providing cost effective services. Community based correctional programs include several types of probation and numerous programs commonly referred to as intermediate sanctions. Probation is the most utilized community and correctional program. There are several types of probation including informal or unsupervised probation and many types of formal and more stringent types of probation such as suspended-sentence probation, standard probation, shock probation, split-sentence probation, and intensive supervision probation. Offenders on probation are supervised by a probation officer who monitors and supervises the conditions of probation that are imposed by the court. Probation officers also prepare presentence investigations (PSI) and are responsible for ensuring that the conditions of probation are not violated. Violation may result in a recommendation for revocation of probation and could lead to a modification or strengthening of probation conditions or incarceration. Intermediate sanctions are alternative sanctions and fall between probation and incarceration. These sanctions are seen as more palatable by many because they are seen as being more punitive than probation. These sanctions include restitution, fines, mental health and drug courts, boot camps, home confinement and electronic monitoring, halfway houses, day reporting centers, and forfeiture. Intermediate sanctions can be combined or used in conjunction with probation. Adherence to these sanctions is oftentimes supervised by a probation officer and violation of the sanction can result in more stringent sanctions or incarceration. Community corrections will be an integral part of the criminal justice system for many years to come. These programs reduce prison overcrowding, provide offenders with services not available in prisons, and appear to be a cost effective alternatives.

Key Terms

Alternative sanctions
Boot Camps
Community Service
Day Reporting Centers
Direct Service to Victim
Drug Courts
Electronic Monitoring
Fines
Forfeiture
Formal Probation
General Probation Conditions
Halfway Houses
Home Confinement
Informal Probation
Intermediate Sanctions
John Augustus
Mental Health Courts
National Probation Act
Parole
Pre-sentencing Report
Probation
Probation Officer
Probation Violation
Restitution

References

APPA (2010). *Probation and parole in the United States*. Lexington, KY: AmericanProbation and Parole Association.

Bureau of Justice Statistics (2013). *Correctional populations in the United States, 2013*. Retrieved from http://bjs.ojp.usdoj.gov.

Bureau of Prisons (2013). *Residential reentry management*. Retrieved from www.bop.gov.

Center for Effective Public Policy (2013). *Collaboration and the community corrections field*. Retrieved from www.collaborative justice.org.

Contino, J. (2011). *Bucks County department of corrections day reporting program*. Washington, DC: National Institute of Corrections.

DOJ (2013). *Assist forfeiture program*. Washington, DC: United States Department of Justice.

FAMM (2009). *Alternatives to incarceration*. Families against mandatory minimums. Retrieved from www.famm.org.

Government Accountability Office (2012). *Growing inmate crowding negatively affects Inmates, staff, and infrastructure* . Washington, DC: US Government Accountability Office.

Hillsman, S. & Greene, J. (1991). *The use of fines as an intermediate sanction.* Vera Institute of Justice. Retrieved from www.vera.org.

James, D. & Glaze, L. (2006). *Mental health problems of prison and jail inmates.* Bureau of Justice Statistics. Washington, DC: Department of Justice. Office of Justice Programs.

James, N. (2011). *Offender reentry: Correctional statistics, reintegration into the community, and recidivism.* Congressional Research Service. Retrieved from www.nationalcia.org.

Justice Center (2008). *Mental health courts.* Retrieved from www.bja.gov.

Justice Policy Institute (2009). *Pruning prisons: How cutting corrections can save money and protect public safety.* Washington, DC: Justice Policy Institute.

Klein-Saffron, J. (1995). Electronic monitoring vs. halfway houses: A study of federal offenders. *Alternatives to Incarceration.* 24-28. Retrieved from www.bop.gov.

Legal Information Institute (2013). *Conditions of probation.* Retrieved from www.law.cornell.edu/uscode/text/18/3563.

MA Courts System (2013). *Massachusetts job description.* Retrieved from www.mass.gov/courts/probation/po/html.

National Center for the Victims of Crime (2012). *Restitution.* Retrieved from victimsofcrime.org.

NCJRS (2013). *Correctional boot camps: Lessons from a decade of research.* Retrieved from www.ncjrs.gov.

Norman-Eady, S. (2007). *Electronic monitoring of probationers and parolees.* CT OLR Research Report. Retrieved from www.cga.gov.

NYC Board of Corrections (1973). Pre-sentence reports: Utility or Futility? *Fordham Urban Law Journal, 2,* (1), 25-53.

OJJDP (2013). *Types of programs and services.* Retrieved from www.ojjdp.gov/pubs/restta/ types.html.

Petersilia, J. (1998). *Probation in the United States.* Lexington, KY: American Probation and Parole Association.

Probation Officer (2013). *The different types of probation.* Retrieved from proba-tion- officer.org/types-of-probation/.

Seiter, R. & Seiter, K. (2003). Prison reentry: What works, what does not, and what is promising. *Crime and Delinquency, 43,* (3), 360-388. Retrieved from http://sagepub.com.

Tonry, M. (1997). *Intermediate sanctions in sentencing guidelines.* Washington, DC: National Institute of Justice, U.S. Department of Justice, Office of Justice Programs.

Urban Justice Center (2013). *Mental health courts.* Retrieved from www.urban justice.org.

CHAPTER 8

GENERAL PRINCIPLES OF LAW

Ignorance of the Law is no Excuse

Of course you know about laws. We were all taught that laws are made to protect us, for example speed limits, or laws against violent behavior or drunk driving. We were taught that if you break a law you will be punished, possibly even going to jail, and that laws apply to everyone regardless of age, race, social status, and gender. We were taught to respect the law, the police, courts and judges who uphold the law. Sound familiar? Maybe so, but do you really know what laws are and how they are created? Let's take a look and see if we can expand your knowledge.

Introduction

Barron's Dictionary of Legal Terms defines law as "1.The legislative pronouncement of rules to guide one's actions in society; 2. The total of those rules of conduct put in force by legislative authority or court decisions, or established by local custom" (Gifis, 2008, p.289).

Merriam-Webster dictionary defines law as "1. a binding custom or practice of a community, a rule of conduct or action prescribed or formally recognized as binding or enforced by a controlling authority; 2. the whole body of such customs, practices, or rules" (Merriam Webster, 2005). These rules and guidelines for conduct are meant to protect society and individuals. Laws define behavioral expectations and if the laws are broken there will be consequences. As has previously been said, our system is based on the premise that one is entitled to the due process of law, and that there will be a fair and balanced application of the rules and laws to everyone. In the United States we pride ourselves in being a society which is governed by the rule of law. "Taking the law into your own hands" is highly discouraged and is illegal. Gone are the days of vigilante justice, so often portrayed in Western movies. Now, gang members who exact "justice" on rival members are held accountable through the court system. You might not feel that the system works as well as it should, or that some may be getting away with murder. However, the law must keep up with the fast-paced changes of our time. For example, the internet has forced judges, legislators, and elected officials to define and create laws to deal with the plethora of technological change: Are emails public or private? How far does free speech extend when someone else is hurt? Is there a criminal or civil cause of action against those who may have caused someone to commit suicide if internet harassment preceded the death? Think about the young man in New Jersey who committed suicide after his college roommate posted a video on the internet of him engaging in sexual activity with another young man. There are so many aspects of our society that require the law to be constantly updated and monitored.

Broadly speaking the lawmakers of our country are our elected officials, legislators, senators, and congress people at the national and state levels, and city councils and other elected people at the local level. We see and hear reports in the media about proposed laws ("death with dignity" is hotly debated in many states), and laws which have just been enacted (your local media covers what new laws your state legislators have passed or those which "died in committee"). There is probably also news coverage of those laws that have been challenged in the courts. President Obama's 2011 controversial health care law was challenged, and then following oral arguments at the United States Supreme Court in the spring of 2012, the new law was upheld in June 2012 by a 5 to 4 Court. The impact of the decision and implementation of the law, which went into effect in 2014, is still hotly debated.

Not only must a judge follow the law, for example in mandatory sentencing cases, but the judge must also examine the facts of the case to determine if the allegations are covered by the law. For example, a slanderous comment about you might or might not be actionable (called "libel") depending on who you are (public or private person), who heard the comment, and other factors. A judge's job is far from a black-and-white analysis, which is why some rulings are overturned on appeal.

Types of Laws

Statutory Law

Laws which are enacted (approved by the legislative bodies which have control over the topics) are codified (arranged into a systematic code) in what are called statutes. Barron's Dictionary of Legal Terms defines statute as "an act of the legislature, adopted under its constitutional authority, by prescribed means and in certain form, so that it becomes the law governing conduct within its scope. Statutes are enacted to prescribe conduct, define crimes, create inferior government bodies, appropriate public monies, and in general to promote the public welfare." (Gifis, 2008)

Statutes defining crimes and criminal behavior are called criminal laws and are handled by the criminal courts. When someone is convicted of a crime the statutes not only define what the elements of the crime are, but may also define the sentence or punishment that the judges must apply. There are many crimes which do not have mandatory sentencing, and in these crimes there is allowance for the judge's sentencing discretion. As you have previously read, statutes governing certain non-criminal interactions between people, such as divorce, property and contracts are called civil laws. There are a wide range of civil laws, and the courts that handle those cases are known by many different names- such as civil, family, probate , and superior courts, to name a few.   In many civil cases there are no jury trials, and although there may be monetary damages, there is no criminal "punishment." Civil courts offer a wide-variety of remedies befitting the case before the court and the specific facts of each case.   Sometimes the courts are asked to issue injunctive relief, which is an order to stop behaviors such as illegal dumping or trespassing.   In family and probate cases courts may issue various orders, for example, assigning custodial rights and responsibilities for children, payment of child and spousal support, division of assets and debts, and the distributions of assets from estates.   There are never jury trials in these kinds of cases.   Judges hear the evidence and decide.   The courts are anxious to have parties reach their own agreements in family and other civil matters.   The courts are overloaded and it is well known that agreements made by the litigants are more readily adhered to than court imposed orders following contested hearings. This is especially true in family matters and courts are encouraging, if not mandating, mediation in these cases.   Mediation is an out-of-court process whereby the parties attempt to reach agreement which the court will then use to issue its order.   Some states mandate mediation or some other form of alternative dispute resolution prior to trial in all of its civil cases, and even subsidize family mediation for income eligible parents.

Common Law
Common law is "the system of jurisprudence, which originated in England and was later applied in the United States, and is based on judicial precedent (court decisions) rather than legislative enactment (statutes) and is therefore derived from principles rather than rules" (Gifis, 2008).

Historically, beginning in the 11th century, judges travelled throughout England and held court in various locales several times per year. The judge would decide which cases could be brought before him using local custom and rules of conduct to then impose a sentence. This system is known as "stare decisis," Latin for "to stand by that which was decided" (Gifis, 2008). As time passed and the same rulings were applied in similar cases legal precedent was established and the judge would follow the prior rulings in deciding new cases.   Eventually the Parliament or legislatures supplemented these judge-made rulings and enacted laws/statutes to codify the body of work which had been developed through the common law practice (Siegel, 2010).

Case Law
Just as common law sets a precedent for courts to follow, the term case law refers to judicial decisions which are then taken into consideration by judges and courts issuing future decisions. The concept of stare decisis applies. This helps everyone involved in a case, the judge, attorneys, and defendants, to predict an outcome.   It is expected that lower-level trial courts will follow

the decisions of the appellate courts. The rulings of the highest court of the land, the United States Supreme Court, are expected to be adhered to by lower courts, and, the Supreme Court too must of course follow its own case decisions. However, since no two cases are exactly alike, attorneys and judges can use case law to bolster their arguments/decisions or compare and contrast their cases with case law to show why a similar or different result should be reached.

Procedural Law
Procedural law is the body of rules and practice which govern the legal process. The federal rules of criminal procedure and evidence will govern criminal trials in federal court systems while states set their own rules of criminal procedure and evidence. There are separate rules governing the legal process in civil, family and other types of courts. The bankruptcy court, for example, is a federal court and has its own rules. Procedural rules define how evidence is introduced, what happens during a trial, and what the process is for an arrest. These rules are designed to protect the rights of the accused by mandating specific processes which must be followed. For example, a police officer may not enter someone's home just because they heard from someone that "Joe" is selling drugs from his kitchen. The officer must follow the specific rules by which a search warrant is obtained in order to enter Joe's house. The officer will submit an affidavit (sworn statement) to a judge who will decide if there is enough evidence to issue a search warrant. If a case is begun with illegally obtained evidence the case may be thrown out of court on that basis alone, even if the accused did commit a crime.

Administrative or Public Law
Administrative or public law governs the regulation of federal and state government agencies, state, city and county proceedings. For example, California's Office of Administrative Law "ensures that agency regulations are clear, necessary, legally valid, and available to the public. This office is also responsible for reviewing administrative regulations proposed by over 200 state agencies for compliance with the standards set forth in California's Administrative Procedure Act. Finally the office is responsible for transmitting these regulations to the Secretary of State and for publishing regulations in the California Code of Regulations" (OAL, 2007).

This agency publishes those California rules and regulation which are being considered, while allowing for public comment to be generated. There are literally tens of thousands of agencies, boards, and municipalities each of which are governed by specific rules of how business is conducted. These rules provide the public with information and advance notice of how various issues are handled.

Substantive Law

Substantive law is the statutory or written law that defines rights and duties, such as crimes and punishments in criminal law, and civil rights and responsibilities in civil law. It is codified in legislated statutes or can be enacted through a voting referendum or petition process which begins at the grass roots level by being voted on in elections. Substantive law stands in contrast to procedural law. Procedural law comprises the rules by which a court hears and determines what happens in civil or criminal proceedings, as well as the method and means by which substantive law is made, administered, and enforced.

U.S. Constitution, Bill of Rights, the Fourteenth Amendment

The U.S. Constitution

You may remember memorizing parts of the United States Constitution which begins: "We the People of the United States in Order to form a more perfect Union, establish Justice, insure domestic Tranquility, provide for the common defense, promote the general Welfare, and secure the Blessings of Liberty to ourselves and our Posterity, do ordain and establish this Constitution for the United States of America." Well, maybe you don't remember it word for word, so let's take a look at this incredible document. The Constitution defines our federal government and the process by which the United States came into being as a group of states which joined this common union. The first three Articles describe the duties, authorities, and obligations of three of the branches of the federal government: the legislative branch (Senate and House of Representatives), the executive branch (President, including the designation of Commander in Chief of the armed forces), and the judicial branch (the US Supreme Court.)

Article 4 is the full-faith-and-credit clause which guarantees that a judicial order made in one state shall be acknowledged by all other states.

Article 5 provides for the process of amending the Constitution.

Article 6 states that the federal laws shall be the supreme "laws of the land" and adhered to by all the states. Members of congress, the president and judges, and their state counterparts are required to swear an oath to the Constitution.

Article 7 established the ratification process by which the then-existing states could approve the Constitution in order for a federal government to become effective. Eleven ratification conventions adopted the proposed Constitution for their states on September 13, 1788, and the new Constitutional government of the United States began on March 4, 1789.

What may be more relevant to you as a criminal justice student are the first 10 amendments to the Constitution, known as the Bill of Rights.

Bill of Rights

The first 10 amendments to the Constitution are known as the Bill of Rights, and the Bill was ratified by three-quarters of the states in 1791. Incredibly it wasn't until 1939 that there was full ratification. The last three states to ratify were Massachusetts, Connecticut, and Georgia. These first 10 amendments were designed to protect citizens from an overreaching centralized government. The revolutionary war had just been won, and the newly formed United States wanted to ensure a balance of powers between the federal and state governments and also to ensure the rights of each citizen. Today there are a total of 27 amendments.

You probably know about the First and Second Amendments. The first provides for freedom of religion, speech, and the press, and the Second is best known as the guarantee of a citizen's right to "bear arms." However, probably the most important amendments for students of criminal justice are the Fourth, Fifth, Sixth, Eighth, and Fourteenth.

Fourth Amendment

"The right of the people to be secure in their persons, houses, papers, and effects, against unreasonable searches and seizures, shall not be violated, and no Warrants shall issue, but upon probable cause, supported by Oath or affirmation, and particularly describing the place to be searched, and the persons or things to be seized."

The phrases "unreasonable search and seizure" and "probable cause" have generated thousands of cases in both the federal and state courts as defendants assert that evidence seized should not be allowed in court if it was unreasonably seized. Naturally, prosecutors argue just the opposite. The exclusionary rule provides that evidence obtained through a violation of the Fourth Amendment is generally not allowed to be presented to the court by the prosecution. In *Katz .v the United States*, 1967, the Supreme Court ruled that a search occurs when 1) a person expects privacy in the thing searched and 2) society believes that the expectation is "reasonable." If there is a reasonable expectation of privacy then the police must get a search warrant in order to conduct the search. A search warrant is a court order permitting a search by law enforcement based on specific written information upon which probable cause is established by the court. It is not enough to guess about what the officer might find, because it has to be objective evidence in order to meet the probable cause standard. If there is no expectation of privacy, then a search may be conducted without a warrant.

Case law is constantly evolving to keep up with technology in our ever-changing society. The authors of the Constitution had no inkling of the internet and whether gathering information through someone's email, computer or other web-based accounts could be considered to be an "unreasonable search and seizure." Courts are called upon to tackle these tough issues. Here are some recent decisions:

On January 3, 2011, in *The People v. Gregory Diaz*, the Supreme Court of California ruled for allowing warrantless search by the police of suspects' cell phones at the time of the arrest, on the grounds of preventing destruction of evidence such as text messages. The Court found that the loss of privacy upon arrest extends beyond the arrestee's body to include "personal property... immediately associated with the person of the arrestee" and that this loss of privacy entitles police not only to "seize" anything of importance they find on the arrestee's body, but also to open and examine what they find.

This decision had a strong dissent from a minority of justices and courts across the country are divided on this, and many other issues *(People v. Diaz, 2011)*.

On January 30, 2007 the United States Court of Appeals for the 9th Circuit decided that an employer who observed an employee viewing child pornography at work and gave the FBI copies of the hard drive did not violate the defendant's Fourth Amendment rights. After reviewing the relevant Supreme Court opinions on a reasonable expectation of privacy, the court acknowledged that the employee, Mr.Ziegler, had a reasonable expectation of privacy at his office and on his computer. However, the court found that the employer could consent to a government search of the computer without infringing on the Ziegler's Fourth Amendment rights *(United States v. Ziegler, 2007)*.

On December 14, 2010 the United States Court of Appeals for the 6th Circuit ruled that a person has a reasonable expectation of privacy in emails and that the government violated a defendant's Fourth Amendment rights by compelling the internet provider to turn over emails without first obtaining a warrant based upon probable cause *(United States v. Warshak, 2010)*.

The most common exceptions to the requirement to obtain a warrant prior to a search are if a person consents to the search or if the evidence is in plain sight, which includes being visible through a window.

Fifth Amendment

The Fifth Amendment has several key rights:

No person shall be... "compelled in any criminal case to be a witness against himself." This is typically referred to as the right against self-incrimination. In *Griffin v. California*, 1965 the Supreme Court ruled that the government cannot punish a criminal defendant for exercising his right to silence, by allowing the prosecutor to ask the jury to draw an inference of guilt from the defendant's refusal to testify in his own defense. Justice Douglas wrote the majority opinion and said, "We ...hold that the Fifth Amendment, in its direct application to the Federal Government, and in its bearing on the States by reason of the Fourteenth Amendment, forbids either comment by the prosecution on the accused's silence or instructions by the court that such silence is evidence of guilt" *(California v Griffin, 1965 p. 616)*.

No person shall "be subject for the same offense to be twice put in jeopardy of life or limb." This is the so-called right against double jeopardy. The government may not bring a new case on the same charges if there is an acquittal (finding of not guilty) of the offense.

"No person…. shall be deprived of life, liberty, or property, without due process of law." This is the due process requirement as previously discussed.

Sixth Amendment

Our Constitution's Sixth Amendment affords persons accused of crimes in which a case is filed with a court procedural rights including: the right not to self-incriminate, the right to cross examine witnesses, the right to have a jury of one's peers, the right to a speedy trial, and the right to have an attorney.
These numerous procedural guarantees allow for anyone who is accused of a crime to know what the charges are, to be able to have an attorney to represent them even if they cannot afford one, to have the government's witnesses be questioned in front of the defendant, to subpoena witnesses in defense, to have a jury which is not prejudiced, and to have a speedy trial. Each of these elements have been litigated and ruled on since the inception of the Bill of Rights as courts are asked to decide what all of these procedural rights mean.

Eighth Amendment

The Eighth Amendment ensures that bail is not "excessive" and that "cruel and unusual punishment" is not inflicted. The case of *Furman v. Georgia*, (1972), is an important case on the issue of cruel and unusual punishment and involved the first significant challenge to capital punishment. In a 5-4 decision, the Supreme Court overturned the death sentences of Furman for murder, as well as two other defendants for rape. Of the five justices voting to overturn the death penalty, two found capital punishment to be unconstitutionally cruel and unusual, while three found that the statutes at issue were implemented in a random and capricious fashion, discriminating against blacks and the poor. *Furman v. Georgia* did not actually say that capital punishment is unconstitutional, although it was interpreted that way by much of the legal community as well as the public.

The Court has ruled on punishments which are considered to be cruel and unusual and are banned regardless of the crime. For example, in *Wilkerson v. Utah* (1878), the Supreme Court commented that the drawing and quartering, public dissection, burning alive and disembowelments constituted cruel and unusual punishment regardless of the crime. The Supreme Court declared executing the mentally handicapped in *Atkins v. Virginia* (2002), and executing people who were under age 18 at the time the crime was committed in *Ropper v. Simons* (2005), to be violations of the Eighth Amendment, regardless of the crime.

In *Graham v. Florida* (2010), the Supreme Court declared that a life sentence without any chance of parole, for a crime other than murder, is cruel and unusual punishment for a minor. Terrance Graham, then 16 years old, attempted to rob a restaurant in Jacksonville, Florida. He was charged with attempted armed robbery and armed burglary and severed a 12 month sentence. Six months after his release, on December 2, 2004, Graham was arrested again for a home-invasion robbery. Though Graham denied involvement, he acknowledged that he was in violation of his probation. In 2006, the presiding judge sentenced Graham to life in prison, and because Florida abolished parole, it became a sentence without parole. The Supreme Court found that the Constitution prohibits the imposition of a life without parole sentence on a juvenile offender who did not commit homicide. In February 2012, Graham was resentenced to a 25 year sentence.

In March 2012, the Court heard arguments in the case of *Miller v. Alabama* (2012) concerning the constitutionality of mandatory life without parole sentences for juvenile offenders in cases including murder. The Court issued its ruling on June 25, 2012, striking down the mandatory sentences as cruel and unusual punishments in violation of the Eighth Amendment. The holding of the court applies to all those under 18, and doesn't either automatically free any inmate or forbid life terms for young murderers. Instead judges have to consider the defendant's youth and the nature of the crime before sentencing the defendant to imprisonment with no hope for parole (Savage, 2012).

The Fourteenth Amendment
The Fourteenth Amendment to the Constitution is the lynchpin of key elements of the legal system – due process and equal protection under the law. Simply put, the Fourteenth Amendment's due process clause requires states not to deprive anyone of "life, liberty or property" without taking steps to ensure fairness in application of the law (due process). In addition this amendment requires states not to "deny to any person within its jurisdiction the equal protection of the laws." The meaning of due process and equal protection of the law have been litigated and defined in many court cases.

Due Process
The Warren Court (1953-1969) led by Chief Justice Earl Warren is considered to have been an activist court and during that time undertook many cases which reviewed the guarantees of due process. This was done to ensure that defendant's rights were not trampled upon by the state in criminal matters. That Supreme Court set standards for criminal procedure which have far-reaching effects on today's practice of criminal law.

In *Gideon v. Wainwright*, (1963), the Supreme Court decided that the guarantees of the Fourteenth Amendment required the state to provide counsel for all defendants who could not afford an attorney in criminal proceedings. Prior to this ruling no such requirement existed and some innocent folks were convicted. Gideon was arrested based on a claim by an eyewitness who said he saw Gideon leaving a restaurant early one morning with alcohol and cash in his pockets. The restaurant later reported broken windows and vending machines with alcohol, cigarettes, and cash missing. At his arraignment the judge advised Gideon that he could not appoint counsel for him since it was not a capital case. The jury convicted. Gideon went to prison and there wrote and filed his own appeal on the basis that the US Constitution guaranteed him the right to have an attorney. The Supreme Court accepted the case and assigned counsel for Gideon. The Court held that the right to counsel was a fundamental right, essential for a fair trial, and that no one should be charged with a crime and be forced to face his/her accusers in court without the guidance of counsel. Gideon got a new trial with assigned counsel who was able to bring in a witness who provided an alibi for Gideon, and to discredit the prosecution's witness, who the attorney asserted, had been a lookout for the group who committed the thefts. A jury acquitted Gideon within an hour.

Equal Protection
The Fourteenth Amendment's equal protection clause was also the basis for *Brown v. Board of Education* (1954), the Supreme Court decision which led to the dismantling of racial segregation in education schools in the United States. In *Reed v. Reed* (1971), the Supreme Court also ruled that laws arbitrarily requiring sex discrimination violated the Equal Protection Clause.

The legal requirements that we in the United States are entitled to due process and equal protection is rooted in the Constitution. The Bill of Rights specifies rights which may not be abridged. The Fifth Amendment's statement that no person shall be deprived of life, liberty, or property without due process of law is made binding on the states in a similar statement in the Fourteenth Amendment. These rights are not just applicable to those being charged with crimes, but to all people. For a student of criminal justice the most important rights are the right to an impartial jury, a speedy and public trial, counsel, the right against cruel and unusual punishment, self- incrimination, excessive bail and/or fines, and double jeopardy (being tried for the same crime twice if acquitted the first time). If these rights are violated it may be cause for dismissal of evidence, or dismissal of the case itself. Due process is both substantive and procedural. Substantive due process is the right not to be subject to laws which are unfair or discriminatory. Procedural due process is the right to have fairness applied in each case. It is the courts which have explored and defined the scope of substantive and procedural due process as it applies to the rights specified in the Constitution. As our society changes so too have court decisions reflected these societal norms. The Supreme Court wields an inordinate amount of power when it comes to deciding cases which set a precedent for future cases. Likewise, the conservative or liberal make-up of the court influences these decisions.

In the case of *Lawrence et al. v. Texas*, (2003), the Supreme Court declared a Texas law outlawing sodomy to be unconstitutional based on the law's discrimination against gays and lesbians. Certainly, even 50 years earlier, it would have been highly unlikely for any court to find such a constitutional prohibition in an anti-sodomy law. In contrast consider one of the most famous of all cases- *Dred Scott v. Sanford*, (1857). Dred Scott, the plaintiff, was an African-American slave belonging to Army surgeon Dr. John Emerson, both of whom resided in Missouri where slavery was allowed. Dr. Emerson moved to Illinois, taking Dred Scott with him even though Illinois did not allow slavery. After 12 years Dr. Emerson moved back to Missouri and wanted to take Mr. Scott with him. Mr. Scott refused and sued for unlawful detainment. At the time of the lawsuit Dr. Emerson was no longer alive and his estate was represented by John Sanford. Mr. Scott stated that since Illinois outlawed slavery, he was a free man and could not be forced to go back to Missouri and slavery. He argued that the Fifth Amendment of the Constitution prevents the unlawful and unethical abuse of power. The court found in favor of Sanford explaining that since slaves were not considered to be citizens of the United States, the Constitutional provisions were not applicable. Dred Scott was forced to return to slavery. In today's world a Dred Scott ruling is unthinkable, not only because slavery was outlawed in the United States following the Civil War, but also because the Supreme Court has interpreted the Fifth and Fourteenth amendments as prohibiting discrimination based on race and ethnicity.

A PERSON OF INTEREST: CLARENCE THOMAS

Judge Clarence Thomas is the second African American to serve on the U.S. Supreme Court. A descendant of American slaves, Thomas grew up in extreme poverty. His father left the family when Thomas was only two years old, and although his mother worked a variety of jobs she was poorly paid. When he was seven years old, he was taken in by one of his grandparents in Savannah, Georgia. He became an outstanding student and his academic diligence led to a number of college scholarship offers. He chose to go to Holy Cross (Worcester MA) for his undergraduate education and then Yale (New Haven CT) for his law degree. In 1989 he was nominated for the Supreme Court, and although the confirmation hearings went smoothly at first, a former aid suddenly appeared and alleged that Thomas had once made an unwanted sexual comment to her. This led to a bitter and contentious debate, with Thomas accusing the Senate committee of "high tech lynching." When the dust finally settled, he was confirmed by the full U.S. Senate. He is known as a strict constitutionalist, arguing always for the court to stay within the framework of the U.S. Constitution and interpret the law rather than legislate. In one of his more famous opinions, he argued that polygraph (lie detector) evidence should not be admissible in federal court. He based his argument on the fact that the scientific community had not found it to be completely reliable or valid. Thomas has aligned himself with the conservative wing of the court and believes government should not be so powerful as to rule all individual actions and circumstances. He acknowledges being strongly influenced by conservative novelist Ayn Rand.

Judicial Review

As you have already seen in the discussions above, the Supreme Court's power is broad and far reaching. The highest court of the land has the power to review lower-court decisions. This authority for judicial review is not specifically mentioned in the Constitution, but was discussed in the writings of the founders of the Constitution. However, it was not until 1803 in one of its most important decisions that the Court asserted its authority of judicial review.

In *Marbury v. Madison* (1803), Chief Justice John Marshall wrote, "It is emphatically the province of the judicial department to say what the law is. Those who apply the rule to particular cases must, of necessity, expound and interpret the rule. If two laws conflict with each other, the Court must decide on the operation of each. If courts are to regard the Constitution, and the Constitution is superior to any ordinary act of the legislature, the Constitution, and not such ordinary act, must govern the case to which they both apply." This decision played a key role in making the Supreme Court a separate branch of government on par with the legislative and executive branches.

During the Warren era the landmark case of *Griffin v. Illinois* (1956) was decided. Griffin was convicted of a bank robbery by an Illinois state court. He wanted to appeal the decision, but could not afford to pay for a court transcript. He asked for a free transcript and his request was denied by the state court, so he appealed the decision to the Supreme Court. The Supreme Court found that Illinois had violated the Constitution and ruled that Illinois defray the costs of the transcript. This gave precedent for the 1963 decision in *Gideon v. Wainwright* referred to above. The Court stated, "From the very beginning, our state and national constitutions and laws have laid great emphasis on procedural and substantive safeguards designed to assure fair trials before impartial tribunals in which every defendant stands equal before the law. This noble ideal cannot be realized if the poor man charged with crime has to face his accusers without a lawyer to assist him."

In 1966 the Warren Court also decided *Miranda v. Arizona* (1966), which demands that people taken into custody be "read their rights," (to remain silent and have an attorney), but this decision only applied to those persons who were under detention. If you were free to leave, you were free to talk.

Then in *Chimel v. California* (1969), the Supreme Court found that Mr. Ted Chimels' burglary conviction could be overturned because, although the police found the stolen items in his home, they didn't have a search warrant even though they did have an arrest warrant. As you can see, police work is not easy. The police were able to locate Chimel, get an arrest warrant, enter his home, find him and the stolen loot, and all to no avail. Chimel walked! These rulings have significantly impacted how the police conduct business as you will no doubt learn in your future careers in this field.

A PERSON OF INTEREST: SANDRA DAY O'CONNOR

The first woman to ever serve on the United States Supreme Court, Sandra Day O'Connor was born in Texas and raised in Arizona on her family's ranch. She later selected Stanford University in California as her college of choice. She received her bachelor's degree in economics in 1950 and her law degree (also at Stanford) in 1952. She then went back to Arizona and served as a prosecutor as the state's Assistant Attorney General. In 1979 she became a judge in Arizona's Court of Appeals (Maricopa County), and only two years later was selected by President Ronald Reagan to fill a position on the U.S. Supreme Court. Her reputation as a highly knowledgeable and fair jurist won praises from both sides of the political spectrum. However, although nominally a Republican, one of her decisions went against conservative philosophy when she voted to uphold the Roe vs. Wade abortion rights decision (which she maintained was supported by the right to determine one's own reproductive destiny as set forth in the Fourteenth Amendment to the U.S. constitution). One of her most famous quotes is that "At the heart of liberty is the right to define one's own concept of existence, of meaning, of the universe and of the mystery of human life". Justice O'Connor retired from the court in 2006 after a series of health problems, and in 2009 President Obama honored her with the prestigious President's Medal of Freedom.

Latin Anyone?

The legal system uses a lot of Latin phrases, and it really is best that you familiarize yourself with some of these basic phrases and concepts. Not only will it help you in your career, but it will also lend legal authenticity to your vocabulary and make you sound as though you're on top of your game.

Actus Rea means to commit a guilty act. In order for someone to be accused of a crime there has to be an illegal action. For example, saying that you are a drug user does not in and of itself give the police authority to arrest you for drug use. But if you are caught using drugs then that act may be sufficient to arrest you for a crime. Also, serious threats of certain actions may result in arrest, such as threatening to kill someone.

Mens Rea means a guilty mind or the intention to commit a criminal act. In order to find someone guilty of a criminal act there must be both the action and the intent. Thinking about committing a crime is not enough. In addition, if must be shown that the person knows, or should have known, the consequences of the criminal act.   Even if the intention was not to hurt someone, knowing that certain acts might lead to harm may be enough to find someone guilty of a crime. Mens rea does not apply when someone is insane at the time the act is committed. In the early 1800s an Englishman, Daniel McNaughton, shot and killed the secretary of the British Prime Minister, believing that the Prime Minister (Sir Robert Peel) was conspiring against him. In this case Mr. McNaughton was found not guilty by reason of insanity and the "McNaughton Rule" became a legally viable defense. Further, the rule created a presumption of sanity, unless the defense proved "at the time of committing the act, the accused was laboring under such a defect of reason, from disease of the mind, as not to know the nature and quality of the act he was doing or, if he did know it, that he did not know what he was doing was wrong." This defense is rarely used today, and when it is used, it is rarely successful.

Specific intent means the person intended the act, that it was not just accidental.

General intent means that the person knows or should have known that an act would cause harm, for example, assault and/or rape.

Malice is when the act is done intentionally with reckless disregard for the consequences, for example, arson.

Criminal negligence is when the person is aware that the act may result in harm and there is a gross lack of care for the potential harm, for example, involuntary manslaughter.

Strict liability applies when there is no need to show that the person was aware that the act would result in harm. For example, statutory rape and selling alcohol to minors.

Mala in se means the act is wrong or evil in and of itself. Most human beings believe that murder, rape, and theft are wrong, regardless of whether a law governs such conduct. That is, mala in se means it's bad because its bad. This is in contrast to "**Malum Prohibitum**," or bad because it's prohibited by law.

Habeas corpus means "you have the body," but by implication means "is it legal?" Habeas corpus is best known as the means by which a prisoner tries to be released from confinement by submitting what is called a "writ of habeas corpus," or the argument that there is no legal reason for their detention. Prisoners have the right to challenge their detainment by asking a judge to consider whether the imprisonment violates the law. Thousands of habeas corpus petitions are filed with the U.S. Supreme Court each year by prisoners who seek to be released from jail. Also, a writ of habeas corpus petition is common when a death row prisoner awaits execution and requests a stay of execution so that the attorneys can proceed with further appeals.

The case of a person convicted of murder and sentenced to death is detailed in the enthralling book "The Innocent Man" (Grisham, 2006). Grisham writes about the case of Ron Williamson who in 1988 was convicted of murdering Debra Sue Carter. Days before his scheduled execution in 1994 his newly-assigned death penalty attorneys filed a habeas petition with the U.S. District Court in Oklahoma. The attorneys not only argued for a stay of the execution, but for a new trial based on what they alleged were errors in the 1988 trial. They presented clear evidence that at the time of his trial Mr. Williamson had been insane, and that the question of his sanity had not been raised during his 1988 trial. The petition argued that he was the victim of ineffective assistance, and that the prosecution had withheld exculpatory evidence. They also said that the hair analysis was "junk science." Although it is rare for a court to grant a new trial, in this case Oklahoma U.S. District Court Judge Seay did just that one year after staying the execution. The case also caught the attention of attorney Barry Scheck's Innocence Project. Mr. Scheck is noted for his expertise in forensic DNA evidence and work as one of O.J. Simpson's defense attorneys. The Innocence Project is committed to working on exoneration of wrongly convicted defendants using DNA testing as its primary tool. The hair, blood and semen samples from Debbie Carter's murder scene were analyzed, and because there were no matches Williamson was exonerated and released from prison, after having served 12 years for a crime he did not commit. The judge seemed very relieved that he had previously ordered a stay of execution.

Subpoena duce tecum is a court ordered writ or document served on witnesses requiring them to appear in court. Witnesses who have been served with a subpoena and fail to appear may be brought before the court on contempt charges (ignoring a court order can lead to the court finding someone in contempt and issuing sanctions).

Pro Se means to represent oneself or to be one's own attorney. In criminal cases it is rare that a defendant will proceed pro se, but there are times defendants insist on acting as their own attorney. It is much more common in civil and family court matters that litigants chose to proceed pro se. This is because most courts do not appoint attorneys in civil or family cases, and if someone cannot afford an attorney they can represent themselves.

In forma pauperis is a request based on financial hardship that the court waive or reduce fees for a court appointed attorney (in criminal cases), or fees to file petitions or motions with the court. If the applicant meets the court's income eligibility standards for appointment of a free attorney, an attorney will be appointed.

Writ of certiorari is when the Supreme Court agrees to hear a case and orders the lower court to send the records of the case for review. This only happens in cases that have substantial impact or questions of law and which have been decided by lower courts which may conflict with each other. Of the thousands of requests the Supreme Court receives each year to review cases from the lower courts it accepts only a few hundred.

Now that our Latin lessons are over, we will return to our favorite language and get back to action in the court

The Grand Jury

Prosecutors may convene a grand jury to begin the process of charging someone with a crime. The jury (called "grand" because it is larger, up to 23 citizens, than the typical jury of only 12 or even 6). The grand jury is comprised of community members whose primary role is to determine if the state has sufficient evidence to justify charges being issued, and if it does, to then issue an indictment. About half of the states use grand juries and then only for serious crimes. Federal prosecutors use a grand jury as required by the Fifth Amendment that says, "No person shall be held to answer for a capital, or otherwise infamous crime, unless on a presentment or indictment of a grand jury." The proceedings of the grand jury are secret and neither the suspect nor the suspect's attorney can attend or present any evidence. Reforms have been suggested to make this process fairer to the suspect.

Types of Crimes

There are three categories of crimes: infractions (least serious), misdemeanors, and felonies (most serious). Infractions typically do not include jail time and have fines issued for charges such as traffic violations, disturbing the peace, and other offenses where there is no injured person. Misdemeanors can involve jail time (typically less than a year) as well as fines and are crimes such as theft under a certain dollar amount, simple assault, or driving under the influence. Felonies are the most serious and can include serious jail time, fines and even the death sentence. Murder, rape, arson, robbery and burglary are a few examples of felonies.

FBI Classification

The FBI classifies crimes as Part I (more serious) and Part II (less serious) crimes. The FBI compiles reports of crimes and analyzes these to predict and track crimes and their trends. Reporting is done through its Uniform Crime Reporting (UCR) and the National Crime Victimization Survey (NCVS). The UCR gathers data directly from law enforcement agencies throughout the entire country, and the FBI has standardized definitions of offenses and terminology. The problems associated with the UCR include accuracy and completeness of reports since reporting is voluntary, and if multiple crimes are committed by one offender only the most serious is reported. NCVS data are collected on the basis of an annual survey of approximately 100,000 persons and are designed to uncover information about crimes that may not have ever been reported to the police. The major criticism of the NCVS is that its data are impossible to verify, and there is a strong suspicion that some of the responses are not quite reliable.

Corporate and White Collar Crime

Corporations can be convicted of crimes and convicted corporate executives are called white collar criminals. These types of crimes include bribery, embezzlement, extortion, forgery, price-fixing, violation of environmental law, and tax evasion. One of the most famous was levied against British Petroleum (BP) for the explosion and oil spill in the Gulf of Mexico which killed 11 workers. In November 2012 the U.S. Justice Department entered into the largest criminal settlement in U.S. history with BP, which pled guilty to 14 criminal counts and was levied a fine of $4 billion to be paid over the next five years.

The White Collar Criminal

A few years ago, Bernie Madoff, chairman of a wall-street investment company, plead guilty to a Ponzi scheme that is considered to be the largest financial fraud in U.S. history. A Ponzi scheme is a fraudulent investment operation that pays returns to its investors from their own money or more often the money paid by subsequent investors, rather than from profit earned by company. The Ponzi scheme usually entices new investors by offering higher returns than other investments. Clients included banks, hedge funds, charities, universities, and wealthy individuals. Notable clients included Steven Spielberg, actors Kevin Bacon, Kyra Sedgwick, and John Malkovitch, Hall of Fame pitcher Sandy Koufax, the family who owns the New York Mets, broadcaster Larry King, and the World Trade Center developer Larry Silverstein. The Elie Wiesel Foundation for Humanity lost $15.2 million, and Wiesel and his wife, Marion, lost their life savings.

Liability and Defense

In order to be convicted of a crime there must be three basic elements: action, intention and causation. Remember, that in order to convict someone of a crime the prosecution must prove "beyond a reasonable doubt" that the defendant committed the crime. The job of the defense counsel is to show that the defendant should not be convicted. There are many types of legal defenses, but they are all used to convince the judge or jury that there is reasonable doubt in the prosecutor's case. Besides the defense of "you got the wrong person, I didn't do it!" there are defenses which attempt to justify the crime (e.g., self-defense), those which assert that there was something wrong with the defendant at the time the crime was committed (e.g., mental capacity/intoxication), and "yeah I did it but there was consent" (e.g., rape), or "yeah I did it but I was insane" (NGRI). Other defenses include the prosecution having done something wrong – a misleading prosecution, or police entrapment. Justification may often be raised in claims of self-defense, defense of others, or defense of property and home. Essentially the defense is arguing that while what happened was wrong there was a good reason for it.

Self-Defense is probably the most well-known of these defense arguments. Self-defense has been used as a defense in the killing of an abusive spouse or when the person was attacked and fought back causing harm. In 2012,

George Zimmerman was charged with second degree murder and pled self-defense in the highly publicized killing of Florida teenager Trayvon Martin. A second-degree murder charge in Florida carries a maximum sentence of life in prison. It is typically charged when there is a fight or other confrontation that results in death, and where there is no premeditated plan to kill someone. Zimmerman's arrest was delayed partly because of Florida's "stand your ground" law, which gives people wide leeway in the use of deadly force without having to retreat in the face of danger. Zimmerman's shooting of the 17-year-old African American teenager set off a nationwide debate over race and self-defense. Civil rights groups and others have held rallies around the country, saying the shooting was unjustified. Many of the protesters wore the same type of hooded sweat shirt that Martin had on that day, suggesting his appearance and race had something to do with his killing. Martin was walking through Zimmerman's neighborhood when Zimmerman started following him. Zimmerman told police dispatchers that Martin looked suspicious. At some point, the two got into a fight and Zimmerman used his gun. Zimmerman told police Martin attacked him after he had given up chasing the teenager and was innocently returning to his truck. He told detectives that Martin knocked him to the ground and began slamming his head on the sidewalk. A jury later acquitted Zimmerman of all charges – second degree murder and manslaughter. At the time of this writing, these "stand your ground laws" have been enacted in 31 states, and the concern is that they may lead to an increasingly armed and trigger-happy citizenry.

Defense of Others may sometimes be claimed when one intervenes to help another being victimized and causes harm to the attacker. Unfortunately this was not the case when an on-looking crowd took no action when Kitty Genovese was attacked and murdered. The lack of action was later called "bystander apathy."

Defense of Property and home can also be used when one causes injury to a person invading one's home or property. This is not as simple as it sounds. Killing someone who has broken into your home does not warrant the defense of property claim if the degree of force used to prevent the intrusion or attack is more than the need to repel the attack. For example if the robber is armed, then killing the robber may be justified, whereas if the robber was unarmed this defense could fail. This is still another example of the subtleties and nuances in the criminal justice system – the rights of the individual balanced against the security of society.

Consent is used as a defense when the victim agreed to the act. This defense is most often raised in sexual assault and rape cases, where the defendant argues that the victim consented to the act and therefore no crime was committed. According to the American Medical Association's Sexual Assault in

America study, sexual assault cases, and rape in particular, are of the most underreported violent crimes. This is because rape victims are often blamed for the attack, being questioned about what they were wearing, whether they had "come on" to the attacker, and other such questions posed by defense counsel in trying to prove consent. While the rape laws endeavor to protect victims from such questioning, public perception and a society in which sex and violence are linked in the media, makes changing the perception of who may or may not have consented to be problematic.

Resisting an unlawful arrest may be argued as a defense when the officer uses excessive force in an illegal arrest or search. This is not a popular defense especially when used by someone who was caught by the police in the act of committing a crime

Mental Capacity
Under the general heading of "mental capacity" there are actually four different potential pleas, all based on the idea that the suspect did not have self-control and shouldn't be blamed: Not guilty by reason of insanity, Diminished capacity, Mental incompetence, and even Intoxication

Not guilty by reason of insanity is used when a defendant can show they were insane at the time the crime was committed, and therefore did not know the action was either right or wrong. Contrary to popular opinion, it is not a "get out of jail free card" as the insane defendant may spend more time institutionalized than they would have had there been straight jail time. The insanity defense is used in only about 2% of felony cases, and of those, only a tiny percentage actually prevail by using this defense. You may have heard of John Hinkley who was found not guilty by reason of insanity when he attempted to assassinate President Reagan in 1980. He still remains institutionalized to this day and the uproar which ensued following the not guilty verdict caused several states to abolish this defense altogether: Kansas, Idaho, Montana and Utah.

Diminished capacity is used as a defense when the person does not have a full understanding of the wrongfulness of the behavior, or perhaps cannot control the wrongful behavior. Unlike the insanity defense, however, this defense cannot produce a not-guilty verdict, but can often lead to lowering the severity of the charges levelled at the defendant.

Mental incompetence is assessed at the time the defendant is supposed to stand trial for the charges, rather than an after-the-fact guess as to their mental state at the time of the crime. If a psychologist/psychiatrist reports that the defendant does not understand the nature of the proceedings and cannot assist in his/her own defense, then the defendant may be found to be mentally incompetent to stand trial at that time. The defendant may be institution-alized until such time as they are able to comprehend the nature of the pro-ceedings. This status can create a dilemma when an institution declares that the defendant is no longer in need of being hospitalized, but the person re-mains incompetent to stand trial. Courts can use non-hospitalization court orders requiring community-based services, supports/ therapy and orders not to reoffend while the criminal charges are put on indefinite hold. Sometimes if the competency status does not change, the state may simply give up and just dismiss the charges.

Intoxication can be used as a defense if it was not considered to be volun-tary intoxication, as in a defendant insisting that they did not know the drink was spiked, or that the munchies contained marijuana. This is difficult to prove, especially with alcohol. However if the intoxication is voluntary it can still be used to assert that the mental state or specific intent was missing when the crime was committed. This is a very tricky defense and it depends on what the crime was and what the elements of proof were. Although often attempted, voluntary intoxication is not typically a successful defense to a rape charge (Sax, 2009).

Procedural Defenses
Unlike the defenses covered in the previous section, procedural defenses are based on the premise that the prosecutor's charges themselves are inappro-priate or perhaps even illegal. This is not like saying "I didn't do it," or "I did it but I couldn't help it," or "The devil made me do it." In fact, this defense is not based on guilt or innocence at all, but only on the argument that the person in question can't be held liable. These include denial of a speedy trial, entrapment, prosecutorial misconduct, and double jeopardy.

Denial of a Speedy Trial
The Sixth Amendment to the U.S. constitution guarantees the right to a speedy trial. In their wisdom our founding fathers understood that justice delayed is justice denied. If a suspect languishes in a cell during pre-trial in-carceration, the right to speedy trial has been violated. Obviously, the longer the delay, the more time there is for memories to fade, for witnesses to be-come lost, for evidence to be mislaid and mishandled and therefore combine to diminish the fairness of the trial. The delay required to negate the right to a speedy trial is understood to be at least a year.

Entrapment
This is when someone is tricked and lured into committing a crime by the police. If the suspect only decided to break the law, for example buy drugs from the undercover officer after excessive pressure and would not have normally done so, then entrapment could be a successful defense. If the

prosecution can show that the defendant was predisposed to commit the crime before the police came along, then the defense will fail.

Prosecutorial Misconduct

This charge can be used by the defense for a variety of reasons. For example it becomes appropriate for the defense attorney when it can be shown that law enforcement employed false suggestion when conducting the identification procedures, or coerced false confessions, lies or intentionally misleads jurors about their observations, fails to turn over exculpatory evidence to prosecutors, provides incentives (money, reduced jail time) to secure unreliable and distorted evidence from informants. It also becomes appropriate when the prosecution withholds exculpatory evidence from defense, deliberately mishandles, mistreats or destroys evidence, allows witnesses to testify even though known to be lying, uses fraudulent forensic experts who they know are relying on "junk science"

Double Jeopardy

This defense is the tied to the Fifth Amendment that states that no person may be tried twice for the same offense. If someone is acquitted, found innocent or convicted, they cannot be tried again for the same offense. Also, the double jeopardy clause does not prevent a civil lawsuit, even if the defendant was found innocent in criminal court. In the famous O.J. Simpson case, Simpson was found not guilty of murdering his wife, Nicole Brown and her friend Ronald Goldman. However, the double jeopardy clause did not prevent his wife's family from successfully suing Simpson for wrongful death in civil court and receiving an enormous monetary award of 33.5 million dollars.

In Conclusion

After finishing this chapter, you probably feel like you've just spent a few years in law school and it's all just too much to comprehend. Yes, it was a lot, but it was necessary, and it wasn't overdone. If you're planning a career in criminal justice, these issues are going to become part of your life and part of your vernacular (Latin and all) over and over again. Also you have to stay abreast of changes. Laws are constantly being written and rewritten, and how they are applied and interpreted by courts are constantly changing. Your career demands that you stay current and stay aware of these changes. It's also important to have colleagues who can share information about best practices. Knowing how to gather evidence, interview witnesses and the accused in a manner which is consistent with legal requirements is absolutely necessary. The last thing you want to have happen in a case in which you have spent time and effort to collect information and evidence is for the court to throw it out for mistakes in the process or procedure.

Summary

Laws govern all aspects of our society from defining criminal behaviors to regulating what goes into our food. Laws are enacted by our legislative and regulatory bodies, including statutes passed by state and federal legislators, rules governing administrative and public agencies, and procedural and substantive laws governing the legal process. Common law and case law precedent is also a means by which laws are defined when court rulings create legal precedent which must be followed.

The U.S. Constitution sets a framework within which the United States was established, governed, and created the three branches of the federal government: legislative, executive and judicial. Key to you, the student of criminal justice are the first ten amendments to the Constitution known as the Bill of Rights which details rights of all citizens. The Fourth Amendment guarantees us privacy and freedom from unreasonable search and seizure without probable cause. The Fifth and Sixth Amendments give us rights if we are accused of a crime to ensure we are treated and being judged fairly. The Eighth Amendment affords citizens just punishment, not excessive or cruel and unusual punishment. The Supreme Court has not banned capital punishment as cruel and unusual, but does ban mandatory life sentences without parole for juvenile offender convicted of murder. The Fourteenth Amendment guarantees all citizens equal protection of the law following a fair process (due process). During the Warren era of the 1950's and 1960's the Supreme Court decided a number of cases which set precedent in criminal cases and greatly impacted how law enforcement and prosecutors must work in order to assure that persons accused or being tried for crimes are treated fairly . As an example, the Supreme Court ruled that those who cannot afford counsel must be appointed defense attorneys (*Griffin v. Illinois*, 1956 and *Gideon v. Wainwright*, 1963) that one must be read their rights when taken into custody (*Miranda v. Arizona* 1966), and that evidence which is illegally gathered must be excluded during trial (*Mapp v. Ohio* 1961, and *Chimel v. California* 1969).

The Fourteenth Amendment's right to equal protection of the law means that the government cannot discriminate because of race, ethnicity, gender, and other protected classifications. As noted in the Due Process section, the Court's decisions change over time with respect to these issues.

In 1857 it was not considered discriminatory to command Dred Scott to slavery after having been a free man for some years, finding that since he was a slave he was not considered to be a citizen and the Constitution did not apply to him. Contrast that case with the 1954 decision in *Brown v. Board of Education* in which the Court ruled that racial segregation in education was in violation of the Fourteenth Amendment. How the courts will apply case precedent and interpret laws in the future is not always known and while one can rely on past rulings there are always nuances to be argued as well as the ever changing nature of our society and the need for the legal system to keep up with technology. The power of the third branch of government, the judiciary, was established in the 1803 seminal case of *Marbury v. Madison*, in which the Supreme Court emphasized that it is the "judicial department to say what the law is." Since that time judicial review has dramatically affected the application of laws and procedure.

The use of Latin phrases is common parlance in the law and those related to criminal law include: actus rea, mens rea, mala in se, habeas corpus, subpoena duce tecum, pro se, in forma pauperis and writ of certiorari to name a few.

A grand jury is convened to begin the process of charging someone. A prosecutor can select its members, conduct the proceedings in secret and the person who might be charged has no rights during that process. Reforms to the grand jury process are being discussed to make it more transparent and fair.

There are various types of crimes. The least serious are infractions, but misdemeanors are more serious, and the most serious of all are felonies. The FBI classification systems for reporting crimes analyze these data to track and predict crimes. Agencies and state programs which implement and report to the Uniform Crime Reporting (UCR) and National Crime Victimization Survey (NCVS) are both being sharpened and expanded as they come into compliance with the federal reporting standards. Corporate and white collar crimes are also types of crimes. Civil cases are often filed simultaneously with criminal charges, such as in the case of the British Petroleum oil spill in the Gulf of Mexico and also the case of O.J. Simpson who was found innocent in a criminal trial for the double murders of his wife and her friend , but then being held responsible in a civil lawsuit. Bernie Madoff pled guilty to a Ponzi scheme in one of the largest fraud cases in the United States. At the time of this writing, civil cases against Mr. Madoff are still pending.

While the prosecution has the burden of proving that the crime was committed beyond a reasonable doubt, defenses are key to any case. Types of defenses include: self- defense, defense of property and others, consent, resisting an unlawful arrest, not guilty by reason of insanity, diminished capacity, mental incompetence, and intoxication. Procedural defenses include entrapment, prosecutorial misconduct, and double jeopardy.

Key Terms

Actus Rea
Administrative Law
Bill of Rights
Case Law
Common Law

Constitution
Corporate Law
Criminal Negligence
Double Jeopardy
Due Process
Equal Protection
FBI Classifications
Felony
Grand Jury
Habeas Corpus
Infractions
Judicial Review
Legal Defenses
Mala in se
Malice
McNaughton Rule
Mens Rea
Miranda Rights
Misdemeanors
Probably Cause
Procedural Defense
Procedural Law
Pro Se
Search Warrant
Self-Incrimination
Stare decisis
Statutes
Substantive Law
White Collar Crime
Writ of certiorari

References

Los Angeles Times. (1995). *AMA deplores increase in sexual assaults and family violence.* Retrieved from articles.latimes.com.

Atkins v. Virginia, 536 U.S. 304 (2002)

Bennett, C., Rosario, F. (2008) . Zuckerman sounds off on Madoff. *NY Post.* December 15.

Brady v. Maryland, 373 U.S. 83 (1963)

Bray, C. (2009). Madoff pleads guilty of massive fraud. *The Wall Street Journal,* March 12.

Brown v. Board of Education, 347 U.S. 483 (1954)

CA Office of Administrative Law (2007). *CA code of regulations.* Retrieved from www.oal.ca.gov.

Chimel v. California, 395 U.S.752 (1969)

Simon, M., & O'Neil,A. (2012). Unstable ground: The fine line between self-defense and murder. Retrieved from www.cnn.com.

Dred Scott v. Sanford, 60 U.S. 393 (1857)

Egelko, R.(2011). Court OKs search of cell phones without warrant. *San Francisco Gate* January, 2011.

FBI Uniform Crime Reports (2012). Retrieved from www.fbi.gov.

Fleury, M, (2009). *Madoff victims count their losses.* Retrieved from news.bbc.co.uk.

Furman v. Georgia, 408 U.S. 238 (1972)

Gideon v. Wainwright, 372 U.S. 335 (1963)

Gifis, Steven H. (2008). *Barron's dictionary of legal terms A simplified guide to the language of law, Fourth Ed.* New York: Barron's Educational Series, Inc.

Graham v. Florida, 560 U.S. ___ (2010)

Graybow, M.(2009). Madoff mystery remains as he nears guilty plea. Retrieved from www.reuters.com.

Griffin v. California, 380 U.S. 609 (1965)

Griffin v. Illinois, 351 U.S. 12 (1956)

Grisham, J. (2006). *The innocent man.* New York: Dell.

Katz v. United States, 389 U.S. 347 (1967)

Lawrence et al. v. Texas, 539 U.S. 558 (2003)

Lenzer, R. (2014). It's a scandal that early on fraudsters Bernie Madoff and Robert Allen Stanford were not shut down by the SEC. *Forbes,* March 30

Mapp v. Ohio, 367 U.S. 643 (1961)

Marbury v. Madison, 1 U.S. 137 (1803)

Merriam-Webster's Collegiate Dictionary (11th ed). (2005). Springfield, MA: Merriam Webster

Miller v. Alabama, 567 U.S. ____ (2012)

Miranda v. Arizona, 384 U.S. 436 (1966)

People v. Diaz, 51 Cal.4th 84,244 p.3D 501,119 Cal. Rptr. 3d 105 (Cal. January 3, 2011)

Randall, D. (2008). *Rich investors wiped out by Wall St. fraud.* Retrieved from www.independent.co.uk.

Reed v. Reed 404 U.S. 71 (1971).

Robinson v. California, 370 U. S. 660 (1962)

Roper v. Simmons , 543 U.S. 551 (2005)

Savage, D. G. (2012). *Supreme Court rules mandatory juvenile life without parole cruel.* Retrieved from articles.latimes.com.

Sax, R. (2009). *The complete idiot's guide to the criminal justice system.* New York: Penguin.

Siegel, L. J. (2010). *Introduction to Criminal Justice.* California: Wadsworth Cengage

Strom, S. (2009). Elie Wiesel levels scorn at Madoff. *The New York Times*. February 27.

United States v. Warshak, 631 F.3d 266 (2010)

United States v. Ziegler, 497 F.3d 890 (2007)

Wilkerson v. Utah, 99 U.S. 130 (1878)

CHAPTER 9

JUVENILE DELINQUENCY AND THE JUVENILE JUSTICE SYSTEM

The focus now turns to a specific group, a group that is defined solely on the basis of age, an age sometimes identified as simply being "under the age of majority." And that age is? The answer actually depends on what state you call home, but for most of you and for most jurisdictions in the United States, that age is 18. The group so defined is made up of what are known as juveniles, and our concern in this chapter is to examine a sub-group of juveniles who unfortunately become delinquent. Now even you, as you read this text book, may be a juvenile (especially if you're a freshman), but you are probably not a "juvie" – the affectionate name given to that subset of juveniles who do become delinquent. As you go through this chapter you will find out what a lot of young people do today that strays from the path of legality. You will also learn what society's responses are, and what happens to the wayward youth who become embroiled in the criminal justice system.

Historical Perspectives

Research on juvenile delinquency is voluminous. Although formally and systematically examined since the 1800s, delinquent and defiant behavior by juveniles was noticed and commented on centuries before. Indeed, Socrates observed: Children now love luxury, they have bad manners, contempt for authority, and they show disrespect for elders, and love chatter in place of exercise. Children no longer rise when elders enter the room. They contradict their parents, chatter before company, gobble up dainties at the table, cross their legs and tyrannize over teachers (cited in Stullken, 1956, p.33).

Juveniles have exhibited unmanageable and deviant behavior for centuries, but the manner by which these behaviors have been addressed has changed considerably and generally for the better. Until the nineteenth century juvenile offenders in the United States were treated as adults and they were processed through the adult system of criminal justice. The adult criminal justice system was modeled after the European system, particularly English Common law. In this system, juveniles were seen as little adults, and were considered the property of their parents. They were often treated severely and harshly if they engaged in criminal or untoward activities, and were imprisoned with adults. Juveniles were also exploited sexually by older inmates, and spent much of their prison time fearing for their safety. Some juveniles learned to become hardened criminals during their period of incarceration.

Actually, the juvenile period or adolescence as we know it, was not even viewed as a formal and distinct stage of human development until the psychologist G. Stanley Hall (1844-1924) labeled it as "adolescence" and identified it as a period of storm and stress. Hall saw this period as replete with emotional upheaval, conflict with authority, and engagement in high risk behavior (Hall, 1904; Arnett, 1999).

Institutionalization of Juveniles
The beginning of nineteenth century America saw a significant increase in immigration numbers particularly in major east coast cities. This population explosion created many opportunities and positive developments, but at the same time, caused a dramatic increase in social problems such as poverty, child abuse, and child abandonment. Deviant activities such as drunkenness, vagrancy, and other crimes began to plague these cities. These were not just adult problems as many children were homeless, poor, maltreated and engaging in criminal activities. Concern that these children were being treated poorly and like adults, resulted in the establishment in 1817 of "The Society for the Prevention of Pauperism." This Society published a working paper, titled "The Penitentiary System in the United States," which stated, in part, that wayward juveniles should be treated differently from adults and, if necessary, should be housed and reformed in institutions separate from their adult counterparts. In response to these developments, institutions referred to as "Houses of Refuge" were developed (NRCIM, 2001; Sullivan, 2007; Crowe 2000; Hewitt, Regoli & Delisi, 2001).

Houses of Refuge.
The first House of Refuge was established in New York City in 1825 to protect, reform, and educate. Houses of Refuge then expanded to other major cities such as Pittsburgh, Philadelphia, and Boston. Their major mission was to provide supportive services and a sanctuary for children who were poor, abandoned, or maltreated. Thus, they were designed to provide a safer and more appropriate alternative to prison. A child could be placed in one of these facilities by a parent, guardian, or government official. In theory, the services that these Houses could provide were positive, but the actual environment was too often rather harsh and grim. They were essentially penal institutions that required strict adherence to rules, stringent physical discipline and punishment through hard labor and rigorous militaristic regimens. Yes, these Houses provided a setting separate from adults, but they certainly were not a refuge as children continued to be mistreated, abused, and exploited. Also, many children who were involved in criminal activities continued to be placed in adult prisons. Because these Houses did not live up to their theoretical goals and conditions, they became virtually nonexistent by the middle of the nineteenth century. Notwithstanding, alternative placements for juveniles in need began to surface (Sullivan, 2007; Ventrell, 1998).

Placing Out

The first of these alternatives was called "Placing Out", sometimes referred to as the Orphan Train. Reformers who were disillusioned by the relative failure of Houses of Refuge believed that children who were offenders, vagrants, or who could not be with their families should, nevertheless, be in another type of family setting. These juveniles were placed on trains and sent to live and work on farms in the West and Midwest. It was thought that removing children from the dangers of city life and oftentimes from abusive parents would be advantageous. Further, living with a family in a simple, rural agrarian environment was seen as promoting a positive work ethic, discipline, family values, and moral development. Placing Out was a positive experience for many juveniles and for the receiving families. Some of these children, however, were not as fortunate as they were sometimes maltreated, abused, and forced to work long hours. Some never returned to their home towns.

Reform Schools.

The Lyman Reform School for Boys was the nation's first reform school and was established in 1846 in Westborough, Massachusetts. Reform schools were residential facilities that were staffed by surrogate caregivers known as 'house parents' or 'cottage parents.' The primary purpose of these schools was to provide educational, moral, and vocational training to youthful offenders. The underlying premise of the reform school movement was that juvenile offenders should not be punished as adults since they were still young enough to be rehabilitated and reformed. The reform school movement quickly spread throughout the United States, yet programming at these schools, similar to Houses of Refuge, continued to be punitive and correctional in nature.

Industrial Schools.

Industrial Schools were actually another type of reform school, but the emphasis was on industrial labor. Juveniles housed in these facilities were required to pay for room and board and companies would contract with these facilities to have the juveniles perform manufacturing and other types of manual work. While the assertion was that the juvenile would develop a positive work ethic, in essence, these children were forced to work long hours at difficult jobs, in harsh conditions, and often under the watchful eye and brutal hand of their supervisor. The institutionalization of juveniles, while perhaps well intended, did little to prevent their mistreatment Children continued to be homeless, live in poverty and be abused, abandoned and imprisoned with adults.

Child Savers and the Development of the Juvenile Court

At the end of the nineteenth century a group of individuals, primarily prominent women, started a campaign that came to be known as the "Child Savers

Movement" (Platt, 1969). They believed that children were not miniature adults, and that they had the capacity to change. This movement sought to develop a system of services that would provide rehabilitative, supportive, and just services to high risk youth (Sullivan, 2007; Ventrell, 1998). This was a movement that emerged primarily because of the following concerns: child labor, child homelessness, maltreatment of children, juvenile crime, and problems with institutional care.

At that time, children were considered miniature adults and were expected to work. According to the Labor Center Public Education Project (2004) children were used on farms as indentured servants. They were being used in factories because they were cheaper to employ, easier to discipline and manipulate, and were not inclined to strike. Children who committed crimes were punished and housed with adult offenders or placed in other institutional settings. Those who were homeless, abused, or neglected were also segregated and oftentimes brutally punished or even apprenticed to the government. Often these children who were abused or neglected by their caregivers were afforded no protection at all. The Child Savers Movement attempted to change all of this and improve the lives of these children. Child labor was seen as inappropriate and cruel, and they viewed youthful offenders as immature children in need of assistance, not as hardened criminals. Homeless children and those abused and neglected by their caretakers were in need of intervention to protect them and also as a way to prevent them from engaging in criminal activities. The Child Savers Movement believed that juveniles should be treated differently than adults, and they advocated for a system to deal with high risk youth - the juvenile justice system (Ventrell,1998; Platt, 1969).

One of the first major steps toward the establishment of a separate system of juvenile justice began with a Supreme Court case, *People v. Turner* (1870). In this case, the Illinois Supreme Court heard that Dan O'Connell, a juvenile, had been placed and held in a Chicago reform school against his parent's wishes. His parents contested this placement indicating that he was being illegally incarcerated and punished and that they should have responsibility for their son. The Court agreed, ruled for his parents, and ordered the release of their son. This case, together with the influences of the Child Savers Movement, prompted the passage of the Juvenile Court Act and the establishment of the first juvenile court in 1899 in Chicago, Illinois. The Illinois Juvenile Court Act was broad-sweeping legislation that allowed the State to develop a system of justice separate from the adult system. This new system was not stern but just, and it was a system that promoted treatment, rehabilitation, and education as opposed to punitive interventions. This newly established juvenile court had jurisdiction over any juvenile under the age of 16 who committed an offense. The Act also gave juvenile courts control over any juvenile under the age of 16 who was abused, abandoned, neglected or otherwise dependent.

Juvenile court proceedings were rather informal and did not have to follow the formalities of criminal proceedings. A formal trial was not held in a courtroom, and there was no due process. The Judge was given considerable latitude, as they are today, in sentencing and could place a child in an institution, issue a warning, or put a juvenile on probation. Juveniles who were in contact with the court were presumed to be from families who could not or would not care for them or who could not or would not provide them with proper guidance and direction.

Parens Patraie

The court was given the authority to intervene unconditionally in the lives of children under the doctrine of something called "parens patraie." Parens patraie (state as parent) is the doctrine that the state will act as the parent if it is determined by the juvenile court that the parents cannot or will not care for or control their children (Sickmund, 2007; NRCIM, 2001).

The juvenile court was respected for quite some time and operated relatively unchallenged until the 1960s. At that time, a number of questions began to emerge regarding the legitimacy of these proceedings. In particular, the absence of due process was seen as a violation of the constitutional rights of juveniles.

Reforming the Juvenile System Yet Again

Four benchmark cases significantly changed the juvenile justice system by establishing procedural safeguards for juvenile court cases. These cases ushered in legislation that held that juveniles had the same constitutional rights as adults and it incorporated the due process clause of the United States Constitution. Due process guarantees all citizens freedom from any arbitrary governmental attempts to deprive them of life, liberty or property and it applies to both federal and state governments (Tannenhaus, 2011).

Kent v. United States (1966).

Morris Kent was a 16 year old adolescent from Washington, D.C. who was taken into custody and charged with robbing and raping a woman in her apartment. Because of these charges and because he was already on probation from a previous charge of burglary, the juvenile court judge transferred Kent's case to adult court where he was tried, convicted, and sentenced to a maximum of 90 years in prison. If tried in juvenile court his sentence likely would have been confinement until his twenty first birthday. These actions were legally challenged, citing that Kent's due-process rights were violated and that a waiver hearing should have been conducted before he was transferred to adult court. The United States Supreme Court ruled in favor of Kent and the conviction was reversed.

In Re Gault (1967)

Gerald Gault was a 15 year old adolescent from Arizona who was taken into detention for allegedly making a lewd and obscene phone call to a woman. Gerald was already on probation for his previous involvement in a wallet snatching. Two hearings were conducted at juvenile court, but at each hearing the alleged victim was not present, defense attorneys were not present, and written documentations of the proceedings were not maintained. At the second hearing the judge found him to be delinquent and remanded Gerald Gault to the State Industrial School until he reached the age of twenty one. This case also eventually reached the United States Supreme Court and, like Kent, the Court ruled that Gault's constitutional rights, particularly his right to due process, were not upheld.

In Re Winship (1970)

In this case the Supreme Court found that delinquency charges must be proven beyond a reasonable doubt, particularly when there was a possibility that the juvenile could be placed in a secured facility. Prior to this finding, the burden of proof standard of preponderance of evidence was required.

In McKeiver v. Pennsylvania

In 1971 the Supreme Court ruled that juveniles did not have the right to a trial by jury. The Court argued that a trial by jury would make the juvenile justice system identical to the adult criminal justice system and remove the more casual atmosphere of juvenile proceedings. Individual states could, however, use the trial-by-jury system in certain situations.

These four Supreme Court cases provided juveniles with the following safeguards:

1. The right to retain an attorney.
2. The right to question witnesses in their defense.
3. Trial by jury is not required in juvenile justice proceedings.
4. The right to be informed of the issues surrounding self- incrimination.
5. Delinquency charges must be proven beyond a reasonable doubt.
6. Waiver hearings must be conducted before transfer to adult criminal court.

Although the state must continue to act in the best interests of the child, as influenced by the doctrine of parens patraie, these Supreme Court cases demand that the states must also employ due process in all juvenile justice proceedings. These due-process safeguards serve to uphold and protect the constitutional rights of juveniles, just as in the adult criminal justice system. Concomitantly, the juvenile court remains a somewhat informal entity that attempts to be less adversarial and more benevolent.

Defining Delinquency

Definitions

Although considerable research has been carried out on the subject of juvenile delinquency, problems in definition remain. Mental health professionals sometimes consider juvenile delinquency to be a psychopathological disturbance or disorder of conduct where the youngster engages in behavior that violates societal conventions and the rights of others (Maxmen & Ward, 1995; APA, 2013). Educators will often, but not always, view delinquency as a type of serious emotional disturbance or social maladjustment where the child is exhibiting inappropriate behaviors, having relationship difficulties, having learning problems, and having a serious mental illness (Hochbaum, 2011; Kauffman, Cullinan, & Epstein 1987). Many sociologists see delinquency as a type of social deviance, of social disorganization, community disintegration, social strain, and poor socialization practices (Hughes, Kroehler, & Vander Zander, 2002; Gough, 1948). Still, the layperson may consider an adolescent to be a delinquent if he smokes, stays out late, curses, or drives too fast. From a legal perspective, juvenile delinquency can be seen as criminal activity committed by a person who has not yet reached adulthood or the age of majority. If this criminal activity were to be committed by someone who has reached the age of majority then that person would be processed in the adult criminal justice system. Most states have set the age of majority at 18, but a number of states have established lower age limits. Nevertheless, in addition to the above criteria, a juvenile can also be considered an offender when adjudicated for a status offense.

Status Offense

A status offense is an act that is only considered an offense when committed by a juvenile. These are offenses such as truancy, being beyond parental control, running away, drinking, smoking, or promiscuity. While this designation is certainly controversial, most states still consider youths who engage in these behaviors to be offenders. Indeed, the most recent data from the National Center for Juvenile Justice (NCJJ) found that in the year 2011 courts that presided over juvenile matters heard over 116, 200 cases involving status offenses (Hockenberry &Puzzanchera, 2014). Other states may no longer use the term status offenders, but do classify these youngsters under other labels such as CHINS (Children In Need of Services), or perhaps refer to them as abused and/ or neglected and therefore under the supervision of social or protective services (Puuzzanchera, 2007; DeFrancesco, 1984).

One does need to exercise caution when using the legal definition of juvenile delinquency as there are 51 juvenile justice entities in the United States in addition to over 500 recognized native American tribes (with many operating under their own systems of juvenile justice). Each of these juvenile justice systems is unique, and many have their own methods of interpreting the juvenile laws established by their lawmakers (NCJJ, 2011). So, generally speaking delinquency can be defined legally as juvenile crime, but with the caveat that it is a definition that is still open to interpretation (NCJJ, 2011).

Juvenile Crime

Juvenile crime can be delineated into broad categories of offenses: status offenses, property offenses, offenses against person, drug-law violations, and public-order offenses.

Status offenses, as described above, are acts that are considered crimes for juveniles but are not considered as such for adults. These offenses are termed status offenses because of the person's juvenile status. Status offenses, such as truancy, curfew violations, and incorrigibility, are not necessarily serious crimes but are seen as being correlated with a future life of more serious criminal involvement. Therefore, court intervention with these youngsters is seen as desirable and preventative (McNamara, 2008; DeFrancesco 1984). As noted above, in 2011 juvenile courts in the United States processed an estimated 116,200 status-offense cases. This represents a 7% decrease since 1995. Table 1 shows the percentage of status offense cases petitioned (handled formally by the juvenile courts) by offense type for the years 2002 and 2011 (Hockenberry &Puzzachera, 2014).

Table 1.1 Profile of Petitioned Status Offense Cases

Offense Type	2002	2011
Runaway	11%	9%
Truancy	33	40
Curfew Violations	10	10
Ungovernability	11	12
Liquor Law Violations	21	20
Miscellaneous	13	9
TOTAL	100%	100%
NUMBER OF CASES	193,700	116,200

Source: Adapted from Juvenile Court Statistics 2011, National Center for Juvenile Justice, Pittsburgh, PA (2014)

There have been some decreases and increases involving truancy and runaway cases respectively, however, the actual overall number of petitioned status offense cases has decreased. Of these petitioned cases the number of youth who were adjudicated (judged) as a status offender also decreased. Table 1.2 shows the percentage of adjudicated status offense cases by offense type for the years 2002 and 2011.

Table 1.2 Profile of Adjudicated Status Offense Cases

Offense Type	2002	2011
Runaway	8%	7%
Truancy	33	38
Curfew	11	10
Ungovernability	10	11
Liquor Law	23	22
Miscellaneous	15	11
TOTAL	100%	100%
NUMBER OF CASES	119,300	66,400

Source: Adapted from Juvenile Court Statistics 2011, National Center for Juvenile Justice, Pittsburgh, Pennsylvania (2014)

Truancy and liquor law violations, by far, make up the largest percentage of adjudicated status offense cases in both 2002 and 2011. Overall there was a decrease in the number of juveniles adjudicated for status offenses. Nevertheless, these numbers continue to show that a societal problem exists, and the youngsters involved in these activities are in need of legal and supportive services.

Technically speaking, status offenders are not considered juvenile delinquents. In other words, they are adjudicated as status offenders and not as delinquent. The vast majority of cases in the juvenile justice system are concentrated in the areas of property crime, crimes against persons, drug law violations, and public order offenses. These are serious offenses that, if committed by an adult, would result in prosecution in the adult criminal justice system. But for someone under the age of majority, the offense would result in juvenile justice involvement and possible adjudication as a delinquent. Approximately 1,236,200 delinquency cases were handled by juvenile courts in 2011. This translates to about 3,700 cases per day and represents an increase since 1985 (Hockenberry & Puzzanchera, 2014).

Delinquency Offenses.

Crimes against another person are considered to be violent offenses. These types of offenses are crimes committed against another person, usually, but not necessarily, with a weapon and include such acts as rape, robbery, aggravated and simple assault, and homicide. Property offenses involve the illegal transfer, taking, or destruction of private or public property. These include such offenses as burglary, shoplifting, larceny, theft, vandalism, arson, trespassing, and motor vehicle theft. Drug law violations are the unlawful use, sale, possession, distribution or cultivation or manufacture of illegal or controlled drugs or drug paraphernalia. This category also includes the use of inhalants. Public order offenses include such acts as obstruction of justice, weapons offenses, liquor law violations (public intoxication), disorderly conduct, and non-violent sex law violations (NCJJ, 2011; US Department of Education, 2011; Snyder, 1982). The percentage of offenses by offense type for the years 2002 and 2011 are noted in the following table.

Table 1.3 Profile of Delinquency Offenses by Offense Type

Offense Type	2002	2011
Person	24%	26%
Property	40	36
Drug Law Violations	11	12
Public Order Offenses	25	26
TOTAL	100%	100%

Source: Adapted from Juvenile Court Statistics 2011, National Center for Juvenile Justice, Pittsburgh, Pennsylvania (2014)

Crimes against persons or violent offenses, drug law violations, and public order offenses all showed increases from 2002 to 2011 while property offenses showed a decline for the same period. According to Juvenile Court Statistics 2014 (Hockenberry &Puzzanchera, 2014) the estimated 1,236,20000 cases involved with juvenile courts showed that:
1. The number of delinquency cases processed increased 7% from 1985 and 2011.
2. Juveniles under the age of 16 accounted for slightly more than half of all cases.
3. Males constituted 72% of the cases in juvenile court in 2011 and females 28%
4. In 2011 white youth made up 76% of youth under juvenile court jurisdiction, African American youth 16%, American Indian youth 2%, and Asian youth 5%
5. While the estimated number of cases handled by juvenile courts was 1,236,200 the number of cases that were actually adjudicated delinquent in 2011 was far less, or approximately 391,700 (Table 1.5).

Table 1.4 Profile of Adjudicated Delinquent Cases

Offense Type	2002	2011
Person	23%	25%
Property	38	34
Drug Law Violations	11	11
Public Order Offenses	28	29
TOTAL	100%	100%
TOTAL ADJUDICATED DELINQUENT CASES	592,200	391,700

Source: Adapted from Juvenile Court Statistics 2011, National Center for Juvenile Justice, Pittsburgh, Pennsylvania (2014).

The overall number of juveniles adjudicated delinquent showed a decrease from 2002 to 2011. Slight increases were seen in crimes against person and public order offenses, while a decline occurred in property offenses. White youth were adjudicated more often as were juveniles under age 16, and males more often than females.

Juveniles who are taken into custody for any of the offenses listed in the above tables certainly have due process safeguards, but they are also afforded protections under the Juvenile Justice and Delinquency Protection Act (JJDP) of 2002 (DCJS, 2011). The JJDP of 2002 amends the original JJDP of 1974 but the intent of the act remains essentially unchanged. There are four major components of the act:

1. Jail Removal Component. Juveniles should not be housed (jailed) with adult offenders (with some extremely limited exceptions).
2. Sight and Sound Component. Juveniles who are jailed with adult offenders must be separated by sight and sound from the adult population.
3. Disproportionate Minority Confinement Component. States must attempt to decrease the disproportionate number of minority youth currently in the juvenile justice system.
4. Deinstitutionalization of Status Offenders Component. Juveniles who commit status offenses, as well as non-offenders, such as abused and abandoned children, should not be detained in secure juvenile or adult facilities.

Compliance with these four components would ensure that juveniles are protected and appropriately processed in the juvenile justice system. Further, states that do not comply with the above requirements are not eligible for Federal grant funds to operate juvenile justice programming.

Today's Juvenile Court

Mission of the Juvenile Court

The juvenile court attempts to be less formal, less adversarial, and more benevolent than the adult criminal justice system. The major mission of the court is to rehabilitate, strengthen, and empower the juvenile rather than to punish and penalize. Through diversion, monitoring, supportive services, and related interventions the court attempts to encourage pro-social development and prevent troubled youth from engaging in a future life of crime and possible involvement in the adult criminal justice system. This philosophy is even evident in the nomenclature (Behavioral Institute, 2012) that is used by the courts. Terminology that is used in the adult system such as criminal, verdict, sentencing, and incarceration is seen as somewhat threatening and accusatory and is generally not used in the juvenile justice system (Table 1.6).

Table 1.5 Juvenile versus Adult Terminology

Juvenile	Adult
Delinquent	Criminal
Taken into Custody	Arrested
Detention	Jail
Petition	Charge (indictment)
Hearing	Trial
Finding	Verdict
Adjudicated	Convicted
Disposition	Sentenced
Committed	Imprisoned (incarcerated)

Source: Adapted and retrieved from Juvenile Justice Terminology http://behavioralinstitute.org February 1, 2012

It is generally accepted practice that diversion is preferred to processing a youngster through the juvenile courts. Diversion (Sheldon, 1999) involves finding alternatives, such as placement with caregivers or guardians, before subjecting a youngster to the sometimes protracted processing and procedures of the courts. Nevertheless, diversion is not always appropriate or desirable and, as statistics cited above indicate, the juvenile courts still handle thousands of cases per day.

Operation of the Juvenile Court
The manner by which a youngster is processed (Figure 1.1) through the juvenile court can be unique to each state or jurisdiction but tends to proceed through the following general steps (Sickmund 2007; Crowe, 2000):
1. Referral
2. Intake
3. Detention
4. Petitioning
5. Adjudicatory Hearing
6. Disposition

Referral
A referral to juvenile court can be made by someone in the community such as a school official, parent or guardian, mental health or social service worker, or a law enforcement officer. Police officers, however, are responsible for the majority of referrals, typically because they received a complaint from someone about delinquent activity or they observed the delinquent activity first hand. The police would prefer not to make the referral and would rather handle the situation informally through, as mentioned above, diversion. This means, for instance, that they would prefer to issue a warning to the juvenile, or refer the juvenile to a community or police-intervention program.

Figure 1.1 Case Flow Diagram of the Juvenile Justice Process

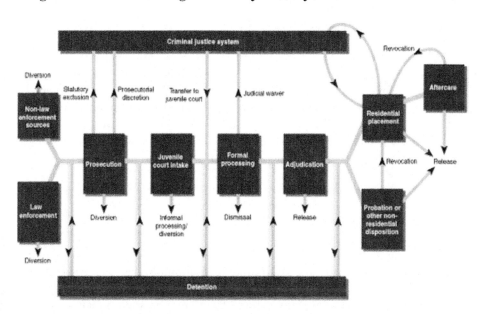

Source: Retrieved from Office of Juvenile Justice and Delinquency Prevention, Statistical Briefing Book www.ojjdp.gov January 2015

These referrals may also come from the youngster's parents or caregivers. Many of these referral sources attempt to prevent the juvenile from being taken into custody. Other diversion activities might include a social service worker who may become aware of an adolescent's high risk activity and, rather than filing a formal complaint might recommend that the youth begin a course of treatment with a therapist. Diversion came to the forefront in 1967 when The President's Commission on Law Enforcement and the Administration of Justice promoted the development of youth service bureaus to assist in creating programs in the community for juvenile delinquents (Sheldon, 1999). Oftentimes the decision to divert is not an easy one. The police will typically base their decisions to divert or take the youngster into custody on a variety of factors including:

1. The seriousness of the offense
2. Oppositional defiant behavior exhibited by the juvenile
3. The juvenile is known to the police department from prior contacts
4. The juvenile is homeless or from another jurisdiction
5. They believe the juvenile is a threat to the community
6. They believe the juvenile is in danger

Once the police officer makes the decision to take the youth into custody, the juvenile is usually brought to the police station where contact with juvenile authorities is made and the intake process is initiated. When taking the youth into custody, due process, as previously discussed, is followed just as it would be for an adult.

Intake
The intake is conducted at the juvenile court, juvenile detention center, or similar facility depending on the policy of the jurisdiction. Intake workers are commonly juvenile probation officers who have had some training in mental health, social services, or forensic psychology. Intake is a screening process that will determine if the juvenile will need court intervention. After interviewing the juvenile and reviewing the specifics of the case, the intake worker, using specific criteria, must decide whether to:
1. Dismiss the case.
2. Handle the matter informally.
3. Transfer the case to adult court (criminal justice system)
4. Formally handle the matter in juvenile court by filing a petition.

If a case is dismissed, the juvenile may be released to his parents. Sometimes a voluntary referral may be made to a social service professional where arrangements are made for restitution or community service. Also, there might be a recommendation for some sort of informal monitoring by the probation officer. And as shown above, there are even some situations when the intake worker decides that a judicial waiver to adult court is necessary. This usually occurs when the juvenile has been involved in a serious crime against persons or property, or if it is determined that the juvenile cannot benefit from services provided by the juvenile court. Alternately, if the intake worker decides that the case warrants formal juvenile court intervention, then a petition is filed and the case is placed on the juvenile court docket. Once the decision is made to file a formal petition, a date is set for an adjudicatory hearing. A petition is a formal charging document stating the allegations against the juvenile and the need for a hearing.

The intake worker also needs to determine if the petitioned juvenile can be released pending the adjudicatory hearing or if the juvenile needs to be held in detention. A juvenile detention facility is a secure placement that ensures that the juvenile will be confined during the juvenile court handling of the case. The decision to place a youth in a juvenile detention facility is typically based on the seriousness of the offense or some other specific determinant. A detention placement does require a hearing before a judge to determine the legitimacy of the intake worker's decision. In most states, the detention hearing is usually held within 24 hours. Before the adjudicatory hearing is held, the court must be ensured that the juvenile will be represented by counsel. Adjudicated means to hear and judge a case. During an adjudicatory hearing, due process, similar to adult court, must be followed. Attorneys are present, evidence is offered, and if necessary, cross-examination is conducted. The judge is able to question the youth directly and usually a jury is not involved. There are situations, although rare, where the defense strongly contests the allegations, and a jury is impaneled. Nevertheless, the judge, based on the information presented, then renders a decision to adjudicate the juvenile as delinquent, or a status offender, or dismiss the case. If the youth is adjudicated a predisposition report is prepared and a disposition hearing is scheduled. While waiting for the predisposition report to be prepared and the disposition hearing to take place, the juvenile may be held in detention or released to the custody of trusted caregivers.

At the disposition hearing the judge imposes sanctions based on information presented at the adjudicatory hearing and on information contained in the predisposition report. The predisposition report is an informative document that is prepared by the probation office of the juvenile court. This comprehensive report tends to focus on how the courts can assist the juvenile by providing services that will rehabilitate rather than punish the youngster. Notice that throughout the process the emphasis is on helping the youngster rather than handing out punishment. Information from the intake interview and adjudicatory hearing is contained in the report. The report will also contain basic demographic information, along with a psychosocial history that encompasses any educational, medical, or family history concerns. Finally, the report will show any prior delinquent activities, and any past attempts at rehabilitation. The probation office may also contract a psychologist to conduct a psychological assessment that evaluates the mental status, emotional stability, and cognitive functioning of the juvenile. Other professionals such as social workers, speech and language specialists, or a psychiatrist may also be contracted as deemed necessary. Further, significant others in the juvenile's life who may be able to support and assist the youth may be identified. The probation officer compiles and integrates all of this information into the predisposition report and then will make specific recommendations to the court regarding disposition of the youth. These recommendations can include treatment options, probation, placement, commitment, community service, restitution, fines or some combination of these sanctions. The judge seriously reviews the predisposition report and usually follows the recommendations made by the probation officer. The judge certainly takes the 'best interests of the child' into consideration but also needs to consider the safety of the general public. In rare circumstances the case will be dismissed.

Probation, by far, is the most common sanction with 250,100 adjudicated youth being placed on formal probation in 2011. This represents 64% of all adjudicated delinquency cases. Residential placement is next with 24% (95,900), while other sanctions such as community service, restitution or fines were given in 12% (45,800) of the cases (Hockenberry & Puzzanchera, 2014).

Types of Sanctions

Probation
Probation is the least restrictive sanction that can be imposed on an adjudicated delinquent. This option allows the youth to remain in the community, optimally with family, rather than being placed in an out-of-home program. Probation provides an opportunity for the youth to access community-based programming and treatment, such as a day treatment program, while being monitored by court staffs. Monitoring is typically carried out by social workers, caseworkers, or probation officers.

Probation can be either standard or intensive.

1. Standard probation
Standard probation might involve periodic monitoring by the court to ensure that the juvenile is participating in the recommended programming and not continuing to engage in delinquent activities.

2. Intensive Probation
Intensive probation, as the name implies, is more restrictive and requires an increased level of monitoring by the probation officer. Sometimes community service, restitution or other types of sanctions can be imposed as part of the probation agreement.

Out-of-Home Placements
The out-of-home placement is another alternative available to the court. These placements are more restrictive than probation, but not as restrictive as commitment to a state training school. Out-of-home placements typically include residential treatment centers, group homes, and foster homes.

Residential Treatment Centers
Residential treatment is certainly more restrictive than probation as it involves removing the youngster from his home and the community and placing him in a 24 hour residential treatment center. The residential treatment center is designed to offer programming and treatment of the delinquent youth. These centers are usually large and may be composed of several cottage-style units or dormitory-type structures, and they are staffed by direct-care workers, often called 'child-care workers' or 'residential counselors.' These workers are usually responsible for the general care and everyday routine of the youth and are also responsible for the scheduling and programming of activities. The residential treatment center would also employ a multidisciplinary team of individuals such as psychologists, social workers, nurses, psychiatrists, pediatricians, teachers, recreation staff and others who are responsible for providing medical and mental health treatment and/or educational services. The major mission of the residential treatment center is

to provide long-term support and treatment in a safe and positive environment. The stated goal is to return the juvenile to his home and community, or, at least move him to a less restrictive setting (DeFrancesco, 1990).

Group Homes

A group home is also a 24 hour out of home placement but is usually reserved for juveniles who do not need the support, structure, and supervision provided by a residential treatment center. A group home is smaller with a limited number of residents, and is typically staffed by 'house parents' who provide supervision and support. Group homes can be located in regular neighborhoods, and they attempt to provide a family-like environment. The residents have a bedroom and access to a kitchen, dining room and similar such amenities. Educational and treatment programming can occur at the group home or in the community. Arrangements for other activities, such as medical appointments, recreation, and family visits can be made. Like the residential treatment center, the group home attempts to prepare the youth to be ready to rejoin his family and the community, or in some instances, to live independently.

Foster Homes

Foster homes, more so than group homes, attempt to provide a more family-like setting. Foster families volunteer to take a juvenile, sometimes more than one at a time, into their homes and attempt to offer support and encouragement while also undertaking responsibility for ensuring that these youngsters have the mental health, medical and related services that they require. Although these families are volunteers, they are reimbursed for expenses incurred. Most foster families are licensed to provide services. Placement in a foster home is usually made when the juvenile's relationship with his own caregivers is severely dysfunctional, and the youth needs a 'surrogate' set of parents for a period of time.

The Juvenile Training School

The most restrictive sanction that can be imposed by the court is commitment to a juvenile training school. Generally, this placement is reserved for youth who have committed serious juvenile offenses. A juvenile training school can be fairly similar to an adult correctional facility and, indeed, many, such as the Connecticut Juvenile Training School, are modeled after adult facilities. These are expansive institutions with a focus on security. While many will state that the purpose of a juvenile training school is to rehabilitate and train the juvenile to become more prosocial, in reality, it is more of a punishment and a way to keep the community safe. These facilities do employ a full complement of support staff such as psychologists, educators (including vocational education), psychiatrists, medical personnel and other professionals. Nevertheless, security personnel are also employed. There are also persons working as direct-care personnel, sometimes referred to as "youth services officers" whose primary responsibility is behavioral control. The length of the juvenile's commitment is based on the seriousness of the offense, but the length of stay could be abbreviated in certain situations, especially when the youth is seen as demonstrating good behavior. Other reasons may not be as functionally positive. Sometimes the length of incarceration is reduced because of alternative placement availabilities or institutional overcrowding. A juvenile released from a training school might return to his family or to a less restrictive placement and would typically be followed by an aftercare worker. The after-care worker would attempt to monitor the juvenile and ensure that the youth continues to receive support and the necessary interventions. If the youth does not comply with aftercare requirements or becomes involved in further delinquent activity then a revocation hearing may be held, and the youth can then be returned to the training school. While juvenile training schools are certainly an improvement over the early Houses of Refuge, they can still be austere, and prison-like. Unfortunately, sometimes these environments harden and corrupt the youngster. Also there are still instances of mistreatment and abuse.

There is also alternative programming for adjudicated youth. These include:

1. Wilderness Programs.
These are outdoor programs that are designed to challenge and empower youth.

2. Boot Camps.
Boot camps are militaristic-type programs that are supposed to promote discipline and self- reliance. Programs of this kind have many critics who decry the militaristic overtones that permeate these camps.

3. Day Treatment Programs.
These are partial, full, or extended-day educational and treatment programs that allow the youth to remain in the community and return home in the evening.

4. Home Detention.
Home detention allows the youth to remain at home, but only under certain parameters (e.g., drug testing).

5. Electronic Monitoring.
As the name implies, this involves monitoring a youth with an attached electronic device. This is often used in conjunction with Home Detention.

All of these alternative programs have seen mixed results with proponents hailing them as groundbreaking, and detractors arguing that there are no data to support their effectiveness.

Waiver to the Adult System

Perhaps the most controversial answer to the juvenile dilemma is the decision to transfer the juvenile directly to the adult criminal court. An intake worker may look at the seriousness of a juvenile's offense or the youth's long record of offenses and then file a petition to waive the juvenile court's jurisdiction of the case. A judge must then review the petition and decide if the case should be transferred to the adult-court system. This process varies from state to state, but in general certain criteria must be met before the transfer can take place. These criteria can include: age, seriousness of the offense (usually a felony), prior record of offending, danger to the community, association with known adult offenders, serious gang involvement, prior placement, and treatment failures in the juvenile system. There are also cases, unfortunately, where the youth is remanded to the criminal court because of the current unavailability of specific programming in the juvenile justice system. There is also the factor of recent societal pressure to "get tough on these kids." Nevertheless, there has been a decrease in 2011 in the number of cases that have been waived. This decline may be attributed to the fact that some states have barred certain types of cases from juvenile court control and still others have allowed the filing of charges directly to adult criminal court (Hockenberry & Puzzanchera, 2014)

Transfer to the adult court is controversial because it tends, according to some, to violate the basic tenets of the juvenile system. That is, it does not consider what is in the best interests of the child, but instead assumes that a juvenile can be treated as an adult despite the argument that a juvenile has not fully developed the cognitive capacity to act in a rational, mature, and adult manner. Nevertheless, some juveniles are being transferred to and processed in adult court. Although this practice is declining, it continues to indicate that society is willing to punish juveniles in adult court for serious deviant activities.

CASE STUDY: The Case of Sandy S.

Sandy is a 13 year old female residing in a medium sized city in New England. She lives with her mother Susan, and her mother's longtime boyfriend Peter. Her parents were never married and only lived together for a few years. They separated when Sandy was 3 years old because of dad's drinking, his violent outbursts, and physical abuse of her mother. Sandy has no contact with him and his whereabouts are unknown. Mom became involved with Peter shortly thereafter and it is reported that Sandy was left alone often when they went out for the evening. There was no supervision and limited discipline. Mom also worked full time which left little time for Sandy. During her preschool years Sandy was withdrawn, appeared sad and sometimes had temper tantrums and nightmares. When she began elementary school her teachers noted that she did not appear to be learning like the others and she was beginning to exhibit defiant and oppositional behaviors. She was referred for special education assessment and was diagnosed as having a Serious Emotional Disturbance (SED) and a language based Learning Disability. She required special education services and also received counseling for several years. These services appeared to be helping but when Sandy entered Middle School her academic and behavioral difficulties worsened as she befriended peers who negatively influenced her behaviors. On the home front, Susan and Peter's relationship began to sour. They were intoxicated daily and arguments were becoming frequent and more intense. Sandy's relationship with her mother and Peter became quite toxic and contentious. Sandy began to stay away from home and would hang with her new friends after school and into the evening hours. They began skipping classes and then eventually began to skip full days of school. They would smoke cigarettes and hang out at the mall. On one occasion, one of the group shoplifted some make-up from a drug store. She was caught by store surveillance and her mother was called but no formal charges were filed. On another occasion, however, Sandy shoplifted a video game and was caught on video surveillance. This store wanted to press charges and called the police. When the police arrived Sandy became loud, disruptive, and belligerent and when the police attempted to take her into custody she struggled with one of the officers. Because of her demeanor, the police brought her to the juvenile detention intake center alleging disorderly conduct, breach of peace, and threatening. The Intake Worker conducted an interview with Sandy and also called in her mother as part of the process. The Intake Worker did find Sandy to be somewhat unstable but since she was only 12 years old at the time and this was Sandy's first contact with the juvenile justice system the Intake Worker recommended that Sandy attend school every day, attend individual and family counseling with her mother at the local youth services bureau and agree to informal monitoring by a probation officer. Sandy was released in her mother's custody. Sandy and her mom attended counseling regularly for about six months and Sandy stated that she was attending school but her grade report indicated that she had missed numerous days and she was performing poorly in many of her subjects. Nevertheless, she was promoted to the eighth grade. The summer before beginning eighth grade was uneventful but the beginning of the school year proved to be a difficult time for Sandy. She showed no motivation and little interest in her classes. She and her friends again began to skip school, smoke cigarettes and get high on marijuana daily. School officials became concerned about her absences and academic failures and contacted her mother. When mom returned from work that evening, Sandy was talking on her cell phone. Mom asked her to get off the phone so that she could talk to her about the call she received from the school. Sandy became irate and threw a glass at her mother, hitting her in the face. A brief struggle ensued and Sandy stormed out and went to her friend's house. Mom called the police to report the incident. At the friend's home Sandy and her friend began smoking marijuana and drinking beer. Sandy became increasingly agitated and angry and got into an altercation with her friend's sister which resulted in breaking several objects in the room. Sandy left but this time she was high and quite intoxicated. She was stumbling and falling on the sidewalk when the police noticed her, apprehended her and again brought her to the juvenile detention intake center alleging public intoxication, disorderly conduct, and assault. The Intake Worker conducted an interview and this time found that the situation warranted formal juvenile court intervention. The worker filed a formal petition and arranged a date for an adjudicatory hearing. The worker also recommended that Sandy be held in detention and this decision was approved by a judge. At the hearing the judge questioned Sandy directly about her activities, and although she was counseled by her attorney to be respectful in the courtroom, she was somewhat defiant and exhibited a rather surly attitude. Based on her courtroom demeanor, her history of illegal activities, and the nature of these activities, she was adjudicated delinquent and held in detention until a predisposition report could be prepared. The predisposition report examined her family, educational, and peer relationships, and also noted her prior contacts with the court. A psychological examination was also requested and included in the predisposition report. The psychologist diagnosed Sandy with a Learning Disorder and Oppositional Defiant Disorder. The recommendations made in the predisposition report included one year of intensive probation with strict monitoring by a probation officer, random drug/alcohol testing, individual and family counseling with monthly progress reports submitted to the probation officer, and the provision that Sandy attend school daily and that her academic progress and attendance be reported to her probation officer. This was thought to be the best option for Sandy. Because of her age the judge did not want to commit her to the state training school or other more restrictive residential type setting. Rather, she is now being provided with the monitoring and tools necessary for her to succeed. The rest is up to her.

The Future

Evaluating how juvenile delinquents have been treated and handled over the decades is a daunting task. It does appear that in the early 1800s and before, children were seen as property and treated as miniature adults, but that awareness of the distinctiveness and innocence of childhood and adolescence began to gradually emerge shortly thereafter. With the establishment of homes, institutions, and the juvenile justice system, the march toward more humane and appropriate treatment of juveniles was beginning to take place. We have, as a society, made great strides to ensure that juveniles are handled fairly, with due process, and with the understanding that they should be treated differently than adults.

But deficiencies and controversies remain. Preventing youth from entering the system at all should be a priority. Along with revisiting and seriously reviewing the provisions of the Juvenile Justice and Delinquency Prevention Act we should also be attempting to identify high risk youth and finding ways to save our youth from a future life of delinquency and crime.

Summary

The beginning of the nineteenth century saw an awakening in the humane treatment of wayward and high risk juveniles. Prior to this time children were seen and treated as miniature adults and housed in institutions with adult offenders. The early 1800s witnessed the establishment of institutions such as Houses of Refuge and Reform Schools designed specifically for youth. In theory, the development of these institutions was well intended but children continued to be abuse, abandoned, and imprisoned. The "Child Savers Movement" then ushered in the creation of the juvenile court and later, several Supreme Court cases were paramount in the formation of due-process safeguards for juveniles who engage in criminal activity.

Criminal activity by individuals who have not reached the age of majority is considered delinquent. While problems in defining delinquency remain, the numbers of youth who come in contact with juvenile authorities is a significant societal problem. Juvenile crime is often delineated into broad categories: status offenses, property offenses, offenses against person, drug law violations, and public-order offenses. The total number of delinquency cases handled by juvenile court is substantial.

The major mission of the juvenile court is to rehabilitate, strengthen, and empower the juvenile rather than to punish and penalize. The juvenile court attempts to be less formal, less adversarial, and more benevolent than the adult court. In fact, attempting to divert the juvenile from the juvenile court process is preferable to a court referral. If diversion is not possible then the juvenile may be processed through referral, intake, detention, petitioning, adjudicatory hearings, and disposition. Disposition can include probation, out-of home placements such as group or foster homes, or commitment to a juvenile training school. Waiver to the adult criminal justice system is another option particularly for youthful offenders who have a history of committing serious offenses. The contemporary juvenile court is certainly an improvement over the earlier and more punitive ways of processing and treating juveniles. Continued efforts at identifying high risk youngsters and preventing them from entering the system at all should be a priority.

Key Terms

Adjudicatory
Child Savers Movement
Custody
Delinquency
Detention
Disposition
Diversion
Due Process
Drug Law Violations
English Common Law
Foster Homes
Group Homes
House of Refuge
Industrial Schools
In Re Gault
In Re Winship
Intake
Judicial Transfer Waiver
Juvenile Court Act 1899
JJDP
Juvenile Training School
Kent v United States
McKeiver v Pennsylvania
Parens Patraie
People v Turner
Person Offenses
Petition
Placing Out
Probation
Property Offenses
Public Order Offenses
Reform School
Referral
Residential Treatment Centers
Status Offenders

References

American Psychiatric Association. (2013). *Diagnostic and statistical manual of mental disorders-5th Ed*. Washington, DC: Author.
Arnett, J. (1999). Adolescent storm and stress. *American Psychologist, 54*, (5), 317-327.

Austin, J., Johnson, K., & Weitzer, R. (2005). *Alternatives to the secure detention and confinement of juveniles*. Juvenile Justice Bulletin. Washington, DC: Department of Justice. Office of Juvenile Justice and Delinquency Prevention.

Crowe, A. (2000). *Jurisdictional technical assistance package for juvenile corrections*. Washington, DC: Office of Juvenile Justice and Delinquency Prevention.

DeFrancesco, J. J. (1984). *Socialization and delinquency: Construct validation of the socialization scale of the California Psychological Inventory*. (Doctoral Dissertation).DissertationAbstractsInternational.(UMI No. DA8417679).

DeFrancesco, J.J. (1990, August). *Quality assurance and the residential treatment center*. Paper presented at the 98th annual convention of the American Psychological Association. Boston, MA.

Department of Criminal Justice Services (2011). *Juvenile justice and delinquency prevention act*. Retrieved from http://www.dcjs.virginia.gov/juvenile/jjdp.

Gough, H. (1948). A sociological theory of psychopathy. *American Journal of Sociology, 53*, 359-366.

Hall, G.S., (1904). *Adolescence. Its psychology and its relations to philosophy, anthropology, sociology, sex, crime, religion, and education*. New York: Appleton.

Hewitt, M., Regoli, R. & Delisi, M. (2011). *Delinquency in society*. Burlington, MA: Jones & Bartlett.

Hochbaum, D. (2011). *Emotional disturbance and social maladjustment. Doing away with the Social maladjustment clause*. Retrieved from www.luc.edu/law/ academics/special/center.

Hockenberry, S. & Puzzanchera, C. (2014). *Juvenile Court Statistics 2011*. Pittsburgh, PA:National Center for Juvenile Justice.

Huges, M., Kroehler, C. & Vander Zander, J. (2002). *Sociology: The core*. New York: McGraw Hill.

In re Gault, 387 U.S. 1 (1967)

In re Winship, 397 U.S. 358 (1970)

Behavioral Institute. (2011). *Juvenile Justice System Terminology*. Retrieved from http://www.behavioralinstitute.org.

Kauffman, J., Cullinan, D. & Epstein, M. (1987). Characteristics of students placed in special Education programs for seriously emotional disturbance. *Behavioral Disorders, 12*, (3), 175- 184.

Kent v. United States, 383 U.S. 541 (1966).

Labor Center University of Iowa (2004). *Child labor public education project*. Iowa City, Iowa: University of Iowa.

Maxmen, J. & Ward, N., (1995). *Essential psychopathology and its treatment*. New York: Norton.

McKeiver v. Pennsylvania, 403 U.S. 528 (1971).

McNamara, R. (2008). *The lost population*. Durham, NC: Carolina Academic Press. National Center for Juvenile Justice. (2011). *Juvenile justice is local*. Retrieved from http://www.ncjj.org/Research Resources/ nationaloverview.aspx.

National Research Council and Institute of Medicine. (2001). *Juvenile crime juvenile justice.* Panel on juvenile crime. Joan McCord, Cathy Widom, Nancy Crowell (Eds.). Committee on Law and Justice and Board of Children, Youth and Families. Washington, DC: National Academy Press.

Office of Juvenile Justice and Delinquency Prevention (2013). *Case flow diagram.* Washington, DC: Office of Justice Programs, US Department of Justice.

Platt, A. (1969). The rise of the child saving movement: A study in social policy and correctional reform. *Annals of the American Academy of Political and Social Sciences, 381,* 21-38.

People v. Turner, 55 ILL 280 (1870).

Puzzanchera, C. (2007). *Trends in juvenile justice system response to status offending.* Pittsburgh, PA: National Center for Juvenile Justice.

Shelden, R. (1999). *Detention diversion advocacy: An evaluation.* Juvenile Justice Bulletin. Washingon, DC: Department of Justice, Office of Juvenile Justice and Delinquency Prevention.

Sickmund, M. (2007). *Juveniles in Court.* Juvenile Offenders and Victims National Report Series. Washington, DC: Department of Justice, Office of Juvenile Justice and Delinquency Prevention.

Snyder, H. (1982). Violent juvenile crime. *Today's Delinquent, 1,* 7-24.

Stullken, E. (1956). Misconceptions about juvenile delinquency. *Journal of Criminal Law, Criminology, and Police Science,45,* 33-36.

Sullivan, P. (2007). *Building the foundation for juvenile justice.* Retrieved from http://www.connections.com/article/15285-building-the-foundation-for-juvenile-justice.

Tanenhaus, D. (2011). *The constitutional rights of children.* Lawrence, KS: University of Kansas Press

United States Department of Education Office of Postsecondary Education. (2011). *The handbook for campus crime reporting.* Washington, DC.

Ventrell, V. (1998). Evolution of the dependency component of the juvenile court. *Juvenile and Family Court Journal, 48,* (4), 17-37.

CHAPTER 10

DRUGS AND CRIME

Background

It is seemingly impossible to watch a TV program or browse the Internet without seeing several advertisements by pharmaceutical companies promoting their most recent miracle drug or without watching hip and popular people drinking vodka or swilling beer. Drugs (including alcohol) are everywhere. The promulgation of drugs and alcohol, however, is not really a new phenomenon. Most people associate the use and abuse of substances with the turbulent 1960s free love and hippie drug culture. In fact, the use and abuse of drugs was popularized and even romanticized in music and by iconic figures of the era. The lyrics sung by John Lennon in the song Lucy in the Sky with Diamonds from the psychedelically adorned and infused Beatles album Sergeant Pepper's Lonely Hearts Club Band (The Beatles, 1967) was thought to be reflective of the effects of using LSD. Dr. Timothy Leary, a native of Springfield, MA and a Psychologist and Lecturer at Harvard also touted the benefits of LSD and the drug psilocybin. He initiated experiments using these drugs with Harvard faculty and students and he believed that these substances could have therapeutic potential for psychiatric patients, could treat individuals suffering from alcoholism, and could also reform the antisocial personalities of criminals (i.e., Concord Prison Study). He influenced and encouraged a generation of youth to "tune in, turn on, drop out" (Greenfield, 2006).

Although the 1960s certainly reflected a drug culture, the use of intoxicating substances dates back many thousands of years. There is ample documentation that the ancient societies of Egypt, Rome, Greece, and China all used wine, beer, marijuana, and other substances such as opium, that the Aztecs regularly used natural hallucinogenics, and that the Indians of Mexico preferred peyote. There is even evidence that Neanderthal man used mind altering substances (Gahlingher, 2004; McGovern, Mirzo & Hall, 2009; Drug-Rehabs, 2012; Shultes & Hoffman, 1992). Drugs are certainly pervasive and seemingly have been consumed since the beginning of time.

Nevertheless, drugs are mind altering, intoxicating, can be addictive and are strongly associated with criminal activity. Further, many drugs are regulated and many are illegal to possess. Therefore, the implications for the criminal justice community are twofold. First, the actual possession, sale, and use of an illicit drug can, in and of itself, be a criminal offense and second, substance abuse is oftentimes strongly correlated with criminal behavior.

Defining Drugs and Substance Abuse

It is difficult to specifically define what a drug is primarily because the term is used in many different and varied contexts. Drugs are used in the pharmacological treatment of diseases and other medical conditions. Drugs, such as alcohol and marijuana, can be used recreationally and still other drugs such as sleep medications can be used to improve the human condition. Further, The Drug Enforcement Administration (DEA) identifies certain drugs regulated by the Controlled Substances Act and defines these drugs as being "...utilized to alter mood, thought, and feeling through their actions on the central nervous system" (DEA, 2012). Perhaps the most comprehensive definition of a drug is offered by the U.S. Food and Drug Administration (FDA). According to the FDA (2012) a drug is defined as:

1. A substance recognized by an official pharmacopoeia or formulary.

2. A substance intended for use in the diagnosis, cure, mitigation, treatment, or prevention of disease.

3. A substance (other than food) intended to affect the structure or any function of the body.

4. A substance intended for use as a component of a medicine but not a device or a component, part or accessory of a device.

5. Biological products are included within this definition and are generally covered by the same laws and regulations, but differences exist regarding their manufacturing processes (chemical process versus biological process.)

For the purposes of this chapter number 3 above is probably most applicable. That is, a drug is any substance or chemical compound that can affect the processes or functions of the body. This substance can be an over-the-counter-drug (OTC) such as Nyquil, a prescribed medication such as the pain killer Hydrocodone, an illegal substance such as lysergic acid diethylamide (LSD) or cocaine, or alcohol.

Substance abuse can be seen simply as the harmful use of prescription, over-the-counter, or illicit drugs, or alcohol. Other substances such as inhalants and solvents, which are not technically considered drugs, also need to be included in our discussion of substance abuse. The types of substance use disorders are formally documented in the Diagnostic and Statistical Manual of Mental Disorders-IV-Text Revision (DSM-IV-TR). The DSM-IV-TR (APA, 1994) identifies, broadly speaking, two major types of substance use disorders: Substance Abuse and Substance Dependence.

"The essential feature of Substance Abuse is a maladaptive pattern of substance use manifested by recurrent and significant adverse consequences related to he repeated use of substances. There may be repeated failure to fulfill major role obligations, repeated use in situations in which it is physically hazardous, multiple legal problems, and recurrent social and interpersonal problems" (p. 182). Examples might include an adolescent who is constantly late for school because of excessive drinking and morning hangovers, an adult who drives a fork lift while under the influence of marijuana, someone who has lost his license because of repeated DUI convictions, or a relationship on the brink of divorce because of substance abuse issues.

"The essential feature of Substance Dependence is a cluster of cognitive, behavioral, and physiological symptoms indicating that the individual continues use of the substance despite significant substance related problems. There is a pattern of repeated self- administration that usually results in tolerance, withdrawal, and compulsive drug taking behavior" (p.176).An individual who regularly uses heroin, for example, will eventually develop a tolerance for the drug. That is, their body habituates to the drug and they will then need to use increasing amounts of the drug in order to maintain the same effect. The same individual may experience withdrawal symptoms when the drug is not readily available. These symptoms can include nausea, vomiting, psychomotor agitation, and muscular pain. In order to avoid these symptoms the individual begins using the substance throughout the day and night and begins to spend inordinate amounts of time attempting to obtain their next dose. All important role obligations are curtailed and despite obvious related physiological and/or psychological concerns such as cardiac problems, hepatitis, or depression the use of the substance continues.

The newest revision of the Diagnostic and Statistical Manual of Mental Disorders is now in its fifth edition and is referred to as the DSM-5. This newest edition does not separate Substance Abuse and Substance Dependence into two distinct disorders. Rather, all symptoms are now included under the diagnosis of Substance Use Disorder but the essential elements, as described, remain intact (APA, 2013).

Further, substance use, in particular substance dependence, is oftentimes conceptualized as an addiction that evolves and progresses through a series of stages. Substance abuse researchers and practitioners have identified four stages of addiction. Not everyone who uses a substance will progress to the final stages of addiction, however, individuals who enter the final stages do not have control over their substance use and typically will require specific drug abuse intervention and rehabilitation (Hovnanian, 1994; Gahlingher, 2003). These stages are:

1. Experimentation: Here the individual may use a drug out of curiosity, to have fun, to bow to peer pressure or simply because they believe the drug will help them deal with a stressful event. Many individuals, particularly young people, will experiment with a variety of substances but will never progress to the next stage. Others may enjoy the intoxicating high or believe that the drug is helping them deal with their stressors. In this case the person may progress to the next stage.

2. Regular Use: The user may begin to use on a regular basis. The drug may be used recreationally or as a way to relieve stress. During this stage the individual may begin planning to use the substance with peers, after work, or on the weekends. Many individuals are still in control of their use and may not progress to the next stage but regular use increases risk taking behavior. Risk

taking might include driving under the influence or being high or intoxicated at work.

3. Risky Use: The user who enters this stage can now be considered an abuser. The substance becomes increasingly important and the individual begins to plan to obtain and abuse the substance despite the probability that their behavior is negatively affecting others and their own well- being. There may be legal, occupational, and relationship difficulties resulting from the abuse but some people can function and are able to confine their substance abuse to specific times or days.

4. Addiction: During this stage the individual is dependent upon the substance. There is a need to be consistently intoxicated or high and the appearance of withdrawal symptoms begin to appear. The person will experience significant interpersonal, legal, occupational, and relationship difficulties as well as physical and mental health disorders. Dependence on the drug will continue, however, and the individual will be unable to control their need to obtain and abuse the substance. It is during this stage that treatment is necessary or the addiction will continue to worsen.

The National Institute on Drug Abuse provides a definition of addiction as a "chronic, relapsing brain disease that is characterized by compulsive drug seeking and use, despite harmful consequences. It is considered a brain disease because drugs change the brain, its structure and how it works" (NIDA, 2010, p5). Focus on part of that sentence – "drugs change the brain." To make this clear, let's take another quick and painless look at just two parts of the human brain (our first look was in the Chapter on Personality and Crime). The two areas of the brain most involved in addiction are (1) the frontal area of the cerebral cortex, which contains the thinking part of the brain (including executive functioning) and (2) the limbic system (which contains the feeling part of the brain). In the Chapter on Personality and Crime there was considerable coverage of the limbic system because of its crucial role in regulating both positive emotions (our feelings of pleasure) and negative emotions (our feelings of fear and dread).

The limbic system contains both the hippocampus and the amygdala, both of which are critically involved in the control of emotions. The limbic system is especially important in understanding substance abuse because it can be activated by drugs, and its circuits can be physically and functionally altered by continued drug use. Drugs also change the chemicals that provide the basis for the brain's ability to send messages to and from its various structures. These chemicals are called neurotransmitters, and in the study of drug abuse one of the most important of these is "dopamine." Dopamine regulates the brain's reward system by creating feelings of pleasure and even euphoria. Some drugs, such as cocaine or amphetamines, can cause the brain to produce abnormally high amounts of dopamine, causing intense feelings of pleasure. Heroin (called an opiate drug) also creates strong feelings of euphoria and relaxation, and these strong feelings can be activated very quickly when the drugs are injected. Other opiate derivatives are Vicodin, Oxycontin, and morphine. Continued use of any of these drugs causes the user to keep increasing the amounts of the drug just to get the same original feelings of pleasure, and without the drug the user feels tired, depressed and pessimistic about life. As one opiate abuser who was in a drug rehabilitation unit said "I'm sick and tired of being sick and tired." Taking increased levels of these drugs to get the same "high" is, again, called tolerance. Because of the neural communication networks between the limbic system and the pre-frontal cortex, continued use also causes damage to the brain's cognitive areas, or the thinking structures in the brain. Although taking any of these drugs is initially probably a voluntary action, it becomes less and less voluntary with continued use. The changes in the brain that coincide with abusing drugs can impair the abuser's ability to control his/her behavior and too often lead to the destructive actions of addiction. Thus, the addict may lose self-control and then find it very difficult to make rational choices at many of life's important decision points. These bad choices may unfortunately lead to criminal activities.

Drugs, their use and abuse, have become relatively commonplace in our increasingly complex society. Substance abuse knows no boundaries. It is not relegated to a specific social class, gender, culture, race, or income level. Drugs, of all types, are easily accessible to people of all ages (DeFrancesco, 1996). Illicit and sometimes legal drugs are sold or obtained illegally (a criminal offense), purchased illegally (a criminal offense), and abused (a criminal offense). Further, a significant number of crimes are committed when the perpetrator is under the influence. But how significant and widespread is the relationship between substance abuse and criminal activity? Before addressing this relationship let us examine the prevalence of drug usage in the general population.

The Prevalence of Drug Usage

The primary and most comprehensive source of information regarding the prevalence of drug use in the general population is the National Survey on Drug Use and Health (NSDUH). The NSDUH, formerly called the National Household Survey of Drug Use, has been conducted annually since 1971 by the Substance Abuse and Mental Health Services Administration and assesses the substance use of individuals 12 years and older in the United States. This survey is based on a representative stratified random sample of U.S. households: The most recent available results and estimates are from the 2013 survey (SAMHSA, 2014). Some of the major findings indicate that:

1. About 22.6 million Americans aged 12 or older were current users of illegal drugs. This represents 9.4 percent of the population aged 12 or older. Illicit drugs are defined as marijuana/hashish, cocaine (crack included), hallucinogens, heroin, inhalants, or prescription-type drugs used illegally.

2. Marijuana was the most commonly used illicit drug. In 2013, there were 19.8 million current users of the drug.

3. There were 2.0 million individuals aged 12 or older who used prescription type drugs illegally in the 12 months prior to the survey.

4. About half (52.2 percent) of the surveyed aged 12 or older reported drinking alcoholic beverages.

5. Binge drinking was reported by 22.9 percent. The survey defines binge drinking as five or more drinks on the same occasion in the past 30 days.

6. Approximately 3.8 percent of individuals aged 12 or older drove under the influence of alcohol at least once in the past year. Driving under the influence of alcohol was highest in the 21 to 25 year old age group (23.4 percent).

These results do seem to indicate that millions of individuals are using illicit drugs, alcohol, and prescription medications. This is a disturbing trend particularly when considering that many users of illicit drugs, prescription drugs, and alcohol initiated use in their teens and early 20s. It is certainly true that possession and use of an illegal drug is a crime. But does the actual use of a substance also predispose someone to engage in criminal activity? Everyone who uses drugs does not engage in criminal behavior. Drugs affect individuals in many different ways depending upon many complex variables interacting with each other. Drugs begin work at the cellular level, enter the bloodstream and, as previously mentioned affect the brain, heart, lungs and other major system of the body. But a number of other variables also need to be taken into consideration (Gahlingher, 2003; Jacobs, 1987):

Dose. The actual amount of the drug that is used.

Ingestion Method. How the drug is ingested. The typical means of ingestion are smoking, orally, injection, or inhaling.

Psychological State. The mental condition of the person at the time of ingestion (e.g., stressed or anxious).

Physical State. The physical condition of the person including weight, height, body fat index and, metabolism rate.

Genetics. The predisposition of some individuals to be vulnerable to the adverse effects of drugs (e.g., alcoholism running in families).

Situation. Where the drug is ingested. Drinking beer at a Yankee's game is legal if you are over 21 while drinking beer while driving is not.

Drug Type. The type of drug that is ingested. Not all drugs have the same impact (see Table 1.1)

Most of the drugs in Table 1.1 initially produce a euphoric effect where the person's sense of wellbeing is enhanced, however, this is typically short lived with the negative effects quickly predominating. Tolerance and withdrawal symptoms will also produce negative consequences and behavioral abnormalities. Again, not everyone who uses drugs will engage in criminal activities, but as can be seen drugs certainly alter behavior and emotions and can be contributing and accompanying factors.

Table 1.1. Drug Types and Effects

Substance Type	Effect
Marijuana (includes THC and Hashish)	Moderate use results in feelings of relaxation, passivity. Heavy use can cause paranoia and anxiety.
Hallucinogens (includes LSD, Peyote, PCP)	Perceptual distortions, extreme anxiety and restlessness, feelings of invincibility, disorientation, impulsivity, volatility.
Cocaine (includes crack cocaine)	Euphoria, hyperactivity, alertness, nausea, insomnia, irritability,
Heroin	Euphoria, drowsiness, detachment, irritability, depression, disorientation.
Inhalants	Feelings of wellbeing, confusion, disorientation, psychomotor impairment, poor judgment.
Amphetamines	Alertness, confidence, speeding, depression, fatigue, volatility, insomnia.
Barbiturates	Sedation, fatigue, drowsiness, lack of responsiveness, confusion, disorientation.
Ecstasy	Feelings of wellbeing, irritability, restlessness, anxiety, confusion, memory impairment.
Alcohol	Euphoria, confidence, sedation, fatigue, confusion, volatility, psychomotor impairment, nausea.

Source: Adapted from www.thegooddrugsguide.com. 2012

The Drug-Crime Connection
As previously mentioned the actual possession, use, sale, or purchase of a drug is a crime. The Federal Bureau of Investigation (FBI) provides a comprehensive definition: "The violation of laws prohibiting the production, distribution, and/or use of certain controlled substances. The unlawful cultivation, manufacture, distribution, sale, purchase, use, possession, transportation, or importation of any controlled drug or narcotic substance. Arrests for violations of state and local laws, specifically those relating to the unlawful possession, sale, use, growing, manufacturing, and making of narcotic drugs. The following drug categories are specified: opium or cocaine and their derivatives (morphine, heroin, codeine); marijuana; synthetic narcot-

ics—manufactured narcotics that can cause true addiction (demerol, methadone); and dangerous nonnarcotic drugs (barbiturates, benzedrine)" (FBI, 2012).

But drugs are also connected to crime in that drugs are frequently implicated in the commission of criminal activities. Drugs can alter behavior and often lead to disinhibition. Disinhibition refers to a lack of restraint or to the loss or lessening of inhibitions, of impulses, self- control, psychomotor, cognitive, or physical capacities. Table 1.2 explicates some of the way in which criminal activity and substances are correlated.

Table 1.2 Relationship of Substances and Criminal Activity

Drugs and crime relationship	Definition	Examples
Drug-defined offenses	Violations of laws prohibiting or regulating the possession, distribution, manufacture of illegal drugs.	Possession or use. Marijuana cultivation. Methamphetamine production. Selling cocaine, heroin, or cannabis.
Drug-related	Offenses in which drug's effects contribute; offenses motivated by need for money for continued use; offenses connected to distribution.	Deviant behavior produced by drug effects. Stealing for cash to buy drugs. Violence against competing drug dealers.
Drug-using lifestyle	Drug use and crime are consistent with a deviant lifestyle. Probability of involvement in crime is increased. Users may not participate in the legal economy and may be exposed to situations that promote crime.	Focused on short-term goals supported by illegal activities. Increased probability of offending because of contacts with other offenders. Criminal skills learned from other criminals.

Source: Bureau of Justice Statistics, Office of Justice Programs, Washington D.C. 2012

Our discussion of the drug and crime relationship will focus on the three areas listed in Table 1.2: drug-defined offenses, drug- related offenses, and drug- using lifestyle.

Drug Defined Offenses. According to the FBI, nationwide, overall crime rates declined. Violent crimes decreased 5.1percent while property crimes decreased 2.8 percent. Nevertheless, in 2013 there was an estimated 11,302,043 arrests made by law enforcement. Of those arrests, 1,505,043 were for drug abuse violations and 1,166,824 arrests were for driving while intoxicated, 354,872 for liquor law violations, and 443,527 for drunkenness. The number of arrests for possession of marijuana exceeded arrests for heroin, cocaine and their derivatives, synthetic or manufactured drugs, and other nonnarcotic drugs (FBI, 2014). The number of individuals arrested for drug and alcohol defined offenses is substantial and likely represents a continued and significant societal concern and a continued challenge to the criminal justice community. Yes, drug law violations are crimes in and of themselves, but the link between drugs and crime is further strengthened when examining how drugs are implicated in criminal activities.

Drug Related Offenses. Approximately 17% of state prison inmates, 18% of federal prison inmates, and 16% of local jail prisoners indicated that they committed their most recent offense to obtain money for drugs while 32% of state inmates, 26% of federal inmates, and 29% of convicted jail prisoners reported using substances at the time of the offense (BJS, 2012). These statistics do seem to indicate a link between drugs and crime. Further evidence of this link is also provided when examining the prior history of substance abuse in these populations. Approximately 68% of local jail inmates reported using drugs regularly while consistent drug use was indicated by 83% of state inmates and 79% of federal inmates. The drugs of choice for these populations were primarily marijuana and cocaine or crack (BJS, 2012).

The National Crime Victimization Survey (NCVS) also provides supporting evidence of the drug-crime relationship. This survey details significant characteristics regarding criminal victimization in the United States. Further, the survey inquires about whether the victim perceived the offender to be under the influence of alcohol or drugs at the time of the offense. In 2007 (only available data) approximately 26 percent of the victims of violent offenses indicated that the perpetrator was using alcohol and/or drugs (BJS, 2007, 2012; NCADD, 2014). The perceived use of substances during the commission of a crime provides additional data regarding the drug-crime relationship.

Drug Using Lifestyle. Andy Dufresne, played by Tim Robbins in the prison movie Shawshank Redemption (Marvin & Darabont, 1994), uttered "Yeah. The funny thing is-on the outside, I was an honest man, straight as an arrow. I had to come to prison to be a crook." This quote appears to reflect the position that the probability of engaging in deviant and criminal activities is increased if an individual associates with other offenders and that criminal skills can be learned through these associations. This position was first developed in the 1930s and 1940s by famed sociologist and criminologist Edwin Sutherland and reflected in his book Principles of Criminology (1947). His Differential Association Theory posited that individuals tend to learn criminal behavior primarily through associating with other criminals in small, intimate groups. The process includes learning specialized techniques "of the trade" and also includes acquiring the deviant attitudes, motivations, and other cognitions needed to engage in criminal activities. This position seems to be particularly applicable to those who are involved with drugs as the use and abuse of substances is congruous with a deviant and antisocial lifestyle. For example, the selling of drugs will often mean that the individual will learn to carry and use a firearm to protect himself and his stash. It may also mean that a major drug dealer will need to learn the processes of trafficking or money laundering.

The drug-crime correlation does seem multifaceted and distinctive from other types of illegal activities in that the relationship can be drug-defined, drug-related, or the result of a drug using lifestyle. Nevertheless, drugs and crime coexist on many levels and have a significant impact on the resources of the criminal justice system such as the need for increased surveillance, investigation, and monitoring of suspects; increased number of arrests; impact on the adjudication process; incarceration in overcrowded prisons; need for substance abuse treatment for inmates; and post-release monitoring. But drug abuse also places a significant burden on several other societal functions including (DOJ, 2010):

1. Healthcare. Substance abuse often leads to specific types of psychological and medical interventions, increased number of visits to emergency rooms, and sometimes inpatient treatment at rehabilitation facilities, psychiatric hospitals, or general hospitals.

2. Workforce Productivity. Substance abuse leads to absenteeism, abuse of sick days, legal difficulties resulting in absence from work, loss of work productivity, and diversion of federal dollars to the treatment of substance abuse rather than to other more productive endeavors.

3. Environmental. The use of chemicals, toxins, and waste materials from the cultivation of marijuana or the manufacture of other drugs such as methamphetamine presents serious environmental concerns.

4. Family. Substance abuse causes significant familial discord often resulting in dysfunctional family systems, separation and divorce, domestic violence, abuse, and neglect.

According to the Department of Justice National Drug Threat Assessment (2010) the economic damage alone is estimated to cost 215 billion dollars. Obviously drugs and crime can have an immense impact on all facets of society.

Drug Courts

Because of the prevalence of substance abuse and crime the need to mitigate the burden that drug abuse had on the criminal justice system and society in general became a pressing issue for criminal justice administrators. In the 1980s the Miami, Florida area was overwhelmed by a crack cocaine epidemic that significantly impacted and flooded the court system. Realizing that the courts were being inundated prompted a group of criminal justice administrators to establish the first drug court. Drug court was established to alleviate pressures on trial courts but the primary purpose was to treat rather than prosecute the drug abuser. The assumption was that therapeutic interventions would assist in severing the drug-crime connection and consequently ease the burden on the criminal justice system and on society (King & Pasquarella, 2009; DOJ, 2010). The first operational drug court was established in Miami in 1989. Since that time the drug court model has gown and is now in all 50 states and several US territories. At the beginning of 2012 there were 2,633 drug courts in operation. There are a variety of models but most adhere to the philosophy that substance abusers (including alcohol) can be diverted from the criminal justice system by treating their substance abuse problems. Most states and jurisdictions have fairly similar eligibility guidelines for referral to drug court but there can be some subtle differences. Generally, the individual must have been charged with a drug-defined or drug-related offense to be referred to drug court. The majority of states, however, will not refer someone who is a violent offender. Once referred and accepted the individual is expected to actively participate in intensive substance abuse treatment, have their behavior consistently monitored by a court official, undergo frequent urinalysis, and regularly appear in court to have their treatment progress reviewed. If the individual successfully completes the program and has no prior criminal charges then his case will not be prosecuted. The case is then considered "Nolle Prosequi" meaning that the prosecutor will no longer consider legal action against the individual (King & Pasqaurella, 2009; DOJ 2010; Public Defender, 2012).

Drug courts have been in existence for over 20 years and, although there were some detractors at first, performance data overall has been quite positive. The Urban Institute (2011) conducted an evaluation of 23 drug courts in seven states and found that drug courts produce significant reductions in substance abuse and crime. Drug court participants were about one-third less likely to abuse drugs and engaged in half as many criminal activities 18 months after completing the program. It was estimated that drug court participation saved about $5680 per participant. Similar studies were conducted in California (Carey, Finigan, Crumpton, & Waller, 2006) and Oregon (Finigan, Carey, & Cox, 2007) and also produced positive outcomes for drug court participation. For example, the California study found recidivism rates of 17 percent for drug court participants as compared to a 41percent recidivism rate for those not participating in drug court while the Oregon study noted that drug courts saved taxpayers about $79 million over a 10 year period. Data compiled by the National Association of Drug Court Professionals

(NADCP) reveals that drugs courts are cost effective and significantly reduce substance abuse and crime (NADCP, 2012):

1. Nationally, 75% of individuals who successfully complete drug court programs do not recidivate for at least two years after program completion.

2. Long term studies of successful completers have shown that the positive effects of the drug court program have resulted in crime reduction for more than 14 years.

3. Nationally, every $1.00 invested in drug courts results in a $3.36 savings in criminal justice expenditures.

4. Drug courts provide more comprehensive supervision and monitoring than any other community-based option.

5. Drug courts are six times more likely to maintain the individual in treatment for longer periods of time and consequently improve their chances for a successful treatment outcome.

The data supporting the efficacy of drug courts seems promising. Drug courts do appear to be a serious alternative to criminal court and do tend to be cost effective and beneficial to the participant and to society. Unfortunately, drugs courts are underutilized and only serve a small percentage of offenders (Reentry Court Solutions, 2012). Notwithstanding, there are alternatives to drug court. Individuals involved in the criminal justice system can be involved in various types of substance abuse treatment and education programs.

Substance Abuse Education and Treatment

Whether a substance abuser participates in drug court or is involved in some other facet of the criminal justice system there are several substance abuse education and treatment options that are available. These options can be implemented in drug court programs, prisons, juvenile facilities, as a condition of parole or probation, in aftercare programs, or in any other criminal or juvenile justice facility or program (McAvay et al., 2000).

Substance Abuse Education is not treatment per se but is an important component in the rehabilitation of the abuser. Education aims to provide the abuser with specific knowledge about the stages of addiction, risk factors, how drugs (including alcohol) affect the body, how drugs interact with other drugs, how drugs are used and abused, how drugs can foster dependence, and how to avoid becoming an abuser. Education programs can also assist the individual by providing information on the types of treatment programs that may be available. In the criminal justice system, however, the type of treatment program may be mandated by a judge or other court official.

There are several types of Substance Abuse Treatment interventions. The most common and popular interventions are Alcoholics Anonymous (AA) and Narcotics Anonymous (NA). These are 12 step self-help programs that require attendance at meetings with other abusers. These meetings offer non-judgmental support, encouragement, hope, and optimism by fellow abusers who are also in or attempting 'recovery.' Most attendees have a 'sponsor' who is typically in recovery and will attempt to provide additional guidance and support to the individual. AA and NA programs are widely offered in communities but many meetings are also held in correctional facilities (Alcoholics Anonymous World Services, 2013; Narcotic Anonymous World Services, 2013).

While AA and NA programs have helped many individuals recover from addictions and lead productive and substance free lives another type of treatment regimen, cognitive behavioral treatment, is viewed as one of the most effective interventions, particularly with correctional populations. Cognitive behavioral treatment is an intervention that reflects both a behavioral and cognitive approach to the treatment of addiction and other disorders. Cognitive behavioral approaches were originally conceptualized and cultivated by Aaron Beck and associates (1979) and Albert Ellis (1972). These techniques assume that faulty thought or cognitive patterns and irrational and illogical ways of thinking contribute to the development of negative behaviors and emotional distress. The primary aim of treatment is for individuals to recognize these patterns and ways of thinking and to restructure their cognitions by adopting a more positive and rational manner of thinking and responding. The cognitive behavioral approach with substance abusers examines the faulty thoughts and irrational cognitions that might be contributing to substance abuse. Triggers are identified and strategies to decrease use of the drug are offered. The individual is taught how to anticipate negative situations and learns how to utilized more adaptive methods to deal with their abuse and addictions. The Bureau of Prisons (2012) has promoted and utilized cognitive behavioral treatment for about 20 years and has found it to be quite effective in treating substance abuse. Specifically, cognitive behavioral treatment programs have been found to reduce relapse and recidivism, and to improve the overall health and mental health of inmates.

Treatment also has the benefit of reducing the spread of diseases such as HIV/AIDS and hepatitis (NIDA, 2006). Further, the American Psychological Association (2004) reported on several outcome studies of substance abuse effectiveness in prisons and found that substance abuse programs with aftercare components significantly reduced recidivism rates. Substance abuse treatment with individuals involved in the criminal justice system works but treatment needs to be consistent and intensive and an aftercare component is crucial. Aftercare refers to monitoring, encouragement, follow-up, and reinforcement of the progress made and skills learned during treatment. Aftercare is imperative to increase the probability that the individual will not relapse or recidivate but unfortunately this is the one component of the treatment process that is most often eliminated or not fully implemented (McAvay, et al 2000).

The Cannabis Conundrum

As previously discussed, marijuana or cannabis, is the most commonly used illicit drug in the general population. Marijuana is also one of the most commonly used drugs in criminal justice populations. Arrests for the sale, manufacture, and possession of marijuana exceeds arrests for other types of drugs and when we examine the prior history of substance abuse among prison inmates marijuana is the drug used most often. Needless to say, marijuana is a popular drug for those involved in the criminal justice system and for those who are not involved. There has been consistent debate regarding the effects and status of marijuana. Is it a harmful drug? Should it be legalized? Should it be decriminalized? There are a number of states that have decriminalized and legalized marijuana. Although the guidelines vary from state to state most will not prosecute someone who possesses a small amount of the substance, usually under an ounce. Further, many states have approved marijuana for medical purposes as the drug seems to relieve anxiety and stress, nausea, and the discomfort and pain associated with illnesses such as cancer. Proponents also argue that marijuana is a safer drug than other illicit drugs, alcohol and tobacco and that there are no definitive long term studies on the deleterious effects of the drug (NORML, 2012). It has also been postulated that the criminalization of marijuana forces courts to spend an inordinate amount of resources prosecuting individuals for simple possession and use. Therefore, decriminalization and legalization of marijuana would reduce the backlog in the courts, would reduce the number of inmates in overcrowded correctional facilities, and would allow police to attend to more serious crimes (NORML, 2012). Opponents argue that marijuana is a gateway drug, that it disinhibits and can lead to criminal behavior, and that minors will be able to access the drug. They also note that it is morally wrong, that use of the substance can lead to health and mental health problems, and that people will resort to crime as a way of paying for the drug (Hartnett, 2005; NORML, 2012).These debates will continue as it appears that many more states are considering decriminalizing and legalizing marijuana. The long term implications for the criminal justice system have yet to be determined.

CASE STUDY: Robbie

Robbie is a 29 year old single male residing outside of Hartford, CT with Rosie his partner of three years. Robbie was a federal employee for almost seven years but lost his job 2 years ago because of federal cutbacks. His unemployment benefits have expired and he has been unable to find full time employment since that time. He has been working 25 hours per week in a restaurant as a kitchen helper. Robbie does not have a college degree. He did attend a local college for two years but because of constant partying he was unable to maintain an acceptable grade point average. Rather than attempting to raise his grades he decided to quit and took a job as a data specialist with the federal government. He expected to keep this job for the long term but the layoff changed his plan. While working at his current job Robbie befriended several co-workers at the restaurant and they would all go out drinking after closing. Robbie always enjoyed drinking. Even when he worked for the federal government, he and his co-workers would go to happy hour every day. But his drinking behavior began years before. He began drinking in high school and the drinking continued once he began college. During his first year at school he was arrested for DUI which resulted in a fine, a restricted license, and mandatory attendance at substance abuse classes. During his second year of college his drinking became more intense and he began to miss his early morning classes because of hangovers. It was also at this time that he was asked to leave the dorms because of several incidents of drunkenness where furniture was broken and some minor altercations occurred. Robbie quit college shortly thereafter. Currently he drinks every night until intoxicated and recently began smoking marijuana and using cocaine with his co-workers. Sometimes they use cocaine and marijuana while at work. His relationship with Rosie then began to unravel and she gave him the ultimatum to quit drinking and using drugs or she would leave. Further, Robbie recently had a promising interview for a full time position with a delivery company but the company required a drug test. He tested positive for marijuana and cocaine and was not offered the job. He became distraught over this incident but rather than curtail his substance abuse he began drinking and smoking more often. Eventually, he began calling in sick to work and also began having bouts of depression that would last for days. When he did go to work his performance was lackluster which resulted in a reprimand from his boss. Despite this warning his drinking and marijuana use did not stop and his performance at work, combined with his frequent absences, resulted in him eventually losing his job. On the day that he lost his restaurant job he and his friends went to a local pub, drank heavily, and he ended up fighting and getting arrested for assault and public drunkenness. This arrest and losing his job was the last straw for Rosie. She ended the relationship and moved out of the apartment. Robbie became increasingly depressed about the break-up and continued drinking and smoking. Eventually, he could no longer afford the apartment because he no longer had a job and he had mounting legal bills because of his arrest. He had to move in with his parents. Currently, he is unemployed, has no relationship, and is living in his old room at his parent's home. Robbie, at this time, does not appear to be substance dependent but he is certainly a substance abuser. That is, he continues to abuse substances despite adverse consequences. He has legal problems (DUI), academic difficulties, interpersonal and relationship conflicts, and occupational problems as the result of his substance abuse. He does not yet experience any type of symptoms typically associated with dependence such as withdrawal. Nevertheless, Robbie is certainly in need of substance abuse treatment but he has been reluctant to access assistance. His parents do not believe that he has a significant problem only that he is going through "a rough patch." Without substance abuse treatment, however, Robbie will likely descend into dependence. Hopefully, the court will mandate treatment.

Summary

Drugs are omnipresent and have been used and abused since the beginning of recorded history. A drug can be defined as any substance that can affect the processes or functions of the body. While many drugs are used legally and for medical reasons many of these substances are mind altering, intoxicating, and strongly associated with criminal activity, particularly when they are abused and the abuse leads to addiction or dependence. Substance abuse and substance dependence are two related but serious conditions. Substance abuse is the maladaptive use of a substance resulting in significant negative consequences related to the consistent use of the substance while substance dependence is the repeated use of a substance that can cause physical or psychological dependence and result in the development of tolerance and withdrawal symptoms. Several studies and surveys indicate that millions of individuals in the general population are using illicit drugs, alcohol, and prescription medications and that individuals involved in the criminal justice system are also seriously involved with drugs. The actual possession and use of illicit drugs is, in itself, a crime but the use of drugs may also predispose an individual to engage in criminal activity. These drug and crime related activities are defined as drug-defined offenses, drug related offenses, and offenses committed because of a drug-using lifestyle. Drugs and crime coexist on many levels and have a significant impact on the criminal justice system, the healthcare system, workforce productivity, the environment, and family systems. Because of the prevalence of substance abuse and crime several programs have been utilized to treat and educate the substance abuser. These programs include drug court, AA and NA, drug education, and treatment regimens such as cognitive behavioral interventions. When combined with aftercare, these programs can have positive effects for the abuser and for the overburden criminal justice system.

A recent development has been the decriminalization, legalization, and medical use of cannabis. Proponents indicate that it will reduce crime and reduce the burden on the criminal justice system while opponents note that marijuana is a gateway drug and that individuals will resort to crime to pay for the substance. This debate will continue until more research is conducted.

Key Terms

Aaron Beck
Albert Ellis
Alcoholics Anonymous
Cognitive Behavioral Interventions

Concord Prison Study
Cannabis Decriminalization
Dose
Drug Courts
Drug Enforcement Administration
Drug-defined Offenses
Drug-related Offenses
Drug Types
Drug-using Lifestyle
Food and Drug Administration
Genetics
Ingestion Method
John Lennon
Narcotics Anonymous
National Survey of Drug Use and Health
Nolle Prosequi
NORML
Physical State
Psychological State
Stages of Addiction
Substance Abuse
Substance Abuse Education
Substance Abuse Treatment
Substance Dependence
Substance Use Disorders
Timothy Leary
Urban Institute

References

Alcoholics Anonymous World Services (2013). *Guidelines*. New York: Author

American Psychiatric Association (1994). *Diagnostic and statistical manual of mental disorders-IV*. Washington, DC: Author.

American Psychiatric Association (2013). *Diagnostic and statistical manual of mental disorders, Fifth edition*. Washington,DC: Author.

American Psychological Association (2004). *Inmate drug abuse treatment slows prison's revolving door*. Retrieved from http://www.apa.org/research/ action/aftercare.aspx.

Beck, A.T., Rush, A., Shaw, B., & Emery, G. (1979). *Cognitive therapy of depression*. New York: Guilford Press.

Bureau of Justice Statistics (2012). *Drug related crime*. Washington, DC: Office of Justice Programs, US Department of Justice.

Bureau of Justice Statistics (2012). *Drug and crime facts.* Washington, DC: Office of Justic Programs, US Department of Justice.

Bureau of Justice Statistics (2007,2012). *National crime victimization survey.* Washington,DC: Office of Justice Programs, US Department of Justice.

Bureau of Prisons (2012). *Substance abuse treatment.* Retrieved from http://www.bop.gov.

Carey, S., Finigan, M., Crumpton, D., & Waller, M. (2006). California drug courts: Outcomes, costs and promising practices: An overview of Phase II in a statewide study. *Journal of Psychoactive Drugs,*3, 345-356

DeFrancesco, J. J. (1996). Delinquency and substance abuse: A brief analysis. *Journal for Juvenile Justice and Detention Services, 11,* (2), 77-78.

Department of Justice (2010). *National drug threat assessment.* Washington, DC: National Drug Intelligence Center.

Department of Justice (2006). *Drug courts: The second decade.* Washington, DC: Office of Justice Programs.

Drug Enforcement Administration (DEA). (2012). *Drug classes.* Retrieved from www.justice.gov/dea/concer/drug_classes.html.

Drug-Rehabs (2012). *The history of drugs.* Retrieved from www.drughistory.org.

Ellis, A. (1972). Rational Emotive Psychotherapy. In J. Huber & H. Millman (Eds.).*Goals and behavior in psychotherapy and counseling* (216-235). Columbus, Ohio: Merrill.

Federal Bureau of Investigation (FBI). (2012). *Crime in the U.S. offense definitions.* Retrieved from www.fbi.gov.

Federal Bureau of Investigation (FBI). (2013). *Cime in the US.* Retrieved from www.fbi.gov.

Finigan, M., Carey, S., & Cox, A. (2007). *The impact of a mature drug court over 10 years ofoperation: Recidivism and costs.* Retrieved from www.npcresearch.com.

Food and Drug Administration (2012). *Drugs@FDA glossary of terms.* Retrievedfromwww.fda.gov/Drugs/informationdrugs/ucm079436.htm#

Gahlingher, P. (2003). *Illegal drugs: A complete guide to their history, chemistry, use, and abuse.* New York: Plume-Penguin Group.

Greenfield, R. (2006). *Timothy Leary-A biography.* Orlando, FL: Harcourt

Hartnett, E. (2005). Drug legalization: Why it wouldn't work in the United States.*ThePoliceChief,72,*(3). Retrieved from www.policechiefmagazine.org.

Hovnanian, L. (1994). *The four stages of drug addiction.* Abstract retrieved from http://www.ncbi.nlm.nih.gov/pubmed/7994578.

Jacobs, B. (1987). How hallucinogenic drugs work. *American Scientist. 75,* (4), 386-392.

King, R. & Pasquarella, J. (2009). *Drug courts: A review of evidence.* Washington, DC:The Sentencing Project.

Marvin, N. (Producer), & Darabont, F. (Director). (1994). *Shawshank Redemption* [Motion Picture]. United States: Castle Rock Entertainment.

McAvay, D., Armstrong, S.S., Russolillo, P.,DeFrancesco, J.J., Kaminer, Y., Sheehan, J., Rockholz, P., & Martin, G. (2000). *The substance abuse program manual.* Washington, DC: U.S. Department of Justice, Bureau of Justice Assistance.

McGovern, P., Mirzo, A., & Hall, G., (2009). Ancient Egyptian herbal wines. *Proceedings of the National Academy of Sciences, 106,* (2), 7361-7366.

National Association of Drug Court Professionals (NADCP). (2012). *Drug courts work.*Retrieved from http:///www.nadcp.org/learn/facts-and-figures.

NCADD-National Institute on Alcoholism and Drug Dependence (2014). *Alcohol and Crime.* Retrieved from: www.ncadd.org.

National Institute on Drug Abuse (2010). *The science of addiction.* Washington, D.C: National Institute of Health Publication 10-5605.

National Institute on Drug Abuse (2006). *Treatment for drug abusers in the criminal justice system.* Retrieved from http://www.drugabuse.gov.

Narcotics Anonymous World Services (2013). *White book.* Van Nuys, CA. Author.

NORML (2011). *Marijuana decriminalization.* Retrieved from http://norml.org.

Public Defender(2012). *Drugcourt.* Retrieved from http://pdmiami.com/drug_court.htm.

Reentry Court Solutions (2012). *Prison based reentry court models.* Retrieved from www.reentrycourtsolutions.com.

Substance Abuse and Mental Health Services Administration (SAMHSA). (2014). *National survey on drug abuse and health.* Retrieved from www.oas.samhsa.gov/nhsda.htm.

Sutherland, E. (1947). *Principles of criminology* (4th ed). Philadelphia, PA: Lippincott.

The Beatles(1967). *Sargent Peppers Lonely Hearts Club Band.* Hollywood: Capitol Records.

The Good Drugs Guide. (2012). *Drug Types.* Retrieved from www.thegooddrugsguide.com.

The Urban Institute (2011). *The multi-site adult drug court evaluation.* Washington, DC: The Urban Institute Justice Policy Center.

CHAPTER 11

FORENSIC SCIENCE AND LAW ENFORCEMENT

Introduction

If you're planning a career in any area within the field of law enforcement, you are going to be faced with a number of scientific detection devices and procedures. But relax. You don't have to have some esoteric science degree in order to use these instruments. You do, however, have to spend some time learning how to use them. They range from some relatively simple devices to some that will require considerable training. It must be remembered, however, that most of the techniques to follow provide circumstantial evidence, not direct evidence. As you will recall from the section on evidence, circumstantial evidence demands an assumption or inference that is based on an observation, whereas direct evidence is the observation itself. Someone walks into your house and is covered with drops of water. You say "it must be raining outside." Perhaps it is, but your observation is an inference and doesn't prove it. The person may have been splashed by a sprinkler or a child playing with a hose. However, if you go outside and observe that it is actually raining, the evidence is now direct. Because evidence is circumstantial doesn't necessarily make it less reliable. Witnesses who provide direct evidence have been known on occasion to be mistaken, and, in fact, it is often easier to challenge the credibility of a direct witness than to challenge a circumstantial inference based on, say, DNA. And even confessions aren't always reliable and can be challenged. Persons have been known to confess to crimes they couldn't possibly have committed. The reasons vary, but the three major themes are the publicity that it generates, police coercions, or a neurotic (perhaps psychotic) need to be cleansed by confessing to anything. In one celebrated California case, a woman was brutally murdered and then sliced in half. The newspapers dubbed her the "Black Dahlia," and the media attention was so great that more than fifty men confessed to the killing, probably men who thought this notoriety was the only way to be become known and sadistically important. But false confession can lead to major legal problems. Confessions can corrupt other evidence from both witnesses and forensic experts and may lead to false convictions (Kassin, 2012).

Forensic

Throughout this discussion the word "forensic" will be in constant use, and it simply means anything that is used or is suitable for use in a court of law. Many types of very ordinary and prosaic work can lend themselves to forensics. For example, an accountant may work for a company doing the detailed work of checking the books, but when this same skill is applied to a legal issue it could then become forensic accounting. That is, the job may entail both checking of the books and also looking to see if there has been any "cooking" of the books.

A PERSON OF INTEREST: DR. HENRY LEE

Considered by many to be the world's foremost forensic scientist, Henry Lee was born in China but came to the United States in 1972. He has degrees in both Forensic Science (John Jay College) and Biochemistry (PhD from NYU.) He serves as the director of the Connecticut State Police Forensic Laboratory and is the state's chief criminologist. He has his own TV show on the TruTV network and is the author of many books and articles. He has been involved in over 6000 cases world-wide, including many high-profile cases in the United States, such as the Jon Benet Ramsey murder, the OJ Simpson trial, the Scott Peterson murder case, the Casey Anthony case and the suicide of President Clinton's White House Counsel, Vince Foster. Vince Foster was found dead (an apparent suicide) a few months after Clinton took office. Because Foster had been rumored to have had some illegal financial dealings with Hillary Clinton there was some doubt as to whether Foster had taken his own life. However, a suicide note was found that seemed to indicate that this was no fault of the Clintons. One line read "No one in the White House to my knowledge violated any laws or standards of conduct." And further, "the public will never believe the innocence of the Clintons and their loyal staff." Henry Lee was then brought in and after reconstructing the death scene maintained that "the data indicate that the death of Vincent W. Foster Jr. is consistent with a suicide." Lee was again thrust on the national scene when he testified in the OJ Simpson case. He has wide-spread public recognition and is highly respected by law enforcement. Although an expert in virtually all areas within forensic science, including fingerprints, computer crimes, and crime scene reconstruction, his expertise in blood and DNA analysis has become legendary. Lee has used DNA to convict the guilty, but just as important, to exonerate the innocent. His blood and DNA analysis techniques have also been used in nonviolent cases, such as the Mick Jagger paternity suit and the identification of the body of Nazi war criminal, Joseph Mengele. Much to Lee's credit, DNA analysis has now become routine in all areas of law enforcement.

It's Still Hard Work

The scientific techniques to be presented here can be of inestimable value to law enforcement, both during the collection of evidence as well as its presentation in court. However, don't be misled into assuming that the scientific collection of evidence is easy, sexy and flashy. We have all seen the crime shows on TV like CSI where the resident geek creates visual miracles by feverishly typing on a keyboard and rendering a few pixels into a full-fledged sharply defined crime solution. This makes for good TV, but it's just not consistent with reality. Investigations can be hard, painstaking work, like sorting through trash, or examining hundreds of head-shot photos. It's time-consuming and demanding. The problems may loom large, but that can often add to the excitement of the challenge.

Combinations of Evidence

It must also be kept in mind that these techniques and devices may not be the sole providers of evidence. For example, an arresting officer may have observed the suspect driving erratically, and may have also smelled alcohol on the suspect's breath. Then when the results of the breathalyzer are also added in, the combination of the three pieces of evidence make the case far more compelling and reduces the probability of a false positive.

A PERSON OF INTEREST: BARRY SCHECK

Barry Scheck is a defense lawyer who founded and serves as the Director of the Innocence Project, a group dedicated to the scientific use of DNA to exonerate persons who have been wrongly convicted. The movie "Conviction" (2010) was based on one of his most celebrated cases - the proof of innocence for a man who had served 18 years for a crime he did not commit. Overall, Scheck has used DNA evidence to rescue well over 200 persons who had been previously convicted. The Innocence Project rests its cases solely on DNA evidence rather than any legal technicalities or dramatic presentations. Scheck has worked on the defense team of such luminaries as O.J Simpson (1995) and the British au pair Louise Woodward (1997). Simpson, an ex- professional football player and millionaire, was charged with the slaying of his wife and one of her friends. Although it seemed that the prosecution had an iron-clad case against him, Simpson's defense team convinced the jury that he was innocent. In the Woodward case Scheck was the lead lawyer, and although Woodward was charged with the second-degree murder of an infant left in her care, the conviction was appealed and lowered to involuntary manslaughter (for which she served an incarceration time of less than one year). Barry Scheck also teaches law at the Benjamin Cardozo School of Law in New York City.

Is It Admissible?

Whether scientific evidence may be admissible in federal court cases depends on two important court decisions, Frye and Daubert.

The Frye Standard (1923) - *Frye v United States, 293 F1013*. The Federal Court of Appeals in 1923, in a case involving the use of the polygraph lie detector ruled that all scientific evidence must meet acceptance by a consensus of the members of the relevant scientific community. Thus, the Frye, general-acceptance standard, demanded that the scientific basis of the evidence be proven to have general acceptance in the particular field involved. Thus, if the consensus of scientists believes it to be true, then the court will accept it.

Daubert Standard (1993) –*Daubert v Merrill Dow Pharmaceuticals*. In this case the court ruled that the scientific evidence involved not only must have the acceptance of a consensus of the scientific community, but also that the evidence be derived from the application of the scientific method, and that it be both reliable and valid. The original case was brought against a pharmaceutical company by a woman who had taken a certain drug during pregnancy which was alleged to have caused abnormalities in the fetus. It also stated that the Daubert rule would supersede the Frye rule in all federal cases. Defense attorneys may raise a Daubert motion aimed at excluding unqualified scientific evidence or the testimony of an expert in the field. It is then up to the federal judge to determine if the evidence has a scientific basis derived from the scientific method. There are, of course some problems involved in this ruling, the most important was voiced by Justice Rehnquist when he said "I defer to no one in my confidence in federal judges, but I do not think we should make them obligated to become amateur scientists."

The State Courts
Daubert may currently be the law of the land, but the state courts have not all fallen in line. At the time of this writing, only about a third of the states have adopted Daubert, another third have remained with Frye, and the rest have combinations of Daubert, Frye and even some that are unique to a particular state. A convenient summary of admissibility requirements under both Fry and Daubert follows (Kiely, 2006):
1. Are there any published peer-reviewed articles and books covering the subject?
2. Is the science involved taught at universities or at scientific meetings and conferences?
3. Has the method been tested for accuracy?
4. Is it generally accepted in the scientific community?

The Forensic Techniques of Science

The Breathalyzer
The breathalyzer is used to detect alcohol levels in the body. Though not testing the blood level directly (which would require the analysis of a blood sample), the blood-alcohol content (BAC) is measured indirectly by measur-

ing the suspect's breath alone. The two most common types are the desk analyzer, usually used at the home base, and the field analyzer, a hand-held device often kept in the patrol car and used to test the suspect immediately (as in a field-sobriety test). The legal limit in the United States is a reading of .08 or higher (the .08 refers to the grams of alcohol per 210 liters of breath). When stopped, the suspect should not be allowed to put anything in his/her mouth from the time of the stop to the time of the testing. The time between the stop and the test must be carefully noted, as it can impinge on the results. Also, watch the suspect closely since there are ways persons can lower their true readings, for example by vigorous exercise, such as climbing stairs, doing jumping jacks or hyperventilating. Also, for the average man, you can get a rough estimate of his BAC even the morning after by simply subtracting .02 per hour. For example, a suspect might be arrested and tested at 8 AM and the police want to estimate his BAC for the night before. If his 8 AM BAC is .02 his midnight BAC would have been about .18 (well over the legal limit).

The use of the Breathalyzer is not without some controversy, especially when used in conjunction with random stops. Some courts have ruled that a warrant should be obtained before the device is used, despite the fact the effects of the alcohol could have worn off by the time the warrant is signed and obtained. This an extremely important issue because drunk driving has led to an enormous number of fatalities. Data from the Fatal Accident Reporting System have been analyzed for various BAC levels. A BAC of 0.15 or higher presents a fatality risk 400 times greater than for a sober driver, and drivers with a BAC of between 0.10 and 0.14 were 50 times more likely to have a fatal accident (Zador, 1991).

Thinking Inside the Box

The chemical fuel cell and infra-red technology inside these devices, although perhaps interesting to some science types, need not be studied carefully by the arresting officer. If you are ever brought in to testify in court, remember the following case study (absolutely true story).

CASE STUDY-Breathalyzer

A young police officer was on the stand being badgered by a slick defense attorney who was attempting to refute his client's DWI charge. The suspect had blown a .10 (obviously above the .08 limit).

Defense Attorney: "And what is the specific chemical reaction that goes on inside that so-called alcohol tester, and how do you know this has anything to do with my client's alleged blood-alcohol level"?

Police Officer: "I'm sorry sir, but I really don't know the scientific chemistry of the breathalyzer."

Defense Attorney: "So you are admitting in front of this court that you have absolutely no idea how this thing works, and you expect to convict my client?

Police Officer: "Yes sir I do". And then lifting his wrist high in the air said, "I don't' know what's going on inside my watch either. But I know what time it is." The now red-faced attorney sat down amid raucous court-room laughter. The suspect was convicted.

Polygraph

The polygraph is used in an attempt to identify whether a person is lying. The first lie detector was a crude device that was created way back in the 1800s by Cesare Lombroso (whom we met before when discussing personality and accompanying physical characteristics). With the current machine, the analyst looks for physiological reactions, such as changes of blood pressure, respiration, pulse rate and GSR (Galvanic Skin Response, which is a measure of the skin's electrical conductivity caused by sweating). During the testing, the examiner begins by asking a series of non-threatening, innocuous biographical questions, like what's your name?, are you married?, where do you live? The answers to these questions then become the control questions and are interspersed with the relevant questions. A not-too-subtle sequence could go like this:

Is your first name Joe?

Are you married?

Did you steal the car?

A needle records the physiological reactions on a graph, with little variation in the line during the control questions, but if the subject is lying, it's supposed to show a big jump during the relevant questions. The line may look like a flat plateau during the control stage, but then gyrate upward and look like a picture of Mount Olympus if a lie is detected. However, there is some concern about the reliability and validity of the modern polygraph, and in many courtrooms its results are not admissible as evidence (Iacono & Lykken, 1997). Said Justice Thomas,"there is simply no consensus that polygraph evidence is reliable" (Thomas, 1998). Despite the court's view, the polygraph is still often used by law enforcement during the investigation process, and at times provides valuable information. Also, many companies use it before hiring a new employee.

Voice Stress Analyzer - VSA

This device analyzes the suspect's voice, with a special emphasis on what are called "voice micro tremors." It has become a very popular instrument in police departments throughout the country, because it is inexpensive and has the look and feel of super science. Although voice analysis has definitely been proven to be able to identify an individual's voice patterns and therefore the identity of the speaker, and has also easily been able to support a charge of high levels of alcohol (through the detection of the slurred speech), its efficiency in detecting deception is far from being proven. In fact, one study uses the term "charlatanry" for describing voice analysis techniques (Eriiksson & Lacerda, 2007). Also a scientific study conducted at the University of Florida, found the voice analyzer to have very low reliability for detecting deception. (Hollien & Harnsberger, 2006). One study found almost 100% agreements between the results of the voice analyzer and the polygraph, which is certainly not a rousing endorsement, because of the known reliability problems that have been demonstrated with the polygraph (Tippett, 1997). The VSA is now used largely during the questioning-investigative process rather than in the court-room, and in this role it is said to have become an effective tool in prodding the suspect into admitting to distortions in his/her/story, and sometimes even a full confession. In some states, however, (i.e., Massachusetts) any hint of deception on the part of the interrogator may invalidate the confession.

Plethysmography

Plethysmography **is** a technique used to measure changes occurring within a person's body, including lungs, limbs and genitalia. When applied to the genitals it is called either Penile Plethysmography or Vaginal Plethysmography. Investigators have used this for assessing sexual arousal and sexual orientation. Evidence gleaned from these data is not currently admissible in court, but may result in important investigative information.

Forensic Web Analysis – The Use of the Internet

Any of the internet web communications services, such as Google, Twitter, Facebook, and other encrypted web sites are now required to build trapdoors into their encryption systems. This will be of great help to law enforcement since it will allow the monitoring of all web conversations (as can also be done now with a court ordered wire- tap on a phone).

Forensic Document Analysis

This is the science of hand-writing analysis and is based on an expert's ability to detect forgeries or the author of hand-written notes, such as a ransom note or a last will and testament. The hand writing analyst also uses such things as word choice and spelling peculiarities. In the famous case of the kidnapping and murder of the infant son of the legendary aviator Charles Lindbergh, hand-writing analysts were used to determine the author of the ransom note found in the baby's crib. The ransom note read, in part, "Have 50000$ redy…we warn yu from making anyding public or for notify the police the child is it gut care." It was confirmed that the note was written by an out-of-work carpenter by the name of Bruno Hauptman. When Hauptman's home was searched investigators found fourteen thousand dollars in marked ransom money. Hauptman was convicted and later executed. The document analyst may also be called on to identify the origin of a typed note or a computer-generated print-out (which printer was used). Hand-writing analysis should not be confused with Graphology, which is the alleged analysis of an individual's personality on the basis of a signature.

Forensic Dentistry
Forensic dentistry is the study of teeth and teeth marks as an aid in a criminal investigation and is utilized as follows:
1. Both the victim and the suspect may be identified on the basis of a comparison of the dental structure, past X rays, and other dental records.
2. By examining the calcification process, teeth can be used to estimate age.
3. An examination of bite marks may show a match between the marks and a suspect's own teeth.
4. Structure. In fact, it was structural evidence of this kind that helped convict the notorious serial killer, Ted Bundy, killer of 30 young women. Teeth marks on the buttocks of one of the women were a perfect match with Bundy's tooth structure.

Forensic Osteology
This is the study of bones and bone fragments in determining such things as the time and cause of death. This is especially helpful when the body has gone through serious decomposition, or was severely mutilated. Forensic osteology has also been used to determine the sex, size, and ethnicity of the person, as well as any evidence of trauma or disease.

The Forensic Autopsy
A skilled coroner can be of value to law enforcement by extracting a great deal of evidence from an examination of the corpse. The autopsy may reveal the cause of death, whether by trauma or disease, and whether the death was natural, accidental, or due to homicide or suicide.

Forensic Fingerprint Analysis
Fingerprints can be used for identifying any specific individual, since no two people, including identical twins, have exactly the same prints. Therefore law enforcement can use the prints for identifying suspects, witnesses, or victims. Even today, despite the remarkable strides in DNA analysis, finger prints are still the most commonly used forensic tool in this country. Crime-scene fingerprints can be extracted from any surface using a dusting powder that locates and then adheres to the print.
Exemplar Prints
When a print is deliberately taken in person from an individual, it is called an exemplar print. This can be taken either by rolling the inked fingers onto a pad, or more recently, and more conveniently, using a 3D scanner. Any print that is not taken directly from the subject, but is instead taken from a surface that the subject has touched is called a latent print. These can be

either visible or even invisible to the naked eye. Prints of this type are typically found by dusting, although today's electronic devices have become increasingly popular. If only a partial print is found, it may still be of some value. Even the partial print can often be salvaged by print-enhancing techniques now used in many crime labs. Although generically called finger prints, prints can also be lifted from other parts of the hand and even from the feet and toes. As long as some friction ridges, or raised portions of the epidermis, can be found, the individual can be traced.

The Integrated Automated Fingerprint Identification System (AFIS)
The FBI is responsible for keeping a huge data base of fingerprints for comparison with the specific prints that are sent in for identification. Currently this master file contains the prints and names of about 60 million persons. Fingerprinting is definitely here to stay.

Fingerprints As Scientific Evidence
Although it is said that all fingerprints are unique, this assertion has sometimes been challenged. For example, one could argue that all the possible prints have never been compared. Since there are about 7 billion persons living on the planet and if each person were to have ten fingers, that would add up to 70 billion prints. Nobody has ever compared 70 billion prints for uniqueness. However, in over 100 years of gathering prints, two persons with identical prints have never been found, and as said before that includes identical twins. Finally, the National Institute of Justice did a study of 50,000 prints and concluded that the chance of a false match was "effectively zero" (NIJ, 2000). As of this writing, fingerprint evidence is allowed by both Frye and Daubert.

Impression Evidence
Impressions are produced when an object is pressed against another with enough force to leave the impression. Tire marks, foot prints, shoe prints, bite marks, lip prints, and tool marks are commonly identified on the basis of an impression that has been generated from a plaster cast, a photograph, or sometimes an ink print. A skilled investigator can estimate a person's size and foot speed when analyzing foot or shoe prints. Fingerprint analysis, which was discussed above, is also basically impression evidence.

Forensic Ballistics: A Job for the Ballistician
Every single firearm on the planet, other than a smooth bore shotgun, leaves its own characteristic marks on a spent round and/or cartridge casing, and the job of the ballistician is to match the round or the casing with the weapon of origin. Inside every gun barrel are spiral grooves called rifling, which cause the bullet to spin and makes the gun more accurate (like a football quarterback spiraling a pass). Also the gun's firing pin and extractor can leave an

impression. These markings on the spent shell or cartridge casing then leave a virtual fingerprint that may narrow the search down to a single weapon. The weapon may also be deliberately fired at the departmental range and its output compared to evidence found at the crime scene. The ballistician is also able to tell if a sound-suppressor (silencer) was used. The National Firearms Data Base has the serial number for every firearm sold in this country.

Cell Phone and/or GPS
Anytime a cell phone or GPS is used, the location of origin can be immediately known by law enforcement. The accuracy of this location-identification is unerringly accurate and has led to many suspects unwittingly giving away their positions and then being brought to justice.

Thermal Imaging
Another important forensic tool is the thermal imager (heat seeker) that can be used to look behind closed doors and down through a building's roof. The devise has been used to spot such things as the use of heat when marijuana is being grown indoors, and in the 2013 case of the Boston bomber, it located a body inside a covered boat. In the latter case, the heat signature proved that the subject was not only in the boat but also still alive.

Photographic Evidence
In this age of digital photography it is easy now to take dozens (sometimes hundreds) of pictures at the crime scene. If you are the one taking the pictures, don't confuse quantity with quality. It is important that there be enough light and that there are no obstacles in the way. The camera can't see it if you can't. Also you want the best pictures you can get, so take your time. Fewer sharp photos are better than a lot of blurred images.

Covert Cameras
Last year the National Retail Federation reported that losses due to theft added up to more than 35 billion dollars. During the last few years stores have also increased the number of cameras set up over cash registers and exits. The problem is that thieves seem to be getting smarter, rendering the overt cameras less effective. Transactions around the cash register are often the scenes of fast action, and the professional shop lifter will always seek out the busiest registers, hoping the cashier doesn't notice the items stuffed in the umbrella, underneath the cart, under the heavy bag of dog food or deliberately mislabeled. Also, cashiers may be in on the deal and coordinate their actions with their friends who are posing as customers. Thus cashiers may undercharge their accomplices or perhaps even not charge at all. One solution is to set up covert cameras, hidden in clocks, smoke detectors and anything else that doesn't look out of place. This deliberate use of camera camouflage (covert photography) could also be extended to the warehouse, self-serve

areas, and storage or lay-away areas. Honest employees should be alerted to being on the look-out for potential shop lifters, like people entering the store carrying an umbrella on a sunny day, or wearing large, baggy clothing.

Photo Enhancement

Courts are beginning to allow computer-aided photo enhancement as evidence. Remember, however, that there has to be an original of fairly decent quality. Even the best photo enhancement techniques can't salvage a photo or video so poorly done that the faces couldn't be discerned or the license plates unreadable. The message here is to be careful when photographing the crime scene. Photo enhancement can help, but it's not a panacea.

Some Numbing Numbers: Demographics and the Numbers Game

Before going on to the next topic, there has to be a brief look at how scientific evidence is combined, based on both demographic characteristics and the concept of probability. When assessing the probability of a specific person being involved, the level of probability is grounded in the theory of random sampling.

Percentages

Percentages are based on a standardized denominator of 100. Thus 10% means ten out of 100 and 50% means 50 out of a hundred and so on. Percentages can also be used to determine rates, such as interest rates, crime rates, and execution rates. Rates can be percentages that are set in fixed intervals, usually time intervals. It is important when looking at rates to carefully examine the time frames since carefully culled time frames can tell almost any story the author wished to convey. For example, by selecting the years 1942 to 1952, it could be shown that the number of TV sets in American homes increased by 10,000% (since 1942 predated the dawn of the TV era). If the same rate were extrapolated out another ten years to 1962, there would have been more that 40 TV sets in each and every U.S. home!

Demographic data allows law enforcement to look at the percentages in the population that share certain characteristics, such as the percentage of Caucasians, Hispanics, Catholics, or Baptists. This often helps the law to narrow the search for a suspect.

Probability

In examining evidence, especially circumstantial evidence, it is important to combine all the evidence so that, if needed, it can then be strengthened by putting it in probability terms. Probability is the number of times a specific event can occur out of the total possible number of events. In flipping a fair coin there are only two possible outcomes, heads or tails. The probability of getting a head (the specific event) is 1 and the total possible number of events is 2, therefore, the probability of flipping a head is 1 divided by 2 or .50.

With dice, the probability of rolling a 6 with one die is 1(for the specific event) divided by 6 (for the total possible number of events), $1/6 = .17$.

Percentages and Probabilities.

Any time you have a percentage value it can be easily and quickly converted into a probability format by simply dividing the percentage of cases by 100 and then dropping the percentage sign. Thus, 67% becomes .67, and 34% becomes .34 and so on.

The Product Rule

The only mathematical method ever approved by a court of law is the product rule. In the *People vs. Axell* (1991) the court ruled that the use of statistical methods for determining probability was permissible in a court of law and that when combining probabilities for independent events occurring together the separate probabilities should be multiplied. Since probability levels can never be greater than 1.00, the multiplication process therefore reduces the resulting, overall probability. The Supreme Court has even ruled on whether a combination of separate non-criminal behaviors can alert law enforcement to a "probable-cause "conclusion. Drug Enforcement agents stopped a man as he arrived in Hawaii, and the following events occurred:

1. The man was travelling under an assumed name.
2. His original destination was Miami, a source area for illegal drugs.
3. He stayed in Miami for only a few hours, even though his flight to Hawaii took 20 hours.
4. He checked no luggage, but had a carry-on in his hand.
5. He had paid $2100 for two airline tickets.
6. He appeared to be anxious when stopped.

Because of these six occurrences, the agents used a dog to sniff his carry-on, and "bingo" it contained well over a thousand grams of cocaine. The suspect complained that because there was no warrant or any reasonable suspicion of criminal activity that his Fourth Amendment rights had been violated. The case eventually went to the Supreme Court, and it was ruled that in evaluating a series of actions taken by a suspect, even though any one of the factors is not by itself proof of any illegal conduct, taken together they amount to reasonable suspicion (*U.S. v Sokolow*, 1989).

CASE STUDY: Probability

A woman was brutally murdered by means of repeated stab wounds. Three eye-witnesses saw a white male running from the crime scene, and all three described him as being white and somewhere between 20 and 40 years old. It was discovered by the serologist that one of the blood samples found at the crime scene did not match that of the victim, and it was therefore assumed to having been left by the assailant. The blood stain showed the following characteristics: On the ABO system it was AB, and on the PGM system it was a

FORENSIC SCIENCE AND LAW ENFORCEMENT

1+. It was also found to be Rh negative. Obviously, any suspect typed as A, B or O, or typed as anything but a 1+, or was Rh positive had to be eliminated as the donor. From the demographics it was found that in the general population, 4% are AB, 19% are 1+ and 15% are Rh negative. Using the procedure shown above, the percentages were converted to probabilities and then multiplied, so that (.04) X (.19) X (.15) = .00114. Then the other evidence had to be factored in, such as the fact that the suspect was seen as white (census figures show the white population to be 85%), and the perceived age range of 20 to 40 (again the census data indicate that an age range of 15 to 59 includes 62%). Thus the above probability of .00114 had to be multiplied by .85 and then by .62, which equals .0006. However since the population is only about half male the previous value has to be multiplied by .50, which then equals .0003, or a probability that only 3 persons per 10,000 could fit all these characteristics.

Forensic Serology

The science of forensic serology is the study and analysis of bodily fluids (blood, saliva, semen, vaginal fluids) to investigate a crime scene and aid in the identification of the victim and/or perpetrator. Blood samples may be of two types:

1. Transfer Blood. This is the blood stain that has been transferred to an object, such as a piece of clothing, furniture, or floor.

2. Projected Blood. This is blood that comes directly from the person involved.

In the case study above, notice that both direct evidence (eye-witnesses) and the circumstantial evidence were combined in arriving at the final probability value. Blood samples have been used to determine if the donor was human or even to estimate the exact time of the crime. In the case shown above three blood categories were used: (1) the ABO system, (2) The Rh system and (3) the PGM system.

1. The ABO system. This is a four-category system based on whether an antigen appears in the blood. If the A antigen is found the person is a type A, and if the B antigen is found the person is a B. If both the A and B antigens are found, the person is AB and if neither is found the person is an O.

2. Rh Factor. In this method the individual is typed as to whether the Rh factor is present, Rh+ if found and Rh- if absent.

3. PGM System. The PGM system is based on a polymorphic enzyme, and the population demographics show only about 19% to be PGM1+.

Luminol

When only trace amounts of blood are left, often undetectable to the naked eye, the forensic investigator may use a spray containing a substance called luminol. Luminol reacts to the blood traces by producing a bluish glow that can be clearly seen in a darkened room. This reaction doesn't last long, but photographs of the glow are admissible in court. Thus, the tiny but telling droplets of blood can be scraped off at the crime scene and brought to the lab for forensic analysis. Although DNA is the preferred analysis today, the previous mentioned blood categories are extremely useful in determining if a certain suspect should be totally excluded. And in this case it is a 100%, direct-evidence exclusion. Notice above that the blood was categorized as AB, meaning that a suspect who was A, B or O could not possibly have been the donor.

DNA: The Gold Standard

DNA, which stands for deoxyribonucleic acid, is found within all living organisms, and contains each organism's unique genetic instructions for both its development and continued functioning. As with the breathalyzer, you don't have to have a PhD in neuroscience to be able to collect DNA samples, but you do need some special training in the collection techniques. DNA analysis has become the gold standard for individual identification. The ABO typing shown above was supplanted on or about 1990, when forensic science took a quantum leap forward. Not only will DNA identify the felon, but it can also tell us for example, if a succession of murders in a given location were committed by the same assailant. And, finally, DNA is extremely useful in identifying a murder victim, as long as the body was found before serious decomposition sets in. DNA can be used to identify persons and also to look for matches between DNA samples and the person who left the samples, both being very important to police work. With a DNA match, for example, the guilt or innocence of a suspect can be determined beyond a reasonable doubt. Although the DNA match is never 100% guaranteed, the probability of a false identification is so astronomically low that it can be assumed to be beyond the limits of any reasonable doubt. The collected evidence can come from a variety of sources, such as skin cells, blood or blood stains, saliva, urine, semen, pieces of any tissue (such as fingernails, hair, bones or teeth) or even objects that the person may have touched, such as clothing, drinking cups, straws, cigarette butts. The specimens do require careful handling (latex or nitrile gloves), and once collected must be carefully protected from any source of contamination. If you happen to ever be the first investigator to arrive at the scene, the main message is "do no harm," which in this case means don't contaminate the crime scene with your own DNA. There are collection kits available, even for touch DNA. The specimen is carefully covered with a chemical solution and then swabbed, capped and sent on to the crime lab. Incredibly, in 2012 DNA was used to identify the remains of a body buried under a parking lot in Leister, England, only to discover it belonged to King Richard III who had been killed in battle in 1485. He had been buried in a monastery that was now covered over by the parking lot.

The DNA Markers

Forensic scientists look at 13 different DNA markers, markers that vary from individual to individual. A match of only one marker does not determine a match, but when thirteen line up, side-by-side, the odds of a match become overwhelming. The procedure first involves the extraction of DNA from small bits of blood, hair, tissue, or semen found at the scene of the crime, and then matching that specimen to the DNA taken from the suspect, called a probe. The statistician then determines the probability of a false match by using the Product Rule (discussed above) to make the final determination. As you may recall, the product rule uses the multiplication process to determine the outcome. Since no probability value can be greater than 1.00, we are virtually always dealing with values less than 1.00 and therefore when combining the probabilities (one event and another event and another event) the values keep getting smaller. For example if the probability of one event is .50 and the probability of a second event is also .50, the combined probability of both events occurring together would be .50 times .50, or .25. This is how the DNA combinations are handled. With DNA, as the number of probes increases, typically 13, the probabilities continue to decline, and the result of a false match becomes so low that it becomes, although still a probability statement, a virtual affirmation of truth. A sample match at one site is approximately 1 in 10, or .10. The probability of a match at two sites would be (.10) (.10) = .01, for 1 in a hundred. For all 13 sites it would be:
$(.10)(.10)(.10)(.10)(.10)(.10)(.10)(.10)(.10)(.10)(.10)(.10)(.10)$
$=1/10,000,000,000,000$ or one in ten trillion. The Supreme Court in *Maryland v King* (2013) ruled that DNA cheek-swabs can be obtained from anyone who has been placed under arrest, and can then be used to create an individual DNA profile which can be put in storage and checked for other crimes.

A PERSON OF INTEREST: SIR ALEC JEFFREYS

If anyone can claim the title "Father of Modern Forensic Science" it has to be Alec Jeffreys. Born in Oxfordshire, England in 1950, Jeffreys went on to become one of the world's most prominent geneticists, and for forensic science, perhaps its greatest innovator. For his invention and pioneering work in creating the process of DNA fingerprinting and DNA profiling, he was knighted by Queen Elizabeth II and accorded the title "Sir Alec Jeffreys." In September of 1984, he was casually examining some DNA test results that his laboratory had recently collected. Although what he called the "banding pattern" from each sample seemed to form a random pattern, Jeffreys suddenly (in what he called a "Eureka Moment") saw both systematic differences and similarities in the patterns. He called each unique pattern a DNA fingerprint, and he soon realized that he had stumbled upon the genetic code that could be used to identify each specimen and, therefore, each person (Jeffreys, 1985). This is one of those rare but classic examples of serendipity which, of course, became extremely important for law enforcement as well as for resolving paternity and immigration issues. In fact one of the first times this new identification system was ever used concerned the immigration case of a young man returning to England after a visit to Africa.. He needed to prove his identity in order to be let back into England, and he used his DNA as verification. A few years later, the German government asked Jeffreys to determine if the remains of a German who died while in South America could be those of the notorious Nazi, Dr. Joseph Mengele. Mengele had worked at the Nazi death camp at Auschwitz and had performed hideous experiments on the bodies of dead and nearly-dead Jewish prisoners. Jeffreys was able to show that the remains were indeed those of Joseph Mengele, a result that pleased the German government since it helped close that horrific chapter of Nazi brutality. The first time DNA was used to solve a criminal case occurred in 1986 when it was used to confirm both guilt and innocence - the guilt of Colin Pitchfork as the rapist and killer of two English teen-agers, and the innocence of the man who had been the main suspect, Richard Buckland. DNA identification has gone through several up-dates since then, but it is due to the scientific curiosity and genius of Alec Jeffreys that the door was opened for this cutting-edge technology.

CODIS

The FBI has a huge data base of DNA profiles that are stored in a computer program called CODIS (Combined DNA Index System). Every U.S. state requires that DNA profiles for many types of felony convictions (for example homicide and sex offenses) be sent to CODIS, and some states are now demanding that the DNA be collected at the time of arrest, not just after a conviction. CODIS contains two types of DNA profiles, the DNA taken directly from the suspected felon, and the DNA recovered from the crime scene as well as from missing and/or unidentified persons. At the time of this writing there are well over 9 million convicted-felon profiles in the FBI data base. Since the Supreme Court's decision in Maryland v. King, 2013, when a new arrest is made the police can now send the suspect's profile directly to CODIS for a possible match. This has put an incredible strain on the system, and a large backlog has accumulated. There is now a priority-based system in the following order: homicide, sexual assault, aggravated assault and battery, burglary, vehicle crimes.

CASE STUDY: Alonzo King

In 2009 Alonzo King was arrested for aiming a loaded shot gun and threatening to kill a group of persons in what looked like an imminent mass murder. The police arrived quickly and King was arrested before any further crimes were committed. While being booked, the police took a cue-tip swab of his mouth, collected his DNA and sent it off to the FBI's DNA base (CODIS). King's DNA matched the DNA found at a 2003 case in which a woman was brutally raped. The rapist-assailant was now known to be Alonzo King. King had broken down the woman's front door, and both raped and robbed her. She was not able to personally identify King because he was masked and wore a hat pulled down over his head. After he left her, the woman went immediately to the hospital and underwent a forensic exam in which semen was collected and a DNA sample extracted. From that day on the woman lived in fear and had even nailed down her windows and bolted shut her doors. When she was told, six years later, that the attacker had been found and was now under detention, she was relieved. However, at his trial it was argued that taking his DNA sample after the shotgun arrest violated his Fourth Amendment rights against unreasonable search and seizure. Although the defense argued strenuously that extracting his DNA was illegal since there was no direct evidence linking King to the rape, the court did find him guilty. The court said that taking the DNA swab was no more unreasonable than taking fingerprints. His lawyers then appealed the decision, but to no immediate avail, and he was sentenced to life in prison. But then in April of 2012 the Maryland Court of Appeals reversed the decision, saying that collecting the DNA evidence was indeed unconstitutional and violated King's right to privacy. King was then free to go, despite the fact that law enforcement and the victim knew he had committed this heinous crime. But then a new twist occurred. The State of Maryland had appealed the appellate court's decision to the Supreme Court of the United States, and in June 2013, the Supreme Court ruled that the police can use cheek swabs and collect the DNA of arrested suspects (Maryland v. King, 2013). King's rape conviction was, of course, reinstated. Law enforcement praised the Supreme Court's decision, believing that DNA swabbing was no more intrusive than finger-printing or photographing and that it would be extremely helpful in solving cold cases and preventing future felonies. Also, had this been allowed on all arrestees early in their crime careers, they could not have committed the large majority of their later crimes. Again the dilemma – the rights of the individual versus the protection of society.

Surviving Parents
There is a group called the Surviving Parents coalition that has urged that DNA samples be taken at the time of arrest, not just after the conviction. Had this been the case, they argue, many cases of sexual assault, especially child assaults, would have been solved, and even possibly prevented. This initiative has not been welcomed by members of the ACLU, as they feel it is a threat to privacy, to individual freedom, and might even foster racial inequalities. Since the 2013 case of *Maryland v. King*, however, the issue has been settled, and it is now legal throughout the country to extract DNA from pos-

sible suspects who have not yet been convicted – a victory for the Surviving Parents.

DNA and the Proof of Innocence

Although DNA evidence can certainly be used for convictions, it is important to stress that it can also be used to prove innocence. In one high-profile case, a 6-year –old child, Jon Benet Ramsey, was murdered by a blow to the head and strangulation. She was an exceptionally beautiful child, and had participated in a number of beauty pageants. Her parents were the first suspects, but they were exonerated on the basis of DNA testing. The murder is still unsolved. At the time of this writing well over 200 persons have been exonerated based on the analysis of their DNA.

CASE STUDY: Lula Cora Hood

Lula Cora Hood, mother of 14, left her home in Illinois back in 1970 after a family dispute. It wasn't the first time she had left home, but in the past she had always returned. This time she did not return. Then in the early 1990s the family was told by police that some female skeletal remains had been found near where Lula had lived, and that it had been established that Lula's body had been found. A funeral service was held, and the family went through with the burial. However in 2008 one of her daughters read about recent advances in DNA testing and wanted more definite proof. She asked to have new DNA testing done on the remains, and the new analyses performed at the FBI laboratory in Quantico, Virginia, proved that it was not Lula who had been buried. The earlier science was primitive by today's standards and led to a misidentification. But the story doesn't end there . Suspecting that she might still be alive, the family pushed for a full investigation, and in 2011 the police, using her full name, birth date, and other personal information, discovered that Lula, now age 84, was still alive and well and living in Florida. Now the question is, whose remains were buried, and how did she die?

Scientific Jury Selection (SJS): Trial or Error

As was shown in a previous Chapter, the use of scientific methods for the selection of a jury has become a big business in the United States and seems to be getting bigger every day. Jury consultants, such as Dr. JoEllan Dimitrius, use their knowledge of personality, demographics and past experience in the selection of a jury that will be most sympathetic to their clients. These consultants have been used both by defense attorneys as well as the prosecution. The famous Clarence Darrow quote that the verdict is in once the jury is empanelled may have been hyperbole, but Dimitrius has probably validated that assertion on many occasions, as in the O.J. Simpson case.

Body Language – Actions May Speak Louder Than Words

During the interrogation phase of an investigation, much can be learned about the suspect by observing the non-verbal reactions with as much care as listening for the verbal responses. The suspect's posture, gestures, eye movements, and facial expressions may reveal at least as much as what is actually being said. Experts in this field, such as Janine Driver, president of the "Body Language Institute," have provided evidence of the value of these non-verbal communication modes. In fact, it is her opinion that over 50% of any communicated message is sent through body language rather than just through words alone. Reading body language has also been used by expert interrogators from the FBI, who add that reading people is a skill that should be learned by anyone working in law enforcement (Navarro, J. & Karlins, M., 2008). These techniques are also used by the scientific jury selectors. During the interrogation the major indicators of lying are as follows:

1. Constant blinking of the eyes, or just as important, the total absence of blinking.

2. A great deal of facial touching during the interview (but not touching the chest).

3. Avoiding eye contact with you.

4. Gestures and facial expressions that are inconsistent with what you are being told, such as an inadvertent start of a smile when describing a very sad event.

5. Is uncomfortable when facing you directly. Tries to turn away from you.

6. Placing objects between the two of you, such as a newspaper, pen or coffee cup.

7. Answering your question by using your words exactly, as in "Did you steal the car?" "No I did not steal the car". The truth teller would be more apt to say "I didn't steal a car."

The Psychic Detective – In the Name of Science

This section would not be complete without at least some mention of the so-called psychic detectives, those persons who claim to have extraordinary paranormal powers that can be used to solve crimes and find bodies. When one of these psychics seems to anticipate some criminal behavior or seems to know where a corpse is buried it grabs enormous media attention, but police departments tell us that this never really happens. Talk shows often present persons alleging to have psychic abilities, and these shows do get ratings. However, any time these paranormal gifts are submitted to the scientific method, they have not proved to be significant (Sprinthall 1964). Even the "great" mentalist Edgar Cayce failed when confronted with controlled conditions (Sprinthall & Lubetkin, 1965). As Joseph Nickell says "We hear a lot about psychics' alleged successes, but less about their notable failures" (Nickell, 2004).

Science and Criminal Justice

Science is here to stay in the field of criminal justice, and the scientific method has become the hall mark of most law enforcement efforts in both detection and prosecution. As you have seen, the Frye and/or Daubert standards must pass judgment for evidence to be introduced in many courtrooms, especially Federal Court Rooms. Although more will be presented on the scientific method in the next Chapter, it is enough here to make you aware of the fact that the methods of science have become important contributors to current law enforcement. You should also bite the bullet and review the section on probability, especially how probability estimates are combined in the court-tested "product rule." Again, more on probability will be covered later. I'm sure you can't wait. Rest assured, however, that it will be presented in conversational style, and is not difficult to understand. It is very important in criminal justice today.

Summary

Science and the scientific method have become law enforcement's most important partners. As a student of criminal justice you are not expected to also get a degree in one of the sciences, but you are obligated to learn the fundamentals of how science is used in law enforcement and what techniques are available. And not just anything with the word science attached can be brought into a court of law. It must be recognized and accepted by the scientific community, Frye, and/or it must be proven to have been established via the scientific method, Daubert. Thus, the rules governing courtroom admissibility in most cases are the Frye and Daubert standards, both approved by the Supreme Court of the United States. This is meant to prevent some outrageously inane evidence, posing as science, from being thrown in as a courtroom distraction. So it's not just anything "in the name of science" that can be introduced into a court of law. This chapter lists a large number of these procedures, from the breathalyzer to the gold standard DNA analysis.

Science has even been used effectively in the selection of the jury, but not so effectively when "in the name of science" psychics attempt to intrude on law enforcement. .And again be reminded that you don't need to know the science underlying each of these techniques, but you may have to be trained in their use. For example, you don't have to take courses in advanced biology to be able to know how and when to collect DNA evidence, nor do you need to know all the internal mechanics occurring within your watch, but you do have to know how to tell time.

Key Terms

Behavioral Profiling
Breathalyzer

CODIS
DNA
Document Analysis
Fingerprint Analysis
Forensic
Forensic Autopsy
Forensic Ballistics
Forensic Dentistry
Frye and Daubert Rules
Impression Evidence
Osteology
Photography and Photo Enhancement
Plethysmography
Polygraph and the Voice Stress Analyzer
Probability
Science and Jury Selection
Serology
The Product Rule
Thermal Imaging
Web Analysis and the Internet

References

Darby, B.W. & Jeffers, D.J. (2000). The effects of defendant and juror attractiveness on simulated courtroom trial decisions. *Society for Personality Research, 16,* 67-84

Eriksson, A. & Lacereda, F. (2007). Charlatanry in forensic speech science. *Journal of Speech, Language, and the Law,14,*2, 169-193

Griswold, M.E. & Murphy, G.R. (2010). *It's more complex than you think: A chief's guide to DNA* . Police Executive Research Forum, Washington, DC.

Hastie, R. , Penrod, S.D. & Pennington, N (1983).*Inside the jury.* Cambridge, MA: Harvard Univ. Press.

Hollien, H, & Harnsberger, J.D. 2006, Detecting truth deception stress from the voice. *IASCEP,* Univ.of Florida.

Iacono, W.G. & Lykken, D.T. (1997) Lie detectors and detection. *Journal of Applied Psychology, 83,* 426-433.

Kassan, S.M. (2012). Why confessions trump innocence. *American Psychologist, 67,* 431-445.

CHAPTER 12

RESEARCH METHODS IN CRIMINAL JUSTICE

Introduction

As a criminal justice student you may never have to actually conduct original research, but you will definitely have to learn to read and understand research results. This is a field of study that is brimming with boat-loads of statistical reports and analytic studies. And since some of these studies may actually be misleading, it is up to you to learn the fundamentals of the research enterprise. It may be true that "figures don't lie," but as you've heard many times, "liars can figure." By the time you finish reading this chapter, the figures should not be lying to you. In this chapter, there will be a discussion of various statistical tests, but you won't have to calculate them! Just try to appreciate them and know what story they are telling. And don't be taken in by the wise guy who tells you that 62.375% of all statistics are made up on the spot. Since we're taking the "numb" out of the numbers, you will not need either a calculator or a computer to read through this chapter. Just think of it as a basic logical tool for ferreting out what can and cannot be legitimately proven by these research studies. In today's high tech world, you may never have to actually calculate a statistical test. With programs such as SPSS and Excel all you have to do is type in the numbers, and then point-and-click your way to the answers (Sprinthall, 2009). Thus, this chapter will focus on the methods used in criminal justice research, not the mathematics involved. The research techniques in criminal justice are based on the very basic notion of trying to discover the most appropriate techniques for gaining new knowledge. The advances we have seen in the physical sciences, in biology, and in medicine, are obvious and have increased our longevity as well as the quality of our lives. In criminal justice these advances have not always been as obvious, yet they have occurred. We now know more about criminal behavior than we did just a few years ago, and this progress has largely resulted from the refinement of the research process. Our field, unlike say physics, is constantly being subjected to public scrutiny and is often vilified by a public (and press) who feel that they already know most of the answers while the professionals don't even know what the questions are. Imagine a headline that screams "Physics Confesses to a Lack of Full Understanding of Aperiodic Crystals." The average reader will probably then yawn and turn to the sports page. In the long run this may be seen as both a blessing and a curse; a blessing since it shows a strong concern about the safety and security of society, but a curse because there are so many self-proclaimed experts. It is the solid contention of this book that an increase in genuine understanding in any field that is even remotely concerned with the scientific endeavor must be solidly grounded in the same basic strategies and knowledge-gathering techniques as are used in every scientific area. And this, after all should be the goal of all researchers in the field of criminal justice - to increase the size of our book of knowledge.

Targeting the Traps – Seven Deadly Research Sins
Before getting to the specific research strategies, let's look at some of the more blatant traps sitting out there in research land just waiting for your arrival.

1. The Family Plot.
The FBI's UCR (Uniform Crime Reports) clearly show that over half the murders in this country are committed by family members and/or acquaintances. Should we therefore feel much safer if we always surround ourselves with strangers? No, since murderers who know their victims is a huge category and includes such groups as rival gang members who, of course, are acquainted with each other at some level. And in large cities, where most murders take place, gangs often shoot each other in turf wars, usually over drugs (and in this context "family" can take on a whole new meaning) (Lott, 2000).

2. Auto Inspections: Young Males and Speeding
In another study, researchers compared the number of driver citations issued by the police to the number of persons in the driving population for a variety of demographic characteristics. They found, among other things, that males, especially young males, were being stopped, searched and cited at a rate that was highly disproportionate to their total numbers (Farrell, 2004). One major newspaper's interpretation of these data was that the police were "profiling" young male drivers, in effect ambushing young males in general rather than using any individualized suspicion of the driver's behavior. Can you think of any other reason that might help explain these results? Could it be that driving behavior itself may differ across age and gender groups? Driving patterns may not be the same for a 21-year-old male and his 60-year-old grandmother. Other studies have found that those young males are also over represented when it comes to risk-taking behavior in many areas. In fact in one government study of over 40,000 drivers, it was found that males between the ages of 18 and 25 are three times as likely not to be wearing seat belts. The study also found seat belt use lower among low-income groups with low levels of education (Chu, 2005). Also the police may use many other exterior cues on automobiles before ordering a stop, such as broken taillights, and missing license plates. Could it be that young males are less careful about vehicle repairs than other demographic groups?

3. Prison Discipline: Does It Matter?

In a study of the enforcement of disciplinary rules in prisons, two equivalent prison populations were compared, one where the rules and regulations were strictly enforced and one where the rules were less invasive and enforcement more casual. It was found that strict enforcement of the rules resulted in more, not fewer, disciplinary problems than in the prison where conditions were more lax. Also, the inmates were asked before being released whether they thought they would be likely to reoffend. The results indicated a significant difference between the groups in favor of the prison with more lenient rules. The results were interpreted by some as showing that increased discipline and strict enforcement were seen as causing more disciplinary problems than they solve and may even add an increased risk of recidivism (Stevens, 1997). Stop for a moment and just think about these conclusions. Perhaps the increased number of infractions in the strict prison was at least partly a function of the increased number of rules that could be broken – that is, the more rules there are, the greater the opportunity for infractions to occur. Also, in the lax prison even those rules that were in place appear to have been enforced in a more random fashion, stated as "casually enforced," It might also be important to find out if the groups were truly equivalent to begin with. Could it be that those with more serious felonies were sent to the strict prison? Also, an inmate's opinion regarding recidivism may not be a realistic bottom line. The comparison should be based on who actually later recidivated. It may be that the lesson learned (as so often stated by Sheriff Michael J. Ashe of Hampden County, Massachusetts) is that prisons should adopt "reasonable rules that are strictly enforced."

4. Happiness in the Neighborhood

In a study based on how an impoverished neighborhood could affect mental health and "happiness," researchers found that persons living in low-income areas become happier and better adjusted when they move to more affluent areas (Ludwig et al, 2012). The authors say it was like giving them $15,000. Could it be that there was already an increase of at least that much in the family's income, an increase that made the move to the new neighborhood possible in the first place?

5. Clothes for the Occasion: Uniforms Count

New York City released figures showing that the uniformed police made only 30% of the subway arrests, while the plainclothes police hit the 70% mark. Does this mean that the plainclothes police work that much harder? Or could it possibly be that officers in uniform were indeed a deterrent, and that the uniform itself may have reduced the number of subway infractions?

6. If You Drink, Don't Park: Accidents Cause People

A study released by the US. Center for Disease Control (CDC) suggested that increasing taxes on beer could lower sexually transmitted diseases (STD), especially gonorrhea. The CDC said that there was a 9% reduction in gonorrhea rates following tax increases on beer by many of the states. The implication was that the increase in the price of beer makes it more difficult for the teenager to buy and that without the beer's influence on impulse control the teen is less likely to be sexually active. The data did not show that teens were buying less beer or having less sex. This was simply assumed. Perhaps the reduction in STD rates was the result of other factors, such as the states using their increased beer revenues for increasing sex education, or using more TV and radio spots extolling the virtues of "safe sex." Finally since there was no evidence indicating that the teens in those states were less sexually active, would it be a stretch to ask if the beer influenced the teens' readiness to use condoms?

7. Beware of Vague Time Lines and Indefinite Population Sizes

A recent study regarding the alleged conviction of innocent individuals states that during the last "several decades" (is it 20 years or a century?) more than 250 citizens have later been found innocent after having been convicted of major felonies. Now without a time line or the total number of convictions we are left unable to interpret this statement. Perhaps 250 citizens are 10% of the total, or perhaps it's a tiny fraction of one percent of the total. Also, when did these convictions occur, prior to DNA testing, prior to fingerprint analysis? We don't know, but the implication is obvious, especially since the article identifies the major issues as being problems and tunnel vision within the criminal justice system. Perhaps the devil is in the details, but this article may just keep the devil at bay.

The Dirty Analogy

You must be alert to what is called the "dirty analogy," the seemingly reasonable proof that suddenly changes direction mid- stream. An example is the argument that starts off "If we can put a man on the moon, then" and follows this with a list of non-sequiturs, such as "we can end crime" or "we can solve the problem of the homeless." Notice how the conclusions have nothing to do with the premise. A successful space launch does, of course, take engineering skill and plenty of money, but unlike crime doesn't take a change in attitudes or personal behavior. Other alleged solutions to beware of include "In a country as rich as ours, we can..." or "It is cheaper to send someone to Harvard than to keep that person in prison." What should the conclusion be for this one? Should we teach our citizens to commit felonies in order to get a free college education?

What is Science?

What is the meaning of this thing called science? In a very real sense science is what science does, which means that science and the scientific method are really inseparable. We can accumulate scientific knowledge only by practicing science. Although the origin of the English word "science" is derived from the Latin word scientia, which translates into English as "knowledge," today's use of the term goes beyond that envisioned by the early Romans.

Definitions of the word knowledge can vary, as can the techniques to acquire knowledge. It is one thing to set up a long list of guiding principles to live by, as the second century Roman Emperor Marcus Aurelius so thoughtfully did. But although these Stoic maxims were considered by the Romans to contain "truth and knowledge" (and maybe they still do), they were not arrived at by the process of scientific inquiry. In fact, Marcus Aurelius even titled his book after the method he used: he called it "Meditations." And although today's criminal justice scientists may spend part of their day meditating, there is certainly more to the scientific method than that. Even today there is no absolutely agreed upon definition of science. To some it is the scientific knowledge itself and to others it is the method used to obtain the knowledge. The majority opinion, however, clearly sees science as both the knowledge and the knowledge-gathering technique, or that the method of science cannot be separated from the scientific knowledge itself. The scientist seeks to find and impose order on what is often an unordered world. As Einstein once said, "science is the attempt to make the chaos of the diversity of our own sense experience correspond to a logically uniform system of thought." (Einstein, 1940, p487).

The Scientific Method

Back in a previous Chapter in a discussion of what evidence is admissible in court, it was pointed out that the Daubert Rule stated that the only evidence that the court should allow is that which is based both on the scientific method and also considered as reliable and valid. The scientific method is always listed under the heading of "Empiricism," a philosophy that insists that truth and knowledge can only be obtained through sensory observation, not just reason and logic alone. The scientist thus attempts to provide empirical proof through the scientific method. This method involves Observation, Induction, and Hypothesis Testing.

Observation. Events are observed, sometimes with instruments and measuring devices, and sometimes with the naked eye. These observations must be measured in some way so that the data can be quantified. This allows for observations to be more directly repeatable (perhaps by other scientists) and it also allows for the later statistical analysis of these measures.

Induction. From those original observations, the scientist uses a logical technique called induction, or the process of arguing from the specific to the general. That is, using those very specific observations a general hypothesis, or educated guess, is developed to help explain how those observations might be related.

Hypothesis Testing. The resulting hypothesis is then tested, through the logical process of deduction, or arguing from the general back to the specific. The test is used to help ensure that the hypothesis conforms to the reality of other measures of specific traits or characteristics. Thus, the hypothesis generates testable predictions, predictions that can be confirmed through more observations. The great sleuths of fact and fiction, for example Sherlock Holmes and the TV character Colombo, were always shown to have great powers of deduction. The resulting test predictions might be done in a laboratory situation, or by comparing these observations on site with the predicted outcome.

Thus, the scientist begins by making specific observations, then thinks about what these observed data might mean (the hypothesis), and then tests the hypothesis against more observations. Therefore, the scientific method is anchored at both ends (first step and last step) in observation. It is also very important to keep in mind that scientific proof is based ultimately on a probability model. It's a matter of proof without certainty, which most agree is better than certainty without proof. Conclusions may be "beyond a reasonable doubt" but to the scientist there is always the probability, slim as it may be, of the conclusion being due to chance.

Methods of Testing.
There are two methods for testing a scientific hypothesis, the experimental method and the post-facto method. These two methods will be discussed in full a little later in the chapter, but suffice it to say here that the scientist doesn't just rely on a single observation, but makes repeated observations. This helps to ensure the consistency of these measures, which is what the scientist calls "reliability."

Reliability
Reliable measures are consistent measures. If a person of a given height and weight were to drink exactly the same amount of alcohol on several different occasions, and the breathalyzer consistently read, say .05, then the results would be considered to be reliable. Similarly, if you were to weigh yourself for several straight days and the scale consistently read as 180 pounds, then the scale would be shown to be reliable. But if the scale showed 210 pounds one day and 140 pounds the next day it would be obvious that the scale was not scientifically reliable. But reliability alone is not enough. Because it al-

ways produces exactly the same time, a broken clock may be reliable, but don't use it to set your alarm.

Validity

In addition to being reliable, good measuring instruments must also be valid. That is, they should actually measure what they are supposed to be measuring. If a personality test is said to be measuring the trait of hostility, we must be sure that persons with high scores exhibit more hostility than persons with low scores. That broken clock we talked about above is only valid two times a day, but the problem is you don't know which two times. Valid measures should represent with as little error as possible, the real-world traits or characteristics they are supposed to represent.

As previously stated, the Daubert rule for the admissibility of scientific evidence demands that measures must be reliable and valid. That is, your scale cannot only be reliable (consistent), but must also be valid. If the scale constantly reads 210 pounds no matter whether you dieted or went on an eating binge, it may be reliable but is certainly not valid. This has been a real troublesome issue with the polygraph, because it is sometimes reliably consistent, but doesn't always indicate whether the subject is actually lying.

Compared To What?

When an old-time vaudeville comic was asked how his wife was, he always replied "compared to what"? This is a question you should keep upper-most in mind whenever you read research results. For example, many have argued that capital punishment has no deterrent effect, and as proof offer the fact that back when pickpockets were publicly hanged, other pickpockets were on hand stealing from the assembled crowd. Can you see any problem with the logic of this argument? The fallacy here is that there is no comparison group, or what we will call "control" group. Thus, we must always ask, "Compared to What"? Compared to the number of pockets picked at less grisly events, such as horse racing, carnivals, or sporting events? If there is no control group the research comparison is meaningless. No conclusion is possible if the comparison is between sample a and sample b, and there is no sample b.

Group Comparisons: Size Matters

It is extremely important to know the sizes of groups when comparisons are made. For example, it might be argued that compared to New York City, small towns in Alaska are far healthier places in which to live. Did you know that in New York City last year over 700,000 people died, whereas in Ugashik Alaska only 22 people died? (the other 8 probably moved to Fairbanks). However, by converting to percentages a far more meaningful comparison might be made. Another example, the death rate in the peacetime army is lower, by far, than the overall death rate in Florida. Therefore as a health precaution Floridians should all join the army, right? Wrong, because again, two qualitatively and quantitatively unequal groups are being compared. The army is composed of young, largely healthy persons who are not likely to be subject to chronic diseases and are certainly not going to be affected by infant health problems or ravaged by the diseases of old age.

Percentages
The percentage is an important term in criminal justice, and it must be understood as a statistical tool because it is such an important descriptive measure. Percentages are actually standardized ratios or fractions, all containing the same denominator (the number below the line in a fraction) and that denominator is always 100. Thus, in order to read a percentage only the numerator (the number above the line in a fraction) is necessary. A percentage of 40 means 40/100, or a percentage of 95 means 95 out of a hundred. In one Massachusetts county, it was found that 60% of the children with an incarcerated parent will end up in jail themselves. We might conclude that these children are following in their fathers' fingerprints.

Percentages and Percentage Changes
Finding percentage changes is really very simple. To find the percentage, just divide the number in question by the total number. For example, to establish the percentage of persons speeding on a holiday weekend, divide the number of speeders by the total number of drivers. Thus, if 800 cars pass the checkpoint, and of these there were 96 speeders, the percentage would be 96/800 or .12, which, by then multiplying by 100, translates to 12 %.

Percentage Increases and Decreases
To find percentage increases or decreases, use the following: N for new number–O for old number, divided by old number N-O/O. If the percentage of speeders went from 12 (old number) to 15 (new number), then the change would be 12-15/12= 3/12= .25 or 25% decrease in speeders. If, however the percentage of speeders went from 16 to 8, then it would be -8/16 = -.50. or a 50% decrease in speeders.

Beware Percentage Gains and Losses: From What to What?
Whenever you read a report on percentage changes, be on the alert for some statistical creativity. Percentage changes can be very misleading if you're not given the numbers that answer the question **"from what to what?"** It would be like going into a store and being told an item was reduced by 50%, without telling you the original price. You'd want to know "50% less than what?" Saying that a new drug reduces the risk of some disease by 50% does not actually tell you much. For example, suppose a new drug therapy has been introduced that alleges to reduce the risk of heart problems. Let's say the new drug reduces the risk of a fatal heart attack by a whopping 50%. Now that's eye catching, but delving into the numbers you find that 1.5 % of pa-

tients on the placebo had fatal heart attacks whereas only 1% of patients on the new drug had a fatal heart attack. Now although going from 1.5% to 1% is indeed a 50% reduction, it hasn't changed the lives of many people. Anytime you read about some treatment reducing risk, look at the original numbers. As shown, a risk reduction from 1.5% to 1% is a 50% reduction, as is a reduction of from 60% to 40%. But in fact a reduction from 60% to 40% would save a lot more lives than the change from 1.5% to 1%.

Variables

A variable is anything that varies and can be measured, such as height, weight, crime rate, or number of felony arrests. If it doesn't vary it's called a constant, such as the number of inches in a foot or the number of pints in a quart. There are two types of variables that are of great concern to the researcher, and they are called the independent variable (IV) and the dependent variable (DV). In any directional relationship, the independent variable is antecedent (comes first) and the dependent variable is consequent (comes second). For example, if we were using height to predict weight, height would be the independent variable and weight would be the dependent variable. Or if we wished to determine if men and women differ with regard to IQ, gender would be the independent variable and intelligence the dependent variable. Or if it were suggested that a strong police presence in a community reduces the crime rate, the IV would be the strength of the police presence and the DV would be the crime rate.

Independent Variables: Two Types

In scientific research there are two types of independent variables, those that are under full experimental control, called Active IVs and those traits or characteristics that the subjects of the study already possess, called Subject IVs. Let's examine the difference, and when it comes to the conclusions, the difference is crucial. An Active IV is under the full control of the researcher and is based on the fact that the subjects in the study have been treated differently by the experimenter, not just by the vagaries of life. Suppose a large group of convicted, male drug felons are randomly divided into two groups. Assume that the researcher then provides intensive counseling therapy to one of the groups but leaves the other group untreated. The IV in this situation is whether the subjects did or did not receive the counseling treatment. Then let's say one year after release, both groups are compared with regard to rates of recidivism, which in this case is the DV. In this situation, it is the researcher, not the felon, who decides who is to be involved in the treatment program. Thus, this would be an Active IV. Compare this with a situation where the researcher selects a group of felons and asks each one if he has ever on his own sought counseling. Then, again, one year after release the researcher compares the recidivism rates between those who had previously reported having been in counseling with those who had reported no counseling. In this latter scenario, it was the felon who chose whether to have counseling, not the researcher. Thus, this is called a Subject IV because it's not under active experimental control.

Two Basic Types of Research

The two types of research are Experimental and Post Facto and these are determined on the basis of the type of independent variable that was involved, Active or Subject. If the independent variable is under active experimental control, then the research is considered to be experimental. In the study mentioned above (the situation in which the researcher decided which group was to receive counseling), we have an example of experimental research, whereas the situation where the felons reported whether they had on their own chosen counseling is an example of post-facto research. Try this one. Assume that a pharmaceutical company ran a study to determine if some newly discovered drug could act as a cure for heroin addiction. In this case the independent variable would be the drug (antecedent) and the later level of addiction would be the dependent variable (consequent). To test this, the researcher selects two groups (samples), and then presents all the members of one group with a given dosage of the drug, whereas the members of the second group are each given a placebo (a non-active identical-appearing pill). Whether the group received the drug or the placebo would define the independent variable. Then perhaps six weeks later all the subjects were checked for continued addiction. Take a moment to think it through. Was this an Active IV (an example of experimental research), or was it a Subject IV (an example of post-facto research)? You were right on if you said an Active IV. Notice it was under full experiential control, that is the experimenter, not the subjects, determined who was going to get which version of the pill. The dependent variable would be based on whether the addiction had continued addiction six weeks later. In experimental research in the behavioral sciences, the independent variable is some form of a stimulus, an environmental input or change, whereas the dependent variable is a measure of the subject's response. Knowing the difference between these two types of research, experimental and post-facto, is of extreme importance to the researcher or research consumer, because only results from the experimental method may be used to form a cause-and-effect conclusion. The post-facto method doesn't address the issue of causality. It doesn't affirm it or rule it out. Only the experimental method, called the "gold standard" by researchers, should be used to suggest causation.

Time Out to Think

Case One. You and a friend are both randomly selected (along with over 100 others) to take part in a study conducted by the federally sponsored NAAC (National Alcohol Awareness Commission). First, everyone in the group must drink a ten-ounce glass of Vodka within a period of 30 minutes. Then, by luck of the draw, you find yourself randomly assigned to the experimental group and your friend to the control group. You are given a newly created miracle drug (made up largely of a heavy dose of caffeine) called the SSU (Super-Sober-Upper), while your friend in the control group is given a non-active placebo. Both groups are then timed to see when all hangover symptoms disappear.

Question: Is this experimental or post-facto research? This is a true experiment, because the subjects were randomly assigned to either the experimental or control group. The IV, the stimulus (whether receiving the SSU or the placebo) was under full experimental control, and the DV (the response variable) was measured on the basis of the time it took to be fully sobered up. Notice again, that the independent variable was controlled by the experimenter, whereas the dependent variable was the response time of the subjects. In this type of research a causal factor may be assumed. That is, if the group taking the new pill sobered up more quickly, then the researcher could affirm that the pill was the causal factor.

Case Two. Suppose a researcher asked a large group of freshmen which of them had coffee this morning, and then separated them on that basis, assigning coffee drinkers to one group and non-coffee drinkers in the other. The researcher then gives everybody the same amount of Vodka and later examines them to see which group sobered up first.

Question: Is this experimental or post-facto research? This is post-facto research. The students, not the researcher, decided on their own whether to have the coffee. The coffee in this example is still the independent variable, and the dependent variable is still length of time to sober up, but it is no longer clear that this is based on a causal relationship. The students who had decided to drink coffee this morning may differ from those who didn't in many ways, perhaps they are older or bigger or perhaps they got up earlier. With post-facto research a cause and effect relationship is no longer either provable or disprovable. A prediction is still possible, but not an etched-in-stone causal relationship

Probability

As we saw in Chapter 11, the term probability is used to explain the likelihood of an event or series of events occurring. It sums up the relationship between the observed, specific event and the total possible number of events. Using s for specific and t for total, probability can be defined as the number of specific events divided by the total number of events, or s/t. Since coins and dice are familiar to everybody, let's start there. With a fair coin, there are only two possible events, heads or tails. So for this examples $t = 2$. When the coin is flipped and you call "heads" that's the specific event, $s = 1$. The probability of the head turning up therefore is s/t or ½. As for the dice, each die (singular for dice) has six sides. So if you roll one die and call, say a five (which is on only one of the sides), the probability of being right is again s/t or in this case 1/6. Not to confuse matters, but with statisticians the fraction is always divided out, so 1/2 becomes .50 and 1/6 becomes .17. This definition of probability assumes that each of the specific events is equally likely. When you read about a probability (p value) of .05 or less, it means that the coincidence explanation has been limited to only 5 chances out of a hundred, or less. And when the p value is .01 or less, it's limiting the coincidence explanation to only one chance out of a hundred or less.

Percentages and Probabilities.
Percentages convert into a probability format by simply dividing the percentage of cases by 100 and then getting rid of the percentage sign. Thus, 25% becomes .25, and 5% becomes .05 and so on.

Combining Probabilities – Sums and Products
There are two methods for combining the probabilities for independent events. First, if you're trying to find the probability of one event OR another event, the separate probabilities are added (called the summation rule). For example if there were one hundred people in a room, half male and half female, the probability of randomly selecting a male would be .50, and the probability of selecting a female would also be .50. Thus, the probability of selecting a male OR a female would be .50+.50 = 1.00 (which is a certainty). Second, if the problem is to find the probability of one event AND another (as in combining DNA probabilities), then the separate probabilities are multiplied (called the product rule). Let's go back to the room of a hundred persons. If you had to select two persons at random and in succession, one male AND one female, then the combined probability would be .50 X .50 = .25. If you're having trouble with any of these probability combinations, relax. You're not alone. Just take a short time-out to think through the logic of these combinations. One event AND another sounds intuitively very much like (probably too much like) a problem in addition, as in how much is two AND two? The key to unlocking this puzzle is to try to remember that the combination of "one event OR another event" increases the probability, through addition, as in .50 + .50 = 1.00, whereas "one event AND another event" decreases the probability through multiplication, as in .50 and .50 = .25. We previously discussed probabilities and their combinations as they related to DNA. The major message in that discussion was that as each DNA match was combined the probability of a false match was reduced. Forensic scientists examine 13 different DNA markers, all of which are independent of each other, and when all the separate probabilities are combined through multiplication, the probability of a false match becomes very close to zero. Many crime-scene investigators seem to know the product rule instinc-

RESEARCH METHODS IN CRIMINAL JUSTICE

tively. They say that a given piece of evidence taken alone often means nothing, but when put together with other evidence, it narrows down the suspect list significantly.

Probabilities and Insurance

To make the case as blatant as possible, check out the following, though certainly apocryphal, story. A young couple had just purchased their first home, and had immediately and prudently bought a fire-and- theft insurance policy. About a month after they moved in, their home was broken into and money and personal belongings were stolen. To make the situation worse, the burglar trashed the house and threw broken glass and gasoline all over each room. He then lit the gasoline and hurried out of the house. When the young couple called their insurance company, they were told to their dismay that they weren't covered. Unfortunately their policy was a fire AND theft policy not a fire OR theft policy. Thus, they were only covered if the house had burned down while the burglar was inside - a far less frequent combination of events.

Joe the Accountant

Joe was a business major in college, quiet, introverted, intelligent and rather conservative politically. However, he did have something of a wild side. He loved to party, and he liked to drink. During one of his sprees, campus security caught him repeatedly driving his car across the football field and leaving huge ruts in his wake. For that infraction, Joe's license was suspended and he had to leave school for one full semester. Several years later he did return to college and graduated. Which of the following has a higher probability? Joe is now working as an accountant OR Joe is now working as an accountant and his continued drinking problem has cost him several jobs over the years.

The answer is that the former rather than the later, is more probable, since a single event is always more probable than the combination of one event AND another. Notice that the second option is saying that Joe is an accountant AND that Joe still drinks AND that his drinking has interfered with his career. It's like asking, which is more probable – rolling a six with one die or getting three sixes in a row on three consecutive rolls? If you can't answer that one, don't go near a casino. In fact don't go near a casino anyway, regardless of whether you answered the dice question correctly. You have to lose in the long run.

The "Law" of Averages: A Word of Warning

As you know, the probability of you being correct when flipping a coin is .50, or a frequency of 50 percent. With a fair coin each flip is totally independent of every other coin flip. So don't think that after a long series of losses that the law of averages will come to your rescue. You remember your long string of losses, but the coin doesn't remember. Successive coin flips are totally independent of each other. They cannot influence or be influenced by one another. Gamblers often convince themselves that after a long series of losses their next bet has to be a sure thing. This is called "The Gambler's Fallacy." While it is true that if an unbiased coin is flipped an infinite number of times, heads will turn up 50% of the time, it doesn't change the probability for any single coin flip. The so-called law of averages is really a description of what generally may happen in the very long run, not enforcers of what must happen in the short run. The theory of probability is a mathematical expectation of what can happen in an infinite run, not a law that states that certain things are inevitable. And don't ever be fooled into thinking that after you were lucky enough to win a few dollars at the casino that you are now playing with "their money." Once you win, it's no longer their money. It's your money. And for any of you who may think you have a system for beating the odds, the casinos have only one word – "welcome." Remember the story of the guy who drove to the casino in a $70,000 Mercedes and came home in a $200,000 bus.

PERSON OF INTEREST: SIR FRANCIS GALTON (1822-1911)

Galton is considered to be the person most responsible for developing the basic ideas for the methods for quantifying the data of today's behavioral sciences. He was born into a wealthy and highly educated English family, and among his relatives were many of England's most influential citizens, including his cousin, Charles Darwin, founder of the modern theory of evolution. In 1869 he published his first major work, "Hereditary Genius" in which he stressed the enormous importance of heredity in determining various human traits, including intelligence. It was Galton, perhaps the world's first forensic psychologist, who introduced the world to fingerprinting, and many of his methods are still used today by law enforcement agencies. Galton's emphasis on the relationship between sensory inputs and intellectual growth foreshadows much of today's research on the importance of sensory stimulation during a child's early years in encouraging cognitive growth. Galton also made major contributions to statistical analysis with his creation of what he called "the index of correlation." It was left to one of his younger colleagues, Karl Pearson, to work out the mathematical equation for this index, known now as the Pearson r. To gain an understanding of the importance of the interaction between heredity and environment, Galton performed psychology's first research on the studies of MZ (identical) and DZ (fraternal) twins. In 1909, just two years before his death, Galton was knighted. Galton's place in the history of psychology and statistics is ensured because of the importance of his work in setting the behavioral sciences on the road to data quantification and statistical analysis

Populations and Samples
The Population

The researcher always needs one or more groups of subjects for any research project. The method used to obtain the subjects and assign them to groups influences the kinds of conclusions that can be made when the testing is completed. The groups of test subjects must be drawn in some fashion from a larger group, with the goal of obtaining groups of subjects who are representative of the larger group, or, at the very least, groups that are equivalent to one another. If the groups of subjects are truly equivalent at the beginning of the study, then any possible difference between these groups at the end are likely to be due to the active manipulation of the IV. The term population refers to the entire group of persons, things or events that share at least one common trait. If you wish to identify the population of, say, college students, the factor of being a college student would be the shared trait. If you wanted to add another trait, you could limit the population to U.S, college students, or by adding a third trait, U.S. college students majoring in criminal justice. Obviously the more traits being added, the more the population becomes limited, and as the population becomes increasingly limited so too does the group to which your findings can be extrapolated. Since we're interested in generalizing our sample results in order to apply them to the population at large, it is important that we know as much as possible about the population from which the samples are drawn.

The Sample

A sample is a smaller number of subjects or observations taken from the total number making up the given population. Thus, the sample is a subset of the population. That is , if the entire population of first-year college students in the United States were to add up to, say, one million, selecting any number of students from that population would constitute a sample, that is any number from 1 to 999,999. Obviously the larger the sample, other things being equal, the more accurately the sample will reflect the characteristics of the population. A sample of only one person has far less chance of being an accurate representation than a sample of 999,999. However, although a sample of one person may yield a highly distorted picture of the population, the sample 999,999 is so unwieldy as to be very impractical. In fact, if you have a sample of this magnitude, why not make the effort to find that last millionth person and thus have the entire population and nothing left to predict?

How is the Sample Selected?

The surest way to get a representative sample is by using the technique called random sampling, that is selecting in such a way as to ensure that every single member of the population has an equal chance of being included in the sample. Thus, if you needed to get a random sample of the student body at your college, you can't simply select from those who are free enough in the

afternoon to meet you at the behavioral laboratory at 3PM. This would exclude all those students who work in the afternoon or who have their own
classes or labs to meet, or who are on athletic teams. Nor can you create a
random sample by selecting every tenth person entering the cafeteria at noon
time. Again, some students eat off campus, or have classes during the noon
hour, or have cut classes that day to provide themselves with an instant mini
vacation – the reasons are endless. The point is that if any students were
systematically excluded the sample is not random.

Significance

The next thing to get acquainted with is the concept of statistical significance.
When reading a research article, this may be the most important concept you
will need to understand. The studies that are out there waiting for you are all
constantly talking about whether the results are significant. In statistics the
word significant does not mean profound or deeply meaningful. It only
means that the researcher has concluded that the results being reported are
probably not due to chance. That is, significant results strongly suggest that
the results are not just a matter of mere coincidence. Further, since virtually
all the studies in our literature are based on sample measures, once the results
are considered to be significant they can legitimately be extrapolated to the
population from which the sample was selected. For example, if it were
found that among a sampling of shoplifters in a series of large discount stores
it was observed that a significant number were wearing rain coats on sunny
days, then it may be inferred that this result would hold true for the population of shoplifters at all similar discount stores. The point is that significance
is a statistical term that suggests that the results of the study are probably not
just a matter of chance. You will also find that significance is always presented in the context of probability, and the only two possible conclusions are
either that the results are probably not due to chance (i.e., significant) or the
results are probably just a matter of chance (i.e., not significant). If you want
to sound super-stat sophisticated, use the term "null hypothesis" in place of
chance and say it with a self-aggrandizing sneer. Thus if chance does not
explain the results, you could haughtily say that you "rejected the null hypothesis." Also, if chance is the likely explanation, you could rub it in by
saying that you "failed to reject the null hypothesis." Most of the time the
researcher is hoping to have significant, non-chance results. Significance
testing has even been taken up by the Supreme Court in the case of *Matrixx
Initiatives v. Siricusano* (2011). The case involved the claim that ZICAM, a zinc-
derived pharmaceutical product that is supposed to shorten the length of
colds, produced a side-effect called "anosmia," or the sensory loss of smell.
One physician had reported that a "cluster" (was it seven or seven thousand?)
of patients had lost the sense of smell while on Zicam. Another researcher
found a total of eleven patients so afflicted. In any case the results were not
statistically significant. And even if they were, the Zicam and anosmia were

not proven to be causally linked. Could it be that the cold itself might some-how be involved in the nasal passage blockage that then causes the smell disorder, with or without ZICAM? The researcher who sadly concludes that the results of the study were just a matter of coincidence (fails to reject null) is not likely to do a victory dance or get in line for a Nobel Prize.

Levels of Significance

A result is deemed significant if it can be assumed to have occurred at a probability level of .05 or less (a probability of .05 or less indicates a frequency of 5% or less). At that level, .05, the researcher can be 95% certain that chance can be ruled out. You will discover that some studies result in a probability value of .01 or even .001, but never a flat-out zero. The probability level and the confidence level are inversely related, such that the lower the probability the higher the confidence. That is, the lower the probability value the greater the confidence that coincidence is not the culprit. Going from a probability of .05 to a probability level of .01, lowers the probability but increases the confidence level from 95% up to 99%. Researchers set the probability level by using what they label as the p value. "It is safe to say that a p value provides assurance, not certainty – it tells us whether the result is a real effect, or just a random occurrence" (Bakalar, 2013). For example, a study might conclude that the significance level had a p value of .027 (which of course is less than .05) and leads to a decision to rule out chance as the explanation (reject the null hypothesis). If on the other hand the p value had been .45, or .25, or even .06, then the decision would have to indicate a failure to rule out chance (a failure to reject the null hypothesis). The probability level needed for significance has long been established at .05 or less. If this sounds like nit-picking then maybe it is, but at least you won't wind up hip-high in nits. Notice again that the probability level can never be zero, since there is always a chance, slight as it might be, that the decision to reject chance is wrong. That is, the decision is always based on chance expectations, not speculation. As has been said so often, it is better to have proof without certainty than certainty without proof.

Testing Hypotheses- Hypotheses of Difference and Association

The Hypothesis of Difference

When testing the hypothesis of difference, the researcher tries to find out if the groups being tested differ on the dependent variable(s). For example is there a difference in rates of recidivism between men and women? Or, is there a difference in the rates of violent felonies between crack-cocaine users and powder-cocaine users? The hypothesis of difference can be tested in either experimental or post-facto research. For example, the post-facto study mentioned above (on gender and recidivism) was designed to discover if there is a difference in rates of recidivism based on a person's gender. In this case gender, the independent variable, is clearly a subject variable, a characteristic inherent to the subject. The possible differences in rates of recidivism (the dependent variable) would then be statistically tested for possible significance. Or as an example of the experimental method a researcher may suspect that the drug Ritalin may reduce the rates of juvenile delinquency among hyperactive, male adolescents. In this instance, two groups of hyperactive adolescent males would be selected and then randomly assigned to either the experimental group (where daily doses of Ritalin would be administered) or the control group (where an identical-appearing, but non-active placebo would be substituted). Whether the subjects received Ritalin or the placebo would define the independent variable and since this was determined by the experimenter, this is an active independent variable. The responses, which in this case would be counted as the possible differences in delinquency rates, would define the dependent variable. A statistical test would then be used to determine if these dependent variable differences were significant, (i.e., not due to chance).

The Hypothesis of Association

The hypothesis of association is aimed at determining if variables co-vary. Do the variables occur together, that is "do they correlate?" For example, do scores on a test of conduct disorder correlate with the number of arrests? That is, do high scores on the test associate with a higher number of arrests, and do low scores on the test associate with fewer arrests. Thus, the hypothesis of association uses the method of correlation to determine the possibility of a significant relationship. When testing the hypothesis of association, the research method is always post-facto.

The Four Major Statistical Tests

Although there are seemingly countless statistical tests out there in research land, the four basic tests (and there are many variations on these) are t, F, r, and chi square.

The t test (Tea for Two ♫)

This test, often called "Student's t test," is used to compare two groups on some measured variable. Try to remember the old song "tea for two," and if you can hum it you've got it made. When you see the results of a t test, you will know that two groups have been compared and the hypothesis of difference has been tested. When you look at the probability level, you can determine if the results are significant. As shown above, if the accompanying probability level is given as $p \leq .05$, meaning that the probability is .05 (five chances out of a hundred) or less, then the results are significant and the null hypothesis has been rejected. However, if you read the probability as $p > .05$, then the researcher failed to reject the null hypothesis and the study probably will languish in the file drawers in the researcher's back office. For example, a study attempts to find out if there is a significant difference between scores of men and women on a test measuring hostility (H). The average H scores from each group (the means) are then compared via the t test, and if the p value is shown to be .05 or less, displayed as p ≤.05, then the null hypothesis would be rejected and the difference between the groups considered to be significant. Had the p value been greater than .05 (p > .05) the researcher would have failed to reject the null hypothesis and no significant difference could be claimed.

Example: (To t or not to t – that is the question)

A forensic researcher suggests that phallometry (the measurement of penis erection) can distinguish between a group of male child molesters and a group of men who have not committed sexual offenses against children. Though controversial, the device used, called a penile plethysmograph, seems to be here to stay (Albernaz, 2005). A large group of male inmates from a medium –security state facility, all about the same age, were selected and placed in two groups. Group 1 represented 120 men who had all been incarcerated for molestation of male children and Group 2 by 120 men incarcerated for auto theft and with no previous pedophile issues. Both groups viewed pictures of young boys in various stages of dress, and measures were recorded on the basis of increases in penile circumference (in millimeters). Group1 had an average measure 2.51 millimeters and Group 2 averaged 1.63 millimeters. There will then be a line in the article in the "results" section that says: $t_{(238)} = 4.974$ p<.001. Thus, the t ratio was 4.974 and had a significance probability of less than .001. For any of you math fans, the subscript value next to t, in this case (238), is a number that is based on the size of the two samples, the larger that number the larger the sample size. That particular number, 238, is technically called the "degrees of freedom" and equals the number of persons in group 1 plus the number in group 2, minus the constant 2 (which is the number of groups.)

Question: Was there a significant difference in the group scores?

Solution: Since the probability value of .001 was clearly below the critical value of .05, the difference in measures between the two groups was significant, with the child molesters scoring significantly higher. Because the independent variable was not under the experimenter's control, this is clearly post-facto research. The independent variable in this case was a subject variable, since the men were assigned to the groups on the basis of their past records.

The F ratio or ANOVA (which stands for Analysis Of Variance)

Just as the t test shown above is used to assess possible differences between two groups, the F ratio tests for differences among 3 or more groups. This means that with the F ratio, the researcher can set the independent variable at more than just two levels. Remember, it is "t for two" but " F for more."

For example, if a new drug is being tested, the t test could only assess the difference between the two groups, the group taking the drug and the group on the placebo. Thus the drug itself would have been tested at only one dosage level. However, with the F ratio, the drug could be administered at varying levels, allowing the researcher to hopefully obtain the optimal levels. Again, the p value would determine whether the null hypothesis could be rejected (.05 or less), or if there were a failure to reject (.05 or greater).

Example:
A pharmaceutical researcher wanted to test the effects of a new drug on a person's level of impulsivity. Three groups of men, all of roughly the same age and size, were randomly selected from a large group of incarcerated male inmates, all of whom had been convicted of crimes of violence. The drug, thought to impact part of the brain's limbic system, was administered as follows: Group 1 received a low-dose level, Group 2 a high-dose level, and Group 3 was given a zero dose level (a non-active placebo). After the drug treatments were completed, each man was measured on the "Levels of Impulsivity Test," and the group means were 4.83 for Group 1, 7.98 for Group 2, and 8.81 for Group 3. The higher the scores, the more impulsive the man is, and the lower the scores the less impulsive. And now in the "Results" section of the article you will see a line like the following: $F_{(2,106)} = 12.672$ p< .001 Thus, an F ratio of 12.672 was computed on the mean differences, and it was shown to have a probability value of .003. The degrees of freedom (the subscript numbers next to the F) are based on both the number of groups and the sample size.

Question: Did the drug produce significantly lower Impulsivity scores?

Solution: Since the F ratio had a probability value of less than .05, the differences were clearly significant and the null hypothesis (chance) was rejected. Also notice that this is an example of experimental research, since the independent variable (the drug level) was all under the experimenter's control. The drug was interpreted as having caused the lowered impulsivity levels.

The Pearson r
Unlike the tests shown above the Pearson r does not attempt to find differences, but instead tries to detect the possible correlation between two sets of measurements. The r can tell us if two measured variables systematically co-vary.

Correlation: The Three Types

There are three possible outcomes when doing correlational research, positive, negative and zero.

The Positive Correlation: This occurs when high scores on one variable link up with high scores on a second variable and low scores on the first link with low scores on the second. The correlation mentioned above between height and weight is an example of a positive correlation – high scores with high scores and low scores with low scores.

The Negative Correlation: A negative association occurs when high scores on the first variable link with low scores on the second and low scores on the first line up with high scores on the second - highs with lows and lows with highs. An example of a negative correlation would be the relationship between age and felony arrests – older people (high in age) tend to have fewer felony arrests and younger people (low in age) tend to have more. The word negative in this sense does not mean faulty, erroneous or bad. It simply means that the relationship is inverse.

The Zero Correlation: The correlation is said to be zero when there is no systematic linkage between the two variables. The high scores on the first variable are just as likely to line up with highs on the second variable as with lows on the second variable. Thus, the zero correlation defines a lack of any systematic relationship between the variables.

Uniform Crime Reports

We will now turn to a data file in order to illustrate each of the correlation types. The following data was sourced from the F.B.I.'s Uniform Crime Report (2012). The data provided by the F.B.I. are per-capita values (i.e., the number of events out of a fixed population of 100,000). The final column, titled "Unemployment" was taken from the Bureau of Labor Statistics (2011) and is given as a percentage of the total.

A YR*	B TC	C IN	D VO	E PO	F UN
1989	5741	276	663	5078	5.3
1990	5820	297	732	5089	5.6
1991	5898	313	758	5140	6.8
1992	5660	332	758	4903	7.5
1993	5484	359	747	4738	6.9
1994	5374	389	714	4660	6.1
1995	5275	411	685	4591	5.6
1996	5088	427	637	4451	5.4
1997	4927	444	611	4316	4.9
1998	4616	461	566	4049	4.5
1999	4267	476	523	3744	4.2
2000	4125	478	507	3618	4.1
2001	4163	470	505	3658	4.7
2002	4125	476	494	3631	5.8
2003	4067	482	476	3591	6.1
2004	3977	486	463	3514	5.5
2005	3901	491	469	3432	5.1
2006	3808	501	474	3335	4.6
2007	3730	506	467	3264	4.6
2008	3669	504	458	3212	5.8
2009	3466	502	429	3036	9.3
2010	3346	526	404	2952	9.6

*Legend: YR=Year; TC=Total Crime; IN=Incarceration; VO=Violent Offense; PO=Property Offense; UN=Unemployment

A Positive Correlation

First we will run a correlation between Violent Crime and Property Crime (columns D and E) two seemingly unrelated categories: $r_{(20)} = .972$ $p < .001$ The Pearson r calculates out to a value of +.972, which has a significance probability of <.001. The subscript value next to r (in parentheses) is calculated as the number of pairs of scores minus the constant 2. Thus from the years 1989 to 2010 (a time span of 22 years) there is a significant positive correlation between violent crime and property crime. That is, the more violent crime there is the more the property crime there is and the less the violent crime the less the property crime. Remember correlation doesn't address causation, meaning we cannot conclude that violent crime causes property crime (nor can we rule it out). If you are familiar with Excel, you can prove this correlation yourself, by typing in the two columns of scores, Violent Crime and Property Crime, onto a work-sheet, clicking on Formula, and then Insert Function. You will then be prompted to select a category, and you should then scroll down until you find Statistical and hit OK. Click on Pearson and OK. For the Array 1 row enter D2.D23 and for the Array 2 row, enter E2.E23. Click the Output Range as D25, and your output screen will yield the above shown correlation of .972.

A Negative Correlation
Next, a correlation will be computed between the Incarceration number (column C) and the Total Crime number, column B (Total Crime includes all the index categories taken together) : $r_{(20)} = -.951$, $p<.001$ Therefore, the Pearson r is $-.951$, and is significant at a probability of $<.001$. The higher the incarceration levels the lower the crime rate, and the lower the incarcerations the higher the crime rate. Does this prove that keeping more people locked up reduces the number of crimes? Again,"no." The correlation itself doesn't prove cause-and-effect, but as said above, neither does it rule it out.

Another Correlation Caution
Another thing to be careful about when dealing with correlation is to be sure the two sets of scores are not mixed together. The scores must be truly independent. For example, using the above data, if we were to run a correlation between property crime and total crime it would compute out as: $r_{(20)} = .999$, $p< .001$. Thus, we would come up with a significant correlation of $+.999$ (which is virtually a 100% association). But here there is just one problem, the two variables are not separate measures, since property crimes are a large component of total crimes.

A Zero Correlation and Prediction
Finally, a correlation will be calculated between Total Crime and Unemployment for that same 22-year time period: $r_{(20)} = -.060$. $p> .05$
Thus, the resulting Pearson r computes to -.060, which is virtually zero and is ns, not significant. Therefore there is essentially a zero correlation between Total Crime and Unemployment during the time period from 1989 to 2010. Thus, for that period of time there is no dependable relationship between the total crime rate and the unemployment.

Prediction: The Goal of Correlational Research
The goal of the Pearson r is not just to establish the correlation but also to indicate if the researcher can predict the scores on a second variable having been given scores on the first. This becomes possible only if the correlation is significant. For example, assume that a researcher reports a correlation of

+.85 between IQ and grade-point average. Let's next assume that the p value is shown to be .03 (which of course is a winning probability because it is less than the magic number of .05). Thus the correlation has been proven to be significant which means that the null hypothesis can be duly rejected. Because the correlation is significant, the researcher can now make better-than-chance predictions by using scores on the first variable to estimate scores on the second. Also, since the correlation was shown to be positive, +.85, the researcher would predict higher GPAs for those with higher IQs and lower GPAs for those with lower IQs. And if the correlation were negative, as is the case with incarceration rates and crime rates, the researcher would predict that the higher the incarceration rate, the lower the crime rate

Correlation: A Final Example

As a "final" example, assume that a researcher is studying the relationship between test anxiety and grades on a Criminal Justice final exam. Assume further that the correlation turns out to be -.80 with a p value of .01. That is, the negative correlation is telling us that students who have high scores on anxiety will have lower scores on the final, and those with low scores on anxiety will have higher scores on the final. Thus, regardless of whether the correlation is positive or negative, if it is significant then better-than-chance predictions can be generated. When using correlation for prediction, researchers assign the variable being predicted as the dependent variable, and the variable being predicted from as the independent variable. Thus, in the previous example, the test anxiety would be considered as the independent variable and the final exam results as the dependent variable. A significant correlation will always produce a reliable prediction. The prediction might not be perfect, but it will certainly beat flipping a coin. For the Pearson r, as with any correlational technique the research method must be post facto.

PERSON OF INTEREST: KARL PEARSON (1857-1936)

Karl Pearson's creations in the field of data analysis are actually too numerous to cover completely in a short biography. However, among his major contributions are the following: the product-moment correlation (now called the Pearson r), the chi-square, the normal curve (previously called the error curve, the multiple correlation, the partial correlation, and the bi-serial correlation). In 1875 he was accepted, on full academic scholarship, at Cambridge University and received his bachelor's degree in mathematics in 1879. His college years were not without controversy, however. Although deeply religious, Pearson got into trouble because of his refusal to attend compulsory chapel. Although this created a major campus stir, the dean finally backed down and the university bent the rule in order to accommodate Pearson's demands. After graduation from Cambridge, he went on to law school and passed the bar in 1881. In 1884 he was appointed to the faculty at the University of London. He was both professor and chair of the graduate department of applied mathematics. In 1889 he befriended and came under the influence of the eminent scholar and researcher, Sir Francis Galton. Pearson was able to develop equations for quantifying Galton's twin concepts of correlation and regression. Later while using his own correlation tool, he discovered a strong correlation between alcoholism and various disturbances, including criminality. He then argued that alcoholism was the result of these disturbances, not the cause (a rather curious conclusion, since it was based on correlation). He spent his last years fighting for what were then considered radical causes, such as the liberation of women and the pursuit of free thought and free speech.

The Chi Square

Finally the chi-square allows for a comparison between non-continuous measures and is based on something called nominal (or sometimes called categorical) data. Nominal data are nose-counting data. We simply count the number of persons who do or do not exhibit the trait in question. Thus, with chi square we are dealing with frequencies within independent categories. With nominal data there are no shades of gray. The trait in question is either observed as occurring or not occurring. In short, nominal data are generated by sorting and counting – sorting the data into discrete, mutually exclusive categories and then counting the frequency of occurrence within each category. For example, a sample of admitted cocaine users (all males) was selected from the county jail. Each subject indicated his choice of cocaine types, crack or powdered. The inmates were then categorized as to whether they had ever been arrested for aggravated assault. The data follow:

	Aggravated Assault	
	Yes	No
Crack Users	120	50
Powder Users	40	130

The chi square test would then tell us if this difference is statistically significant. Thus, the chi square value would result in a p value, and if the p value were .05 or less, the result would indicate a significant difference. In the case of the above data, the computation is as follows: $\chi^2 = 75.556, p < .001$ Since chi square computed to 75.556 and returned a p value of .001 or less, the result would be considered to be statistically significant. Crack users were found to be significantly more likely than powder users to commit aggravated assault. With a slight adjustment, Chi Square can also be converted into something called the Coefficient of Contingency (C) that can be used to assess correlation when the data are nominal. Chi Square has very few restrictions and is therefore an extremely versatile test of significance. Researchers know that when all else fails, there's always Chi Square.

Post Facto Research and The Cause-and-Effect Trap

An important issue in post facto research is the problem of mistakenly assigning causal factors to relationships that are only linked by association. This is especially true in the area of correlational research. Suppose a researcher is interested in finding out whether parental rejection might cause juvenile delinquency among teen-age boys. Furthermore, the researcher has developed an accurate method for assessing perceived parental rejection. That is, the researcher has a tool for determining a given adolescent's perception of his parents' rejection-or-acceptance attitudes. After gathering the data, the researcher checks police records and finds that a strong, positive correlation does indeed exist. The more a boy perceives himself as the victim of parental rejection, the more frequent have been his confrontations with our friends in blue uniforms. But has a cause-and-effect relationship been established? The best way to look at this is to use symbols. Let's use A to symbolize parental rejection and B to designate juvenile delinquency (using letter symbols when analyzing correlation studies is always a good idea, since such symbols do not carry any literary overtones that are often inherent in the word descriptions of the variables). Three possible causal explanations could be used to account for these findings:

1. A→B. It is possible, though not proven by this study, that A (parental rejection) does cause B (juvenile delinquency).

2. B→A. It is also possible that B (juvenile delinquency) causes A (parental rejection). A parent may not always project warm feeling of affection toward a son who is brought home night after night in a patrol car.

3. X→A+B . Finally, it is possible that X (some unknown variable) is the real cause of both A and B. For instance, X could be an atmosphere of frustration and despair that permeates a given neighborhood, leading both parents and children to generate feelings of hostility toward each other and toward society in general.

All three of these explanations are possible, but because the analysis is correlational, it is impossible to establish the direction of the relationship. Without knowing the direction of the relationship, any causation hypothesis remains only at the guess stage. An example of a one-directional relationship would be that although flicking the on-off switch to the on position turns on the light bulb (let there be light), if the bulb were to go out it wouldn't move the light switch. As another example, marriage researchers have found that persons who find their partners attractive have happier sex lives. This does not guarantee that personal attractiveness increases sexual pleasure, for it is just as likely that persons with more fulfilling sex lives tend to perceive their partners as more attractive. Perhaps beauty is in the eye of the beholder. Or perhaps a third variable, say an optimistic view of life in general, causes people to both find their partners more attractive and report having happier sex lives. Let's take a moment to map it out, calling A the perceived attractiveness of the partner, and B a happy and fulfilling sex life, and X will be the optimistic view of life.

1. A→B. It is possible, though not proven by this study, that A (perceived attractiveness) does cause B (happy sex life).

2. B→A. It is also possible that B (happy sex life) causes A (perceived attractiveness).

3. X→A+B. Finally, it is possible that X (an optimistic approach to life) is the cause of both A and B.

The Cause and Effect Ambush

As stated above, the potential for the cause and effect ambush is not just a function of correlational research. It also lurks in waiting any time post facto research is the method of choice, even when testing for differences. The Food and Drug Administration (FDA) did a study comparing suicide rates between teenagers who took anti-depressant medication versus those who did not. Some have interpreted this as a cause-and-effect relationship, and are discouraging the use of anti- depressants among teens (New York Times, 2004). However, this was not based on the experimental method. The researchers did not actively control the independent variable, did not choose which teens should take the anti-depressants. Therefore there is in this case the strong possibility of a mediating variable, that is the depression itself. Perhaps it's the depression that caused both the reason for seeking medical relief as well as for producing a suicidal urge. The bottom line is that just because two things occur together doesn't mean that one necessarily causes the other. Thus, the rooster shouldn't take credit for the dawn, and we shouldn't blame flies for the garbage.

Partial Correlation: Pointing the Finger of Suspicion

One very powerful method in the researcher's tool kit, especially in post-facto criminal justice research, is something called a partial correlation. As is so often the case with correlational research, a two variable correlation may be influenced by other variables making it difficult to untangle the true nature of the relationship. The point is that the correlation between two variables may often be significantly influenced by at least one other important variable, possibly an unknown variable, which we've been calling the X variable. To solve this problem a method has been devised that allows the researcher to rule out the influence of the third variable (or even fourth or fifth) on the remaining two variables in the study. It involves a statistical method for creating equivalent groups of subjects after the fact. For example, suppose we found a correlation between number of years of education and number of arrests, a correlation (negative) that seemed to show that the more years of education the fewer the number of arrests. However, it was then realized that total number of arrests may also be related to age, since older persons have a longer time frame in which to be arrested. The solution was to put all three variables, years of education, number of arrests, and age into a partial correlation and partial out the age variable. That is, we could make all the subjects statistically the same age and then determine if the correlation still exists. Also, since there is a possibility that persons with higher IQs might be less susceptible to arrest, we could run a second-order partial correlation, and partial out the influence of IQ. The subjects could then be statistically the same age and of equal intelligence. This is an especially important tool for the criminal justice researcher, because designing and carrying out the true experiment often presents many real-world difficulties.

For example, there could be legal challenges to a research study in which the experimenter had full control of an independent variable, such as determining if the combination of IQ and whether the felon had been sentenced to prison or probation had any significant effect on recidivism. If the research demanded that there be random assignment of felons to either prison or probation, it might prove to be legally impossible for a judge to allow it to be carried out. One answer to this dilemma would be to use the partial correlation, and then after the fact, partial out the prison-probation variable. Of course this would not be the same as full experimental control, but at least it would be a statistical control that might point a strong finger of causal suspicion.

Survival Analysis

Finally, an extremely important tool for the criminal justice researcher is something called "survival analysis." In fact this is probably the most powerful statistical technique for anyone working in the area of rehabilitation, which of course is important in corrections. Survival analysis is based on what is called "longitudinal" research, where subjects are measured across time periods, sometimes very long time periods. It is modeled on that branch of statistics that has traditionally dealt with medical and biological studies that were focused on the eventual death of the persons under study.

That is, the analyses concerned problems surrounding how long a given person would survive, given various conditions, such as type of medication, age, general health status and so on. Although it was once primarily used by the medical profession and insurance companies, the field has broadened considerably since its introduction and now covers everything from psychology (how long can a patient remain stable without returning to therapy), to criminal justice (how long can a released inmate remain free from reincarceration), to auto design (how long can an engine run before failure), to sociology (how long can a couple stay married before divorce) to economics (how long do auto workers stay employed under varied economic conditions). Thus, survival analysis examines the association between a given period of time and the event in question, and in many criminal justice studies the event is re-incarceration. This technique lends itself to the experimental method, since two groups, experimental and control (treated and non-treated) can be compared on correction's bottom-line of how long (days, months, years) does a treated vs. untreated inmate remain in the community before being re-incarcerated? It is society's hope that the treated inmates are never again incarcerated.

Theories and Quantitative Research

Hard data should always be used to provide the basics of good theorizing. In the area of criminal justice, Capone has suggested that theories are generated by deriving "empirically valid statements about individual, group, or mass behavior" (Capone, 1976). Also, Dillinger, in conceptualizing the psychopathic personality, has argued that its theoretical underpinnings can best be formulated by using item-response theory, as measured by the Psychopathy Checklist (Dillinger, 2008). And finally, both Bonney and Clyde have added important elements to theory building, Bonney (2007) in psychology and Clyde (2003) in geology.

Summary

This chapter focuses on both how research should be conducted and also how to prepare yourself to read the results of research studies that can often be misleading. The chapter begins with a definition of science and the scientific method, stressing that the two cannot be separated. Science is the knowledge and the method of obtaining that knowledge. The scientific method is anchored at both ends in observation. The steps are Observation, Induction, and Hypothesis Testing. The measures used by the scientist should be both reliable and valid – reliability referring to the consistency of the measures and validity referring to whether the measures conform to the realities of the underlying construct (both are key components of the Daubert rule on the admissibility of scientific data in the courtroom). Percentages and especially percentage changes are discussed with a special emphasis on percentage changes. You are warned that when percentage changes are presented you should always ask –from what to what? Variables and constants are then introduced, with the variable defined as anything that varies and can be measured, whereas the constant remains unchanged. The two most important variables for the researcher to consider are the independent variable (IV) and the dependent variable (DV), with the independent variable preceding the dependent variable. The two types of independent variables are the Active IV (under the experimenter's control) and the Subject IV (a trait or characteristic the subject already possesses, such as gender). The type of IV determines the type of research being conducted. The Active IV is under full experimental control, that is, the researcher not the subject determines what level of IV is assigned to the groups. The Subject IV is based solely on whether the subjects already possess a given trait. Whether they possess the trait determines which group they are assigned to. When the IV is under the researcher's control, the research is called Experimental, and when the IV is assigned on the basis of the subject's traits the research is called Post Facto. Legitimate cause-and-effect statements should only be applied to data confirmed by the experimental method (often called the "gold standard" of research). Probabilities and the combination of probabilities are discussed next, the summation rule for the probability of one event or another and the product rule for establishing the probability of one event and another. Populations are defined as the entire number of observations sharing at least one common trait, and samples are defined as any number of observations selected from the population that is less than the population. The best method for obtaining a representative sample is by the use of random sampling, where everyone in the population has an equal chance of being selected. Of critical importance is the concept of Significance. The research reports you will have to read will constantly be referring to whether the results are significant, which means results that are probably not just due to chance. The two most popular significance levels are .05, where the probability of chance is only five chances out of a hundred, or .01 where the results are reduced to only one chance out of a hundred. Four statistical tests are discussed (The Big Four), the t test for assessing differences between two groups, the F test for assessing differences between three or more groups, the Pearson r for determining if a correlation exists between two variables, and the Chi Square for the analysis of discrete (nominal) data. The statistical coverage continues with a discussion of the Partial Correlation, a very popular and useful method for analyzing data for the criminal-justice researcher. Since the criminal justice analyst often finds many legal difficulties involved in gaining full control of the independent variable (especially the creation of equivalent groups of subjects) the partial correlation allows for the after-the-fact control, by statistically creating equivalent groups. It is based on partialing out the effects of one or more variables, and then determining if the original relationship still holds. The student is urged to keep carefully in mind the rules of science and the allowable conclusions when reading the criminal justice literature. Finally, the chapter concludes with a discussion of survival analysis, perhaps the most powerful tool the researcher has available in the area of criminal justice. The analysis is aimed at discovering how long a person can remain free of failure (in criminal justice that would be free from re incarceration), given different treatment conditions or perhaps different personality types

Key Terms

Constants
Deduction
Experimental Research

Hypothesis Testing (Differences and Association)
Induction
Law of Averages
Partial Correlation
Percentage Changes
Post-Facto Research
Reliability and Validity
Samples and Populations
Scientific Method
Significance
Survival Analysis
Tests of Significance
Variables

References

Albernaz, A. (2005). Device prompts controversy. *Mass. Psychologist, 13,* 1-2

Anderson, D.A. (1999). The aggregate burden of crime. *Journal of Law and Economics, 42,* 611-642.

Bakalar, N. (2013). Take a number. *New York Times,* March 12, p D7.

Bonney, N., (2007). Gender employment and social class. *Work Employment Society,* <u>21</u>, 145-155.

Capone, D.L. & Nichols, W. (1976). Urban structure and criminal mobility. *American Behavioral Scientist, 20,* 119-218.

Clyde, W.C. & Christensen, K. (2003). Testing the relationship between pedofacile and avulsion using Markov analysis. *American Journal of Science, 303,* 60-71.

Dillinger, R.J. (2008). An exploration of the interpersonal features of psychopathy. *Dissertation Abstracts International. Section B. 68,* , 19-48.

Farrell, A., McDevitt, J., Bailey, J. , Anderson, C. & Pierce, E. (2004). Massachusetts racial and gender profiling. Final Report. *Northeastern Institute for Race and Justice.*

Ludwig, J., Duncan, G.J., Gennetian, L.A., Katz, L.F., Kessler, R.C., Kling, J.R. & Sonbonmatsu, L.(2012). Feel good effects of changing neighborhoods. *Science, 334,* 1505-1510.

Sprinthall, R. C. (2009). *SPSS From A to Z: A brief step-by-step manual.* Boston MA: Allyn-Bacon

Sprinthall. R.C. (2012). *Basic statistical analysis, 9th ed.* Boston MA: Allyn-Bacon.

GLOSSARY

Actus Rea: Legal term meaning committing a guilty act.

Addiction: This is the fourth of the Four Stages of Addiction. During this stage the individual is considered dependent on the substance. Tolerance and withdrawal symptoms begin to occur and there is significant interpersonal, legal, occupational, and relationship problems as well as physical and mental health distress.

Adjudicate: To judge or hear a case.

Adjudication: The power of a judge or arbiter to make the final decision in a legal dispute.

Adjudicatory Hearing: The actual trial in juvenile cases where evidence contained in the petition is presented. Based on this evidence the judge renders a decision to adjudicate the juvenile as delinquent, a status offender, or dismiss the case.

Administrative/Public Law: The regulation of federal and state government agencies, state, city, and county proceedings.

Age Related Anti-Social Behavior: Most of adult behaviors, good or bad, are formed early in life and have been found to be age-related. Family turmoil and inconsistent parenting can produce an antisocial personality that can be exhibited by age five, and 80% of children who later become criminals can be seen as antisocial by age eleven.

Alcoholics Anonymous: A 12 step recovery program for alcoholics that requires attendance at meetings with other alcoholics. These meetings offer support, guidance, hope, and optimism from others attempting recovery. Most attendees have a 'sponsor' to provide additional guidance and support. A similar program, Narcotics Anonymous, is available for those with drug addictions.

American Correctional Association: A commission formed in 1870 to oversee and evaluate U.S. jails and prisons. It introduced major changes in prison treatment and philosophy by such things as abolishing the silence rules and encouraging vocational training. It also allowed for the possibility of rewarding deserving inmates with an early release. The association is still active, and one of its main responsibilities is the grading and accrediting of the jails and prisons throughout the country.

Amygdala: Small almond-shaped brain structure located on both of the brain's temporal lobes (the area between the ears). It is involved in the fear emotion and the memory of anxiety producing past events. The psychopath often has distinct structural abnormalities in the amygdala.

Analysis of Variance or (ANOVA): Statistical test of significance (also called the F ratio, after its creator Sir Ronald Fisher), designed to establish the probability of true differences among several sample means.

Antisocial Personality Disorder (ASPD): The failure to conform to lawful behavior patterns, including lying, cheating, deceitfulness, impulsivity, and failure to feel remorse.

Appeal: The request to have a higher level appellate court review the lower court's findings. There are specific procedures to be followed and in certain criminal cases appeals are automatic, such as in a first degree murder case.

Appellate attorney: An attorney who handles cases being reviewed by a court of higher authority.

Arraignment: The first step in the court process when a person charged with a crime appears in court, receives copies of the indictment, and enters a plea.

Arrest: The power of authorities to hold a person in detention.

Attorney General of the United States: The nation's chief law enforcement officer.

Auburn System of Corrections (early 1800s): Sometimes referred to as the "New York System," the Auburn philosophy was based on a silent-repentance theme, but unlike Walnut Street (see entry), prisoners were allowed to leave their cells during the day in order to work. And work they did. In fact Auburn prisoners, ironically, built the world-famous prison in Ossining New York that became known as "Sing Sing."

Augustus, John: A Boston shoemaker and temperance advocate who, in 1841, petitioned the Boston Police Court to release an individual charged with temperance law violations into his custody for rehabilitation. He is considered the "Father of Probation."

Autopsy: an examination of the corpse that may reveal the cause of death, as well as such things as whether the death was caused by trauma or disease, or whether by homicide or suicide.

Bail: Money paid to the court to ensure the defendant's appearance at trial.

Balllistics: Every firearm, other than smooth-bore shot guns, leaves distinct marks on a spent round or cartridge casing. The ballistician matches the round or casing with the weapon of origin. Also the weapon's firing pin or extractor leaves a distinct impression.

Behavioral Profiling: A type of profiling which can reduce the size of the suspect pool by examining behavioral patterns that are personally unique. The analysts look for a person's habits, methods, and general patterns of behavior. The profile can actually create a suspect's virtual "signature." This should not be confused with "racial profiling."

Beyond a reasonable doubt: The evidentiary standard which the prosecution must meet in criminal cases.

Bill of Rights: The first ten amendments to the United States Constitution and the cornerstone to citizen rights in this country. These rights protect citizens from an overreaching, centralized government.

Body Language: Suspects often give themselves away by their non-verbal reactions, such as posture, gestures, eye movements, and facial expressions. Reading body language is a skill possessed by many police interrogators, as well as those working as scientific jury selectors.

Bonding Attachment: A symbiotic process usually occurring between mother and child and requiring direct physical contact. It produces a strong emotional connection, and failure to bond may be related to future problematic behaviors for the child.

Boot Camps: An intermediate sanction that is a militaristic like placement involving intensive physical regimens and strict discipline. Typically staffed with former military personnel.

Brady Error: The prosecution may not withhold evidence, called "exculpatory," that could be favorable to the defendant. This helps ensure that the defendant receives due process.

Breathalyzer: An instrument used for detecting blood-alcohol content (BAC) by measuring a suspect's breath. The current legal level is a BAC of .08 (grams of alcohol per 210 liters of breath).

Briefs and Memoranda of Law: Written arguments by attorneys to persuade the court to rule in their client's favor.

Broken Windows: A theory of crime suggesting that an antisocial atmosphere is spawned by a decaying neighborhood, especially an inner-city neighborhood. If windows are left broken, and garbage and trash are left on the street, the conditions are ripe for crime and disorder. When order is restored, graffiti cleaned up, windows repaired, there is said to be less crime.

Bullying: the repeated physical or even psychological mistreatment of a victim who is less powerful than the bully. The victims often develops stress-related illnesses and sometimes even attempt suicide.

Burden of proof: The standards for presenting evidence in a case for it to be legally viable; in a criminal case the burden of proof is "beyond a reasonable doubt," in a civil case it is often "by preponderance of the evidence."

Burglary: Unlawful attempt to enter another person's home or place of business with the intent of taking the owner's possessions.

Bystander Effect: A theory used to explain why people who are part of a large crowd of bystanders are less apt to help out in emergency situations than when alone. The theory says that when there is a diffusion of responsibility, people assume that others will help out, when in fact nobody helps.

Capital Punishment: Society's most severe punishment and involves putting the assailant to death (usually by lethal injection)

Cell Phone and/or GPS: Law enforcement can find the exact location of an individual anytime a cell phone or GPS is used. The suspect, thus, gives away his/her locatable position.

Challenge for Cause: The prosecution or defense attorney may challenge a prospective juror on the basis of a reasonable suspicion of bias. The reason for the challenge has to be publicly stated , as opposed to a peremptory challenge where no reason has to be given.

Chi Square: A statistical test of significance used to determine whether frequency differences have occurred on the basis of chance.

Child Savers Movement: Started by a group of women at the end of the nineteenth century who believed that children were not miniature adults and had the capacity to change. Sought to develop a system of services providing support and rehabilitation to high-risk youth.

Childhood Stress: Stressors occurring in early childhood have more effect on the developing child than had they occurred at a later age/stage. Early stress may even cause hormonal changes that link to later aggressiveness and a heightened probability of offending.

Civil Law: Refers to legal disputes among private parties. Losing in a case of civil law usually results in a financial settlement , rather than detention.

Code of Federal Regulations (CFR): The rules, regulations, and laws of the United States and how they are to be carried out and enforced by the government.

CODIS (Combined DNA Index System): This is the FBI's DNA data base currently containing over 9 million convicted-felon profiles.

Cognitive Behavior Therapy (CBT): A therapeutic technique that assumes that faulty thought or cognitive patterns and irrational and illogical ways of thinking contribute to the development of negative behaviors and emotional distress. Treatment is aimed at helping the individual recognize these patterns and restructure their cognitions. The Bureau of Prisons has promoted the use of CBT for the treatment of substance abuse.

Cognitive Dissonance: A psychological concept that explains what happens when an individual has conflicting thoughts, attitudes and behaviors. People try to resolve this dissonance by looking for consistency to restore their equilibrium. A juror may unconsciously create internal stories and weave them into the actual facts in order to make the explanations of the lawyer, witness, or suspect more consistent and reasonable.

Combining Evidence: When the details of evidence are combined, the total package becomes far more convincing than when looked at separately. Finding combinations of evidence, such as (1) erratic driving, (2) the smell of alcohol on the driver's breath, (3) a failed field-sobriety test, and (4) a high score on the Breathalyzer – all combine to reduce the probability of a false positive.

Community Oriented Policing (COP): A philosophy of policing that involves officers spending time in the community, and involving themselves with the community members and its culture. That is, there should be a co-operative effort between the police and the public to combat crime.

Common Law: The system of jurisprudence, which originated in England and was later applied in the United States, which is based on judicial precedent (court decisions) rather than legislative enactment (statutes).

Community Corrections: An approach to relieving prison overcrowding by providing supervised alternatives to incarceration in the community.

Compassionate Release: Among the sick and elderly there have been situations where a compassionate release from prison has been granted. This only occurs when the inmate is proven to pose no threat to self or society.

CompStat: A data-driven computer system for making calculations regarding the best available police response and identifying the city areas which are most in need of police intervention.

Concord Prison Study: A study conducted by Dr. Timothy Leary in the 1960s to determine if psilocybin could be used to reform and treat the antisocial tendencies of prisoners

Conditions of Release: Terms set by the court prior to trial, these may include restrictions on the defendant's whereabouts or contact with victims, but might also include preventive detention

Conduct Disorder (CD): a disorder of childhood and adolescence that presents as a repeated violation of the social norms and the rights of other persons.

Conflict of Interest: When an attorney is unable to represent someone if there is an actual or perceived conflict. For example, if that attorney represented the opposing side in a past matter.

Contempt of Court: Order of a judge for failure to behave in the courtroom or failure to follow the court's order. Consequences for contempt of court may be jail time.

Control Group: In experimental research the control group is the comparison group, or the group that ideally receives zero magnitude of the independent variable. The use of a control group is critical in evaluating the pure effects of the independent variable on the measured responses of the subjects.

Corporate and White Collar Crime: Corporations can be convicted of a crime and convicted corporate executives are known as "white collar criminals."

Correlation Coefficient: A measure of the strength of an association, rather than detecting a difference, among two or more variables. Correlation alone should not be used to prove cause-and-effect.

Court Clerks: The administrators of the court who must ensure proper functioning of all aspects of the court process.

Court of Last Resort: The U.S. Supreme Court

Court Officer or **Bailiff:** Security staff who assure the safety of the judge, litigants, jury, attorneys, and others in the courthouse. Many courts use metal detectors at the court entrance.

Court Reporter: The person who records all of the courtroom proceedings both on audio tapes as well as on the computer. The reporter will also log all evidence introduced in a case and keep a list of all the exhibits that have been entered.

Criminal Justice: The government's system of institutions that are directed toward societal protection within the confines of individual rights, a delicate balance. The three major components are known as the three Cs: Cops, Courts and Corrections

Criminal Law: Those laws or government rules which if violated can result in confinement for a period of more than one year for a felony, or less than a year for a misdemeanor.

Criminal Negligence: A charge of someone being aware that an act may result in harm and there is a gross lack of care for the potential harm

Custody Levels: The assignment of custody levels within the jail or prison, from minimum security to maximum security. The assignment is based on the inmate's criminal record and, when appropriate, past prison behavior. This is often a difficult judgment for the evaluator to make.

Cyber Crime: Computer hackers from all over the world have been attacking the U.S. military, state department, as well as major corporations (and perhaps even your email account). The FBI has put together a group of high-tech professionals called the National Cyber Investigative Joint Task Force. Their job is to investigate and curtail cyber crime.

DARE – Drug Abuse Resistance Education: This was a program designed to place police officers directly into the schools and teach children the dangers of substance abuse. The program unfortunately met with limited success.

Daubert Standard for Court Admissibility of Scientific Findings: The Daubert rule (since 1993) stated that scientific evidence was admissible in a federal court of law if it was derived from the scientific method and if it has been proven to be both reliable and valid.

Day Reporting Centers: An alternative sanction allowing offenders to live at home but report to the center daily for supervision. Programming such as counseling, education, and groups may be provided at these centers.

Deadly Force: Can only be used as a last resort, or when the officer believes his/her life or the lives of others are in imminent danger. Deadly force may not be used to stop a suspect from escaping.

Death Qualified Jury: A jury that is composed of persons who are not totally opposed to the death penalty, sometimes called a "Witherspooned" jury.

Defense Attorney: The attorney who represents someone charged with a crime, or in civil cases, is representing the defendant.

Dependent Variable: In any antecedent-consequent relationship, the consequence is called the dependent variable and is usually based on a subject's measured response. In experimental research it is the effect half of the cause-and-effect relationship

Deposition: A formal questioning of a witness under oath at an attorney's office where both sides are present; taken prior to trial to aid in the pre-trial discovery process.

Detective: A criminal investigator, usually in plain clothes, who collects evidence at the crime scene and may testify in court. Detectives are usually not first responders.

Detention: A secure placement for juveniles where they can be confined during the juvenile court handling of their case.

Direct and Cross Examination: Interrogation of witnesses in court. The attorney who has called the witness asks direct questions, the opposing attorney asks questions on cross examination.

Discovery: The process of finding out all the facts and information before going to trial. Evidence may be requested in written form (interrogatories), the actual physical evidence may be requested, or sworn testimony (depositions) may be taken.

Disposition: The actual sentence imposed by the juvenile court judge at the conclusion of the adjudicatory hearing.

Diversion: Refers to attempts to divert the juvenile from involvement in the juvenile justice system. Involves finding alternatives, such as placement with caregivers or guardians, before processing a youngster through the juvenile courts.

DNA (Deoxyribonucleic Acid): A tiny substance found in all living organisms and containing an organism's unique genetic instruction code. It is now considered to be the "gold standard" for individual identification. Scientists examine 13 different DNA "markers," and when all 13 line up with another specimen, the probability of a false match is so incredibly small (one in ten trillion) as to provide overwhelming accuracy. DNA is just as effective in proving innocence as it is in proving guilt.

Docket Clerks: Court staff who enter information into computers, assure the judges receive motions and other paperwork, prepare the daily list of cases to be heard, answer phones, and assist the public at the clerk's office.

Document Analysis: Based on the science of hand-writing analysis, it used to verify the author of written content, such as forgeries, ransom notes, or even a last will-and-testament. This is not to be confused with graphology which is a pseudo-scientific attempt to measure one's personality via one's handwriting.

Double Jeopardy: Constitutionally protected right that no person may be charged twice for the same offense.

Drug Courts: An alternative to traditional trial courts, drug courts were first established to relieve the overburdened justice system. The assumption is that therapeutic interventions mandated by these courts would assist in severing the drug-crime connection and consequently ease the burden on the criminal justice system and on society.

Drug-defined Offense: Violations of law prohibiting or regulating the possession, distribution, or manufacture of illegal drugs. An example includes operating a meth lab.

Drug-related Offense: Offenses to which the effects of a substance contribute. An example includes stealing and pawning jewelry for cash to buy heroin.

Drug-using Lifestyle: Adopting a deviant lifestyle because of involvement in the possession, distribution, or manufacture of illegal substances. An example is a drug dealer who learns how to launder money.

Due Process of Law: The concept of fairness and consistency in the application of the law.

Early Experience Theory: A position taken by researchers and theorists who stress the critical importance of an individual's early environmental experiences in determining later adult behavior and characteristics. These theorists argue that the child goes through critical periods when certain traits and skills can best be learned. Developing these traits too early or too late can result in possible problems.

Education Within the Walls: These prison rehabilitation programs provide both academic and vocational education, including basic literacy. The GED, high school equivalency degree, may be earned while serving time and offers the inmate a life-changing opportunity.

Eighth Amendment: Part of the Bill of Rights which demands that government treatment of inmates may not be "cruel and/or unusual." The phrase has been used by countless inmates who have sought legal action against a litany of complaints concerning government actions that have been alleged to violate this amendment. Some of these complaints have been rather frivolous such as the complaint that the scheduling of a dental exam interfered with the time the convict wanted to be in the gym "working out."

Equal Protection Under the Law: The 14th amendment to the US Constitution requires that laws are applied equally to all citizens, however, the courts decide what is constitutionally permissible. The case law in this area is constantly changing and what was once permissible has later been found to be impermissible (e.g., laws which discriminate on the basis of sexual orientation).

Evidence: Physical, documentary, and personal statements presented in court to support or deny a claim, such as the weapon used in the crime and witness statements

Exculpatory Evidence: Evidence that might justify or excuse the defendant's actions which is held by the prosecution. This evidence must be given to the defense.

Exemplar Prints: Fingerprints taken in person from an individual by rolling their inked finger onto a pad or, more currently, using a 3D optical scanner.

Exhaust Remedies: Specific pathways which must be followed in order to appeal a case to a higher authority.

Experimental Research: Research conducted using this method, where an independent variable (stimulus) is under experimental control and manipulated in order to cause a change in the subject's response. Equivalent groups of subjects are formed, then exposed to different levels of the independent variable, and then measured to see if concomitant response differences can be observed.

Experimentation: The first stage in the Four Stages of Addiction. Refers to casual use of a substance possibly because of peer pressure or to deal with a stressful event.

Expert Opinions: Evidence given based on a person's expertise (e.g., medical opinion). Strict rules for determining expertise must be met

Facial Width to Height Ratio (WHR): Researchers in 2011 found a relationship between the width of man's face (assumed to be inherited) with the man's personality. The wider the face the more likely he is to lie, cheat and deceive.

Federal Bureau of Investigation (FBI): Under the auspices of the DOJ (Department of Justice), the FBI is the major country-wide law enforcement agency. It is charged with investigating over 200 categories of federal crime as well as serving as a U.S. intelligence agency. The first director of the FBI was J. Edgar Hoover.

FBI Classification Systems: Data collected by the FBI to track, analyze and predict crimes and their trends.

Federal Courts: There are 94 District Courts (each state has from one to four), 12 U.S. Courts of Appeal which are regionally based, and the U.S. Supreme Court.

Federal Crimes: These are federal violations that are listed in the (CFR) Code of Federal Regulations and includes such violations as kidnapping and bank robbery.

Felonies: Criminal charges of the most serious types of crime, such as murder.

Fifth Amendment: The accused cannot be tried twice for the same crime (double jeopardy), does not have to testify against him/herself, and cannot be deprived of life, liberty, or property without due process.

Fines: A type of alternative sanction where a monetary fine is imposed on an offender. These fines can be tariff fines (fixed fines) or day fines (based on offense and ability to pay).

Fingerprint Analysis: Since no two people, even MZ twins, have exactly the same prints, law enforcement may use fingerprints for identifying suspects and finding possible links to prints left at the crime scene.

First Amendment: Freedom of speech, press, religion, and peaceful assembly

Flint Michigan Study: This was a study to measure the effectiveness of community policing on crime rates. Unfortunately the results showed very limited success.

Force: Any sworn officer has the right to use force if the officer feels physically threatened, and only that amount of force necessary to control the suspect.

Forensic: Virtually anything that is used or is suitable for use in a court of law. For example, forensic accounting would entail both checking the books and/or looking for evidence of someone possibly "cooking" the books.

Forfeiture: The seizure of assets by the government when it is determined that the assets were connected to criminal activity. Forfeiture attempts to discourage crime by taking away the incentive.

Foster Homes: A placement for juveniles that provides a family-like setting. Foster families volunteer to take juveniles into their homes and offer support while also taking responsibility for ensuring that they receive needed services. Although voluntary, foster families are reimbursed for their expenses.

Fourth Amendment: The government cannot be involved in search and seizure without probable cause, and this includes a search warrant.

Freedom of Religion: The Supreme Court has ruled that all inmates have their first amendment rights, including freedom of religion. This issue has become complicated by the fact that some alleged religions are not easy to define, or have practices that threaten prison security. Prisons have a far higher percentage of some of these non-traditional religions than exist in the free population at large.

Frustration-Aggression Theory: The theory that aggression results from environmental causes, especially environmental frustration. When a person's goals are blocked, aggressive behavior is a major result

Frye Standard for Court Admissibility of Scientific Findings: The major standard for many years (since 1923), the Frye rule stated that scientific evidence was admissible in a federal court of law if it had general acceptance in the scientific community.

Gambler's Fallacy: The erroneous assumption that independent events are somehow related. For independent events, such as coin flips, the probability remains the same for each and every coin flip, regardless of the previous outcome. The gambler remembers the past, but the coin doesn't.

Grand Jury: Closed proceedings initiated by a prosecutor to begin the process of charging someone with a crime

Group Homes: A 24 hour out of home placement for juveniles usually reserved for those who do not need the structure and supervision of a residential treatment center. Typically staffed by house parents and located in residential neighborhoods, these placements offer services on site or in the community.

Habeas Corpus: Petitions filed by prisoners to challenge illegal detainment.

Halfway Houses: Sometimes referred to as 'residential reentry centers.' These are community correctional homes that serve as an alternative to incarceration in a jail or prison. Many of these home are offense specific. For example, only housing offenders with drug convictions.

Hearsay: Testimony about what someone else said when the witness did not actually hear it is not allowed except in limited circumstances.

Hearsay Exceptions: There are limited circumstances under which hearsay can be admitted by the court (e.g., an excited utterance) and deemed to be trustworthy

Holding Cells: Police department cells, often called "drunk tanks," where suspects can be held, usually just over night or until they can be transported to a jail or possibly released.

Home confinement: Sometimes referred to as 'house arrest,' this is a sanction where the offender is mandated to remain in their homes rather than be sent to prison. The offender will often be supervised through electronic monitoring. There are preauthorized exceptions to this confinement such as allowing the offender to attend therapy or medical appointments.

Houses of Refuge: Established in 1825 in New York City to protect, reform, and educate wayward juveniles. Designed to provide an alternative to jail for minors.

Hung Jury: When the jury cannot reach a unanimous (or sometimes majority) decision. Also known as jury deadlock

Hypothalamus: A brain structure located at the base of the brain, the hypothalamus controls part of the nervous system as well as the endocrine system. It is a very important aspect of the emotional four Fs. Abnormalities in this area of the brain's structure have been noted among psychopaths.

Impression Evidence: When any object is pressed against another it may leave an impression, such as tire marks, foot prints, bite marks, and so forth. Fingerprinting is actually a form of impression evidence.

In forma paueris: Reduced or waived fees for a court appointed attorney (in criminal cases), or when filing petitions or motions with the court.

Independent Variable: In any antecendent-consequent relationship, the independent variable is the antecedent variable. Whether the independent variable is under full experimental control (manipulated) or assigned determines whether the research is experimental or post facto.

Indictment: The written accusation of the crime being charged.

Industrial Schools: Another type of reform school for juveniles but with an emphasis on industrial labor. Juveniles housed in these schools were required to pay for room and board and companies would contract with the schools to have them perform manufacturing and other types of manual work.

Instinct Theory: A now-discredited theory that attempted to explain behavior by simply describing it and then calling it "instinctive." For example, humans were seen as going to war because of an aggressive instinct, or forming groups because of a gregarious instinct, or twiddling their thumbs because of a thumb-twiddling instinct. These theorists are said to have committed what is now known as the nominal fallacy, that is using the behavior itself as its own explanation.

Institutionalization: A condition brought on by long-term confinement and resulting in a condition in which the inmate becomes so accustomed to the prison situation that reentry into society becomes an authentic problem. The inmate adjusts to prison life so completely that he/she doesn't want to face what they see as the inconsistencies and surprises of the outside world. Prison seems less threatening than life outside the walls.

Instrumental Aggression: Anger that is goal directed, as when someone is beaten by an assailant who is trying to steal a bill-fold or hand bag.

Intake: The juvenile court intake process is a screening that will determine if a juvenile needs court intervention. Typically conducted by juvenile probation officers who have had training in mental health, social work, or forensic psychology.

Integrated Automated Fingerprint Identification System (AFIS): This is an FBI data bank currently containing the finger prints and names of about 60 million persons.

Intensive Supervision Probation: This type of probation requires consistent monitoring and supervision by a probation officer, perhaps on a daily basis, along with the application of strict conditions.

Intermediate Sanctions: These are considered alternative sentences imposed by the court. These sanctions typically fall between court ordered probation and incarceration.

Interrogatories: Written questions to be answered in writing and under oath are sent to and from each side in a case to aid in the discovery process prior to trial.

Jails (Detention Centers): Until tried in court, suspects are held in a jail facility while awaiting trial. Some jails also house short-term offenders, usually less than a year. Levels of security vary widely in a jail, because some of those awaiting trial may be killers, and they can be housed in the same facility as are low-security short-timers. Jails are typically operated at the county level.

John Detail: The police use of women (even female police officers) to pose as prostitutes and lure men (called "johns") into making payments for sexual favors.

Judge: The person presiding over cases who makes decisions based on the law and facts. Judges are appointed or elected.

Judicial Review: The power of appellate courts to review lower courts' decisions.

Jury: A group of local people who are summonsed to court to hear evidence in a case and make decisions based on the facts.

Jury Box: A separated area in the front of the courtroom where a jury will sit during a trial.

Jury Deliberations: Private meetings of the jury after a trial to review the evidence and make decisions.

Jury Instructions: A set of oral or written instructions given to the jury by the judge as they enter their private deliberations.

Justification: Legal defenses raised to assert that while what happened was wrong there was a good reason for it. These include self-defense, defense of others, defense of property, necessity, consent, and resisting unlawful arrest.

Juvenile Transfer Waiver: The process of determining if the seriousness of a juvenile's offense or the youth's long record of offenses warrants the filing of a petition to waive the juvenile court's jurisdiction of the case to adult criminal court.

Kallikaks (The Good Seed and the Bad Seed): A family that was studied in great detail by Henry Goddard during the early 1900s. Goddard traced back two distinct branches of the Kallikaks, both having been originally sired by a Revolutionary war soldier named Martin Kallikak. One branch, the "good Kallikaks," resulted from Martin's marriage to an "upright and worthy Quakeress," and the other branch came from his affair with a feeble-minded bar maid. The good Kallikaks were found to be superior in virtually every human category, but the bad Kallikaks were definitely inferior, composed mostly of alcoholics, prostitutes, and criminals. By today's standards, the account of the Kallikaks is, to put it gently, rather fanciful.

Kansas City Study: A research study designed to test police effectiveness using three different approaches: 1) proactive with a marked increase in police presence and visibility, 2) reactive with a police response only to calls for help and, 3) control situation where the police responded in their typical, business as usual way. Unfortunately none of these approaches made any difference on crime rates.

Latent Prints: Fingerprints taken, not directly from the individual, but from the surface of an object. These prints are not always visible to the naked eye, but can be lifted by dusting and then examined for possible matches.

LEOKA (Law Enforment Officers Killed in Action): The FBI's annual list of those officers who were killed in the line of duty.

Limbic System: A grouping of brain structures (including the amygdala and hypothalamus) that are primarily involved in emotions and the control of emotions.

Lombroso, Cesare: Italian criminologist of the late 1800s who maintained that a person's physical and mental characteristics were inborn, and that certain traits such as a sloping forehead, long arms, and a lack of earlobes described someone who had inborn criminal tendencies.

Luminol: A blood-tracing substance that can be sprayed at the crime scene and reacts to traces of blood by producing a bluish glow. Photographs of the glow are admissible in court.

Magistrates or **Justices of the Peace:** Court officers with limited jurisdiction such as child support Magistrates.

Magnetic Resonance Imaging (MRI): Technique used to create an image of the body's internal structures and activities. With the MRI the brain's emotional reactions to certain events can be clearly viewed, and with the psychopath normal emotional images are sometimes distorted.

Mala in se: Latin term meaning "is wrong or evil in itself."

Malice: Latin term meaning that the act was done intentionally with reckless disregard for the consequences.

Mapp Ruling: The rule that a defendant may have evidence excluded if it was obtained by any violations of the Fourth (unreasonable search) or Fifth (self- incrimination) amendments.

Margaret the Mother of Criminals: A sociologist, Richard Dugdale, published a book in 1877 in which he claimed to have found a family of criminals (the Jukes) all of whom were descended from a woman named Margaret - whom he called the "mother of criminals." Though briefly mentioning the influence of environment, Dugdale attributed most criminality to hereditary influences.

Martinson, Robert: Author of the famous "nothing works" (1974) summary of the results of research and corrections studies spanning back almost 200 years, with the bleak conclusion that neither punishment nor rehabilitation (or anything else) had any effect on recidivism or prisoner behavior in general. Major flaws were later found in Martinson's data and conclusions, and he later recanted his position and announced that there are rehabilitation programs that do have an appreciable effect on recidivism. In 1980 Martinson committed suicide by jumping to his death from a high-rise window as his son looked on.

McNaughton Rule: The case that established the defense of not guilty by reason of insanity.

Measurement: A method of quantifying observations by assigning numbers to them according to specific rules.

Mens Rea: Latin term for "guilty" mind or the intention to commit a criminal act.

Mental Health Courts: An alternative court that attempts to divert offenders with mental disorders from having to be incarcerated. These offenders are placed in strictly supervised mental health treatment programs located in the community.

Mental Incapacity: Legal defenses raised to assert that the defendant is not able to be found guilty of the charged crime by reason of insanity, diminished capacity, mental incompetence, or intoxication.

Miranda Rights: A rule to ensure that suspects must be told that they don't have to incriminate themselves, that they may remain silent, and that they have the right to an attorney. Also if they do answer questions, what they say may be held against them.

Misdemeanors: A less serious type of crime than a felony.

Mistrial: Termination of a case if the jury cannot reach a verdict, or, if there are legal grounds as decided by the judge.

National Crime Victimization Survey (NCVS): These are data based on surveying a representative sample of the population in order to gain information on all crime, even crimes that were never reported to the police.

Neighborhood Watch Program: Persons in their own neighborhoods volunteer to walk through the area, especially at night, looking for any suspicious activities. These volunteers may not accost a suspect but instead are urged to call the police.

New Gate Prison: A famous prison opened in 1773 and located in an abandoned copper mine in East Granby, Connecticut. This is the first known prison on American soil, and it embodied the "punishment" philosophy of how to deal with inmates. New Gate also recorded the first prison riot on American soil, a riot that ended in the shooting deaths of many inmates. Even today, neighbors in East Granby have reported hearing haunting sounds emanating from the ground below the prison. The prison was officially closed in the late 1800s, but has now been reopened as a state-run museum.

New Generation Jail (NGJ): A larger jail using the pod system, or a series of smaller units holding about 40 or 50 inmates. These self-contained units or "pods" within the main jail serve groups of inmates who are housed together and both work, learn, and socialize together.

NGRI (Not Guilty by Reason of Insanity): Used as a defense in a homicide trial and based on the idea that the killer did not know what they were doing, and having no concept of the difference between right and wrong. It has not been a very effective defense, and is actually rarely used today.

Nolo contendere: A plea where the defendant neither admits nor denies the charge. It is Latin for "I will not contest the charge." A plea of no contest can be seen as basically the same as a guilty plea.

Norfolk Island Prison: Notoriously cruel prison (circa early 1800s) located on an island off the coast of Australia. Famous for having housed the mutineers from Captain Bligh's ship "Bounty." When Alexander Maconochie was sent to administer the prison, he changed the conditions in dramatic fashion and he even attempted to use what are now called "behavior modification" techniques, which apparently worked and resulted in a significant drop in recidivism.

Null Hypothesis: The assumption that the research results are simply due to chance or coincidence.

Opening and Closing Arguments: Speeches made by prosecutors and defense counsel at the beginning and end of a trial to attempt to persuade the judge and/or jury of the strengths of their case and the weaknesses of the other's case

Oppositional defiant disorder (ODD): A disorder of children who show an ongoing hostile and defiant pattern of behavior toward adults and/or authority figures. It often includes temper tantrums and persistent anger.

Orientation and Classification: Initial processing of the convicted inmate's entry into detention, where rules and regulations are explained and classification is determined. This includes both the level of security and type of training that is best suited to the inmate's background and potential.

Osteology: The analysis of bones and bone fragments in determining the victim's identity, time of death, type of trauma, disease, and cause of death.

Overcrowding: Because of the large increase in America's jail and prison populations, overcrowding has become an enormous problem for corrections authorities. One answer has been the use of private, for-profit prisons, and the other answer comes from a group calling themselves "abolitionists," who demand the total elimination of all prisons and even the prison system itself. This group claims that prisons don't work, do not deter crime, and are racially biased.

Parameter: Any measure that has been obtained by measuring the entire population. Statisticians use sample measures, statistics to estimate population measures, parameters.

Parens Patraie: A Latin term meaning 'state as parent.' The doctrine that the state will act as the parent if it is determined by the juvenile court that the parents cannot or will not care for or control their children.

Parole: A period of supervision imposed on an offender after the offender has served a prison term. Decisions regarding parole are typically made by a parole board using release guidelines and strict conditions are imposed. A parole officer is responsible for monitoring the parolee.

Peel, Sir Robert (Bobby): In 1826 Peel set up the world's first organized police force in London, England. His police officers (still known as "Bobbies") were paid professionals and were structured as though para military. Peel later went on to become England's Prime Minister.

Peremptory Challenge: During voir dire a jury challenge can be issued by either the prosecutor or defense attorney without having to use any reason whatsoever. It is an automatic dismissal of a prospective juror.

Petition: A formal charging document stating the allegations against a juvenile and the need for a formal hearing.

Photographic Evidence: Photography, especially with today's digital features, is an extremely important police tool for collecting evidence at crime scenes and for basic identification purposes.

Phrenology: The now discredited theory that personality characteristics could be assessed by an examination of a person's skull.

Placing Out: Reformers in the late 1800s believed that wayward children residing in cities should be placed in family-like settings. These children were placed on trains and sent to live with families and work on farms in the West and Mid-West. Often referred to as the Orphan Train.

Plaintiff: Term for someone who brings a lawsuit or petition in a court, such as in a divorce, or wrongful death case.

Plea: Defendant's statement of guilt or innocence at arraignment.

Plea Bargains: Agreements reached between the prosecutor and defense to resolve the case. This slang term is "cop a plea."

Plethysmography: A technique for measuring changes occurring within a person's body, including limbs, lungs, and genitalia. It can be used for assessing sexual arousal and/or sexual orientation. Although used during police investigations, its results cannot be used in a court of law.

Police Academy: A physically and educationally demanding school for young men and women for careers in the law enforcement.

Polygraph: A scientific instrument that attempts to detect whether a person is lying. Although it is commonly used during the police investigative and questioning process, its use in court has become quite limited and open to challenge.

Population: The entire number of persons, things, or events having at least one trait in common. Populations may be limited (finite) or unlimited (infinite).

Post Facto Research: A type of research that while not allowing for direct cause-and-effect conclusions, does help the researcher make better-than-chance predictions. In this type of research, subjects are measured on one response dimension and these measures are compared to other trait or response measures,

Predisposition Report: A document prepared by the juvenile probation office that focuses on how the court can assist the juvenile by providing identified services that will rehabilitate rather than punish the youngster.

Preliminary Hearing: A hearing where the Court can determine probable cause.

Preventive Detention: Defendants are ordered by the court to be held in a corrections facility pending trial. Usually occurs when the charges are serious or violent or the offender has a history of arrests, convictions, or violations of probation.

Prison Industries: Both for vocational training and economic necessity convicts have long worked in such areas as factories, road gangs, and coal mines. Much of the work occurs within the prison walls where inmates make everything from furniture to license plates, and in one prison a line of clothing is made and sold as "Prison Blues."

Prisoner Rights: The Supreme Court has ruled that prisoners have most of those rights specified in the Constitution's Bill of Rights, and prisoners may now use the court system to hear their grievances, including being forced to attend drug-treatment programs. The court also ruled that all prisoners must have free medical and dental care. There are, however, some rights enjoyed by free citizens that inmates cannot demand, especially when they involve security issues or the legitimate use of some punishments.

Prisons (Including Penitentiaries and Corrections Centers): Prisons, both state and federal, typically hold inmates serving more than one year. State prisons hold the large majority of prisoners, while federal prisons only serve those who have been convicted of federal crimes, such as racketeering or bank robbery. Federal prison is alleged to be less demanding, more lax in enforcing the rules, and holding far fewer of those convicted of crimes of violence.

Private Prisons: Because of prison over-crowding, many new prisons have been built and operated by private corporations. By 2014, they accounted for well over 10% of the total inmate population. They are said to save money for the tax payers, but there is still a question as to how professionally trained the private staffs are when compared to state and federal employees.

Pro bono: No fee is paid to the attorney and is Latin for "for the public good."

Pro se: Latin term meaning to "represent oneself."

Probability: A statement as to the number of times a specific event can occur out of the total possible number of events, usually listed as from .oo to 1.oo. The higher the probability, the closer it is to 1.oo, the more likely it is that the event will occur.

Probable Cause: A finding by a court that there is sufficient evidence to charge someone with a crime, or, the facts by which law enforcement determines that the requisite elements are present for a valid arrest or search and seizure.

Probation Officer: An officer of the Court at the Federal or State level who is primarily responsible for monitoring and supervising the behavior of offenders who have been placed in the community.

Probation or Parole Violation: If terms and conditions of parole or probation are violated new criminal charges may be filed

Probation: From the Latin 'probatio' meaning a "period of proof or testing." A sanction that allows for the conditional release of an offender into the community under the supervision of a probation officer.

Procedural Defenses: Defenses raised that impugn the process of charging a crime, including entrapment, prosecutorial misconduct, and double jeopardy.

Procedural Law: The body of rules and practice which govern the legal process.

Prosecutor: The government's attorney who is trying to convict the suspect.

Psychopathy: An emotional disorder characterized by extremely low levels of empathy, a callous disregard for the feelings of others, and a lack of anger controlling mechanisms. The psychopath is often a glib, fast talker who can present a charming persona. Most theorists today believe that psychopathy has both a biological and environmental origin, as opposed to the sociopath who has many of the same behaviors, but is believed to be due almost solely to environmental stresses, such as poverty, poor parenting, and a failure to interject societal norms.

Random sampling: A technique of sampling in which every member of the population has an equal chance of being selected.

Reactive Aggression: An anger reaction triggered by frustration or threat as opposed to Instrumental aggression which is instead based on an attempt to use the aggression for personal gain.

Recidivism: To reoffend. The actions of habitual criminals that lead to re-arrest or re-incarceration.

Reentry: The difficulty an institutionalized inmate encounters when released from prison and re-enters society. Prisons are now becoming more understanding of this problem and are providing assistance to the about-to-be released inmate, some calling them "decompression programs."

Reform Schools: A juvenile residential placement intended to provide educational, moral, and vocational training to youthful offenders. The underlying premise was that juvenile offenders should not be punished as adults since they were young enough to be rehabilitated and reformed.

Regular Use: The second of the Four Stages of Addiction. Refers to the regular use of a substance. The substance can be used to relieve stress and the user now begins to plan to use the substance with peers, after work, or on the weekends.

Reliability: The consistency of measures or theories. Traits or characteristics whose measures yield consistent results are said to be reliable.

Res judicata: A final judgment by a court of competent jurisdiction is conclusive. Latin for "a matter already judged."

Residential Treatment Center: A long term 24 hour out of home placement designed to offer programming and treatment for delinquent youth. Staffed with direct care workers and a multidisciplinary team of support staff such as mental health, educational, and medical professionals.

Rest: The term used to indicate that one side is finished with all of its evidence to be presented to the court, as in "the defense rests."

Restitution: Like a fine, this sanction requires the offender to make a payment to their victim. Restitution can be monetary, community service, or direct service to the victim.

Retainer fee: Money paid to a private attorney before the attorney begins work on the case.

Retribution: A get tough method of prisoner treatment (circa 1980s) that called for stricter prison rules, stronger punishments, and the now-famous "three strikes and you're out" rule, or, that a third felony conviction should result in a life sentence.

Right against Self-Incrimination: The 5th Amendment allows a person to refuse to answer questions if there is a likelihood of criminal prosecution. This right allows a defendant in a criminal trial not to testify and for the jury or judge not to use that lack of testimony as evidence of guilt

Risky Use: The third of the Four Stages of Addiction. The individual can now be considered an abuser. The substance becomes increasingly important and the person plans to obtain and abuse the substance regularly despite the probability that their behavior is affecting others and their own well-being.

Robbery: Unlawful attempt to take property away from another person's possession.

Rules of Evidence: Written rules which define what evidence is allowed to be considered in a court process. There are exceptions to those rules which are also clearly delineated, such as the rule against hearsay and the exceptions to the hearsay rule.

Sample: A group of any number of observations (persons, things, or events) selected from a population that is less than the total population.

Schizophrenia: A serious mental disorder, characterized by delusions and hallucinations. Usually first diagnosed during late adolescence/early adulthood, the individual with schizophrenia has significantly higher rates of violent behavior than the population at large.

Scientific Jury Selection (SJS): Using science to select a jury that is going to be sympathetic to their side (defense) or (prosecution). The selection of jurors is based on such things as demographics, personality assessment, common prejudices, and group dynamics.

Search Warrant: A court order permitting a search by law enforcement based on specific written information.

Second Amendment: The right to bear arms.

Sentencing Hearing: The court hearing at which a convicted defendant is formally sentenced.

Sequestered Jury: When a jury is sequestered its members may not return to their homes but are put up in other accommodations (hotels) to prevent them from being swayed by the news media, or perhaps even approached by someone offering a deal or a bribe. The jury's decision should be based only on what is heard and seen in court.

Serial Killers: Some psychopaths in pursuit of ever-higher levels of excitement commit multiple homicides. The serial killer is defined as someone who has killed at least three people in separate events over the course of just a few months.

Serology: The study and analysis of bodily fluids (blood, saliva, semen, vaginal fluids). Analysis of these fluids can point to the identification of a suspect or victim.

Serotonin: A neurotransmitter that may act to suppress aggression and increase feelings of wellbeing.

Sheldon and his Somatotypes: In the 1950s a psychologist named William Sheldon found what he believed to be a correlation between one's personality and one's physical characteristics, or what he called somatotypes. Physically people were either endomorphs - overweight but jolly and easy going, mesomorphs – muscular, aggressive and daring, or ectomorphs - thin, withdrawn, and sensitive. He also associated these body types with certain personality types.

Sheriff and Sheriff's Deputies: Law enforcement agents at the county level who are involved in managing the county jail as well as responding as police officers. The Sheriff is considered to be the county's chief of police.

Shock Probation: The court sentences the offender to prison but after a short period of time the offender is returned to court and placed on probation. This serves to "shock" the offender into realizing the seriousness of their actions. At the onset, the offender is unaware of this arrangement.

Significance: A statistical term used to indicate that the results of the study are not simply a matter of chance. Researchers talk of significant differences as well as significant correlations under the assumption that on a probability basis, chance has been ruled out. A significant result can be extrapolated from the sample to the population. Significance levels are set at a probability level of at least .05 or lower. Any research result showing a p level of $< .05$ is considered to be significant.

Sixth Amendment: The accused has a right to a fair and speedy trial, to consult with a lawyer, be told of the reason for being tried, and the right to face the accuser.

Skinner, B.F.: A behaviorist who picked up where Watson left off, and again ascribed the vast majority of one's learning and personality formation to environmental stimuli. He said that most learning was based on what he called operant conditioning, as opposed to Pavlov's "classical conditioning." He believed that aggressive behavior is learned, but could also be unlearned (extinguished). He thought he could engineer a society in which all the ills of mankind would be eliminated, especially crime and war.

Social Learning theory: A theory proposed by Albert Bandura who suggested that a large part of what a person learns occurs through imitation or what he liked to call modeling. Individuals copy and modify behavior as a result of how others in the group respond. If group responses are negative, as may occur in a run-down neighborhood, the youngster picks up on what is seen and imitates the destructive behavior, especially when parents are the models. Bandura was especially insistent that aggression is a learned behavioral phenomenon

Special Need Inmates: Because many inmates enter confinement with special needs, such as health problems, substance-abuse issues, mental disorders and age-related problems it has recently become the prison's job to accommodate these varied conditions, especially HIV/AIDS.

Specialty Courts: Courts that hear specific types of cases such as juvenile, drug, traffic or domestic violence matters.

Split-sentence probation: The court will split the offender's sentence between prison time and probation. The offender is sentenced to a specific prison sentence before being placed on probation.

Standard/Straight Probation: The most popular type of probation. The court sentences the offender to probation with specific conditions and supervision requirements.

Stare decisis: Latin term meaning "to stand by that which was decided," In practice this means that a judge will follow prior rulings in deciding new cases thus establishing legal precedent.

State Courts: Each state has a tiered system for its trial and appellate courts.

State Police Department: This is the largest law enforcement agency at the state level. State police are involved in keeping our highways safe from auto violators. State police are also used in locating missing persons, finding escaped convicts, and numerous other law enforcement duties.

Statistic: Any measure that has been obtained by measuring the sample as opposed to the entire population.

Status Offense: An act considered an offense when committed by a juvenile but not an adult. These include offenses such as truancy, running away, smoking, and beyond parental control.

Statutes/Statutory Law: Laws which are enacted (approved by the legislative bodies which have control over the topics) and are codified (arranged into a systematic code).

Sting: A police operation aimed at catching suspects by setting up deceptive ploys to lure suspects into a criminal activity. This technique is legal in the United States as long as it doesn't involvement entrapment.

Strict Liability: For some charges there is no need to show that the person was aware that the act would result in harm, for example, statutory rape and selling alcohol to minors.

Subpoena duce tecum: A document served on witnesses requiring them to appear in court. Latin for "to bring with you."

Substance Abuse Education: Aims to provide the user with information and specific knowledge about the stages of addiction, risk factors, how drugs effect the body, how drugs interact with other drugs, how drugs are abused, how drugs can foster dependence, how to avoid becoming an abuser. Not to be confused with Substance Abuse Treatment.

Substance Abuse Treatment: Consists of the evaluation and diagnosis of a substance use disorder along with therapeutic interventions to assist the individual in addressing and coping with the disorder. Examples include AA, NA, and Cognitive Behavioral Therapy.

Substance Abuse: According to the DSM, a maladaptive pattern of substance abuse as evidenced by ongoing and serious consequences related to the use of the substance, such as repeated DUI convictions or relationship problems.

Substance Dependence: According to the DSM, a group of symptoms indicating that someone continues to use a substance despite significant substance related problems such as tolerance, withdrawal, and sustained use of the substance.

Substance Use Disorder: A new diagnosis included in the DSM-5 that combines Substance Abuse and Dependence diagnoses from the previous edition but incorporates and retains all of the essential elements and criteria.

Substantive Law: Written laws.

Super-Max: Prisons with security of the highest order, such as ADX in Colorado. These prisons house the most dangerous males in all of confinement.

Each prisoner is in an individual cell and is allowed out of the cell for only an hour a day. Prisoners are monitored in an extremely close and controlled fashion. The prison is surrounded by double-fenced electrified barbed wire. These prisons are alleged to be "escape proof."

Suspended-sentence Probation: A type of probation where the court imposes a jail sentence then suspends the sentence on the condition that the offender will meet all conditions of his probation.

t test: A statistical test for determining the probability of whether there is a non-chance difference between two sample means

Terry Stop: A rule that if law enforcement has a reasonable suspicion that criminal activity "may occur," a suspect may be stopped, detained, and searched.

Testosterone: A male, steroid hormone that peaks at just about the same age as do crimes of violence. Among prison inmates, testosterone levels are highest among men who had committed crimes of violence. Although women can carry trace amounts of testosterone, the male levels are far higher.

The Product Rule: This is the only mathematical method ever tested and approved by a court of law. The rule states that when combining probabilities, separate events can be combined through multiplication which then reduces the overall resulting probability. Although these probabilities may be used for "probable-cause" conclusions, it has become a critical tool in DNA identification.

The Super Male (XYY): A chromosomal anomaly first noted back in 1986, in which some men were found to be carrying an extra Y chromosome. They were called "super males" and were found to be rather aggressive and were over represented in the prison population.

Thermal Imaging: A heat-seeking device that can be used to look behind closed doors or down though a roof or any other covering. Is often used to locate marijuana being grown indoors.

Three Strikes Laws: Mandatory prison terms, often long prison terms, for a person convicted of a third violent crime or felony. Many states have these laws but they do foster controversy.

Tolerance: An indicator of substance dependence. Refers to the physiological state in which a person no longer responds to a drug and needs increasing amounts of the drug to maintain the desired effect

Training School: The most restrictive sanction imposed by the juvenile court and usually reserved for youth who have committed serious offenses. These facilities can be similar to adult correctional facilities. The focus is on security but there is typically a support staff of mental health, educational , and medical professionals.

Uniform Crime Reports (UCR): An FBI collection of the year's crimes. The data are collected from law enforcement agencies throughout the country and therefore only count crimes known to have been committed.

Validity: Answers the question of whether the data are measuring what they are purporting to measure. If a scale is supposed to be measuring a trait like aggressiveness, that must remain its sole focus if it is to be considered valid.

Variable: Anything that varies and can be measured.

Voice Stress Analyzer (VSA): A device which analyzes a suspect's voice with a special emphasis on "voice micro tremors" or subtle voice changes that may not be noticed during normal conversation. It can be used to establish the identity of a speaker. It is typically used during the questioning-investigative process rather than in the court room.

Voir Dire: The questioning of potential jurors by prosecution and defense counsel at the beginning of a jury trial. Jurors can be disqualified based on their answers, for example, if they have a family member who is a police officer, or, if they were victim of a crime..

Walnut Street Jail: Established in Philadelphia in 1790. This has been labeled as the first "true" corrections facility in the United States. This was a jail that was known for its treatment philosophy of "silent repentance." Prisoners were not allowed to say a word and were confined to their cells 24 hours a day. The "repentance" theme led to the origin of the term "penitentiary."

Watson, John B. (1878-1958): The founder of a psychological theory called "Behaviorism." Watson was a strong believer in the influence of environment, almost to the exclusion of heredity. He believed that personality resulted from a build-up of stimulus-response connections that were the result of Pavlovian conditioning. He believed he could take any "well-formed" baby and shape it's personality into anything from a college president to a beggar or thief.

Web Analysis: Law enforcement's use of the internet to examine encrypted web sites. This allows for monitoring web conversations and is often used in conjunction with court-ordered wiretaps.

Wickersham Commission: An association formed in the 1930s to evaluate both the corrections system and law enforcement in general. Their first findings led to an indictment of both corrections and law enforcement. Their report aroused the public and produced significant changes in the corrections system, such as an emphasis on rehabilitation.

Withdrawal: An indicator of substance dependence. A psychophysiological reaction that occurs when an individual who is dependent on a drug ceases taking that drug. Examples include nausea, vomiting, tremors, and agitation.

Witness Stand: A seat to the side of the judge where someone who is called to testify will sit when answering questions.

Writ of certiorari: A Petition filed to a higher court to review a case decided by a lower court.

Z score: A measure of how far an individual score varies from the mean in units of standard deviation.

CPSIA information can be obtained at www.ICGtesting.com
Printed in the USA
BVOW06s1812240915

419576BV00010B/55/P

9 781627 340410